Creativity Theory and Action in Education

Volume 4

Series editors
Ronald A. Beghetto, Department of Educational Psychology, University of Connecticut, Storrs, Connecticut, USA
Bharath Sriraman, Department of Mathematical Sciences, The University of Montana, Missoula, Montana, USA

Editorial Board
Don Ambrose, Rider University, USA
David Cropley, University of South Australia, Australia
Vlad Petre Glaveanu, Aalborg University, Denmark
Beth Hennessey, Wellesley College, USA
Maciej Karwowski, Academy of Special Education, Poland
Scott Barry Kaufman, University of Pennsylvania, USA
Todd Lubart, University of Paris Descartes, France
Jean Pretz, Elizabethtown College, USA
Ai Girl Tan, Nanyang Technological University, Singapore
Yong Zhao, University of Oregon, USA

More information about this series at http://www.springer.com/series/13904

Ronald A. Beghetto • Giovanni Emanuele Corazza
Editors

Dynamic Perspectives on Creativity

New Directions for Theory, Research, and Practice in Education

Editors
Ronald A. Beghetto
Neag School of Education
University of Connecticut
Storrs, CT, USA

Giovanni Emanuele Corazza
Marconi Institute for Creativity
University of Bologna
Bologna, Italy

ISSN 2509-5781 ISSN 2509-579X (electronic)
Creativity Theory and Action in Education
ISBN 978-3-319-99162-7 ISBN 978-3-319-99163-4 (eBook)
https://doi.org/10.1007/978-3-319-99163-4

Library of Congress Control Number: 2018960918

© Springer Nature Switzerland AG 2019
This work is subject to copyright. All rights are reserved by the Publisher, whether the whole or part of the material is concerned, specifically the rights of translation, reprinting, reuse of illustrations, recitation, broadcasting, reproduction on microfilms or in any other physical way, and transmission or information storage and retrieval, electronic adaptation, computer software, or by similar or dissimilar methodology now known or hereafter developed.
The use of general descriptive names, registered names, trademarks, service marks, etc. in this publication does not imply, even in the absence of a specific statement, that such names are exempt from the relevant protective laws and regulations and therefore free for general use.
The publisher, the authors and the editors are safe to assume that the advice and information in this book are believed to be true and accurate at the date of publication. Neither the publisher nor the authors or the editors give a warranty, express or implied, with respect to the material contained herein or for any errors or omissions that may have been made. The publisher remains neutral with regard to jurisdictional claims in published maps and institutional affiliations.

This Springer imprint is published by the registered company Springer Nature Switzerland AG
The registered company address is: Gewerbestrasse 11, 6330 Cham, Switzerland

To Jeralynn for your persistent love and support

–Ronald A. Beghetto

Giovanni Emanuele Corazza would like to dedicate this book to his wife

Thank you for sharing your life with me, together we embody our reality, our adventure and our dreams

–Susy

Book Series Foreword

The goal of the book series, *Creativity Theory and Action in Education*, is to explore new frontiers in creative theory, research, and practice in educational settings. The series therefore endeavors to provide an international forum for thinkers from various disciplinary and methodological perspectives to build on existing work in the field and offer new, alternative, and even speculative directions for creative theory, research, and practice in education.

In this way, the series is a creative experiment of sorts, one that is aimed at providing an opportunity for those engaged and interested in the broader project of understanding creativity in education to generate, develop, test out, and learn from new possibilities and multiple perspectives on all manner of creative phenomena in education. Such an experiment has potential implications for how we think about creativity in education and also for how we act on creative opportunities afforded by educational situations and settings.

–Ronald A. Beghetto, Series Co-Editor, University of Connecticut, USA

Current Volumes in the Series

Volume 1: Creative Contradictions in Education: Cross Disciplinary Paradoxes and Perspectives, edited by Ronald A. Beghetto and Bharath Sriraman (2017)

Volume 2: Creativity in Theatre: Creative Theory and Action in Theatre/Drama Education (2018)

Volume 3: Creativity Under Duress in Education? Resistive Theories, Practices, and Action, edited by Carol A. Mullen (2018)

Volume 4: Dynamic Perspectives on Creativity: New Directions for Theory, Research, and Practice in Education, edited by Ronald A. Beghetto and Giovanni Emanuele Corazza (2019)

Acknowledgments

The authors would like to give very special thanks to Natalie Rieborn from Springer for her enthusiasm and support throughout this process, the members of our advisory board, colleagues at our universities, and family and friends.

Contents

1	**Introduction to the Volume** .... Ronald A. Beghetto and Giovanni Emanuele Corazza	1

Part I Dynamic Applications & Emergent Explorations

2	**Unfreezing Creativity: A Dynamic Micro-longitudinal Approach** .... Ronald A. Beghetto and Maciej Karwowski	7
3	**Participatory Creativity: Supporting Dynamic Roles and Perspectives in the Classroom** .... Edward P. Clapp and Michael Hanchett Hanson	27
4	**Emotions: The Spinal Cord of the Creative Thinking Process** .... Sergio Agnoli and Giovanni Emanuele Corazza	47
5	**Estimator Socialization in Design Thinking: The Dynamic Process of Learning How to Judge Creative Work** .... Julia P. A. von Thienen, Steven Ney, and Christoph Meinel	67
6	**Exploration as a Dynamic Strategy of Research-Education for Creativity in Schools** .... Monica Guerra and Federica Valeria Villa	101
7	**Educational Implications of the 'Self-Made Worldview' Concept** .... Alexandra Maland and Liane Gabora	117
8	**Dynamic Creativity: Influential Theory, Public Discourse, and Generative Possibility** .... Carol A. Mullen	137
9	**Content-Driven Pedagogy: On Passion, Absorption and Immersion as Dynamic Drivers of Creativity** .... Lene Tanggaard	165

Part II   Dynamic Conceptions & Future Directions

10   Creativity as a Dynamic, Personal, Parsimonious Process   181
Mark A. Runco

11   Polyphonic Orchestration: The Dialogical Nature of Creativity   189
Ingunn Johanne Ness and Vlad Glăveanu

12   The Dynamic Definition of Creativity: Implications for Creativity Assessment   207
Lindsey Carruthers and Rory MacLean

13   Interdisciplinary Exploration and Domain-Specific Expertise Are Mutually Enriching   225
Don Ambrose

14   Thought Dynamics: Which Role for Mind Wandering in Creativity?   245
Manila Vannucci and Sergio Agnoli

15   From Dynamic Processes to a Dynamic Creative Process   261
Marion Botella and Todd Lubart

16   Navigating the Ideology of Creativity in Education   279
Michael Hanchett Hanson

17   The Dynamic Universal Creativity Process   297
Giovanni Emanuele Corazza

CODA   321
Ronald A. Beghetto and Giovanni Emanuele Corazza

Chapter 1
Introduction to the Volume

Ronald A. Beghetto and Giovanni Emanuele Corazza

Abstract Creativity is a dynamic phenomenon (Corazza, GE. Creativity Research Journal, 28:258–267 (2016)). Indeed, change is central to creativity and results in new thoughts, actions, and products (Beghetto 2016). Moreover, there is an exploratory nature to the creative process, which blends both inconclusiveness and achievement. In this way, the trajectory of potentially creative outcomes dynamically changes across time and is influenced by variations in the social, cultural, historical, and material features of the situation.

Creativity is a dynamic phenomenon (Corazza 2016). Indeed, change is central to creativity and results in new thoughts, actions, and products (Beghetto 2016). Moreover, there is an exploratory nature to the creative process, which blends both inconclusiveness and achievement. In this way, the trajectory of potentially creative outcomes dynamically changes across time and is influenced by variations in the social, cultural, historical, and material features of the situation.

In the context of a classroom, for example, a student's unique perspective may initially be ignored (i.e., temporarily suspended) and then later returned to and built on (i.e., reanimated) by other students as a class discussion unfolds (see Gajda et al. 2017). The inconclusive and dynamic nature of creativity also extends to judgments about the creativity of finished products (Corazza 2016), which can be revisited, revised, and changed. Present actions and reflections can therefore influence creativity episodes from the past.

A teacher who judged a student's alternative solution as incorrect may, upon further reflection, recognize that the solution is indeed creative. In this way, assessments applied to the outcomes of a creative process, require a dynamic approach that can better account for the variations in judgments of creativity across possible situations, contexts, and futures.

R. A. Beghetto (✉)
Neag School of Education, University of Connecticut, Storrs, CT, USA
e-mail: ronald.beghetto@uconn.edu

G. E. Corazza
Marconi Institute for Creativity, University of Bologna, Bologna, BO, Italy

This dynamic nature of creativity, however, is overshadowed by more static conceptions, methodologies, and practices. Indeed, even standard definitions of creativity tend to use more fixed criteria, which have recently been critiqued as excluding creative potential at all levels of accomplishment (see Corazza 2016; Smith and Smith 2017). These critiques extend to more static or "one and done" estimates of the creativity of ideas or products, which fail to account for variations and changes in both the subjective and intersubjective assessments of creativity.

In short, traditional conceptions of creativity and methods for assessing and identifying creativity in educational contexts tend to privilege static creative achievement and fixed creative traits, rather than focus on the more dynamic, developing, and variable nature of creative thought and action.

These static conceptions can have dire consequences with respect to whether and how students' and teachers' potentially creative thought and actions will be recognized and developed in educational settings. Indeed, because creative potential is not as tangible as creative products, potential may be overshadowed by externally recognized creative outcomes (Runco 2004). The consequences of focusing on products or immediate recognition of creative outcomes can have an especially dramatic impact on the students' attitude towards the value of persisting in long term creative endeavors, inducing a preference for early closure.

At present, there is a need for more dynamic conceptions of creativity in educational settings. This is particularly important given the fast evolution of modern society and the widespread consensus that efforts to develop creative potential should be democratized—extending well beyond the boundaries of select individuals and the confines of "gifted & talented" programs (Clapp 2017; Corazza 2016; Hanchett Hanson 2015). There is also recognition that more dynamic perspectives on creativity are necessary for understanding its complexity, value, and meaning in educational contexts (Beghetto 2016; Corazza 2016).

The purpose of this edited volume is to bring together experts who presuppose creativity to be a dynamic phenomenon and thereby introduce new conceptions, methods, and applications in educational settings that are in alignment with that presupposition.

Collectively, the voices and perspectives represented in this volume aim to provoke new directions for thought and action in the field of creative studies. Some of applications and perspectives introduced herein are speculative, whereas others are grounded in many decades of research in the field. All however have the aim of providing a more dynamic way of considering how to think about, study, and engage with creative phenomena in and outside of educational setting.

This volume is organized in two parts. Part 1 focuses on dynamic applications and emergent explorations. More specifically, the essays and chapters included in this section provide an account of the kind of work already underway and emergent efforts by researchers who approach creativity from a more dynamic perspective. Part 2 offers new conceptions and theoretical directions for creativity researchers interested in applying and extending a dynamic perspective to their future endeavours. In this way, the volume offers an overview of the kind of work presently underway and on the horizon as well as maps out new ways of conceptualizing future efforts aimed at realizing the more dynamic nature of creative phenomena within and beyond educational settings.

We hope you enjoy spending time with this volume and find your experience engaging with the ideas contained within this volume both challenging and rewarding.

References

Beghetto, R. A. (2016). Creative learning: A fresh look. *Journal of Cognitive Education and Psychology, 15*, 6–23.

Clapp, E. P. (2017). *Participatory creativity: Introducing access and equity to the creative classroom*. New York: Routledge.

Corazza, G. E. (2016). Potential originality and effectiveness: The dynamic definition of creativity. *Creativity Research Journal, 28*, 258–267.

Gajda, A., Beghetto, R. A., & Karwowski, M. (2017). Exploring creative learning in the classroom: A multi-method approach. *Thinking Skills and Creativity, 24*(250), 267.

Hanchett Hanson, M. (2015). *Worldmaking: Psychology and the ideology of creativity*. London: Palgrave Macmillan.

Runco, M. A. (2004). Everyone has creative potential. In R. J. Sternberg, E. L. Grigorenko, & J. L. Singer (Eds.), *Creativity: From potential to realization* (pp. 21–30). Washington, DC: American Psychological Association.

Smith, J. K., & Smith, L. F. (2017). The 1.5 criterion model of creativity: Where less is more, more or less. *Journal of Creative Behavior, 51*, 281–284.

Part I
Dynamic Applications & Emergent Explorations

Chapter 2
Unfreezing Creativity: A Dynamic Micro-longitudinal Approach

Ronald A. Beghetto and Maciej Karwowski

Abstract Creativity researchers have conceptualized and studied creativity in a variety of ways. One common approach is to treat creative thought and action as if they are static phenomena that can be assessed using fixed measures. In this chapter, we argue for a more dynamic, micro-longitudinal approach to studying creativity in classrooms. We open with a brief discussion of our operating assumptions about creative thought and action, which serve as the basis for our argument. We then discuss examples of how researchers might move from a more static to more dynamic approach. More specifically, we discuss how researchers can study creative phenomena (such as creative confidence beliefs) using more dynamic, micro-longitudinal designs. We also discuss various promising options for analyzing data collected from such designs, including latent growth curve modeling, network-based analysis, and qualitative interpretations of visual displays. We close with a brief discussion of implications for future research and practice.

2.1 Introduction

Scholars have long been interested in nurturing creative thought and action in the context of schools and classrooms. Indeed, some of the earliest conceptions of creativity have their origins in the works of educational philosophers, such as the German philosopher Friedrich Froebel[1] (1887/1906) who asserted, "The young,

---

[1] Froebel's ideas about creativity had an anxious (Pieter Fannes, personal communication) and religious tinge to them, cloaked in the worry that unless young people worked on creative and productive endeavors, they would quickly devolve into destructive impulses (see translators note on p. 31 of Frobel's The Education of Man).

R. A. Beghetto (✉)
Neag School of Education, University of Connecticut, Storrs, CT, USA
e-mail: ronald.beghetto@uconn.edu

M. Karwowski
University of Wroclaw, Wroclaw, Poland

growing human being should...be trained early...for creative and productive activity" (p. 34). John Dewey (2007/1999), the American pragmatist, also recognized the importance of nurturing the creative imagination of students,

> We hear much nowadays about the cultivation of the child's 'imagination.' Then we undo much of our own talk and work by a belief that the imagination is some special part of the child that finds its satisfaction in some one particular direction – generally speaking, that of the unreal and make-believe, of the myth and the made-up story (p. 72)

It should therefore come as no surprise that understanding creativity in the context of the classroom has served as an important line of research in the field of creativity studies (Guilford 1950, 1967; Torrance 1966). Indeed, some of the earliest research on creativity occurred in schools and classrooms. Much of this early work focused on developing and using "creativity tests[2]" to measure aspects of children's creative and imaginative thought (e.g., *Torrance Tests of Creative Thinking*, TTCT, Torrance 1966).

In the years that followed, research on creativity in schools and classrooms continued to serve as a robust and burgeoning line of research in the field of creativity studies. In addition to the TTCT (Torrance 1966), creativity researchers have developed and used a wide array of methods and measures (Reiter-Palmon et al. 2014), including checklists of creative behavior (*Inventory of Creative Activities and Achievements*, Jauk et al. 2014); self-belief measures (e.g., *Short Scale of Creative Self*, Karwowski et al. 2013); teacher perceptions of creativity (e.g., Aljughaiman and Mowrer-Reynolds 2005); observational check-lists of creative teaching (e.g., Schacter et al. 2006); teacher ratings of students (e.g., *Scales for Rating the Behavioral Characteristics of Superior Students*, Renzulli et al. 1976); product rating scales (e.g., *Creative Product Semantic Scale*, O'Quin and Besemer 1989); and expert ratings of creative products (e.g., *Consensual Assessment Technique*, Amabile 1996).

Although there are variations in how researchers have conceptualized and studied creativity, a common approach is to treat creative thought and action as if they are static phenomena, which can be assessed with fixed measures (Beghetto, in press). This is not to say that such work lacks value, but we maintain that it can only provide limited insights into the dynamic and multifaceted nature of creative phenomena (Gajda et al. 2017).

In what follows, we argue for a more dynamic, micro-longitudinal approach to studying creativity in classrooms. We open with a brief discussion of our operating assumptions about creative thought and action. We then focus on examples of how researchers might move from a static to more dynamic approach to studying creative phenomena. More specifically, we discuss how researchers can study creative self-beliefs using more dynamic, micro-longitudinal designs. We also discuss various

---

[2] Torrance's Test of Creative Thinking (TTCT) is actually a measure of divergent thinking, which is viewed as an essential, but not sufficient component of creative thinking or outcomes. In fact, creativity scholars tend to view divergent thinking as an indicator of creative potential (rather than a measure of creativity itself – see Karwowski and Beghetto 2018 for a discussion). The TTCT remains as one of the most popular measure used in the field of creativity studies in general and in schools and classrooms in particular (Plucker and Makel 2010; Reiter-Palmon et al. 2014)

promising options for analyzing data collected from such designs, including latent growth curve modeling and network-based analysis. We close with a brief discussion of implications for future research and practice.

2.2 Basic Assumptions

Prior to describing examples of a more dynamic approach to studying creativity, it is first important to clarify a few basic assumptions about the nature of creativity in classrooms. These assumptions (which have been discussed elsewhere, e.g., Beghetto, in press) include:

- *Uncertainty serves as a creative catalyst;*
- *Creative thought and action results from a dynamic and emergent processes;*
- *Determinations about creativity are based on generally agreed upon criteria; and*
- *Judgements about creativity are dynamic and subject to change across time and contexts.*

In the sections that follow, we briefly discuss each of these assumptions.

2.2.1 Uncertainty as a Catalyst

Although there are many reasons why a person may choose to engage in creative thought and action, creative endeavors always involve some level of uncertainty. Indeed, if you know the outcome of an action in advance, then the result can hardly be called creative.

Consider the musical arts. A musician who is writing a composition starts at the point of uncertainty. The musician does not know exactly how the composition will take shape until it is finished. Once the composition is finished opportunities for creative expression are limited, but not entirely eliminated (see also Corazza 2016). Although it is true that little uncertainty remains in how to perform the composed piece, people can still have new and different "creative experiences" when hearing it performed. Moreover, performers of the composition can introduce additional uncertainty by experimenting with unique interpretations and novel flourishes when playing the piece.

In this way, uncertainty serves as a catalyst for creativity. In the context of the classroom, uncertainty can be encountered or induced (Beghetto in press). In the case of encountering uncertainty, a student may share an unexpected perspective or idea during an otherwise routine class discussion. Such ruptures in otherwise planned lessons, can serve as potentially creative openings (Beghetto 2016a). The potential of such openings can only be realized by engaging with (rather than dismissing) the uncertainty encountered in that surprising moment. Indeed, whenever some experience breaks upon our habit of expectation (Peirce 1958), it is a sign that new thought and action are required (Beghetto in press).

If, for instance, a student shares an unexpected idea, the student's teacher does not know in advance what the outcome will be if class time is used to explore that idea. It is possible that pursuing such an idea will cause confusion for other students and expend class time. It is also possible, however, that exploring the idea will result in a new and meaningful (i.e., creative) contribution to the discussion (see Gajda et al. 2017). The only way to know is to engage with the uncertainty of the rupture.

In addition to these unexpected encounters with uncertainty, teachers can also induce uncertainty. Induced uncertainty refers to teachers intentional and systematic efforts to present students with structured experiences with uncertainty in an otherwise supportive lesson. One way of doing so involves what has been called "lesson unplanning" (Beghetto 2018), which refers to blending *to-be-determined* openings with pre-determined features of learning activities, assignments and tasks. Students are then required to resolve the uncertainty of the to-be-determined aspect by responding in a new and meaningful (i.e., creative) way.

In sum, regardless of whether uncertainty is encountered or induced, it serves as a catalyst for creative thought and action because resolving uncertainty requires thinking and acting in new and meaningful ways. Although it is true that a student's new and meaningful insight might only be considered creative at the subjective level, it is also possible that working with those insights can result in creative contributions to others (Beghetto 2016b). In order for this to happen, educators need to provide opportunities for students (and themselves) to explore the creative potential that uncertainty offers. If the outcomes, procedure for arriving at those outcomes, and problems to be solved are all predetermined, then there is little room for creative expression in the classroom.

2.2.2 Emergent Processes and Products

Given that some level of uncertainty is involved in creative thought and action, it is difficult to predict what will emerge from students and teachers attempts to resolve uncertainty in the classroom. The creative resolution of uncertainty is therefore dynamic and emergent because both the process and the outcomes of creative thought and action change and take shape overtime (Corazza 2016; Beghetto 2016a).

With respect to the process, there are heuristics that people have used to creatively resolve uncertainty. Techniques that involve combining diverse stimuli in an effort to generate creative ideas, insights, and outcomes is a common example. Such heuristics have their basis in work that has explored the combinatorial aspects of the creative process (Finke et al. 1992; Rothenberg 2014). Indeed, creativity researchers have demonstrated that some of the most creative outcomes come from combining highly divergent and even opposing stimuli.

Although creativity researchers have been able to point to several examples of how combinatorial thinking results in creative outcomes, there is no guarantee that using such techniques will lead to creative results. Indeed, combinatorial thinking is a strategy, not an algorithm. Moreover, even in cases where techniques, such as conceptual combination, lead to creative outcomes those outcomes tend not to be known in advance.

One reason that there are no surefire techniques for generating creative thought and action is because creativity has an emergent quality to it. Emergent properties represent new features that are not known to be present in the initial stimuli (Sawyer 2012). It is for this reason that creativity researchers sometimes refer to the processes that lead to creative outcomes as being blind (Simonton 2017). Indeed, if we know the way to a solution in advance, then we don't need to think or act creatively. Rather, we could simply apply a pre-determined set of steps (Getzels 1964).

Consequently, creativity always involves some element of surprise (Simonton 2017). Creative outcomes start to take shape as we take action on them. The creative process "comes to a rest" once an idea or outcome has reasonably resolved the uncertainty being confronted (Peirce 1958). The process can be reanimated at later time points and by different participants (Beghetto 2016a; Corazza 2016; Gajda et al. 2017). A student's unique idea which has been discussed and accepted as relevant, can later be referred to by the teacher in a class discussion with a new group of students who then build on it and transform it into a different insight.

In this way, creative thought and action has a to-be-determined quality to it (Beghetto in press), which even when reasonably resolved, maintains a state of inconclusiveness (Corazza 2016). As students (or teachers) work through the uncertainty of a situation or task, they can resolve that uncertainty by producing new ideas, perspectives, or outcomes that reasonably meet the task constraints. The process is both dynamic and emergent.

If, for example, students are using conceptual combination as strategy to think differently about a problem, then they would not necessarily know in advance the specific combinatorial features that ultimately lead to creative resolution of a problem. Rather students need to develop and test out various alternatives until a reasonable solution takes shape. Students and teachers would also benefit from realizing that even "finished" work can be reanimated, remixed, and transformed into new works (Navas 2012).

2.2.3 *Generally Agreed Upon Criteria*

Although creativity has proven to be somewhat of an elusive concept in education (Plucker et al. 2004), creativity researchers generally agree (e.g., Kaufman 2016; Runco and Jaeger 2012; Stein 1953) that definitions of creativity tend to require two criteria[3]: *originality* (i.e., newness, uniqueness, or novelty) and *usefulness* (i.e., meaningful, meeting task constraints, or effective). Moreover, these criteria are defined within a particular socio-cultural and historical context.

The criteria of this definition implies a somewhat static characteristic to it and thereby might be thought of as applying to creative achievement, rather than the more dynamic aspects of the creative process (Giovanni Emanuele Corazza personal communication, April 26th, 2018). As we will discuss, however, judgments of creativity (even those that rely on these criteria) maintain a dynamic characteristic to them given that they vary by context and can be revisited at a later time and by a new audience.

In this way, creativity in the classroom can be thought of as a dynamic combination of original expression and meeting task constraints. Along these lines, a student's new and personally meaningful insights when learning something new can be considered creative in the context of that student's subjective experience (Beghetto and Kaufman 2007). In order for others to recognize a student's idea as creative, the student would need to demonstrate not only the originality of the idea, but also demonstrate how it fits the particular or situational tasks constraints (Beghetto 2016b). In many cases, the social recognition of creative outcomes is of most importance to creativity researchers because it is this level of creative expression that moves beyond a person's subjective experience and makes a contribution to the learning and insights of others (i.e., peers and teachers) in the classroom context.

2.2.4 Dynamic Judgments of Creativity

Much like the dynamic process that results in creative outcomes, so too are judgments about creative expression in classrooms. Although it is possible for teachers and peers to immediately recognize a student's unique perspective as creative, on other occasions student's unexpected ideas or actions may need to be explored or revisited in order to recognize that connection (Beghetto 2016b).

In the context of a classroom discussion, for instance, a student's unexpected utterance may be initially dismissed and then, only after the student's teacher or peers revisit the idea do they recognize its creative relevance (Gajda et al. 2017). In some cases, this recognition may be delayed over much longer time spans or only by virtue of analysis by outside observers (e.g., researchers analyzing transcripts, video footage or other artifacts from a classroom activity). Indeed, teachers and students may be so focused on attaining expected outcomes and fearing going off-topic that they do not recognize or value potentially fruitful deviations (Gralewski and Karwowski 2013; Kennedy 2005). In yet other cases, what was initially viewed as a creative response, may after consideration be recognized as lacking originality

---

[3] Several scholars have offered variations and elaborations on the two criteria definition of creativity (for recent examples see Corazza 2016; Simonton 2016; Smith and Smith 2017).

or failing to meet the task constraints in the context of the particular assignment or activity (Beghetto 2016a).

Taken together, these four assumptions highlight the dynamic nature of creative thought and action in classrooms. Specifically, uncertainty (which can be encountered or induced) serves as a catalyst for thinking and acting in creative ways. The process of creatively resolving uncertainty is dynamic and emergent, which means creative outcomes are difficult to predict at the outset and start to take shape overtime. This includes the opening of many new possibilities and trajectories along the way.

Given the dynamic nature of judgments about creativity, researchers and educators might benefit from moving away from terminology that implies a more final or fixed state (i.e., judgement, assessment) and toward more dynamic language. Following Corazza (2016), we would suggest that terms like "estimation" might be more appropriate and useful when describing creative phenomena. More dynamic labels highlight the indefinite features of creative judgements and signal the potential for differing perspectives and future possibilities.

In sum, resolving uncertainty when facing one situation can open multiple new areas of uncertainty. In other situations, the uncertainty faced by a student or teacher may not be resolved or only be temporarily resolved. The social judgments of whether a student or teacher resolves uncertainty in a creative way is based on the generally agreed upon criteria of blending originality and meeting task constraints as defined in a particular situation, activity, or task. Finally, estimations of what is or is not creative are also dynamic and can change over time and across contexts.

2.3 Implications for Research

Given these assumptions, how might researchers design studies that take into account the dynamic and emergent nature of creative expression in classrooms? In the sections that follow, we address this question by arguing for the use of a micro-longitudinal approach (Beghetto and Karwowski 2017; Karwowski and Beghetto 2018). More specifically, we briefly define what we mean by a micro-longitudinal approach and then discuss how such an approach can be used to study creative phenomena both at the individual and socio-interactional level.

2.3.1 A Micro-Longitudinal Approach to Studying Creativity in Classrooms

A micro-longitudinal approach is a dynamic approach. It requires taking multiple measurements of the phenomena of interest over a small period of time. Unlike typical longitudinal designs that involve making repeated measures at moderate to long intervals, micro-longitudinal designs take measurements at more rapid intervals (e.g., milliseconds, seconds, minutes). In this way, more dynamic and otherwise ephemeral phenomena can be recorded, analyzed, and interpreted (Beghetto 2016a; Gajda et al. 2017; Karwowski Beghetto 2018). Such approaches can be used with qualitative and quantitative data.

Qualitative Interpretations of Dynamic Visual Displays In the context of the classroom, researchers using micro-longitudinal approaches can develop dynamic visual displays of interactions to represent and analyze different patterns of interactions amongst students and teachers (Tanggaard and Beghetto 2015). Doing so can help explain classroom level variations in creative expression. Figure 2.1 provides an example of a micro-longitudinal display of a segment of class discussion (reproduced with permission from Gajda et al. 2017).

Figure 2.1 is based on a segment of classroom talk which involved 23 utterances (or turns), one teacher and seven students. Although it is beyond the scope of this chapter to provide a full detailed discussion and analysis of this visual display (see Gajda et al. 2017 for details), we want to briefly highlight a few key points germane to our discussion.

Using visual displays like the one depicted in Fig. 2.1 can provide a way for researchers to illustrate and interpret the dynamic patterns of interaction that occur in classrooms, including how ideas sometimes are dismissed (D), suspended (S), accepted (A), and returned to at later points (- - -). Such displays highlight the dynamic trajectories and potential of ideas that otherwise might be missed when relying solely on transcripts. Visual displays can support various analytic and interpretive possibilities, including comparing patterns of interaction between different types of classrooms and subject areas (see Beghetto 2016a;

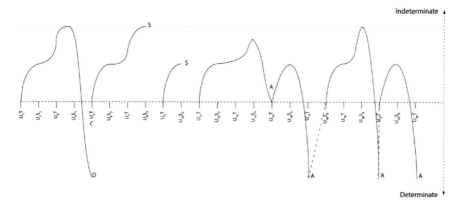

Fig. 2.1 Example of micro-longitudinal visual display. *Note*: U = each utterance. U# = temporal order of each utterance. T = teacher utterances. S = student utterances, S# = number of a particular student in order of the appearance. A = idea accepted or acknowledged by the teacher, D = dismissed by the teacher, S = idea not acknowledged, but suspended. Dotted lines (- - -) represent the teacher or students reanimating and building on a previous ideas

Gajda et al. 2017; Tanggaard and Beghetto 2015 for additional examples and more detailed discussion).

Dynamic Quantitative Approaches In addition to qualitative interpretations of classroom interactions, micro-longitudinal studies can complement and extend traditional approaches that rely on static snapshots to measure creative phenomena (e.g., single measure surveys, pre-post measures) and also compliment delayed interval approaches increasingly used by creativity researchers (e.g., experience sampling, diary-based methods; ecological momentary sampling).

Micro-longitudinal studies lend themselves to the kinds of analyses that allow researchers to examine the more nuanced and variable patterns of within and between subject variation in creative processes and outcomes of interest. Indeed, potentially important variations and patterns that are typically viewed as statistical noise or eliminated through statistical aggregate, can be analyzed and thereby offer new insights into the nature of creative phenomena.

One particularly promising application of such an approach is the examination of how different patterns of students' self-beliefs and emotions might explain differences in students' willingness to share creative ideas and make creative contributions in the classroom. Taking a micro-longitudinal approach to studying creative self-beliefs can help researchers to move from more traditional, static approaches and toward more sensitive and dynamic approaches.

In the sections that follow, we provide further discussion and examples of how micro-longitudinal approaches can be applied to estimating and analyzing creative-self beliefs. We close with a brief discussion of implications for future research and practice.

2.3.2 Creative Self–Beliefs: A Quick Overview

Creative self-beliefs refer to a "constellation of beliefs that shape one's creative self and play a unique role in helping to determine a person's engagement and performance on creative endeavors" (Karwowski and Beghetto 2018). The constellation of self-beliefs that make up one's creative identity can be organized into three broad categories: *Creative confidence* (i.e., beliefs in one' ability to think or act creatively), *creative self-awareness* (i.e., beliefs about the nature of one's creative abilities, including one's creative strengths and limitations), and *creative self-image* (i.e., beliefs about whether and how creative activities, aspirations, and abilities are part of one's sense of self) (Beghetto and Karwowski 2017; Karwowski and Beghetto 2018).

These beliefs vary across several dimensions (Beghetto and Karwowski 2017), including: temporal (i.e., past, present, and future orientation), stability (i.e., dynamic vs. static), and task (i.e., specific vs. general). For the purpose of this chapter we focus on creative confidence beliefs and discuss how taking a more dynamic, micro-longitudinal approach is necessary to measure and better understand the role these beliefs plays in creative behavior.

2.3.3 Measuring Creative Confidence: A Micro-Longitudinal Approach

One way to measure creative confidence beliefs more dynamically, is to incorporate them into a micro-longitudinal approach. As discussed, a micro-longitudinal approach involves taking multiple measures at brief intervals in an effort to more fully capture the variable nature of phenomena of interest. When it comes to creative confidence beliefs, researchers can apply this approach by first identifying a performance situation or task and then take measurements of creative confidence before, during, and after performing that task (Beghetto and Karwowski 2017; Karwowski et al. accepted).

Figure 2.2 illustrates a hypothetical example of how researchers can model components of a dynamic, micro-longitudinal assessment of creative confidence beliefs. The components are based on an activity that the first author (Beghetto) had initially designed for pedagogical purposes (i.e., help workshop participants become aware of the dynamic nature of their own creative confidence beliefs in conjunction with other factors, like emotions). Although the activity was designed for instructional purposes, researchers can easily adapt it for data collection and analysis.

As illustrated in Fig. 2.2, there are several components that can go into designing a micro-longitudinal study of creative confidence beliefs. These components can be organized across three measurement windows: Window 1 (i.e., prior to presenting the task to participants), Window 2 (i.e., immediately before and during task engagement), and Window 3 (i.e., following task completion).

Measurement Window 1 refers to the time period prior to introducing the specific performance task to participants. The goal of measurement Window 1 is to tap into the more general creative confidence beliefs (e.g., creative self-concept) related to the performance domain (e.g., problem solving) and any other variables of interest that might explain variations in confidence during task performance (e.g., background variables, emotional state, physiological arousal, situational variables) or be used as a point of comparison (e.g., general confidence completing tasks).

Depending on the goals of the study, general creative confidence can be estimated using a creative self-concept scale (Beghetto and Karwowski 2017) that taps into cognitive and affective perceptions of creative competence (e.g., I'm good at solving problems creatively; I enjoy coming up with creative solutions). Researchers can ask respondents to indicate their general confidence on a 100-point scale (0 = *not at all confident, 100 = extremely confident*). Importantly, general creative confidence is assessed *prior* to providing participants with a specific task.

Measurement Window 2 refers to the time period when participants are presented with a specific task (including instructions and criteria for success) and during actual task performance. During this time, researchers can assess the more dynamic nature of creative confidence for the specific task (e.g., confidence in producing a creative solution to this task, assessed on a 100-point scale) as well as any other variables of interest that might change across the duration of task engagement (e.g., emotional state, physiological arousal, confidence in completing the task).

2 Unfreezing Creativity: A Dynamic Micro-longitudinal Approach

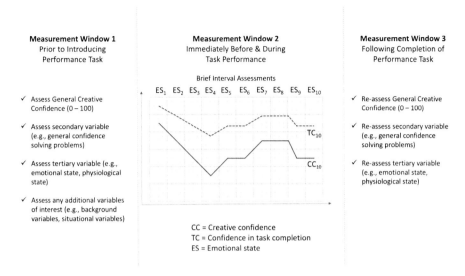

Fig. 2.2 Micro-longitudinal design of creative confidence beliefs

Measurement of variables should commence once participants have been presented with the task and have a clear understanding of what they are being asked to do. Measurements will continue at regular and rapid intervals (e.g., every minute) across the duration of the task. As illustrated in Fig. 2.1, within measurement Window 2, researchers can assess both continuous (e.g., creative confidence measured on a 100-point scale), discrete variables (e.g., reported emotional state), or some combination thereof (e.g., reported emotion and intensity of that emotion).

The task presented to participants should have a clear time limit (e.g., 10 min), specific criteria for successful completion (e.g., "design a visual representation of creative teaching using a total of six pattern blocks and write a 30-word description of your design"), and provide an opportunity for participants to solve the task in their own way and produce their own unique outcome. Put simply, the task should provide enough structure so participants can draw on their efficacy beliefs to predict and monitor their progress (Bandura 2012), but also have to-be-determined elements to afford opportunities for creative expression (Beghetto in press).

Finally, measurement Window 3 refers to measurements taken after the participants have completed the task or time has expired (whatever comes first). Measurement Window 3 provides researchers with an opportunity to re-assess the more general beliefs initially assessed during measurement window 1 and allow researchers to test a variety of theoretical assertions (e.g., the role that specific versus general confidence beliefs have on creative task performance).

Ideally, measurement Window 3 would include measurements taken immediately after task performance *and* at some later delayed interval (e.g., days, weeks, months later). In this way, micro-longitudinal work can complement more traditional longitudinal studies providing researchers with an opportunity to examine the stability of key variables and how performance on specific tasks might influence those variables.

2.3.4 Analyzing Micro-Longitudinal Creative Confidence Data

For decades, creativity researchers relied heavily on correlation-based or comparative (e.g., ANOVA-based) analytic methods to describe the relationships between creativity and its antecedents and consequences. Although these classic methods are still in use, a dynamic perspective requires more dynamic approaches to data analysis.

This dynamism is two-fold. First, it calls for interactive, intensive, longitudinal methods of data collection, as described above. Second, it requires fresh analytical techniques to properly model between and within-person variability in creative process, self-assessment or self-regulation. From a theoretical standpoint, the dynamic perspective is less focused on differences between people (i.e. the question of who feels more and who feels less confident) and more on intra-individual differences.

Consequently, the focus is on collecting and analyzing data that addresses questions of: When, where and under what circumstances the same people experience variations in their beliefs? Multilevel modelling and network modelling are two of the many possibilities to analyze such data.

Multilevel Models Multilevel models (or hierarchical linear models, see Snijders and Bosker 1999) extend typical analyses of regression by taking into account the nested structure of the data at hand. This "nesting" (a procedure that leads to biased statistical estimates) is often observed in research yet ignored. One obvious example of nesting are students clustered in classes or employees clustered in firms. Another type of clustering, more relevant for our discussion in this chapter, is nesting several responses or self-ratings within person.

When a participant provides several self-evaluations during a problem-solving session (see Fig. 2.1), researchers are not only interested in an average level of a person's creative confidence overall, but also in the variability of these intrapersonal changes. The level of within- and between occasion variability may be effectively quantified using the intraclass correlation coefficient (ICC, Bartko 1976). Conceptually, ICC denotes the percentage of the variance that lies between level-2 units – i.e. a person in our example. Consequently, 1-ICC denotes the percentages of variance that lie *within person* or *between occasions* for a specific person. Previous studies in creativity literature that utilized dynamic measurement (e.g. experience sampling method or diary studies (see Conner and Silvia 2015; da Costa et al. 2018; Karwowski et al. 2017) have demonstrated that the level of within person variability of creativity related emotions or beliefs tends to be large. This variability is in alignment with what our dynamic perspective assumes.

In other words, scholars using multi-level models have been able to describe how much people differ interpersonally (ICC) *and* how they differ from occasion to occasion (i.e., intrapersonally: 1-ICC). Importantly, the variance estimated at both levels can be effectively explained by subsequent multilevel models. Thus, researchers can use relatively stable characteristics of participants (i.e., their personality, previous creative achievements, or a creative self-concept) as between person predictors, but they can also include more dynamic, state-like variables collected during the process (e.g., creative confidence, affect or emotional arousal), as within person predictors.

A wide array of advanced, analytic and automated (AAA, see D'Mello et al. 2017) devices that allow for collecting data in real-time are available and may prove useful for creativity researchers. Examples include, measures of facial expression, attention shifts using eye-tracking methods, and emotional arousal based on galvanic skin response. With recent developments in technology, these kinds of data can be collected in a relatively non-intrusive way – without any effort from the participant, thus minimizing the risk of influencing and disturbing the processes the researcher is interested in.

It is important to note that the micro-longitudinal character of datasets makes it possible to explore important "chicken-and-egg" problems (i.e., the questions about possible cause-and-effect relationships and reciprocal links between psychological and social phenomena). Example questions include: Do positive emotions cause stronger creative self-beliefs during solving a problem or does growing creative confidence lead to emotional flourishing? Using micro-longitudinal datasets and applying multilevel models enables researchers to ask and address these more causal and dynamic questions (Conner et al. 2018).

Latent Growth Curve Modeling Latent growth curve modelling (LGC, see: Preacher 2008) is a special case of multilevel models that seems promising for dynamic creativity research. This method, originally developed for longitudinal studies within developmental psychology, bridges two analytical traditions: multilevel modelling and structural equation modelling (SEM). As we have discussed, multilevel modelling allows for a more appropriate estimation of parameters of interests by accounting for the nested structure of data and explaining within person variability.

Conceptually, LGC is based on multilevel modelling, but it also utilizes the SEM approach, whereby main variables of interest are modelled as latent variables. This allows for a proper control of measurement error and the model fit indices are available. In LGC models, two specific latent variables are modelled. The first is *intercept* – namely, the base level of creative confidence or any other variable of interest that is subject to change during the process. The second is *slope,* the average change between people (average slope) as well as the pattern of intra-individual changes (i.e., significance of the variance in slope).

Researchers using LGC can address questions such as: Does creative confidence increase or decrease while handling a creative task? Perhaps it follows a curvilinear trend from a relatively low level before the task, through high level during the task, all the way to a significant decrease after the task (U-curved shape)? Alternatively, maybe a high level of creative confidence from pretest decreases during the task and then increases (reversed U pattern)? Thus, LGC allows the researchers to estimate the overall pattern (shape) and level (the percentage of variance) of intra-individual changes and including intrapersonal and interpersonal factors that might explain this variability.

Both intercept and slope can be regressed on potentially relevant psychological, social or demographic predictors. Moreover, parallel LGC models (Preacher 2008) can be used to explore the extent to which the level and pattern of intraindividual change (hence: the slope) of a single variable, such as creative confidence, is linked to the level and pattern of change of another variable (arousal, affect, effectiveness of problem solving, etc.).

Network-Based Analysis Network psychometrics represent another set of promising analytical techniques that tend to be underutilized by creativity researchers (Constantini et al. 2017; Epskamp et al. 2017). Researchers can use network techniques to examine complex relationships between creative processual variables. Originally, statistical techniques based on network analyses were developed to explore the relationships between individuals in groups (e.g., describing their popularity, strength of social ties, exclusion from the wider social groups; see Wasserman and Faust 1994 or to study within- and between-networks diffusion of different phenomena, like obesity (Christakis and Fowler 2007).

It is important to note, that it is only recently that researchers have used network analyses to examine creativity-relevant phenomena rather than its more traditional and limited uses (Moreno 1960). In the creativity literature, researchers have used network-based analyses to explain the social positions of students with higher or lower creative accomplishments (see McKay et al. 2017; Kéri 2011). Network-based models can be useful for modelling and illustrating the dynamics of various psychological phenomena –from psychopathology, to play, and creativity.

Although researchers have tended to use network models to examine cross-sectional data (e.g., Christensen et al. 2018), there are recent developments to apply network models to simultaneously model both between- and within-person networks (see Constantini et al. 2017). As Constantini and colleagues (in press) have demonstrated, it is possible to model the dynamics of the relationship between different characteristics both between-subject and within-subject. While between-subject networks illustrate the dynamics that involve more stable, trait-like characteristics (i.e., personality), within-subject networks illustrate links between momentary levels of individuals characteristics – for example their moment-to-moment or problem-to-problem creative confidence and affect.

In short, an estimated network of the relationships between different characteristics of variables, provides an overview of the structure of links and interactions between these characteristics. Creativity researchers can use this technique to examine complex and dynamic interaction among emotions, confidence and subsequent micro-actions. Consider the hypothetical example of two simulated networks presented in Fig. 2.3.

2 Unfreezing Creativity: A Dynamic Micro-longitudinal Approach

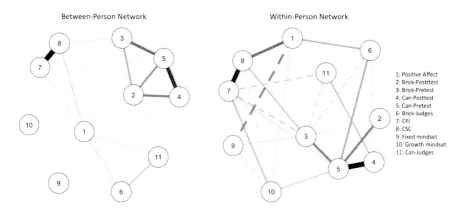

Fig. 2.3 Hypothetical example of between- and within-person network analysis. Simulated relationships between momentary creative self-efficacy while solving DT task and a number of related states. CPI = Creative personal identity. CSC = Creative self-concept

The left panel of this hypothetical example illustrates between-subject networks, while the right panel shows within-subject networks. Imagine that participants were asked to provide their creative confidence ratings in relation to two divergent thinking (DT) tasks – ability to come up with creative uses for a brick and a can. Imagine also that ratings were provided twice in relation to each DT problem – immediately after presentation of a problem (pre-test) and after solving it (post-test) – generated ideas were scored by external judges and a number of relevant characteristics of participants were also collected e.g., creative mindset (see Karwowski 2014), positive affect related to the task, creative self-concept (CSC), and creative personal identity (CPI).

These variables could then be analyzed using network-based analysis and potential similarities and differences of between-person and within-person networks could be identified. As illustrated in the hypothetical example presented in Fig. 2.3, one may conclude that at both between-person and within-person level, creative self-beliefs measures (creative self-concept, node 7 in the diagram) and creative personal identity, node 8 in the diagram) form a common cluster. In addition to helping identify similarities, these types of visual network can also highlight differences (e.g., general self-beliefs are relatively independent from the more dynamic, task related estimate of creative confidence, nodes 2–5). Moreover, the within-person panel of this hypothetical example demonstrates much denser relationships between these momentary assessments, growth mindset (node 10), and judges' ratings (nodes 6, 11). Thus, as this example illustrates, using network-based techniques may prove helpful in exploring whether and how changes occur in different types of beliefs and experiences while solving a problem (e.g., the intra-individual dynamics of creative confidence may be quite different from the aggregated, more stable between-person pattern of relationships).

At this point, we are not aware of any application of network models to study the dynamic of creative action, but as the above hypothetical example illustrates: The potential for using this and other types of dynamic and visually based analytic technique seems very promising for such purposes. Indeed, network models can serve as a useful solution of analyzing and illustrating the within-student and between-student dynamics of self-beliefs-activity links, and help untangle teacher-student interactions in a dynamic way (by modelling those interactions from teacher and student perspectives).

2.4 Concluding Thoughts

Our central argument in this chapter is: Creative phenomena in classrooms, like other contexts, is dynamic and therefore needs to be treated as such by researchers. Although traditional, static approaches have provided some glimpses into creative expression, we now have the theoretical, methodological, and analytic basis for approaching creative expression more dynamically. As we have asserted, micro-longitudinal approaches offer a particularly promising way for researchers to conceptualize, design, and study key features of creative expression within, between, and amongst students and teachers.

Even though such approaches are promising, there are several issues that need to be explored, including how intense micro-longitudinal measurements influence the creative process itself. Indeed, researchers using such methods will benefit from exploring how different types of measures might impact the process and outcomes in expected and unexpected ways. This includes exploring what kinds of less intrusive measures might be better suited for studying the emergent process of creative expression.

On the flipside, real-time measures also have the potential to provide real-time feedback that may be of benefit to people engaged in creative tasks and endeavors (Giovanni Emanuele Corazza, personal communication; see also, Agnoli et al. 2018). In short, there is much exciting and untapped potential in using more dynamic, real-time and micro-longitudinal designs to understand creative phenomena in and outside of classroom settings.

We therefore invite researchers interested in taking a more dynamic approach to studying creative expression in classrooms to join us in developing, testing, and refining the ideas we presented herein. We also recommend that educators rethink their own conceptualizations about the nature of creativity. The assumptions we outlined at the outset of this chapter can serve as starting points for educators to consider how they think about, estimate, and develop opportunities for creative thought and action in their own classrooms. Here's a quick recap of our assertions

- *Uncertainty serves as a catalyst for creative thought and action;*
- *Creative thought and action results from a dynamic and emergent processes;*
- *Determinations about creativity are based on generally agreed upon criteria; and*
- *Judgements about creativity are dynamic and subject to change across time and contexts.*

Building from these assumptions, we have attempted to describe how educators and researchers might approach creativity differently in their work.

A dynamic perspective on creativity is promising, not because it reduces the complexity of how we think about, try to support, or study creative expression in classrooms. Rather, it is promising because it requires researchers and educators to come together in an effort to better understand how, when, and under what conditions creative thought and action manifests in classrooms.

References

Agnoli, S., Zanon, M., Mastria, S., Avenanti, A., & Corazza, G. E. (2018). Enhancing creative cognition with a rapid right-parietal neurofeedback procedure. *Neuropsychologia*. https://doi.org/10.1016/j.neuropsychologia.2018.02.015.

Aljughaiman, A., & Mowrer-Reynolds, E. (2005). Teachers' conceptions of creativity and creative students. *Journal of Creative Behavior, 39*, 17–34.

Amabile, T. M. (1996). *Creativity in context: Update to 'The Social Psychology of Creativity'*. Boulder: Westview Press.

Bandura, A. (2012). On the functional properties of perceived self-efficacy revisited. *Journal of Management, 38*, 9–44. https://doi.org/10.1177/0149206311410606.

Bartko, J. J. (1976). On various intraclass correlation reliability coefficients. *Psychological Bulletin, 83*(5), 762–765.

Beghetto, R. A. (2016a). Creative openings in the social interactions of teaching. *Creativity: Theories-Research-Applications, 3*, 261–273.

Beghetto, R. A. (2016b). Creative learning: A fresh look. *Journal of Cognitive Education and Psychology, 15*, 6–23.

Beghetto, R. A. (in press). From static to dynamic: Toward a socio-dynamic perspective on creativity in classrooms. In I. Lebuda & V. Glaveanu (Eds.), *Palgrave handbook on social creativity*. London: Palgrave.

Beghetto, R. A. (2018). *What if? Unleashing the power of complex challenges in teaching and learning*. Alexandria: ASCD.

Beghetto, R. A., & Karwowski, M. (2017). Toward untangling creative self-beliefs. In M. Karwowski & J. C. Kaufman (Eds.), *The creative self: Effects of self-efficacy, mindset and identity* (pp. 4–24). San Diego: Academic.

Beghetto, R. A., & Kaufman, J. C. (2007). Toward a broader conception of creativity: A case for mini-c creativity. *Psychology of Aesthetics, Creativity, and the Arts, 1*, 73–79.

Christakis, N. A., & Fowler, J. H. (2007). The spread of obesity in a large social network over 32 years. *New England Journal of Medicine, 357*(4), 370–379.

Christensen, A. P., Cotter, K. N., Silvia, P. J. (2018). *Nomological network of openness to experience: A network analysis of four openness to experience inventories*. Unpublished manuscript available at: https://osf.io/47xjp/.

Conner, T. S., & Silvia, P. J. (2015). Creative days: A daily diary study of emotion, personality, and everyday creativity. *Psychology of Aesthetics, Creativity, and the Arts, 9*(4), 463–470.

Conner, T. S., DeYoung, C. G., & Silvia, P. J. (2018). Everyday creative activity as a path to flourishing. *The Journal of Positive Psychology, 13*, 181–189.

Corazza, G. E. (2016). Potential originality and effectiveness: The dynamic definition of creativity. *Creativity Research Journal, 28*, 258–267.

Costantini, G., Richetin, J., Preti, E., Casini, E., Epskamp, S., & Perugini, M. (2017). *Stability and variability of personality networks. A tutorial on recent developments in network psychometrics*. Personality and Individual Differences.

D'Mello, S., Dieterle, E., & Duckworth, A. (2017). Advanced, analytic, automated (AAA) measurement of engagement during learning. *Educational Psychologist, 52*(2), 104–123.

da Costa, C. G., Zhou, Q., & Ferreira, A. I. (2018). State and trait anger predicting creative process engagement: The role of emotion regulation. *Journal of Creative Behavior.* https://doi.org/10.1002/jocb.236.

Dewey, J. (2007). *The school and society.* New York: Cosimo (Original work published 1899).

Epskamp, S., Borsboom, D., & Fried, E. I. (2017). Estimating psychological networks and their accuracy: A tutorial paper. *Behavior Research Methods, 50,* 195–212.

Finke, R. A., Ward, T. M., & Smith, S. M. (1992). *Creative cognition: Theory, research, and applications.* Cambridge, MA: MIT Press.

Froebel, F. (1887/1906). *The education of man.* New York: D. Appleton & Company.

Gajda, A., Beghetto, R. A., & Karwowski, M. (2017). Exploring creative learning in the classroom: A multi-method approach. *Thinking Skills and Creativity, 24,* 250–267.

Getzels, J. W. (1964). Creative thinking, problem solving, and instruction. In E. R. Hilgard (Ed.), *Theories of learning and instruction* (pp. 240–267). Chicago: University of Chicago Pres.

Gralewski, J., & Karwowski, M. (2013). Polite girls and creative boys? Students' gender moderates accuracy of teachers' ratings of creativity. *The Journal of Creative Behavior, 47*(4), 290–304.

Guilford, J. P. (1950). Creativity. *American Psychologist, 5,* 444–454.

Guilford, J. P. (1967). Creativity and learning. In D. B. Lindsley & A. A. Lumsdaine (Eds.), *Brain function, Vol. IV: Brain function and learning.* Los Angeles: University of California Press.

Jauk, E., Benedek, M., & Neubauer, A. C. (2014). The road to creative achievement: A latent variable model of ability and personality predictors. *European Journal of Personality, 28,* 95–105.

Karwowski, M. (2014). Creative mindsets: Measurement, correlates, consequences. *Psychology of Aesthetics, Creativity, and the Arts, 8,* 62–70.

Karwowski, M., & Beghetto, R. A. (2018). Creative behavior as agentic action. Psychology of Aesthetics, Creativity, and the Arts. Advanced online publication, https://doi.org/10.1037/aca0000190.

Karwowski, M., Han, M., & Beghetto, R. A. (accepted). Toward dynamiting the measurement of creative confidence beliefs. *Psychology of Aesthetics, Creativity, and the Arts.*

Karwowski, M., Lebuda, I., Wisniewska, E., & Gralewski, J. (2013). Big five personality traits as the predictors of creative self-efficacy and creative personal identity: Does gender matter? *Journal of Creative Behavior, 47*(3), 215–232.

Karwowski, M., Lebuda, I., Szumski, G., & Firkowska-Mankiewicz, A. (2017). From moment-to-moment to day-to-day: Experience sampling and diary investigations in adults' everyday creativity. *Psychology of Aesthetics, Creativity, and the Arts, 11,* 309–324.

Kaufman, J. C. (2016). *Creativity 101* (2nd ed.). New York: Springer Publishing Company.

Kennedy, M. (2005). *Inside teaching: How classroom life undermines reform.* Cambridge, MA: Harvard University Press.

Kéri, S. (2011). Solitary minds and social capital: Latent inhibition, general intellectual functions and social network size predict creative achievements. *Psychology of Aesthetics, Creativity, and the Arts, 5,* 215–221.

McKay, A. S., Grygiel, P., & Karwowski, M. (2017). Connected to create: A social network analysis of friendship ties and creativity. *Psychology of Aesthetics, Creativity, and the Arts, 11,* 284–294.

Moreno, J. L. (1960). *The sociometry reader.* New York: Free Press.

Navas, E. (2012). *Remix theory: The aesthetics of sampling.* New York: Springer.

O'Quin, K., & Besemer, S. (1989). The development, reliability, and validity of the revised: Creative product semantic scale. *Creativity Research Journal, 2,* 267–278.

Peirce, C. S. (1958). In A. W. Burks (Ed.), *Collected papers of Charles Sanders Peirce.* Cambridge, MA: The Belknap Press of Harvard University Press.

Plucker, J. A., & Makel, M. C. (2010). Assessment of creativity. In J. C. Kaufman & R. J. Sternberg (Eds.), *The Cambridge handbook of creativity* (pp. 48–73). New York: Cambridge University Press.

Plucker, J., Beghetto, R. A., & Dow, G. (2004). Why isn't creativity more important to educational psychologists? Potential, pitfalls, and future directions in creativity research. *Educational Psychologist, 39*, 83–96.

Preacher, K. J. (2008). *Latent growth curve modeling*. Thousand Oaks: Sage.

Reiter-Palmon, R., Beghetto, R. A., & Kaufman, J. C. (2014). Looking at creativity through a Business-Psychology-Education (BPE) Lens: The challenge and benefits of listening to each other. In E. Shiu (Ed.), *Creativity research: An interdisciplinary and multidisciplinary research handbook* (pp. 9–30). New York: Routledge.

Renzulli, J. S., Smith, L. H., White, A. J., Callahan, C. M., & Hartman, R. K. (1976). *Scales for rating the behavioral characteristics of superior students*. Mansfield Center: Creative Learning Press.

Rothenberg, A. (2014). *Flight from wonder: An investigation of scientific creativity*. New York: Oxford University Press.

Runco, M. A., & Jaeger, G. J. (2012a). The standard definition of creativity. *Creativity Research Journal, 24*, 92–96.

Sawyer, R. K. (2012). *Explaining creativity: The science of human innovation* (2nd ed.). New York: Oxford University Press.

Schacter, J., Thum, Y. M., & Zifkin, D. (2006). How much does creative teaching enhance elementary school students' achievement? *The Journal of Creative Behavior, 40*, 47–72.

Simonton, D. K. (2017). Defining creativity: Don't we also need to define what is *not* creative? *Journal of Creative Behavior, 51*, 281–284.

Smith, J. K., & Smith, L. F. (2017). The 1.5 criterion model of creativity: Where less is more, more or less. *Journal of Creative Behavior, 51*, 281–284.

Snijders, T., & Bosker, R. (1999). *Multilevel analysis: An introduction to basic and applied multilevel analysis*. London: Sage.

Stein, M. I. (1953). Creativity and culture. *The Journal of Psychology, 36*, 311–322.

Tanggaard, L., & Beghetto, R. A. (2015). Ideational pathways: Toward a new approach for studying the life of ideas. *Creativity: Theories— Research—Applications, 2*, 129–144.

Torrance, E. P. (1966). *The Torrance tests of creative thinking-norms-technical manual research edition-verbal tests, forms a and b-figural tests, Forms A and B*. Princeton: Personnel Press.

Wasserman, S., & Faust, K. (1994). *Social network analysis: Methods and applications*. New York: Cambridge University Press.

Chapter 3
Participatory Creativity: Supporting Dynamic Roles and Perspectives in the Classroom

Edward P. Clapp and Michael Hanchett Hanson

Abstract This chapter introduces the concept of participatory creativity as a dynamic approach to invention and innovation that is particularly relevant to the field of education. Here, the focus of creativity studies shifts from individual ideation to interactions within complex sociohistorical systems. While acknowledging the roles played by those who successfully commit exceptional energy and resources to creative projects and new points of view, the participatory approach reframes those previously deemed as creative individuals as participants in larger narratives. These complex processes of change are described as the *biographies of ideas*. People play various roles as they contribute to these biographies over time. Such roles are social positions that are neither fixed nor uni-dimensional, but dynamic. After framing this position from a theoretical perspective, the authors offer two examples of participatory creativity in action. These examples show how moving the locus of creativity from individual ideation to social participation makes visible the many ways that young people can participate in the development of creative ideas, while also establishing their own unique "profile of participation" and encouraging creative agency—all while honoring students' diverse knowledge, expertise, background experiences, and sociocultural perspectives. After discussing some of the limitations of this reframing of creativity as a participatory process, the authors conclude by suggesting implications for practice and future research.

E. P. Clapp (✉)
Project Zero, Harvard Graduate School of Education, Cambridge, MA, USA
e-mail: edward_clapp@gse.harvard.edu

M. Hanchett Hanson
Teachers College, Columbia University, New York City, NY, USA
e-mail: mah59@tc.columbia.edu

3.1 Introduction

Throughout the United States—and across the globe—society has changed dramatically over the past few decades, with electronic technologies permeating every aspect of life. How people access information, and who has access; how people work together, at what pace, and over any distance; how identities are constructed, expressed, and reconstructed; whether and how the best and worst of human impulses are expressed; how public opinion is swayed, and by whom—all of these aspects of life have changed in ways that would have been hardly recognizable just 20 years ago. One effect of our interconnected and digital times is that almost every aspect of our lived experiences has become both more distributed and more participatory. In particular, patterns of idea formation and transformation have become more apparent than they have been in the past—and more important. During these changing times, the conceit of lone individuals being the source of innovative ideas has become harder and harder to maintain—and yet it persists. Why?

At the same time as these societal shifts have been re-shaping so many of our lived experiences, theories advocating for sociocultural, distributed, and participatory understandings of creativity have advanced. This work began with early concerns about an over-emphasis on individualism and an interest in the social and cultural dynamics that effect creativity, spearheaded by theorists like Amabile et al. (1996), Csikszentmihalyi (1997, 1999) and John-Steiner (1997, 2015). Today's participatory view of creativity (e.g., Clapp 2017; Glăveanu 2010, 2014a, b; Hanchett Hanson 2015) has built upon that early work as a synthesis, combining sociocultural analysis, developmental psychology, and distributed cognition theory. A participatory view of creativity moves away from the traditional focus on individuals and ideation—and even away from the concept of group or collaborative ideation. Instead, the focus of participatory creativity is on elaboration and integration of ideas at both cognitive and social levels—all via the mechanism of participation. Many social positions, commonly referred to as roles, contribute to this variety of "work," including formal and informal influencers, producers, and audiences, but also teachers, confidants, and so on. Even adversaries, rivals, and adverse conditions may be considered key actors in the development of creative ideas. From the participatory perspective, artifacts, technology, and the natural and constructed worlds also play crucial roles in the creative process.

Earlier views of creativity, focusing on the traits of purported "geniuses," assumed that ideas originated in the minds of individuals. "Having ideas" was the goal of creativity. Participatory views, in contrast, assume that ideas are symbol manipulations that originate in learning the symbol systems of one's worlds[1] and evolve through social and material interactions. In other words, the meaning of any one person's ideas is always mediated by existing symbol systems. Ideas exist in a

---

[1] "Worlds" are the patterns of meaning in which people participate. In other words: historically produced and contextually specific symbol systems through which people make meaning. This usage borrows from both Nelson Goodman's (1978) views of constructionism and Rollo May's (1974) analysis of the creative encounter between people and their worlds.

social space, not within the skulls and skin of individuals. Indeed, because symbols are means of communication, both influencers and audiences are inherent to ideation. Yes, many purported creative individuals may spend much of their lives alone—working on manuscripts, paintings, experiments, or business plans. This solitary work is often productive and important. From the beginning to end, however, they are not actually alone, but drawing on past collaborations (Sawyer 2007), engaging with the tools and technologies of those who have come before them (Glăveanu 2014a), and working in relation to an often complex polyphony of current and historical audiences.

How, then, should we think of Confucius, Murasaki Shikibu, Leonardo da Vinci, Sir Isaac Newton, Jane Austen, Madame Curie, Rabindranath Tagore, Maya Angelou, Pablo Picasso, Frida Kahlo, John Coltrane, Madonna, Jay Z, and on and on? Are they not creative geniuses?

Participatory views of creativity continue to recognize the importance of such creative contributors—but reframe the analysis of their roles in a much broader arc of creative idea development. This reframing of creativity prompts a shift in focus focus from a Promethean narrative of brilliant individuals overthrowing social conventions to individiuals taking up roles among an array of actors who contribute to the evolution of their worlds through various social positions. Singular individuals may commit extraordinary energy and resources to put together, reapply, and champion particular ideas and points of view, and those individuals are important. That being said, in every instance of invention and innovation, such individual work paints little more than a portion of the whole picture. If the interest of creativity theory is to prop up unrealistic views of rugged individualism inherited from nineteenth century Romanticism via the American Cold War (Hanchett Hanson 2015), the current ideational focus of creativity as divergent thinking, social personality traits, giftedeness, genius, or sudden insight might do the trick. But to understand how change occurs in individual points of view and social and material worlds over time calls for a broader perspective.

Like the world of work—and in part because of its changing nature—education has much to gain from a reframing of creativity as a dynamic, distributed, and participatory process. Indeed, the educational need may be even more urgent than in any other domain. Throughout the United States—and in many countries around the world—"school" is largely based on learning driven by individual achievement. This overwhelming emphasis on individual achievement within many teaching and learning environments bleeds into conceptions of creativity in the classroom. (See additional discussion in Dr. Hanchett Hanson's Chapter on the ideology of creativity in this volume.) In this space creativity is too often seen as an individual capacity. Such an individual focus on creativity, and a narrow focus on what creativity is, sets up a scenario where some students may see themselves as more or less creative than others, and some students may see themselves as not being creative at all. What is needed here is a reorientation towards creativity that suggests that *no* students are creative. Instead, *all* students have the opportunity to *participate* in creativity. The primary means by which we suggest making this shift is to introduce a participatory understanding of creativity that honors the diverse knowledge, expertise, background experiences, and sociocultural perspectives that all students bring with them when they enter the classroom, and to show how there are various roles that each student may play when they participate in creativity. By doing so, young people develop dynamic profiles of participation that are unique to each individual.

The reframing we provide below describes the concept of participatory creativity as a broader and more realistic perspective on creative work. First we offer a discussion of the theoretical frameworks that serve as the basis for our reframing of creativity as a distributed and participatory process, then we present two examples of participatory creativity in action, within two different learning environments. Finally, we explore the limitations of our reframing of creativity as a distributed and participatory process, including our suggestions for future research.

3.2 Theoretical Foundations

3.2.1 Sociocultural Systems Theory

One of the most influential theorists to move away from a focus on the individual was Csikzentmihalyi (1997, 1999) whose social systems theory located creativity in the tension between individuals' ideas, the domains (symbol systems) in which they worked, and the field (gatekeepers) who evaluated and integrated the work into the domain. Here, the field is particularly important. These are the people who judge whether or not ideas are of value, and therefore to be considered "creative." Sawyer (2012) expanded the view of the field to include informal audiences, and the participatory approach has expanded this model even further. This view of creativity as a judgment arising from social dynamics of many actors is fundamental to the participatory approach.

3.2.2 Constructivist Developmental Theories

The early-twentieth-century constructivist theories of Piaget and Vygotsky have had enormous influence on developmental psychology. Analyses of creative development have also come directly from their work. John-Steiner and Moran (John-Steiner 1997, 2015; Moran and John-Steiner 2003) have advocated a Vygotskyan view of creative development, emphasizing the role of social context in creative thinking. People develop by internalizing concepts and practices from their social context, including language, customs, aesthetics, notation systems, ethics, and so on. Then they externalize what they learn, expressing themselves through those same meaning systems. In other words, development is socially situated from beginning to end. Gruber et al. (Gruber and Davis 1988; Wallace and Gruber 1989, 1999) came to similar conclusions in extending Piaget's theories to lifelong creative development (the evolving systems approach). These researchers studied creativity as a form of work, a complex behavior with different goals, settings, resources, and personal styles in each case. Through case-study analysis of famous people, these researchers concluded that individuals develop a sense of creative purpose, distinctive points of view, habits of work, and personal styles over time in a dialectical relationship to the work itself. At its core that work is an organization of resources and always embedded in personal and sociohistorical worlds.

3.2.3 Distributed Cognition

Gruber's systemic view of individual development, Vygotsky's dialectics of development in sociohistorical contexts, and Csikszentmihalyi's social systems theory—all of these situate creativity in social and material interactions well beyond the confines of the human skull. Still, the break has not been clean. Old inside-the-head cognitive frames have persisted alongside the alternative views. The last piece of the puzzle is, then, distributed cognition theory itself.

One of the most influential theorists of distributed cognition has been Edwin Hutchins. Hutchins' analysis of the navigation crew of the *USS Palau* provided a paradigmatic example of distributed cognition (Hutchins 1995). No one on a ship knows everything that is going on, not even the Captain. The ship is navigated through people interacting with each other and the technologies of the ship itself (e.g., radar, positioning technologies, etc.). When something goes awry, like an equipment failure, the crew-ship system may have to improvise. Hutchins' research showed how new solutions emerged from both the interactions of the crew with the ship and the interactions of the crewmembers with each other. The thinking was, thus, distributed temporally, socially, and materially.

People do not have to be faced with navigating a naval escort carrier to experience the distribution of thought. Creativity researcher Keith Sawyer and his associates (Sawyer 2010, 2011; Sawyer and DeZutter 2009) have built on experiences in improvisational theater and jazz performances to analyze the social emergence of creativity. Even the most celebrated "creative geniuses" worked in analogous ensembles. For example, Freud's inner circle met regularly to discuss ideas, review cases and, as a group, literally develop the theories and techniques of psychoanalysis. Furthermore, Freud, his colleagues, and critics worked in the material world. The material distribution of thought is particularly important for creativity research. Staying with the Freud example, without letters and books and journals, his ideas would not have spread to those he influenced during his life, much less to people today, more than 80 years after his death. Without the trains that influenced so much of the nineteenth and early twentieth centuries, there would not have been annual, international psychoanalytic conferences. Just as Hutchins analyzed constant interaction between the social and material distribution of thought on the *USS Palau*, the material world plays crucial roles in creative thinking. Books, letters, technologies, works of art, and so on, are actors in the creative process (Glăveanu 2014a; Latour

2005). They store and carry messages across time and space. They accommodate some kinds of work and resist others. They do not have intentions but can carry and inspire them, making the communication and understanding of intention possible.

3.3 Participating Roles

According to the theories described above, thought and the distribution of thought have emergent structures. Participation itself also has structure, commonly called *roles*. These are constructs that loosely codify social positions[2] and mediate the individual and the social, facilitating participation in change. "Artist," "agent," "friend," "reviewer," "CEO," "Creative Director," and "teacher" are such roles for which community norms exist. They affect how people relate to each other, the resources available to them and what will be considered responsible, remarkable, and scandalous behavior. People take up their roles in different ways and sometimes to unexpected ends, however. In other words, although roles are learned and recognizable social positions that help define interactions, they can also provide unexpected affordances.

Roles come in groups. A fundamental point of the participatory approach to creativity is that the world stage does not accommodate true "one-man" shows. (Even the literal theatrical version requires an audience, writers, funders, promoters, and many crew members to focus everyone's attention on the seemingly solo performer.) One way roles are grouped is through complementary positions. For example, teachers work with students, editors work with writers, gallery owners with artists and collectors. Building on the work of George Herbert Mead, Martin (2013, 2014, 2015) has studied how people who do extraordinary work take up roles and develop styles of roles in relation to both particular individuals in their lives (e.g., family, teachers, mentors, etc.) and general others (e.g., historical figures, pop culture icons, community members, etc.). People learn, not just *their* role but also the *complementary* roles. Teachers draw on their experiences as students. Often, gallery owners are, or have been, artists. Editors know good writing from being readers and may coach writers based on their own experience of writing.

---

[2] Today, many theorists avoid the term role, analyzing instead social positions. That approach emphasizes the enacted and physical aspects of social interactions. While recognizing the legitimacy of these points, here, the authors have chosen a different strategy. Because creativity theory is so often applied in everyday settings with non-academic practitioners (e.g., students and teachers), we have chosen to use the more common term of role, while acknowledging the need to research the physical instantiation of roles. Another reason for this strategy is that participatory creativity includes analysis of material actors. In everyday speech, discussing the roles of technology and nature makes sense; whereas, discussing the *social* position of material actors stretches the meaning of terms beyond what we consider helpful.

Beyond complementary pairings, the social organization of any domain comes with a full cast of roles. For example, the domain of music today includes composers, lyricists, performers, producers, agents, record companies, online streaming organizations, reviewers, pirates, fans, and consumers, plus everyone involved in concert venues, ticket sales, instrument manufacturing and on and on. In analyzing any specific creative contribution, three general types of roles are of interest: producers (those who lead the charge, including the individuals formerly called "creators" or "creative geniuses"), the influencers from whom producers draw, and the multiple audiences they address.

Note that the same person can, and usually does, take up many roles in the creative process—the building, integration, and interpretation of ideas. Professional writers often write book reviews, theorists often write peer reviews, and gallery owners may also be artists. In the online space, one may contribute content to a digital platform, like or comment on the contributions of others, or even download, hack, and re-upload content originally contributed by others (Duncum 2013). This is common practice amongst young people and adults throughout the social media sphere. The dynamism of roles moves, then, along several axes, including complementary positions, influencer-audience oscillations and stylistic shifts. The complementary roles that Martin analyzed using Mead's theories are relatively stable social positions in any given situation. People tend to progress from student to teacher of an art or act as writer or editor on a given project. Influencer and audience roles, in contrast, can be very hard to parse. One's teachers are influencers but also tend to become internalized audiences, if not an active audience in the external world.

Note also, the same person will take up the same nominal role in different ways, depending on context. To continue the theatrical analogy, characters may evolve or simply act differently in different scenes, revealing the individual within the role. In everyday life, the same teacher may be nurturing in some situations, unbending on standards in others, and dismissive of inadequate work in yet others. Each role is, thus, only *loosely codified* within social traditions. A role is not just a set of expectations, responsibilities, and limitations but also offers affordances that different people use in different ways, and the same person may use in different ways at different times.

Finally, material worlds play roles in all of these interactions. What is communicated, how it is communicated, to whom, how quickly, and across what timespans and distances—all of these are strongly influenced by technologies and artifacts. The inspiration that Basquiat gives an artist could not be conveyed without physical form, his paintings—and Basquiat could not have made the paintings he did without the tools and materials he worked with, nor without the technologies and artifacts associated with the culture he worked within. To analyze creative work without attention to the roles of technologies and material actors is to leave out much of the picture, both figuratively and literally.

3.4 Biographies of Ideas

One way to shift the focus of creativity research from individual ideation to broader social and material systems is to organize the analysis around the biographies of ideas (Clapp 2017) that come to be seen as "creative." These ideas have histories to which many people contribute. At different points one or another person may take leadership, pulling together resources and ideas and taking risks to make a distinctive contribution, but creative ideas are never finished.

For example, Darwin's name has become eponymous, a synonym for evolution. However, his contribution of natural selection was only one beat in an already well-established debate about evolution (Gruber 1981). The environment in which Darwin matured already included the concept of evolution. (Darwin's own grandfather, Erasmus Darwin, was an evolutionist and naturalist Jean-Baptiste Lamarck had put forth a theory of evolution.) While Darwin's contributions significantly advanced evolutionary theory, this work would not be so powerful without the later contributions of genetics and of all of the research applying his ideas—and taking issue with it—that continues today.[3]

A similar story may be told about the relationship between Dr. Martin Luther King, Jr. and the Civil Rights movement. Like the association of Darwin and evolution, King has long been deeply associated with the Civil Rights movement of the 1960s. It is not a stretch to say that, in popular speech and rhetoric, King has even been portrayed by many as being the father of this movement. But a more careful look at the Civil Rights movement reveals that, like Darwin, King's work in this arena drew upon longstanding historical roots and social momentum. Indeed, the work of the Civil Rights movement did not conclude with the Civil Rights Act of 1964, but instead carries on to this day. While King played a prominent role in the Civil Rights movement—and Darwin a prominent role in the development of evolutionary theory—both arenas were richly filled with a host of other actors before, during, and after these two men made their contributions.

One of the key advantages for developing the biographies of ideas is the power that this approach has to make the creative process visible. More individual-based orientations towards creativity retain a sense of mystique, as they fail to make creativity visible. By contrast, describing the biography of an idea reveals not only the various forms an idea assumes as it takes shape in the world, but also the various actors who have contributed to the development of an idea along the way.

---

[3] Interestingly, that work includes using evolution as a paradigm for cognitive and social dynamics of creativity (see for example Perkins 2000 and Simonton 1999).

3.5 Participatory Creativity and Educational Practice

While it is useful to bring the concept of role to an analysis of the development of creative ideas from academic and historical perspectives, shifting the creativity narrative in the direction of a more participatory perspective has no greater urgency in the world than it does within the educational sphere. It is here that young people develop an identification with—or become alienated from—creativity in ways that have lasting effects. It is therefore imperative that young people become cognizant of the many roles they may play throughout the process of creative idea development. The biography of an idea approach to describing participatory creativity has the power of making creativity visible in the classroom. By making creativity visible in this way, young people may better see how they, too, may participate in creativity in various ways.

3.5.1 Profiles of Participation

As with historical figures, students in classrooms also take on multiple roles, but it is important to note that these roles are flexible and dynamic, not rigid, narrowly defined, or fixed. The roles that young people play when they participate in creativity are often informed by their strengths, as well as their background experiences and sociocultural perspectives. We call the variety of roles a student is apt to play in the creative idea development process the student's current *profile of participation.*

Utilizing the biography of an idea approach, one may develop a sensitivity to the various roles one plays in the development of creative ideas by noting moments of significant participation. This concept does not require difficult methodologies, just awareness of and attention to role dynamics. Because role profiles evolve over time and across contexts, the awareness is more important than measurement precision—at least in actual educational settings. The point is for teachers and students to (a) appreciate all contributions, (b) be aware of each student's strengths, and (c) also be attuned to opportunities to make contributions from roles they have not yet explored.

Each young person's profile of participation is unique, and there is no limit to the variety of profiles of participation that may be expressed by young people when they participate in the development of creative ideas. From this perspective, young people can participate in creativity, rather than "having" creativity. In the participatory framework, *being* creative is not a relevant question. No one *has* creativity, because creativity is always socially situated. No one *is* creative for the same reason, but also because there is no one way to be creative. Quite intentionally, participatory creativity suggests a move away from a *possessive* view of creativity, towards a *participatory* view that honors the knowledge, expertise, background experiences, and sociocultural perspectives that all young people bring to their work in the creative classroom.

3.5.2 Encouraging Creative Identity

In addition to students' roles in the classroom, there is the question of identity. Like many adults, many young people have grown up with an understanding of creativity from a traditional, individual-based perspective that centers on eminent individuals who have achieved a degree of "greatness" for their accomplishments in a particular field or profession. Within the participatory framework, these individuals remain important, now viewed as significant actors within broader narratives. As Corazza (2016) has suggested, the amount of resources put toward creative pursuits is an important factor in identifying creative activity—discussed here as participation in the biographies of creative ideas. The amount of energy and resources that young people commit to invention and innovation is certainly key to students' personal identification with creative work, but to be realistic, these commitments must be understood as part of larger social and material worlds. In education, this understanding can emerge from how key historical innovations are presented.

Within many teaching and learning environments, the social and material dynamics associated with participatory creativity can be easily overshadowed by the "greatness" of historical individuals heralded for their genius, originality, and courage within a particular curriculum. While such creative individuals are often presented as role models for young people, because of the greater-than-thou ways in which these individuals are framed, growing up to be a creative genius like fill-in-the-blank can seem daunting, if not entirely out of reach. This issue is compounded by the racial and gender bias towards white male creative icons (e.g., Albert Einstein, Vincent Van Gogh, Charles Darwin, Steve Jobs, etc.) who literally do not look like the majority of young people in many schools. The emphasis on a particular set of skills, cognitive abilities, or character traits of a particular individual may further estrange young people who do not see themselves as being talented or "gifted" in these same ways. Some educators, however, have found opportunities to teach young people about creativity from a different, more inclusive, and more accessible perspective.

3.5.3 Reframing Creativity as a Participatory Process in Elementary School

One such educator is Julie Rains. Julie teaches within a media center at a public elementary school in the suburbs of Detroit, Michigan. Throughout her work as an educator Julie has engaged with young learners with special needs, as well as within integrated classrooms where young people of various ability levels have come together. As part of the third grade curriculum at her school, Julie's colleagues have taught a unit on Henry Ford as a part of Michigan history, coupled with a unit about biographies—where the life story of Henry Ford often plays a role. Teaching about Henry Ford makes great sense for Julie's colleagues, as he was an instrumental player in the development of the automobile industry that had been a driver of the *Motor City* economy for many years. Being in such close proximity to Detroit, Henry Ford has been framed not only as an outstanding creative individual, but also as a part of the students' history.

Julie understood that creativity is not an isolated human endeavor, but rather a distributed and participatory process. Her concern was that given the individual focus of the unit on Henry Ford, students at her school might develop a great man understanding of creativity that emphasized eminence and even giftedness, which might actually alienate many young people from participating in creativity. She was also conscious that the story of Henry Ford was a story about the accomplishments of one white man,[4] and therefore was eager to disrupt the "dead white guy" bias that is pervasive throughout the dominant creativity narrative. To do this, Julie began to teach a counter-narrative that was equally relevant to her students and their local history. Instead of teach a unit on the biography of Henry Ford, Julie developed a unit exploring the biography of the idea Henry Ford was most known for: mass production.

Julie found a wealth of resources she could use to teach her unit on mass production (e.g., books, local museum exhibitions, online resources, etc.). Many of these resources included a mention of Henry Ford as a participant in the development of the idea of mass production—perhaps even as a prominent contributor—but they also included mentions of a wealth of other actors, materials, environments, and societal issues that all contributed to the development of the process of mass production. By teaching her unit about the biography of mass production, Julie was able to (a) debunk the great man myth associated with traditional, individual-based understandings of creativity, (b) provide her students with more of a systems-based understanding of the development of creative ideas, (c) situate Henry Ford within that greater system, (d) show her students that there were multiple ways to participate in the development of a creative idea, and (e) provide her students with an understanding that they, too, could participate in creativity (Fig. 3.1).

To follow up on this initial experience, Julie intends to have her students develop biographies of themselves as individuals, including an investigation of how they have participated in creativity in the past. She intends to have her students use this information to build their own profiles of participation. Having individually identified their own profiles of participation, Julie will then introduce her students to a set of design challenges that they will engage with, understanding that each of them have a unique suite of talents, skills, and cultural perspectives that they may leverage individually, and within groups, as they pursue this work.

Julie's reframing of creativity as a participatory process is a powerful example of how introducing young people to the distributed and participatory nature of creativity—as opposed to an act of individual genius—may empower young people to see themselves as creative agents in the world—each of whom have their own unique

---

[4] Julie and her colleagues note that many accounts indicate that Henry Ford held racist and antisemetic beliefs, which further complicate him as an icon for aspiring young people of various racial and religious backgrounds.

Fig. 3.1 Students working with Julie Rains watch a video describing the development of mass production and the auto industry

profile of participation, and each of whom are capable of participating in invention and innovation through their interactions with others.

3.5.4 Engaging Young People in the Development of Creative Ideas in High School

Another example of participatory creativity in action comes from Jodie Ricci and her colleagues Rick Tate, Nick DiGiorgio, and Rennie Greenfield. Jodie and her colleagues are educators at the upper school (grades 9 through 12) at an independent pre-K through 12th grade school in the suburbs of Cleveland, Ohio. At the tail end of each academic semester, just as the attention of the average high school student starts to wane, 9th through 12th grade students at the school where Jodie and her colleagues teach take a single course for 3 weeks, earning a semester's credit. These immersive courses, known as "intensives," provide students with an opportunity for in-depth study of a topic. While the variety of intensive experiences that young people may engage in varies, the particular intensive that Jodie, Rick, Nick, and Rennie have developed explicitly focuses on participatory creativity. Throughout these 3 weeks, the students in the creative process intensive engage in an idea development process that is structured around a guiding question. During the fall 2017 run of the creative process intensive, the guiding question that Jodie and her colleagues chose for their students was: "How might we use the next three weeks to create something that makes our community more effective, efficient, beautiful, ethical, or more _____?"[5]

During the first week of the creative process intensive experience, students self-organized into project teams to conduct research and develop initial ideas geared towards addressing the intensive's guiding question. At the same time, the students in the intensive also read seminal texts supporting the theory of participatory creativity, including sample biographies of ideas that have been developed in other teaching and learning environments. This theoretical grounding in the core tenets of participatory creativity was meant to help students understand the academic underpinnings of the process that they were about to engage in, while also scaffolding their idea development.

During the second week of their intensive experience, the students engaged in an "expedition." The expeditions for each intensive have been designed to provide students with real world experiences so that they may connect their learning to everyday life, engage with experts, and share their work outside of the classroom. During the fall of 2016 and 2017, the creative process intensive expedition entailed a trip to the Boston/Cambridge area to meet with creativity researchers at various universities and institutes of technology, to tour school programs that enact distributed and participatory approaches to creativity, and to visit museums, theater companies, and innovative businesses that maintain a creative stance towards their work. All the while, students presented the ideas they were developing and received feedback from the various professionals they encountered. When the students presented their ideas, they did so by describing the biography of their idea development process. This process entailed the many twists and turns that their ideas had undergone in the short span of the intensive program, including the various actors who had contributed to the development of their ideas, and the ways in which they had individually—and uniquely—participated in the process.

During the final week of the creative process intensive, the students continued to hone their ideas, prototype any products or services associated with those ideas, and further presented their ideas and received feedback. Though not a requirement for the intensive, the end result of this work often took the form of a proposal for change submitted by the participating students to their school administration and/or student faculty senate, for potential implementation of their ideas on campus (Fig. 3.2).

One of the most interesting aspects of this work has been the degree to which the students' ideas changed in the short span of just 3 weeks. Taking a participatory approach to creativity has helped the students understand that the ideas that they have developed through this intensive experience exist in a social space. Indeed, the project teams developing these ideas have developed a sense of purpose and investment in their work, but because they understand that the ideas they have developed exist in a space external to themselves, they do not feel overly protective of them—nor unnecessarily proprietary. For this reason, they were comfortable hacking their

---

[5]This is a tweaked application of the "Imagine If…" thinking routine designed by the Agency *by* Design research initiative at Project Zero. For more information about Agency *by* Design and the Imagine If… thinking routine, see: http://agencybydesign.org

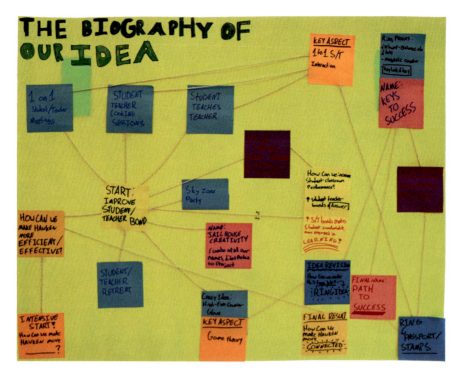

Fig. 3.2 Students working with Jodie Ricci, Rick Tate, Nick DiGiorgio, and Rennie Greenfield map out the biography of their idea over the course of their school's creativity intensive experience

ideas, or entirely letting their ideas go and developing new ones based on the influential feedback they received throughout the process.

The creative process intensive experience that Jodie, Rick, Nick, and Rennie have structured for their students merges participatory creativity with project based learning, maker-centered learning, and design thinking. Though these different approaches to practice are in the mix, the core tenets of participatory creativity are foregrounded for the students. In particular, the students have explicitly framed the story of their idea development as the biography of an idea, they have actively sought out ways to make their idea development process be as distributed and as participatory as possible, and they have been cognizant of the unique ways they each participated in the development of their focal ideas within their diverse project teams. Along the way, participating students constructed—and reconstructed—their profiles of participation.

Like Julie's work in Michigan, the creative process intensive experience that Jodie and her colleagues have structured for their students in the suburbs of Cleveland, Ohio offers a powerful example of how a reframing of creativity as a distributed and participatory process may support students in seeing themselves as active agents of change, while also helping each student understand, appreciate, and develop his or her unique profile of participation. Having established one's own profile of participation by engaging in a structured idea development process, it is hoped that the students who participate in this intensive experience will bring what they have learned about their unique profiles of participation to bear on their other learning—and life—experiences.

3.6 Avoiding the Pitfalls of Participatory Creativity: Don't Go Back to the Box

The examples described above show how participatory creativity can be effective in classrooms. But focusing on the roles that young people play during participatory creativity learning experiences is not without its perils. The main challenge here is that a naïve focus on role may lead one to pigeonholing historical actors—or flesh and blood students—as being uni-dimensional players within the narrative of the biography of an idea. To do so would be to overlook the dynamic nature of participatory creativity, and to potentially limit or thwart the learning experiences young people (and adults) may have by engaging in this work.

This prospective misinterpretation of the function of role in a participatory reframing of creativity resonates with misinterpretations of other theories of mind as applied to education, namely, Howard Gardner's (1983) theory of multiple intelligences. As the field of psychology bucked at the release of Gardner's theory of multiple intelligences in the 1980s (see, for example, Schaler 2006, *Howard Gardner Under Fire: The Rebel Psychologist Faces his Critics*), educators rejoiced. The reason for their enthusiasm was that Gardner had presented a theory that affirmed what educators had known all along: that young people are smart not just in one way, but in many different ways. Gardner's original theory offered eight different intelligences, each of which had to meet a set of criteria.[6] However, despite their enthusiasm, many educators misinterpreted Gardner's theory when they applied it to their home teaching and learning environments. The greatest pitfall was to use Gardner's theory to pigeonhole learners by labeling them as having one or another type of intelligence/being one or another type of learner (Groff 2013). For example, an educator may look across his or her classroom and determine that Jenny is a visual-spatial learner, Malcolm is a logical-mathematical learner, and Maria is a bodily-kinesthetic learner. At the least, putting students into these narrowly defined cognitive boxes was a misinterpretation of Gardner's theory that limited the potential of young learners. At the worst, Gardner's theory was applied with a racist lens, providing greater breadth of potential for white students than for their fellow learners of color. But the theory was never meant to be applied in this way. Gardner (1993) suggested that all people have all of the intelligences in different measures. Jenny may indeed exhibit great strength in visual-spatial intelligence, but

---

[6] Gardner's original suite of intelligences has been expanded to include as many as ten, or more, intelligences.

she is also intelligent in many other ways. Every individual has varying strengths and weaknesses across the multiple intelligences. Each individual's unique arrangement of strengths and weaknesses across the intelligences establishes what Gardner referred to as a *profile of intelligence* (1993)—an approach borrowed here in the idea of profiles of participation (Clapp 2017).

A similar misinterpretation can befall the function of role from the perspective of participatory creativity. As we have noted in the past, "young people play various roles when they participate in creativity, but those roles are neither fixed nor unidimensional" (Clapp 2017, p. 42). From this perspective, we view the function of role in a participatory creativity learning experience as being dynamic, fluid, and multi-directional. Rather than pigeonhole young people and place them into role-defined boxes, it is important to recognize that young people play various roles throughout the process of creative idea development—and that these roles are frequently shifting and changing.

3.7 Opportunities for Future Research

To support educators and their students in understanding and enacting participatory approaches to creativity, further research will be essential. This opportunity space yields multiple possibilities for expanding our understanding of participatory creativity, while at the same time further developing a participatory creativity "tool kit." To that end, below we address four potential areas for future research.

3.7.1 Develop a Research-Based Instructional Framework for Participatory Creativity

The two vignettes described above offer rich examples of participatory creativity in action. These two examples come to us from courageous educators who, through their own ingenuity, have been able to find opportunities to interpret the theories associated with participatory creativity and apply those theories to their classroom practice. These two applications have some commonality, but they are also quite different approaches to enacting participatory creativity in practice. What participatory creativity most lacks is a research-based instructional framework that is both accessible and actionable for educators working in a broad array of teaching and learning environments. Here we are careful to use the word *framework* and not the word *curriculum*. The reason being is that we believe a framework consists of core concepts, general structures, and flexible educator resources that may be applied across grade levels, learning environments, and content areas, whereas a curriculum is more of a prescriptive tool designed to meet specific learning goals within specific learning environments. We envision a framework for participatory creativity as being far more flexible, and dynamic than a prescriptive curriculum designed to meet the learning goals of a specific environment.

3.7.2 Develop Research-Based Documentation and Assessment Strategies that both Support Student Learning and Make Participatory Creativity Visible

It is widely the case in many countries that if new educational structures are to take hold, they must be accompanied by well-founded documentation and assessment strategies. Reservations about the drive to "test" every aspect of students' learning experiences are well-founded, but the need for assessments in education are also a reality—especially those designed to support student learning. To that end, it is necessary to develop research-based documentation and assessment strategies that are formative in nature, while also being carefully designed to make creativity visible.

3.7.3 Develop Research-Based Case Studies of Teachers Placing Participatory Creativity in Practice

As useful as the descriptions of the two creative classrooms discussed above may be, more and different case studies of participatory creativity are needed to serve the greatest breadth of teachers—serving the greatest breadth of students. In this way, educators across the curriculum and across the content areas will be able to see a diverse set of examples of participatory creativity in action, before experimenting with such approaches in their home teaching and learning environments.

3.7.4 Investigate the Interplay Between Participatory Creativity, Roles, and Student Identity

Lastly, it is important to pursue further research on the relationship between participatory creativity and identity. Of particular interest is the connection between providing young people with the opportunity to engage in creative learning experiences in new and unexpected ways, and their identification as creative agents. The concept of role will be essential to such studies. Does broadening the participatory nature of creativity to multiple and fluid roles that young people may play correlate to greater identification of young people as individuals with creative agency?

3.8 Conclusion

Participatory creativity holds great potential for providing young people with a counter-narrative of creativity in their worlds. From this perspective, individual initiative and commitment to creative work remain an important part of the distributed development of creative ideas, but not in the heroic sense that more traditional, individual-based creativity narratives suggest. By recognizing the many contributing roles of individuals and their interactions with the material world, participatory creativity promises to empower students as they develop unique profiles of participation. This approach can provide young people with a new understanding of how they can participate in creativity in ways that honor their unique skills, interests, background experiences, and sociocultural perspectives. The benefits of this new approach to fostering creativity through education also include supporting young people as systems thinkers and helping them see beyond the race and gender biases that are prevalent in the dominant creativity narrative.

More specifically, we have seen four advantages to the participatory approach. First, reframing creativity as the biography of an idea allows young people to see the distributed and participatory nature of creativity, and the various roles that actors play throughout the development of creative ideas. This experience can help debunk the myth of the lone creative (traditionally white male) "genius" for young people. Second, a participatory reframing of creativity in the classroom allows young people to define, redefine, and further develop their profiles of participation. In this way, engaging in the tenets and work of participatory creativity alerts young people to their own multi-dimensionality. Third, taking a participatory approach to creativity in the classroom broadly opens creative participation to the widest breadth of students, making creativity in education—and in life—more accessible and more equitable. Traditional, individual-based approaches to creativity, especially those that narrowly define creativity as a certain set of skills, traits, or cognitive abilities, privilege some students, while alienating a great many others. Lastly, despite its theoretical strength and practical implications, adapting a participatory view of creativity may require an epistemological shift for many educators, researchers, parents, and policymakers. This can be hard work. Nonetheless, that work is worthwhile. The cases described here have shown that the payoffs of applying a participatory reframing of creativity in one's classroom practice can be much richer—and more accessible and inclusive—than other orientations to supporting creativity in various teaching and learning environments.

Acknowledgements We would like to thank Ron Beghetto and Giovanni Emanuele Corazza for supporting this essay. We would like to further thank Raquel Jimenez for her early contributions to the ideas in this essay. We would like to especially thank educators Julie Rains, Jodie Ricci, Rick Tate, Nick DiGirogio, and Rennie Greenfield—and their students—for sharing their classroom work with us.

References

Amabile, T. M., Colins, M. A., Conti, R., Phillips, E., Picariello, M., Ruscio, J., & Whitney, D. (1996). *Creativity in context*. Boulder: Westview Press/Perseus Books Group.

Clapp, E. P. (2017). *Participatory creativity: Introducing access and equity to the creative classroom*. New York: Routledge.

Corazza, G. E. (2016). Potential originality and effectiveness: The dynamic definition of creativity. *Creativity Research Journal, 28*(3), 258–267.

Csikszentmihalyi, M. (1997). *Creativity: Flow and the psychology of discovery and innovation*. New York: HarperPerennial (Original work published 1996).

Csikszentmihalyi, M. (1999). Implications of a systems perspective for the study of creativity. In R. J. Sternberg (Ed.), *Handbook of creativity* (pp. 313–335). Cambridge, UK: Cambridge University Press.

Duncum, P. (2013). Creativity as conversation in the interactive audience culture of YouTube. *Visual Inquiry, 2*(2), 115–125.

Gardner, H. (1983). *Frames of mind: The theory of multiple intelligences*. New York: Basic Books.

Gardner, H. (1993). A multiplicity of intelligences. *Scientific American Presents, Exploring Intelligence, 9*(4), 19–23.

Glăveanu, V. P. (2010). Creativity as cultural participation. *Journal for the Theory of Social Behaviour, 41*, 48–67.

Glăveanu, V. P. (2014a). *Distributed creativity: Thinking outside the box of the creative individual*. New York: Springer.

Glăveanu, V. P. (2014b). *Thinking through creativity and culture: Toward an integrated model*. New Brunswick: Transaction Publishers.

Groff, J. (2013). Expanding our "frames" of mind for education and the arts. *Harvard Educational Review, 83*(1), 15–39.

Gruber, H. E. (1981). *Darwin on man: A psychological study of scientific creativity* (2nd ed.). Chicago: University of Chicago Press.

Gruber, H. E., & Davis, S. N. (1988). Inching our way up Mount Olympus: The evolving systems approach to creative thinking. In R. J. Sternberg (Ed.), *The nature of creativity: Contemporary psychological perspectives* (pp. 243–270). Cambridge, UK: Cambridge University Press.

Gruber, H. E., & Wallace, D. B. (1999). The case study method and evolving systems approach for understanding unique creative people at work. In R. J. Sternberg (Ed.), *Handbook of creativity* (pp. 93–115). Cambridge, UK: Cambridge University Press.

Hanchett Hanson, M. (2015). *Worldmaking: Psychology and the ideology of creativity*. London: Palgrave Macmillan.

Hutchins, E. (1995). *Cognition in the wild*. Cambridge, MA: The MIT Press.

John-Steiner, V. (1997). *Notebooks of the mind: Explorations of thinking* (Rev. ed.). Oxford: Oxford University Press.

John-Steiner, V. (2015). Creative engagement across the lifespan. In V. P. Glăveanu, A. Gillespie, J. Valsiner, & J. (Eds.), *Rethinking creativity: Contributions from social and cultural psychology* (pp. 31–44). New York: Routledge.

Latour, B. (2005). *Reassembling the social: An introduction to actor-network-theory*. Oxford: Oxford University Press.

Martin, J. (2013). Life positioning analysis: An analytic framework for the study of lives and life narratives. *Journal of Theoretical and Philosophical Psychology, 33*, 1–17.

Martin, J. (2014). Ernest Becker at SFU (1969–1974). *Journal of Humanistic Psychology, 54*, 66–112.

Martin, J. (2015). Life positioning analysis. In J. Martin, J. Sugarman, & K. L. Slaney (Eds.), *The Wiley handbook of theoretical and philosophical psychology: Methods, approaches and new directions for social sciences* (pp. 248–262). Hoboken: Wiley-Blackwell.

Moran, S., & John-Steiner, V. (2003). Vygotsky's contemporary contribution to the dialectic of development and creativity. In Marschark, M (Series Ed.). *Creativity and development* (pp. 61–90). Oxford: Oxford University Press.

Perkins, D. N. (2000). *The eureka effect: The art and logic of breakthrough thinking.* New York: W. W. Norton & Co..

Sawyer, R. K. (2007). *Group genius: The creative power of collaboration.* New York: Basic Books.

Sawyer, R. K. (2010). Individual and group creativity. In J. C. Kaufman & R. J. Sternberg (Eds.), *The Cambridge handbook of creativity* (pp. 366–381). Cambridge, UK: Cambridge University Press.

Sawyer, R. K. (Ed.). (2011). *Structure and improvisation in creative teaching.* Cambridge, UK: Cambridge University Press.

Sawyer, R. K. (2012). *Explaining creativity: The science of human innovation.* Oxford: Oxford University Press.

Sawyer, K., & DeZutter, S. (2009). Distributed creativity: How collective creations emerge from collaboration. *Psychology of Aesthetics, Creativity, and the Arts, 3*(2), 81–92.

Schaler, J. A. (Ed.). (2006). *Howard Gardner under fire: The renegade psychologist faces his critic.* Chicago: Open Court.

Simonton, D. K. (1999). *Origins of genius: Darwinian perspectives on creativity.* Oxford: Oxford University Press.

Wallace, D. B., & Gruber, H. E. (Eds.). (1989). *Creative people at work.* Oxford: Oxford University Press.

Chapter 4
Emotions: The Spinal Cord of the Creative Thinking Process

Sergio Agnoli and Giovanni Emanuele Corazza

Abstract In reviewing the huge effort made by the psychological research in defining the main components of the creative process and of the creative potential, rarely we encounter models and theoretical frameworks considering emotional reactions as main determinants of the creative process, except of the widely and broadly defined concepts of motivation and mood. Emotional phenomena are usually intended as strong (intrinsic or extrinsic) forces able to influence the creative thinking process, and in particular the cognitive processes sustaining idea generation. In this chapter, we maintain that emotional phenomena are not simple influencers of creative thinking, but that they are the spinal cord of the creative process. In considering emotions the core of the process, we sustain that emotional reactions are the *conditio sine qua non* by which the creative thinking process can occur, or, in different words, the necessary (although not sufficient) determinant of the process. On the basis of the above, taking into account different theoretical approaches to the study of emotions and adopting a dynamical systems framework, we intend to explain the role of emotions in the dynamic emergence of the creative thinking process.

4.1 Introduction

Sometimes we appear to forget that human beings are intrinsically and fundamentally emotional animals. Or better, we want to forget it. We strongly feel the necessity to define ourselves as logical and self-defined cognitive actors. This despite the

---

S. Agnoli (✉)
Marconi Institute for Creativity (MIC), Villa Griffone, Sasso Marconi, Italy
e-mail: sergio.agnoli@unibo.it

G. E. Corazza
Marconi Institute for Creativity (MIC), Villa Griffone, Sasso Marconi, Italy

Department of Electrical, Electronic, and Information Engineering "Guglielmo Marconi",
University of Bologna, Bologna, Italy
e-mail: giovanni.corazza@unibo.it

empirical and experimental evidences demonstrating that our thoughts and our actions are characterized in any moment by limited cognitive resources (see for example Ariely and Norton 2008; Kahneman 2011; Tversky and Kahneman 1983). Psychological research on creativity is no exception. In reviewing the huge effort in finding the main components defining the creative process and the creative achievement (e.g., Jauk et al. 2014; Hélie and Sun 2010; Lubart 2001), rarely we encounter models and theoretical frameworks considering emotional reactions as main determinants of the creative process, except for the widely used and broadly defined concepts of motivation and mood (Amabile 1983; Amabile et al. 2005; Davis 2009; Zenasni and Lubart 2002). Emotional phenomena are usually intended as strong (intrinsic or extrinsic) forces able to influence the creative thinking process, and in particular the cognitive thinking process sustaining idea generation. They are essentially intended as mediators and moderators of the thinking process. Only recently some valuable works explained the role of specific emotions on creative performance (Baas et al. 2012; Silvia and Brown 2007), or the separate influence of affective valence and affective arousal on creative thinking (De Dreu et al. 2008), suggesting an intrinsic importance of the emotional experience in the control of the creative thinking process.

In this chapter, we suggest that emotional phenomena are not simple influencers of the process, but that they are the spinal cord of the creative thinking process. In this effort, we will concentrate on the individual thinker, leaving extension to social creativity for future work. In considering emotions the core of the process, we posit that emotional reactions are the *conditio sine qua non* the creative thinking process can happen, or, in different words, the necessary (although not sufficient) determinant of the creative thinking process. In formulating this strong assumption, we do not want to suggest that creative processes occur whenever emotions are present in human life. Human creativity cannot emerge without access to knowledge, without interactions with social norms, without the use of some forms of intelligence, without divergent movement in the thinker's mind space, or without evaluation abilities. All these elements together, however, may not be sufficient for the generation of an original and effective idea in a human mind if we do not include emotional phenomena into the process. In other words, we propose a change of point of view in looking at creativity, a shift from a cognition-driven to an emotion-driven point of view. This new perspective is intended to be included in a dynamical systems framework, which would interpret the creative process as a self-organized system controlled and driven by the emotional experience, as we will discuss in the body of this chapter.

The first step into this new proposal will be to outline the complexity of the emotional phenomena as well as their roles for human beings. The aim of this explanation is to enter inside the dynamics of the emotional phenomenology, in order to comprehend its multi-componential nature. The appraisal theory will be in particular used as an explicatory approach to understand the emergence of emotions as a consequence of self-organized interrelations between different components, and in particular between cognitive and affective elements. The dynamical system theory will be the natural framework hosting this explanation. The same theoretical framework will also serve as an interpretative scenario guiding the explanation of the creative thinking process as a complex dynamic system. To this purpose the DIMAI model of creative thinking (Corazza and Agnoli 2015) will be used as a reference model. DIMAI, in particular, represents an acronym for five mental states, which define, according to Corazza and Agnoli (2015) the creative thinking process: *Drive, Information, Movement, Assessment, Implementation.* Within this scenario the role of emotions for the emergence of creative thinking will be highlighted. How emotions can control the creative thinking process and drive the emergence of potential new and effective idea will be outlined. To this purpose, different examples will be provided on how several components defining emotional reactions are able to drive and control the shifts between different mental states within the creative thinking process. Some key questions within the study of creative thinking will be addressed through these examples. However, it worth highlighting that, given the complexity characterizing the dynamic relationships between emotions and creative thinking, this exemplification is not planned to give a comprehensive explanation of these dynamics, but it is meant to provide a first illustration of the theoretical and explanatory utility of an emotional dynamical approach to the study of creative thinking. Finally, considerations on the impact of this new approach on the research and education of creative thinking will be provided.

4.2 Emotions: Multi-componential Controllers

But what are emotions? A broad definition has been proposed by Scherer (2009, p. 3459), who claims that: "emotion is a cultural and psychobiological adaptation mechanism which allows each individual to react flexibly and dynamically to environmental contingencies". Under this definition reside four basic attributes of emotions, which are uncontrovertibly accepted in the emotion literature (Frijda and Scherer 2009): (i) emotions emerge when something relevant happens to the organism, having a direct relation with its goals, values, or general well-being; (ii) emotions prepare the organism for important events, producing states of *action readiness* (Frijda 2007); (iii) emotions engage the entire person, requiring action suspension or urging action accompanied by preparatory tuning of the somato-visceral and motor systems; (iv) emotions bestow control precedence on the states of action readiness, in the sense of giving priorities in the control of behaviours and experiences.

Therefore, emotions are organism's controllers which entail the involvement of five distinct components (Scherer 1987, 2001): appraisal, i.e., a cognitive component; action readiness, i.e., a peripheral efference component; goal-oriented motivation, i.e., a motivational component; overt actions, i.e., a motor expression component; and subjective feelings, i.e., a phenomenological component. We observe emotion when an episode interrelates and synchronizes all or most of these components in response to the evaluation of external or internal stimuli relevant to the organism well-being. Clearly, these attributes highlight the intrinsic overlap between cognition and emotion. Years of research proved that emotional and cognitive phenomena are often separated only for conceptual reasons, but that they are most of the time hardly distinguishable from one another. The inextricable overlap between cognitive and emotional phenomena has led to the modern constructivist theoretical frameworks, which state that emotions are not special mental states, but rather that they are continually modified constructive processes involving basic psychological ingredients, which are not specific to emotion (Feldman Barrett 2017; Gross and Feldman Barrett 2011).

If we had to find a basic role exerted by emotions in human and animal life, we could sustain that they are the multi-componential controllers of our relationships with the world. Starting from the most basic approach/avoidance behaviours, reacting with promptness to safe/unsafe stimuli from the world, emotions allow to understand (or to estimate) the nature of those stimuli, to act with respect to the stimuli, and to communicate to the external world our disposition towards those stimuli. In other words, emotions are emergent acts of meaning-making in our relation with the world (Gross and Feldman Barrett 2011).

4.2.1 *Appraisal Theories and Stimulus Evaluation Check*

Let us consider an example of this controlling role exerted by emotions over our relationship with the world. The example is offered by the appraisal approach. Appraisal theories of emotions propose that emotions are adaptive responses which emerge from the evaluation of features of the environment that are important for the individual's well-being (Moors et al. 2013). While the first approaches within this theoretical framework (Lazarus 1982, 1984) essentially tried to explain emotions through cognitive processes, basically emphasizing the supremacy of cognition over emotion, the following propositions within this framework tended to describe the emergence of the emotional phenomena through the use of dynamic elements. Contemporary appraisal approaches are componential in nature in that they view emotions as involving changes in several organic components and systems. Emotions are therefore processes where changes in one component feed back to other components. For example, changes in the appraisal of an event may produce changes in the physiological response, which, in turn, can lead to a change in the appraisal itself, both directly and indirectly (through other components).

Here we will in particular refer to the stimulus evaluation check approach proposed by Scherer (2001), which considers the appraisal as a process of multilevel sequential checking. This theory explains the differentiation of emotional states as the result of a specified sequence of Stimulus Evaluation Checks (SECs). SECs are a set of criteria underlying the assessment of the significance of a stimulus for the organism (Scherer 2001), which are organized according to four appraisal aims: relevance, checking how relevant is the event for the organism; implications, checking the consequences of the event and how much it can impact organism wellbeing; coping potential, checking the coping abilities to face the event and its consequences; normative significance, checking the meaning of the event with respect to individual's self-concept and social norms. For the purposes of the present chapter, we will limit our action to consider the first appraisal objective, relevance, which, as we will see, is not irrelevant for creativity.

An organism is constantly scanning the environment to check whether the occurrence (or the lack of occurrence) of an event requires deployment of attention, more information processing, interruption of an on going activity, etc. Our relation with the (external or internal) environment is organized according to a progressive incremental complexity following specific evolutionary patterns and sequences, starting from a very basic somato-sensorial level to more complex conceptual levels (Leventhal and Scherer 1987). Relevance checking makes no exception. At the most primitive level in the appraisal of relevance, a *novelty check* can be found. Starting from sensory-motor processing, any sudden stimulus is likely to be detected as novel and attracting attention (the classic orientation response). Beyond this basic level, novelty evaluation can differ greatly for different species, individuals, situations and depends from previous experience and familiarity with the stimulus. On the most complex level of processing, novelty check can be based on predictability evaluations (based on the observation of regularities from the world).

The following evaluation level is based on the *intrinsic pleasantness check*. This check determines the fundamental reaction of the organism, liking/pleasantness feelings, leading to approach behaviour, or dislike/aversion, leading to avoidance behaviour. The intrinsic pleasantness check has been defined by Scherer (2001) as independent from the goals or momentary state of the organism, but as an intrinsic feature of the stimulus itself.

Orthogonal to this check is the *goal relevance check*, which defines the pertinence and importance of the stimulus for the present hierarchy of goals or needs.

These three sequential and different SECs define the relevance of a stimulus for the organism, dynamically and interactively organizing the emotional experience. No modular or predefined experience arises from this dynamic emergence of the emotional experience; on the contrary, emotions emerge as the products of subjective and situational evaluations of the relationship with the (external or internal) world.

4.2.2 Emotions in the Dynamical System Framework

Scherer (2000, 2001) proposes the invariance of the sequence of appraisal checks defining the evaluative or cognitive component of emotions, while bidirectional relationships exist between appraisal, feeling, motivation, action readiness, and expressive components. The relationships between appraisal and the other emotional components define a dynamic interaction in which appraisal sets in motion other components and reacts to feedback from other components, in order to drive the adaptation to a given context or situation (Camras and Witherington 2005). Scherer's approach resides within the dynamical system framework, which represented a true innovation in the study and analysis of emotional phenomena (Fogel et al. 1992; Lewis and Granic 2000). Emotions emerge in this theoretical framework as self-organized systems of interacting components within contextually situated social interactions. New emotional episodes happen when stable emotional patterns break down as a consequence of a critical change in one of the emotional components.

Emotions are however not chaotic ensembles of components, but recursive and stable emotional structures that can be recognized socially and culturally (e.g., basic emotions such as anger, surprise, happiness, sadness, disgust). Indeed, emotional components self-organize into more or less stable patterns (attractors) that manifest a large number of minor variations. Because of the recursiveness and apparent invariance in some emotional patterns across time and space, some authors argue that self-organization in emotions is hard-wired and finds its roots in evolutionary pre-specified processes (Izard et al. 2000). True emergence in the sense of generation of new forms without pre-specified instructions would seem to be hardly applicable to emotions. On the other hand, self-organization seems to be applicable in the context of cognitive-affective interactions, where appraisal components operate as monitoring systems for the organization of other systems (Camras and Witherington 2005): this will be our working hypothesis.

4.3 The Creative Process as an Emotion-Driven Emergent Process

The study of creative thinking, as defined by an ensemble of components the interactions of which lead to the emergence of potentially original and effective products (Corazza 2016), can highly benefit from the use of a dynamical system framework. In particular, in the following, we will look at the creative thinking process following a series of prescriptive steps proposed by Thelen and Smith (1994, 1998), as a specific strategy of investigation within the dynamical system framework. Using this approach we will discover the dynamic relationship between the emergence of emotional reactions and the emergence of new ideas.

Step 1 of the investigation strategy is to establish a collective variable for the study, which is any observable variable that reflects the state of the system. Through the measurement of this variable, the interrelationships between the lower-order components of the system can be identified. Any collective variable can assume a variety of states that emerge from the interactions between the components of the system and which the system seems to be attracted by. *Step 2* requires the identification of the attractor states which characterize the collective variable across different times and conditions. *Step 3* involves the mapping of temporal stability and changes in the collective variable, either through a microgenetic analysis of the variable in real time or by a longitudinal analysis distributed over a longer period of time. Through this analysis a trajectory is established for the collective variable. *Step 4* requires the identification of the phase transitions (or phase shifts) within this trajectory, i.e., when the system transitions from one attractor state to another. *Step 5* involves the identification of the factors underlying these transitions; in other words, the control parameters whose quantitative changes destabilize the relationships between the components of the system leading to a phase shift which conduces to the establishment of a new stable pattern of interrelations. *Step 6*, finally, requires the experimental manipulation and investigation of the control parameters in order to explore the dynamics of the system.

4.3.1 Investigating the Creative Thinking Process in Five (Out of the Six) Steps

Step 1

The creative thinking process represents the highly complex collective variable to be studied. The creativity literature presents indeed a long tradition about the modelling of the creative thinking process (Lubart 2001), as a system composed by a multitude of lower order interacting variables. This tradition has been inserted in the cognitive approach to creative thinking. Representatives of this tradition are the four-stages model by Wallas (1926), the articulation of the mental abilities by Guilford (1950), the eight dynamic stages in the model by Mumford et al. (1991), or the Geneplore model (Finke et al. 1992). All these models describe the process leading to the generation of new ideas, passing through different states or stages attracting the thinker's mind. We do not intend here to propose a new model to conceptualize the creative thinking process, but we will enter in this theoretical tradition in order to understand whether a dynamical system framework can offer new insight on the creative thinking process and in particular on the role exerted by emotions in the emergence of new ideas.

In doing so, we will use the DIMAI model (Corazza and Agnoli 2015; Corazza et al. 2016) as a reference to look at the creative process through a dynamical system framework. The DIMAI model represents indeed a functional description of the creative thinking process that could be applied to any knowledge domain. This model will help us to identify the lower-order components of the system as well as the attractors states, the trajectories, and controllers of the process. DIMAI will be therefore here used as exemplary container, in that it has been proposed as a theoretical model that should encompass all the previously mentioned cognitive approaches (Corazza et al. 2016).

From Step 2 to Step 4

In the description of the DIMAI model we intend to define some attractor states in our collective variable (*Step 2*) as well as to map moments of stability and changes into the system (*Step 3*) and the phase transitions (*Step 4*) from one state to another, determining possible trajectories. This will appear as a sort of journey into the thinker's mind, proposing a dynamic model to understand the emerging and realization of new ideas.

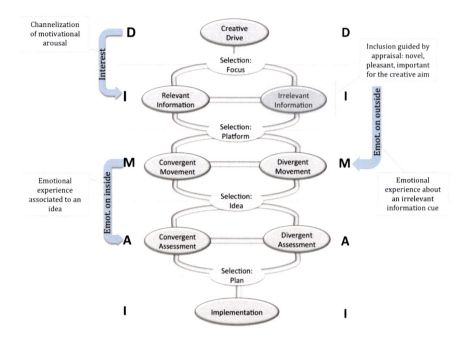

Fig. 4.1 The DIMAI model of the creative thinking process and some examples of possible emotional mechanisms controlling the process

The five mental states of the DIMAI model, *Drive, Information, Movement, Assessment, Implementation* (Fig. 4.1), represent the attractor states which define the creative process, characterizing therefore our collective variable across different conditions and different periods of time. The five mental states can be thought of as recursive states of stability around which the creator's thinking process is organized. The DIMAI mental states should not be however intended as mutually excluding mental states, since they can coexist in parallel and be reiterated. According to this model, during the process the thinker's mind can indeed move between different attractor states in the search of a new equilibrium state.

The first state, *Drive*, involves thinker's main focus area of interest, inside of which the generation of ideas shall take place. In this state the main motivational elements that support the thinker throughout the entire process are stated, defining the action tendencies and the starting arousal level which will be essential to put effort in the generation of a new idea.

In the moment in which these action tendencies are directed towards a specific area of interest, an immediate activation of the attractor state of *Information* occurs, which consists in the activation or gathering of all knowledge elements related to that focus area. *Information* attracts the thinker's mind toward the knowledge about the focus area (which is stored within the thinker's memory, but which is also recruited through an active search). Knowledge elements include meaning, symbology, and/or the physical representation of items related to the focus area. Clearly, the more the thinker has previous knowledge and/or expertise in the selected focus area, the richer the collection of information will be. This kind of information directly activated into the thinker's mind or collected from the state of the art in the focus area is defined as *relevant*, to stress the "semantically direct" connection to the focus. Along with *relevant information*, the DIMAI model includes also the introduction into the thinking process of *irrelevant information*. This kind of information has no apparent relation with the focus area or with the relevant information. It represents a spark, a possible inspiration, forcing the thinker to accommodate the process accordingly to this extraneous or peripheral element, consequently re-organizing the knowledge structure, which leads to the possible generation of new perspectives. Irrelevant information can come from any element surrounding the thinker, even from random causes (Agnoli et al. 2015).

The disequilibrium state produced in information processing by irrelevant information leads the thinker's mind toward the next attractor state, *Movement*. This state defines the search of new meanings within information, exploring the complex network of alternatives, through interpretation, inquiry, insight, and so on. Movement can be convergent or divergent, the former searching for the best possible consequence, the latter exploring multiple alternatives into the information network.

This state moves towards the generation of one or multiple potential new ideas, attracted towards the evaluation of their effectiveness and novelty, i.e., towards the next attractor state, *Assessment*. The Assessment state can take on a convergent modality, which evaluates the utility and effectiveness of the new idea with reference to the initial focus, or a divergent modality, which evaluates the idea independently from the starting focus, applying a multiplicity of judgment criteria. *Assessment* and *Movement* interact iteratively in order to refine the raw idea attracted towards the realization and externalization of the idea, resulting in the final attractor state, *Implementation*, where and when the idea is organized and represented to the external world (in the form of words, a real product, etc.).

Step 5

In the description of the mental states and of the possible trajectories followed by the thinker's mind during the generation of a new idea, the factors that can explain the transitions from one attractor state to another remain to be explained. Here, in particular, we propose that the control parameters whose quantitative changes destabilize the relationships between the components of the system leading to the establishment of a new equilibrium state can be collected under the unified explanatory umbrella represented by emotions. We indeed believe that even if emotions can be defined within a specific and unitary psychological construct, their complex dynamics allow to take into account the extremely different conditions leading to transition shifts within the creative thinking process. In this view, emotions assume the role of controllers of the creative thinking process driving the thinker's mind back and forth iteratively along different attractor mental states. The transition from one mental state to another is therefore permeated with a new emotional meaning.

4.4 Emotions as Controllers of the Creative Thinking Process

In the next sections, we will offer some examples on how quantitative changes in emotional reactions can explain the transition shifts between the different mental states defining the process. When does motivational focus start attracting information from memory and when does it require an active search of new information? When is information enough to start moving across information and why does specific information prime a sudden restructuring of the knowledge leading to a new unexpected idea? Why do some specific alternatives generated within the thinker's mind attract the need to understand, through conscious assessment, whether they can solve the initial creative drive? These are only some of the questions that can be faced and explored assuming that state shifts are controlled by components defining emotional reactions. Let us therefore try to answer to these questions proposing some hypothetical explanatory scenarios derived from an emotional dynamical approach to the process. This will help us to exemplify the involvement of different emotional components and the interaction between them in different moments of the creative process.

4.4.1 Motivational Tendencies and Arousal

Opening with the first question, asking when the motivational focus start attracting information from memory, we can assume that the *Drive* state is mostly defined by creative motivational forces, i.e., by the thinker's motivational tendencies to act on the world in a generative way. These motivational forces find an activation, driving the thinker's creative behavior, only when they find a resonance with a specific attentional focus, which arouses the thinker's action tendencies toward a specific direction. In an interactive modality, motivational tendencies act on the world through a constant attentive alert in the search for relevant events/stimuli, and through a feedback reaction, attention, which focuses on a specific area, channels motivational forces, arousing the process in a specific direction. This emotional dynamic immediately activates in the thinker's memory all information related to that specific focus area as well as the need to collect more information on the focus. In other words, interest emerges in the thinker's mind driving her/his first creative acts.

Emotional reactions belonging to the individual seem therefore to be discriminant variables in explaining this first phase shift. This assumption can explain the huge individual differences characterizing people's creative interests. What can be attractive for a specific person, might not be even perceived by another person. Only when individual action tendencies match a specific external or internal focus, the individual creative drive can activate the process, or, rather, a sufficient level of arousal can be reached to sustain the entire creative process. This proposition finds in part support from research on the synergic interaction between extrinsic and intrinsic motivation, which showed that the impact of extrinsic forces on creativity is determined in an interactive manner by the nature of the task, the receptor of the reward (individual or group), the personality traits of the involved individuals (individualistic or collectivistic), and the level of intrinsic motivation (Agnoli et al. 2018b; Amabile 1993; Eisenberg 2002). In this view, quantitative changes in motivational forces, in terms of the channelization of the spread affective arousal in the direction of a specific attentive focus, can explain the phase shift from the *Drive* mental state to the *Information* mental state (see Fig. 4.1).

The role of the channelization of motivational drive into different attentive and emotional focus areas, which define the individual interests, is evident in the case of many past artists or inventors who grew up together but who were separated by their different interests. A classical example are the lives of Paul Cezanne and Emile Zola, who were close friends throughout their youth and who shared a common undefined passion, as Zola wrote: "certain secret affinities, the still vague promptings of a common ambition, the dawning consciousness of possessing greater intelligence…" (Zola 1886/1993, p. 31). This common ambition (their common drive) was however attracted and pointed in different directions, towards writing in the case of Zola and towards painting in the case of Cezanne. Their different interests led therefore their common drive towards different directions and, finally, towards different lives.

4.4.2 Appraisal Checks

In the attempt to analyze which are the affective components controlling the phase shift from *Information* to *Movement*, let us adopt the appraisal approach. The fundamental question here regards why some information elements from the environment lead to restructuring the thinker's information structure. Why is some information more effective in increasing the probability for a creative idea to emerge? In their seminal work, Goldenberg et al. (1999) showed for example that in the advertisement domain specific methods to handle information are needed to enhance this probability, while randomness is essentially ineffective in this sense. But we could also wonder why in the legendary episode was exactly an apple leading Newton to come up with his theory of gravity and not, for example, the wind in the trees or a random object falling from his hand? We do not have certainly the ambitious goal of answering to these big questions, but what we are going to do is to use an appraisal approach to look at these questions from a different perspective.

Scherer's stimulus evaluation check approach (2001) seems particularly suitable to analyze these questions, since it can help understanding the selection of stimuli on the basis of their relevance. Relevance is here defined on the basis of three sequential SECs that find a precise contextualization within a specific motivational and attentional drive as well as within a specific information network activated within the thinker's mind. The same checks indeed can lead to totally different evaluations if inserted in a different context. It is therefore important to highlight that during the creative process cognitive appraisal interacts with specific motivational tendencies and affective arousal as well as with a specific thinkers' knowledge structure. The first SEC (*novelty check*) scans environment in the search for novelty, i.e., in the search of unfamiliar, unexpected stimuli. All elements responding to this check are able to attract attention. This SEC takes into account the knowledge structure activated within the thinker's mind and detects all elements which are not related to this structure. The second SEC (*intrinsic pleasantness check*) determines then the thinker's reaction toward the novel stimulus, establishing the fundamental like/dislike reaction of the organism toward this stimulus. This SEC is particularly important since it charges the organism with a further arousal source directed toward the stimulus, in order to prepare the organism to approach or to avoid this stimulus. The final SEC is the *goal relevance check* which delineates the importance of the stimulus for the momentary hierarchy of thinker's goals or needs.

It is here important to discriminate between the notion of relevance and irrelevance described within the DIMAI model and the notion of relevance as defined within Scherer's approach (2001). Relevant information is defined in the DIMAI model as the set of items related to the specific focus area, i.e., the state of the art of the knowledge on that specific area. Irrelevant information is instead all information which is not usually included in this state of the art. The distinction between these two forms of information is defined through the first SEC into an appraisal approach. Relevance is instead defined within this latter approach as the organism's aim to maintain the status quo or to reach the desired goals through the active investment of more extensive resources (Scherer 2001). Through this evaluation new energy is actively invested from the organism into the process. We maintain that this new source of energy is able to destabilize the relationships between the components defining the *Information* mental state (in particular the thinker's knowledge structure), leading to a new form of equilibrium, to a new mental state.

We can however assume that only when an information cue passes through all three SECs, it can bring its energy within the process. In particular the last SEC seems to be discriminant in this sense. To attract attention a stimulus should be novel (not familiar), to attract energy it should be charged by a sort of pleasantness or unpleasantness, but to be included in the creative thinking process it should be important for thinkers' motivational goals. These three SECs could explain the mechanisms which are at the basis of the inclusion into the process of only some information cues and not instead of all information coming from the environment (see Fig. 4.1). Moreover, the affective charge deriving from the relevance evaluation can explain the feelings of discomfort or pleasant surprise sometimes emerging when a new extraneous element bursts into the thinking process, producing a temporary restructuring of our knowledge structure. This does not mean that all elements breaking into the process can produce a fruitful (in terms of creative) restructuration of the thinker's knowledge, but we can assume that they can give further energy to the thinking process to explore new paths never considered before.

Classical examples of the restructuring brought about by external elements come from insight episodes described in classical anecdotes of discovery. Many of these anecdotes are based on the ability of an inventor to capture or to be captured by some information in the environment that seemed to be apparently irrelevant and that all other people have discarded or not even noticed. We can hypothesize that this ability is indeed guided by a constant appraisal of environmental information. The discovery of penicillin by Alexander Fleming is paradigmatic in this sense. In looking at a petri dish containing a culture of bacteria which had become moldy, he noticed that the bacteria around the mold had been destroyed. This selective encoding of the environment (Sternberg and Davidson 1999) could be based on the three aforementioned SECs: the destruction of bacteria by the mold was not familiar, it was pleasantly new, and essentially it matched with the motivational goals of Fleming, whose main interest and motivational focus was the discovery of new antibacterial agents. Passing through these three SECs, that apparently irrelevant information captured Fleming's attention and restructured his knowledge structure, and later that of the entire medicine.

4.4.3 The Role of Awareness

A further pressing question is related to how an idea emerges among the virtually infinite alternative ideas that a thinker could produce. In the attempt to analyze this question, we will in the following consider the role of awareness in the emotional experience, i.e., what is usually intended as feelings.

Feelings are typically considered from the common sense to be what emotions are all about. Obviously the question is not so simple. Emotions mostly reflect non-conscious appraisal processes, state of action readiness, psychophysiological responses, which largely occur without an aware experience of their occurrence (Frijda 2005). The same holds for the processes described in the previous paragraphs. Most of them occur without a conscious experience by the thinker. Emotion experience can have indeed different forms, as any other experience. Which form it takes depends on the role of attention, and on thinker's direction of attention (Lambie and Marcel 2002). We have for example two main forms of consciousness, characterized by absence or presence of focal attention. Moreover, attention can be directed either towards the world or towards oneself. Even if during a creative act many specific emotional experiences come into the process, we can try to characterize different forms of emotional experiences into different mental states.

In the case of the focalization of motivational forces on a specific focus area, the thinker can move from a first to a second order of experience. While in the first order of experience there is no separate awareness of here and there, of self and object, the second order of experience involves a focal attention (Frijda 2005). During an emotional experience of the first order the thinker is not aware of her/his feeling, it is an immersed condition, such as in the case of the feeling of being motivated to be creative, which is not related with a specific focus and that most of the time is totally unaware to the thinker. The focalization on a specific focus area moves the thinker's experience to a second order level, which can shift and extend to awareness the intense emotional forces directed toward that specific area. In other words, the emotional experience become reportable only when focused attention intervenes canalizing the affective experience into a perceptible thinking area/object (Frijda 2005). The life of Van Gogh gives us an outstanding example of the importance of the aware realization of our creative focus, to effectively invest on that specific area of interest. This emerged for example in 1880, when Van Gogh realized that all his undefined "driving force behind" his "feeling for beauty", which led him to try different professional experiences, had to finally and definitively result in becoming a "true painter" (Jansen et al. 2009). The aware investment of his driving force towards painting gave rise to some of the most incredible pieces of art humanity has ever seen.

The thinker becomes therefore aware of a personal interest toward a specific focus area. However, this emotional experience is usually characterized by a general feeling distributed on a wide and broadly defined network of semantically related information, defining the focus area of interest. Through the appraisal process described in the previous paragraph, an analytical attentive analysis of information begins. Attention tends to be focalized on one or more specific aspects of the world. When an important information (as evaluated through sequential appraisal SECs) emerges into thinker's consciousness, an emotional experience related to that specific information emerged. The emotional experience becomes in this case an affective meaningful perception of the world (Frijda 2005) and in particular of a specific information which emerged to be relevant for thinker's goals (see Fig. 4.1). In this way, appraisal processes become conscious and an aware feeling toward the information emerges. The information emerged to be attractive, repulsive, surprising, etc. As described by Frijda (2005), the emotional experience is indeed *about* something, not just *of* something. The aware shifting of attention towards an information which apparently does not pertain to our thinking process allows to charge that information with an affective arousal. The aforementioned example of Fleming's episode leading to the discovery of penicillin seems to indicate a shift of awareness from an internal thinking process to an external entity (the bacteria around the mold), which was charged with an affective meaning deriving from the personal motivational goals of the inventor. This information emerged therefore to be attractive and surprising, leading Fleming to explore the phenomenon more in depth.

Moving from *Information* to *Movement* attention turns to be focalized on the self, in the attempt to explore possible alternative ideas inspired by this new information breaking into the process. An internally directed appraisal process checks many alternatives into the thinker's mind. Attention is no more object-centered but becomes thinker-centered, and experience changes accordingly. During this exploration however the thinker might need a signal that has effects even if he/she is engaged in an open-defined cognitive exploration and that can alert a large variety of response processes, including the pre-specified goal settings and purposive behaviours, and cognitive activities like conscious assessment (Frijda 2005). This signal is provided by the emergence of an emotional experience into awareness as soon as an alternative is appraised as relevant to the creative purpose. The main function of feelings during the *Movement* state could be therefore to open the door to consciousness and to the more elaborate functional properties usually ascribed to it. Through an emotional experience associated to a specific idea generated into the thinker's mind, the specific idea becomes aware and can be consciously evaluated in reference to thinker's creative goals. This does not however mean that the idea would be necessarily effective in solving creator's drive (Corazza 2016).

The breaking into consciousness of an emotional experience associated to an idea is highly evident in the insight phenomenon, when a solution or idea is usually accompanied by an intense emotional reaction. This experience has been well documented in recent research that showed that insight is associated to the activation of Nucleus Accumbens, a subcortical area associated to reward (Floresco et al. 2001; Haber and McFarland 1999; Tik et al. 2015, 2018). According to the hypothesis here proposed, therefore, the main role in controlling the phase shift from *Movement* to *Assessment* might be ascribed to the emergence into consciousness of an emotional experience which brings into awareness a specific idea triggering that experience (see Fig. 4.1).

The coupling of an emotional experience with a specific idea or series of ideas generated as a consequence of a personal motivational drive is well defined by Lubart and Getz (1997) when they describe emotional-based mechanisms leading to the generation of new ideas. In particular, they describe a resonance-detection mechanism that controls whether an activated pattern into the thinker's mind enters in resonance with her/his goals, letting it passing into conscious working memory. This experience has been described by past creators as a mechanism that allowed the selection and emergence of their creative ideas. Poincaré (1921/1985) for example was aware that creativity involves a selection mechanism, which he identified as "emotional sensibility" (p. 29), allowing only aesthetically pleasing mathematical ideas to pass into his aware consideration.

4.5 Conclusions: The Sixth Step

In the previous paragraphs we offered a general overview of the role of emotions into the creative thinking process from a dynamical system point of view, as well as some particular exemplifications on the role of specific emotional components in the emergence of creative mental states.

It will not have however escaped the attentive reader that in paragraph 3.1 only five of the six steps described by Thelen and Smith (1994, 1998) have been considered. The sixth step in the investigation of a dynamic system requires an active experimental investigation of the control parameters in order to understand the dynamics of the system. We do believe that this step represents a challenging goal for the future research on creativity. Through this step it will be possible to understand the real empirical validity of the approach proposed in this chapter and whether emotions can be really intended as control parameters into the creative thinking process. Specific experimental paradigms as well as dedicated analysis methods should be developed, building on the valuable micro-analytic research approaches already described in the creativity literature (e.g., Glăveanu and Lahlou 2012). The high complexity of the dynamics involved in the process requires both a parcelled approach to explore the role of single emotional components in the emergence of the creative process and a holistic approach, to understand how the different emotional components interact with specific elements defining the creative behaviour.

Some evidence on the role of emotions as control parameters within the creative thinking process seem already to have emerged from research. Silvia for example described a model of aesthetic emotions (Silvia 2005a, b), which connects emotional responses to art to the cognitive processes that underline emotions, *de facto* explaining how appraisal mechanisms can drive the assessment of artistic ideas. Moreover, in a recent study (Agnoli et al. 2018a) we demonstrated how affective components (and in particular affective arousal) can interact with the attentive processing in determining creative performance. Specifically, we demonstrated that emotional attitudes, defining regularities in how a person feel, regulate, and perceived emotions (i.e., trait emotional intelligence) can drive the creative process through the management of the attentive and emotional resources beneficial to creative thinking.

Beside the impact on the experimental approach to the analysis of creative thinking, we believe that the theoretical framework here proposed can offer new insight also to the education of creativity. Sensitivity to emotions, emotion regulation, perception and awareness of emotions should be included within the educational approaches to creativity. If we believe that the creative process is a mental activity paved by emotional experiences, some of which of intense negative nature, we should give to the young generation the instruments to recognize and manage these experiences in order to take benefit from them during the creative process. The frustration deriving from the low cost-benefit ratio of the creative process, because of the too high investment of energy as compared to the low probability of success, is one of the first causes for the disinvestment from creative activities (von Thienen et al. 2017). Moreover, the powerful negative emotions (sadness, anger, depression, etc.) deriving from negative evaluations of our creative products are disincentives in the undertaking of creative activities.

The management of all these emotional variables should be contextualized within the education of creativity and not allowed to vary according to emotional individual differences. Particularly, we believe that educational programs, along with the teaching of creative thinking abilities and methods, should also consider the inclusion of specific training for the management of the emotional impact of creative activities in everyday and academic/professional contexts. If we do not take into account the emotional burden intrinsic to thinking and acting creatively, we risk that much creative potential will be wasted. The training of adaptive emotional behaviors and traits in schools could give students new and effective tools to regulate and manage the affective charge of creative decisions and acts. As said before, emotional intelligence emerged indeed in recent research to be a fundamental predictor of higher creative performance, especially under creative frustration situations. Specific and reliable trainings do exist for increasing emotional intelligence and specific emotional abilities (e.g., Hodzic et al. 2017). If the teaching of creative thinking were coupled with these methods aimed at the education of the intelligent use of the emotional experiences rising during the creative process, new generations may be more prone to take the risk and to cope with the frustrations associated to thinking and acting creatively. We indeed strongly believe that new educational avenues can be traced adopting an emotional approach to creativity, and further potential can be thereby spotted to face the challenges of the future.

References

Agnoli, S., Franchin, L., Rubaltelli, E., & Corazza, G. E. (2015). An eye-tracking analysis of irrelevance processing as moderator of openness and creative performance. *Creativity Research Journal, 27*, 125–132.

Agnoli, S., Franchin, L., Rubaltelli, E., & Corazza, G. E. (2018a). The emotionally intelligent use of attention and affective arousal under creative frustration and creative success. *Personality and Individual Differences*. https://doi.org/10.1016/j.paid.2018.04.041.

Agnoli, S., Runco, M. A., Kirsch, C., & Corazza, G. E. (2018b). The role of motivation in the prediction of creative achievement inside and outside of school environment. *Thinking Skills and Creativity, 28*, 167–176. https://doi.org/10.1016/j.tsc.2018.05.005.

Amabile, T. M. (1983). The social psychology of creativity: A componential conceptualization. *Journal of Personality and Social Psychology, 45*(2), 357–376.

Amabile, T. M. (1993). Motivational synergy: Toward new conceptualizations of intrinsic and extrinsic motivation in the workplace. *Human Resource Management Review, 3*(3), 185–201.

Amabile, T. M., Barsade, S. G., Mueller, J. S., & Staw, B. M. (2005). Affect and creativity at work. *Administrative Science Quarterly, 50*(3), 367–403.

Ariely, D., & Norton, M. I. (2008). How actions create–not just reveal–preferences. *Trends in Cognitive Sciences, 12*, 13–16.

Baas, M., De Dreu, C., & Nijstad, B. A. (2012). Emotions that associate with uncertainty lead to structured ideation. *Emotion, 12*, 1004–1014.

Camras, L. A., & Witherington, D. C. (2005). Dynamical systems approaches to emotional development. *Developmental Review, 25*(3), 328–350.

Corazza, G. E. (2016). Potential originality and effectiveness: The dynamic definition of creativity. *Creativity Research Journal, 28*(3), 258–267.

Corazza, G. E., & Agnoli, S. (2015). On the path towards the science of creative thinking. In G. E. Corazza & S. Agnoli (Eds.), *Multidisciplinary contributions to the science of creative thinking* (pp. 3–20). Singapore: Springer.

Corazza, G. E., Agnoli, S., & Martello, S. (2016). A creativity and innovation course for engineers. In *Handbook of research on creative problem-solving skill development in higher education* (pp. 74–93).

Davis, M. A. (2009). Understanding the relationship between mood and creativity: A meta-analysis. *Organizational Behavior and Human Decision Processes, 108*(1), 25–38.

De Dreu, C. K., Baas, M., & Nijstad, B. A. (2008). Hedonic tone and activation level in the mood-creativity link: Toward a dual pathway to creativity model. *Journal of Personality and Social Psychology, 94*(5), 739–756.

Eisenberg, J. (2002, July). *Does individual motivation and creativity predict group creative performance? Yes, but with some surprises*. Paper session presented at the International WAM meeting. Lima, Peru.

Feldman Barrett, L. (2017). *How emotions are made: The secret life of the brain*. Boston: Houghton Mifflin Harcourt.

Finke, R. A., Ward, T. B., & Smith, S. M. (1992). *Creative cognition: Theory, research, and applications*. Cambridge, MA: MIT Press.

Floresco, S. B., Blaha, C. D., Yang, C. R., & Phillips, A. G. (2001). Modulation of hippocampal and amygdalar-evoked activity of nucleus accumbens neurons by dopamine: Cellular mechanisms of input selection. *The Journal of Neuroscience, 21*, 2851–2860.

Fogel, A., Nwokah, E., Dedo, J. Y., Messinger, D., Dickson, K. L., Matusov, E., & Holt, S. A. (1992). Social process theory of emotion: A dynamic systems approach. *Social Development, 1*(2), 122–142.

Frijda, N. (2005). Emotion experience. *Cognition & Emotion, 19*(4), 473–497.

Frijda, N. H. (2007). *The laws of emotion*. Mahwah: Lawrence Erlbaum Associates.

Frijda, N. H., & Scherer, K. R. (2009). Emotion definition (psychological perspectives). In D. Sander & K. R. Scherer (Eds.), *Oxford companion to emotion and the affective sciences* (pp. 142–143). Oxford: Oxford University Press.

Glăveanu, V. P., & Lahlou, S. (2012). Through the creator's eyes: Using the subjective camera to study craft creativity. *Creativity Research Journal, 24*, 152–162.

Goldenberg, J., Mazursky, D., & Solomon, S. (1999). Creative sparks. *Science, 285*(5433), 1495–1496.

Gross, J. J., & Feldman Barrett, L. (2011). Emotion generation and emotion regulation: One or two depends on your point of view. *Emotion Review, 3*(1), 8–16.

Guilford, J. P. (1950). Creativity. *American Psychologist, 5*, 444–454.

Hélie, S., & Sun, R. (2010). Incubation, insight, and creative problem solving: A unified theory and a connectionist model. *Psychological Review, 117*(3), 994–1024.

Haber, S. N., & McFarland, N. R. (1999). The Concept of the Ventral Striatum in Nonhuman Primates. *Annals of the New York Academy of Sciences, 877*(1), 33–48. https://doi.org/10.1111/j.1749-6632.1999.tb09259.x PMID:10415641.

Hodzic, S., Scharfen, J., Ripoll, P., Holling, H., & Zenasni, F. (2017). How efficient are emotional intelligence trainings: A meta-analysis. *Emotion Review*. https://doi.org/10.1177/1754073917708613.

Izard, C. E., Ackerman, B. P., Schoff, K. M., & Fine, S. E. (2000). Self-organization of discrete emotions, emotion patterns, and emotion-cognition relations. In M. D. Lewis & P. Granic (Eds.), *Emotion, development, and self- organization: Dynamic systems approaches to emotional development* (pp. 15–36). Cambridge: Cambridge University Press.

Jansen, L., Luijten, H., & Bakker N. (eds.) (2009), *Vincent van Gogh – The letters*. Version: December 2010. Amsterdam/The Hague: Van Gogh Museum/Huygens ING.

Jauk, E., Benedek, M., & Neubauer, A. C. (2014). The road to creative achievement: A latent variable model of ability and personality predictors. *European Journal of Personality, 28*(1), 95–105.

Kahneman, D. (2011). *Thinking, fast and slow*. New York: Farrar, Straus and Giroux.

Lambie, J., & Marcel, A. (2002). Consciousness and emotion experience: A theoretical framework. *Psychological Review, 109*, 219–259.

Lazarus, R. S. (1982). Thoughts on the relations between emotion and cognition. *American Psychologist, 37*, 1019–1024.

Lazarus, R. S. (1984). On the primacy of cognition. *American Psychologist, 39*, 124–129.

Leventhal, H., & Scherer, K. (1987). The relationship of emotion to cognition: A functional approach to a semantic controversy. *Cognition and Emotion, 1*(1), 3–28.

Lewis, D., & Granic, P. (2000). *Emotion, development, and self- organization: Dynamic systems approaches to emotional development*. Cambridge: Cambridge University Press.

Lubart, T. (2001). Models of the creative process: Past, present and future. *Creativity Research Journal, 13*, 295–308.

Lubart, T. I., & Getz, I. (1997). Emotion, metaphor, and the creative process. *Creativity Research Journal, 10*(4), 285–301.

Moors, A., Ellsworth, P. C., Scherer, K. R., & Frijda, N. H. (2013). Appraisal theories of emotion: State of the art and future development. *Emotion Review, 5*(2), 119–124.

Mumford, M. D., Mobley, M. I., Uhlman, C. E., Reiter-Palmon, R., & Doares, L. M. (1991). Process analytic models of creative capacities. *Creativity Research Journal, 4*, 91–122.

Poincarè, H. (1985). Mathematical creation. In B. Ghiselin (Ed.), *The creative process: A symposium* (pp. 22–31). Berkeley: University of California Press (Original work published 1921).

Scherer, K. R. (1987). Toward a dynamic theory of emotion: The component Process model of affective states. *Geneva Studies in Emotion and Communication, 1*, 1–98.

Scherer, K. R. (2000). Emotions as episodes of subsystem synchronization driven by nonlinear appraisal processes. In M. D. Lewis & I. Granic (Eds.), *Emotion, development, and self-organization: Dynamic systems approaches to emotional development* (pp. 70–99). Cambridge: Cambridge University Press.

Scherer, K. R. (2001). Appraisal considered as a process of multilevel sequential checking. In K. R. Scherer, A. Schorr, & T. John Stone (Eds.), *Appraisal processes in emotion: Theory, methods, research* (pp. 92–120). New York/Oxford: Oxford University Press.

Scherer, K. R. (2009). Emotions are emergent processes: They require a dynamic computational architecture. *Philosophical Transactions of the Royal Society of London B: Biological Sciences, 364*(1535), 3459–3474.

Silvia, P. J. (2005a). Cognitive appraisals and interest in visual art: Exploring an appraisal theory of aesthetic emotions. *Empirical Studies of the Arts, 23*, 119–133.

Silvia, P. J. (2005b). Emotional responses to art: From collation and arousal to cognition and emotion. *Review of General Psychology, 9*, 342–357.

Silvia, P. J., & Brown, E. M. (2007). Anger, disgust, and the negative aesthetic emotions: Expanding an appraisal model of aesthetic experience. *Psychology of Aesthetics, Creativity, and the Arts, 1*(2), 100–106.

Sternberg, R. J., & Davidson, J. E. (1999). Insight. In M. A. Runco & S. R. Pritzker (Eds.), *Encyclopedia of creativity* (vol. II, pp. 57–69).

Thelen, E., & Smith, L. B. (1994). *A dynamic systems approach to the development of cognition and action*. Cambridge, MA: MIT Press.

Thelen, E., & Smith, L. B. (1998). Dynamic systems theories. In W. Damon & R. M. Lerner (Eds.), *Handbook of child psychology, Theoretical models of human development* (Vol. 1, pp. 563–634). New York: Wiley.

Tik, M., Sladky, R., Di Bernardi Luft, C., Hoffmann, A., Hummer, A., Banissy M., Bhattacharya J., & Windischberger C. (2015). *Ultra-high field fMRI insights on insight: Neural correlates of the "Aha!"*. 21st meeting of the Organization for Human Brain Mapping, HBM – Honolulu.

Tik, M., Sladky, R., Luft, C. D. B., Willinger, D., Hoffmann, A., Banissy, M. J., et al. (2018). Ultra-high-field fMRI insights on insight: Neural correlates of the Aha -moment. *Human Brain Mapping, 39*, 1–12. https://doi.org/10.1002/hbm.24073.

Tversky, A., & Kahneman, D. (1983). Extensional versus intuitive reasoning: The conjunction fallacy in probability judgment. *Psychological Review, 90*, 293–315.

von Thienen, J., Meinel, C., & Corazza, G. E. (2017). A short theory of failure. *Electronic Colloquium on Design Thinking Research, 17*, 1–5.

Wallas, G. (1926). *The art of thought*. New York: Harcourt Brace.

Zenasni, F., & Lubart, T. (2002). Effects of mood states on creativity. *Current Psychology Letters, 8*, 33–50.

Zola, E. (1886/1993). *The masterpiece*. New York: Oxford University Press.

Chapter 5
Estimator Socialization in Design Thinking: The Dynamic Process of Learning How to Judge Creative Work

Julia P. A. von Thienen, Steven Ney, and Christoph Meinel

Abstract The assessment of ideas is a central activity in creative processes. Since teachers and coaches guide the learning of students, their assessment styles are particularly consequential. We report a longitudinal study, comparing the idea evaluation style of coaches before and after they are trained in the innovation paradigm design thinking. Initially, the coaches display a static idea assessment style. They attribute value primarily based on the requirement that ideas should be immediately effective, regardless of whether students are in the middle or in a late stage of their creative process. After being trained, the coaches have developed a dynamic, process-oriented evaluation style. They also assess ideas in line with design thinking values, with one exception. Contrary to design thinking teachings, the coaches do not come to value idea originality. The chapter closes with considerations how to facilitate the acceptance of original ideas.

5.1 Introduction

The assessment of ideas – finding ideas promising or futile – often decides which path a creative project takes. This happens for good or bad. When assessments go astray, fruitless ideas may be pursued with ample resources until they all too obviously reach a dead end, or ground-breaking ideas may be unnecessarily abandoned.

J. P. A. von Thienen (✉)
Digital Engineering Faculty, University of Potsdam, Potsdam, Germany
e-mail: Julia.vonThienen@hpi.de

S. Ney
HPI Academy, Potsdam, Germany
e-mail: Steven.Ney@hpi.de

C. Meinel
Hasso Plattner Institute at the University of Potsdam, Potsdam, Germany
e-mail: Christoph.Meinel@hpi.de

© Springer Nature Switzerland AG 2019
R. A. Beghetto, G. E. Corazza (eds.), *Dynamic Perspectives on Creativity*, Creativity Theory and Action in Education 4, https://doi.org/10.1007/978-3-319-99163-4_5

In creativity education the handling of ideas is taught both on explicit and implicit levels. What teachers say about the evaluation of creative ideas is one thing. How they handle student ideas is another. When teachers react to student ideas in approving or dismissive ways, they implicitly convey standards how to think and feel about ideas.

The assessment of creative ideas is unlike the assessment of student answers in a math test where teachers can "judge" what is right or wrong according to rather static standards. Corazza (2017) therefore suggests a change of language: In creativity education we don't *judge* the value of creative ideas, we *estimate* it. Yet, the question how teachers can learn to be good estimators of student ideas is still an open one, requiring further research.

> We must progress in the understanding of
> - how educators can be good estimators of creativity
> - how they can foster the development of estimation ability in their students, an essential part of their creative mindset
>
> (Corazza 2017, p. 22)

It has been repeatedly observed that educators who are untrained in creativity paradigms intuitively adopt idea assessment styles, which in fact counter the development of creative mindsets in students. For instance, at school teachers regularly perceive unexpected student ideas as disruptive (Beghetto 2007, 2010). Consequently, teachers are inclined to dismiss these ideas, hoping to ensure seamless on-task work in class. However, unexpected student ideas are potentially creative. To aid the development of creative mindsets, teachers should learn to explore these ideas more frequently (Beghetto 2013). Maybe creativity education for teachers could endow them with revised assessment standards, ideally yielding novel intuitions altogether. Unexpected student ideas would then be perceived as opportunities rather than threats by the teachers, if not always then at least more regularly.

Is this possible? Can estimators learn to perceive ideas in novel ways, such as to better facilitate creative processes and the development of creative mindsets?

In this chapter we report a longitudinal study, tracing how idea assessments of estimators change as they undergo training to become certified innovation facilitators. Study participants attend a one-semester *Certification Program for Design Thinking Coaches* at the Hasso Plattner Institute (HPI) of Potsdam University. Design thinking is an innovation paradigm taught at an increasing number of academic institutions world-wide, including Stanford, Potsdam and Cape Town University. At Potsdam, we presently teach 320 students each year in formats such as the "Design Thinking Weeks" (80 students), the one-semester long "Basic Track" (160 students) and the also one semester long "Advanced Track" (80 students).

In the *Manual for Design Thinking Coaches* (Ney 2016) participants of the *Certification Program* learn about their tasks as innovation facilitators. Preparing and hosting creative processes of design thinking teams are important objectives.

> Team coaches need to apply their judgement about when to adhere to and when to depart from the plan, when to leave the team be and when to intervene, as well as how to best help a team that has got itself stuck. […]

> [T]eam coaches need to forge *links* and create effective transitions from one design thinking phase to the next. Here, team coaches not only have to ensure that teams generate the outputs that enable them to address the tasks of the subsequent phase, they also need to support teams in creating the type of outputs that inspire and promote innovation.
>
> (Ney 2016, p. 9, emphasis in original)

Among other things, the *Certification Program for Design Thinking Coaches* attempts to school the estimation abilities of participants. After the training, coaches shall be expert estimators who reliably sense whether teams progress on trajectories with a high creative potential, or whether teams go astray and potentially need to be redirected by means of coaching interventions. Team coaches shall also estimate to what extent intermediate process outcomes – such as ideas – adequately promote the development of innovation, i.e. creative achievements, in subsequent process stages.

The basic objective of our longitudinal study is anticipated by Beghetto's insinuation: "As with all assessments, when it comes to assessing creativity, what you assess is essentially what you get" (2010, p. 453). This observation yields key questions we hope to clarify. What do people assess when they estimate the value of ideas? Do the assessment styles of estimators change in characteristic ways when people undergo training in a creativity paradigm?

We will first introduce idea characteristics, which are considered important in design thinking education (Sect. 5.2). We will then describe our longitudinal study, including the measurement approach that was developed to analyse assessment styles of estimators (Sect. 5.3). Then study outcomes will be reported (Sect. 5.4) and discussed (Sect. 5.5). As one study result indicates, the handling of idea originality may be especially difficult to learn and teach. This issue concerns creativity educators far beyond design thinking. We will close this chapter with considerations how to facilitate the acceptance of original ideas (Sect. 5.6).

5.2 Valuing Ideas Design Thinking Style

The design thinking community has gradually developed some consensus on how to think and feel about ideas. This consensus certainly does not seek to eliminate all judgement variance that people naturally produce when thinking about ideas. Different valuation perspectives are a tremendous resource to be cherished in creative communities. Instead, design thinking courses shall help trainees develop "antennas" for some aspects of ideas, or evaluative dimensions, to which they may have been insensitive before. Trainees can also expect to develop novel emotional preferences regarding ideas and to unlearn others.

The evaluative style that is characteristic of design thinking culture at present has been shaped over decades. It is informed by personal preferences of pioneering community members, philosophical positions, explicit argumentation and, increasingly often, by empirical studies. While the style is conveyed through implicit and explicit enculturation processes (Sects. 5.2.1, 5.2.2 and 5.2.3), it is not an arbitrary culture. Instead, it is based on clear assumptions and is open to argument-driven revisions. In Sect. 5.2.3 we will discuss some questions where novel data could potentially impact the community's future way of assessing ideas.

We will review four dimensions, on which ideas can vary, to characterize design-thinking-typical ways of assessing ideas. While the discussion serves to clarify design thinking specific patterns of idea assessment, we hope to inspire readers beyond this particular creativity paradigm. The question what dimensions one invokes to estimate the potential of ideas is crucial for creative processes, whatever approach to creativity one pursues. Another important question is how the assessment standards are conveyed to novices, both explicitly and implicitly. Readers with a background other than design thinking are specifically invited to compare the assessment dimensions outlined below, and educational strategies used on their behalf, to the assessment dimensions and respective teaching approaches used in their own field.

5.2.1 Focus on User Needs

Already in the 1950s, when precursors to design thinking trainings began to develop at Stanford University, a humanistic philosophical orientation informed the emerging approach. John Arnold, who pioneered creativity education in the engineering department, discussed societal challenges as important starting points for creative endeavours (Arnold 1959/2016; von Thienen et al. 2017a). He prompted his students to tackle issues such as world hunger or traffic deaths. In Arnold's view, the task of engineers, designers, inventors and generally product developers is to identify bad conditions in the world and to bring about positive change by means of creative solutions. Based on this general philosophy, one of his predecessors in the department, Robert McKim, formulated a design theory based on human needs (McKim 1959/2016; von Thienen et al. forthcoming-a). According to McKim, the task of designers is to satisfy the physical, emotional and intellectual needs of mankind in morally and socially responsible ways. Present-day design thinking education continues these lines of thought. Creative projects evolve around user needs, which shall be gratified in socially responsible ways (Fig. 5.1).

Typically, in design thinking education students get to work in multi-disciplinary teams with three to six members. They work on real-life innovation challenges often provided by external project partners. The task can be, for instance, to create a better airport experience, which may be the wish of an airport operating company. At first the students shall *understand* the airport domain by conducting research about it. In the *observe* phase the students interview travellers, security guards, check-in personnel or even pizza sellers at airports and make careful behaviour observations; they can also build on personal airport experiences. In the *point of view* phase the team specifies key insights and decides who their user shall be. They may decide to create a better airport experience for travellers, in which case security guards, pizza sellers etc. will not be the addressees of their project henceforth. The team then

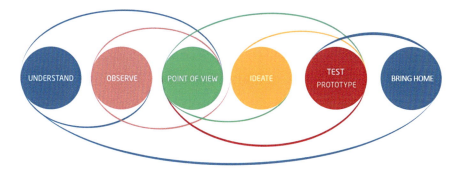

Fig. 5.1 The design thinking process

creates an imaginary customer to facilitate ideation, a so-called "persona". This could be Mrs. Wiggs, 62 years old, who flies regularly but finds it increasingly stressful to wait in long lines where she misses opportunities to sit down. In the *ideation* phase the team begins to think up solution ideas. They seek solutions for Mrs. Wiggs, considering as many and as diverse ideas as they possibly can. Afterwards, one or more ideas are selected. The team may decide to focus on the idea of a trolley to improve the experience of airport security checks: The trolley allows customers to separate fluids, technology, shoes etc. without hurry while lining up for the security check and also provides convenient seating. To test the idea, the team builds a prototype and tests it with persons who resemble the persona. User experiences shall be the ultimate criterion for the team to learn and advance their project. Team members should not defend a solution if users had unpleasant test experiences. In that case, the team should instead learn from the test and iterate their solution, returning to previous process phases if necessary. Finally, in the *bring home* phase a successful prototype is further advanced and potential implementation barriers are tackled.

A strong focus on user needs is taught explicitly basically in every session of design thinking education. The whole creative process, and methods used along the way, all support this purpose. In addition, design thinking novices can learn implicitly about this assessment dimension. Feedback from teachers or more experienced team members usually conveys how addressing user needs is of highest priority.

When a team ideates with a focus on user needs they seek solutions that specifically aid their intended user. In the airport scenario, the team seeks solutions for Mrs. Wiggs – not solutions for check-in personal or security guards at the airport and certainly not solutions, which team members may find "cool" for personal reasons while the approach would disregard the specific situation of Mrs. Wiggs.

Such a strong and consistent focus on user needs has a number of advantages in the creative process.

- **Solution effectiveness:** A consistent focus on user needs ensures that the intended audiences (users) find the outcome of the creative process valuable.

- **Intrinsic motivation:** Students feel their projects warrant much personal effort. They see themselves working towards truly desirable ends (Brown and Katz 2009; Kelley and Kelley 2013) and find the challenges personally meaningful (McKim 1972). Thus, students build up intrinsic motivation and drive (von Thienen et al. 2016, 2017a); they work energetically on their task even when facing difficulties along the way.
- **Teamwork:** The concern for user needs helps teams establish a joint focus and pursue a joint goal. The process is not about "what I want" versus "what you want". Instead, all team members decide together for whom they seek a solution and then the group forges ahead jointly to deliver the best possible outcome for their selected user.
- **Social connectedness, self-efficacy and agency:** The focus on user needs entails empathy and collaboration. Design thinkers experience social connectedness to team mates and users, which is an important resource in creative processes. As Cojuharenco et al. (2016) have demonstrated, social connectedness promotes self-efficacy (the belief of a person that she can make a difference) as well as agency (her taking of action even if positive effects are not immediately visible). This is especially important in creative projects. After all, creative achievements may materialize in the end, but people need to take action with no guarantees of success (Corazza 2016a).
- **Testing opportunities:** The focus on user needs introduces excellent opportunities for creative teams to test and learn. Users should embrace novel solutions like "revelations": Their gnawing, unmet needs would finally be satisfied. If test users do not celebrate a presented prototype, the creative team has something important to learn.

Despite of these advantages, the focus on user needs is not completely uncontroversial in the community. Occasionally people voice their preference that there should be more freedom to pursue personal visions, interests and intuitions. It should be possible to work more in the way artists proceed without having to focus on someone else's user needs. While such art-inspired process models might play a greater role in the future, as they did some decades ago, at present the user-focus is a clear and quite characteristic learning objective in design thinking education.

5.2.2 Balancing Team Interests

Working in teams is everyday-business in many product development units of the industry. Rarely does one individual have all the necessary skills to make inventions for a company alone, where software, hardware, usability and marketing expertise may be required. Such an industry inspired team-based work approach was also adopted early on in Stanford's creativity education for engineers, which is a major root of present-day design thinking. However, initially the team based approach was

Fig. 5.2 Explicit mottos convey design thinking values. Here, the motto "build on the ideas of others" is printed in large letters on the wall. (Photo by Toni Mattis)

just one training mode amongst others. In the late 1990s the emphasis on teamwork was strongly increased (Carleton and Leifer 2009). At present there is no teaching of individuals any more. Design thinking is completely team-based. Throughout their training students work in teams. Analogously, teachers teach in teams (Kelley and Kelley 2013; Roth 2015).

The value of collaborative invention is conveyed in multiple ways in design thinking communities. Explicitly, mottos such as "build on the ideas of others" prompt teams to ideate jointly (see Fig. 5.2).

Implicitly, students learn to think and act collaboratively both by what they witness and by what they don't witness. Experienced design thinkers act as role-models who live and teach in a collaborative spirit. In addition, it is also noteworthy what happens seldom in design thinking environments. Historically, theories of creativity often evolved around figures of "individual creative geniuses" (Beaney 2005; Gaut 2010). However, design thinking communities rarely narrate "hero-stories" of individual inventors. Rather, the community tells stories about both the creative achievements and struggles of creative teams (see, for instance, the collection of design thinking case stories on thisisdesignthinking.net, Hasso Plattner Institute for Digital Engineering 2017).

In creative teamwork, the question how to handle varying interests is a regular issue to come up. For instance, what if some of the team members want to build a technical solution whereas others favour a social solution? In this case, should the team maybe seek a social and technical solution? After all, such a combined approach could help keep all team members engaged in the process.

Coaching novices sometimes interpret the literature on teamwork and social competence as promoting the integration of all team member interests as a high-ranking requirement. Yet, experienced design thinkers do not place questions regarding team member interests centre-stage in the ideation phase. When teams seek solutions, they shall "saturate the solution space", considering as many different approaches as they possibly can. Limiting the solution space to approaches that satisfy all team member interests would seem counterproductive (e.g., considering solutions only that are social and technical). Furthermore, solutions shall be tailored to user needs, not to team member interests. Finally, teams learn to "bias toward doing and making over thinking and meeting" (d.school 2010, p. iii). Teams can trust that subsequent user tests will clarify the potential of ideas. Arguments about the issue featuring personal preferences seem highly unnecessary.

Thus, ideas that balance team interests are at present only slightly preferred in design thinking communities. While social skills are generally accorded great importance, the evaluation of solution ideas should not be overly limited by the need to accommodate diverse private interests of team members.

5.2.3 Originality and Effectiveness

Creative achievements are commonly defined as outcomes of creative processes that are *original and effective,* or, in another parlance, *novel and valuable* (Gaut 2010; Runco and Jaeger 2012; Corazza 2016a). These notions will be discussed in more detail below as they had to be operationalized in our study (see Sect. 5.3.1). For now we trust that a considerable consensus has been achieved as to what the terms mean.

In virtue of being an innovation paradigm, design thinking carefully attends to the originality and effectiveness of solution ideas. Thus, design thinking shares these two evaluative dimensions with many other approaches to creativity and innovation, which helps to draw from a rich corpus of theories and research results, and to jointly advance knowledge in the field.

One resource to draw from is a model of thought trajectories provided by Corazza (2015, 2016b) as part of the *Dynamic Creativity Framework.* The model depicts typical ideation moves in creative processes, illuminating likely time-dynamics of innovation projects. It also provides explanations why the objective of creative projects, to arrive at original and effective outcomes, is often difficult to achieve. Notably, we live in sophisticated cultures where a lot of ideas have been contemplated before. Moving beyond those ideas that someone else has already thought up is therefore a non-trivial task that usually requires time. Persons who enter a creative process can expect to tap a number of non-novel options first. Then, once ideation trajectories enter the realm of novel ideas, effectiveness becomes particularly hard to achieve. Most novel ideas may seem funny, foolish, mad etc. Working out a creative breakthrough – an idea no one else has had before, which in addition proves utterly effective – needs to be acknowledged as a great feat. If creative breakthroughs ever materialize in a project, it is typically after a long creative process where the originator had to persist in the face of numerous inconclusive outcomes, i.e. ideas that did not seem sufficiently original and effective.

Corazza's trajectory model hints at interdependencies between originality and effectiveness. The two dimensions are likely to be non-orthogonal in most natural settings. Effectiveness seems easily achievable with conventional solution ideas. One simply replicates already existing approaches, which should be at least somewhat effective. When, by contrast, untried possibilities are explored, effectiveness is often rather difficult to reach.

Empirical evidence seems to support this view. In a study at the HPI Potsdam (von Thienen et al. 2011), 40 participants worked on a real-life innovation challenge over 1 week. Half of the participants had participated in design thinking courses. The other participants were interested in creative work but had not yet been enrolled in design thinking classes. Design thinking students developed significantly more original ideas compared to untrained students. However, when the effectiveness of outcomes was estimated by domain experts, a negative correlation of −0.55 obtained between idea originality and idea effectiveness, which was statistically significant at a level of $p \leq .01$. Considering only the most original ideas, i.e. those of design thinking students, this negative correlation even amounted to −.70. This data supports the view that originality and effectiveness are non-orthogonal dimensions in many natural settings. The higher the level of originality, the more difficult it becomes to achieve effectiveness.

Similar results were found by Agnoli et al. (under review) who studied patterns in the advertisement domain. They found that, generally, greater originality entailed less recognized creative achievements at work. However, work experience seemed to mediate between originality and creative achievement, so that experienced advertisers in effect benefit from more original ideas. Again, the picture emerges of a *prima facie* negative relationship between originality and effectiveness. However, the difficult task of achieving effectiveness with original ideas seems to be manageable by those persons who can build on a great amount of work experience.

There can be a number of reasons why original ideas face effectiveness-hurdles (von Thienen et al. 2017b). Original ideas may be more difficult to communicate: Audiences may struggle to understand novel concepts, including their value. Furthermore, some – or many – audiences seem to reject original ideas, regardless of the idea content. Blair and Mumford (2007) demonstrate this phenomenon in a study with two samples of undergraduate students. A first group of students generates ideas, then another group of students evaluates the suggestions. In addition, four independent expert raters characterize all ideas on a number of dimensions, such as idea originality, adherence to social norms or expected implementation effort. Notably, the study participants display a strong preference for unoriginal ideas. The authors even speak of an "undeniable disdain for [...] original ideas" (p. 215). They explain the phenomenon in virtue of forecasting difficulties. Highly original ideas make it difficult for audiences to predict the ensuing effects. As the ideas are unprecedented, it is unclear whether hurdles will emerge in the implementation process and social effects are hard to foresee; they could be positive or negative. Thus, the authors describe a contrast between original ideas on the one hand and ideas yielding clear social benefits as well as ideas yielding predictable positive short-term effects on the other. Audiences are said to prefer socially beneficial and immediately effective ideas over original ones.

In addition to cognitive difficulties of anticipating the effects of original solutions, straightforward emotional reactions to novelty can also play a role. In animal innovation research, *neophobia* (being afraid of novel things) as opposed to *neophelia* (being attracted by the novel) is discussed as an important parameter (Greenberg 2003; Kaufman and Kaufman 2014). In human creativity studies, Barron (1955) made related observations. He assessed 100 men and found stable patterns in their orientation towards originality. Some men displayed an emotional preference for simple and conventional stimuli; these men also gave conventional rather than original answers in a number of tests. Other men who preferred more complex, unconventional stimuli also produced more original answers in the test situations. Against this background it is easy to see how audiences of people who emotionally prefer the conventional, who display neophobia rather than neophilia, can make it very difficult for any original idea to achieve full effectiveness. These audiences can function as gatekeepers who reject original ideas and counter their implementation.

Finally, original ideas face a practical, marked disadvantage compared to established ideas when it comes to effectiveness assessments. Established ideas benefit from longer periods of refinement and people are more practiced in their application. To illustrate difficulties novel approaches have to overcome, the high jump may serve as an example. Some decades ago high jumpers used the so-called scissors technique. There is a notable span in how high people can jump with this technique, depending on how practiced they are and how refined their technique is. Then, at some point a person (be that Fosbury or yet someone else) decided to try jumping backwards, which is nowadays known as the flop technique. Today we believe that it is possible to jump higher with the flop technique than with scissors. However, upon first trying it out with an unrefined technique and no practice in its application, surely the person who tried jumping backwards for the first time would not jump as high as professionals using a refined scissors technique. Thus, novel approaches may seem less effective than established approaches in first tests, even if their potential is actually greater (Fig. 5.3).

All in all, the degree of immediately realizable effectiveness is often a bad predictor for potential long-term effectiveness. A novel approach may need refinement to work out; people may need practice to use it effectively. Furthermore, a novel idea may be difficult to understand for others, so that better communication strategies need to be developed first. Also, audiences may need to be exposed to a novel idea for some time to gradually become more familiar with it and thus feel more comfortable about it. This presumed loose linkage between short term and long term effectiveness is of course highly relevant for creativity education.

In the history of design thinking, the belief was adopted early on that ideals of originality and effectiveness should play varying roles over time in creative processes. In the ideation phase, originality is considered a "must-have", whereas immediate effectiveness is only "nice-to-have". Key beliefs in this regard were adopted from the brainstorming pioneer Alex Osborn. John Arnold was personally

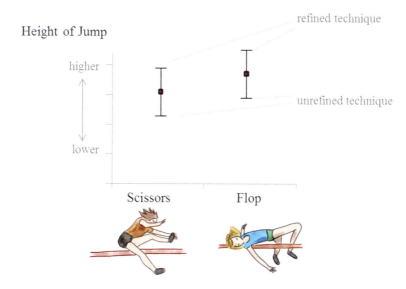

Fig. 5.3 Even if the flop technique has a greater potential effectiveness than the scissors technique in the high jump, it may seem less effective in first tests. Initially, an unrefined novel approach competes with a highly refined old approach. (Figure adapted from von Thienen et al. 2017b)

well-familiar with Osborn's approach, which he discussed in great detail and also critically (Arnold 1959/2016). Nonetheless, regarding originality and effectiveness Osborn's teachings have been maintained mostly unchanged in the design thinking community up to the present. "Osborn claims that it is easier to tame down than to think up" (Arnold 1959/2016, p. 106). Consequently, coaching instructions favour original ideas in the ideation phase. Arnold recapitulates what Osborn would say: "Remember now, men, we want as many ideas as possible – the wilder the better, and remember, no evaluation" (p. 105). Here, the instruction to avoid evaluation is given because evaluative thinking is taken to hinder the generation of multiple and original ideas. Up to the present, design thinking trainees still learn to "encourage wild ideas" and to "defer judgment" during ideation (d.school 2010, p. 28).

While these instructions are deeply engrained in design thinking practices, upon a closer look they actually seem contradictory. On the one hand people shall seek wild ideas, on the other hand they shall not evaluate. However, to seek wild ideas people must evaluate ideas on the dimension of originality, preferring original over unoriginal ideas. The instruction to refrain from evaluation obviously intends only one particular evaluative dimension, namely immediate effectiveness. This dimension shall play no important role in the ideation phase.

Given that design thinking is an innovation paradigm its projects must arrive at original and effective solutions eventually during the project term. This is rendered possible by a dynamically refined assessment strategy. Design thinkers do not aspire to originality and effectiveness uniformly throughout the process, which would mean to statically maintain one assessment style all throughout the project. Instead, assessment strategies undergo a fine-tuned regulation based on the following logic.

(0) Ideation is the process of thinking up ideas.
(I) Innovation requires original ideas.
(II) After ideation, the originality of ideas does not increase.
(III) Therefore, ideation must target original ideas to promote innovation.

(IV) Innovation requires effective ideas.
(V) When ideation targets immediately effective ideas, it tends to produce unoriginal ideas.
(III) Ideation must target original ideas to promote innovation.
(VI) Ideation need not target immediately effective ideas to promote innovation; the effectiveness of ideas can easily be increased through iterative prototype tests after ideation.
(VII) Therefore, ideation shall not target immediately effective ideas.

These arguments include empirically testable beliefs and more related research is likely to emerge. Notably, the development of idea effectiveness has already been investigated (claim VI).

In the design thinking process model (see Fig. 5.1), ideation is followed by the phase of testing prototypes. In practice this entails fast and highly iterative work routines. Prototypes are built quickly, tested and revised based on trial experiences. Indeed, this approach appears to be a reliable strategy to increase the effectiveness of basically any ideation outcome, as an experiment by Dow and Klemmer (2011) suggests. In their study 28 participants were asked to build vessels from everyday materials in 25 min to protect a raw egg from crushing that would be dropped from increasing heights. Task performance was measured in terms of the highest height at which the egg of each participant survived the fall. In the experimental condition, participants received a full carton of eggs and were prompted to test their vessel prototypes roughly every 5 min. Participants in the control condition received only one egg altogether. In the end, the average drop height that eggs survived was almost twice as high in the experimental condition compared to the control condition. Notably, solutions in the experimental condition did not excel because the participants switched their general approach based on test experiences. Rather, almost all participants stuck to their first ideation outcome (e.g., choosing a parachute, capsule or pillow design) and then only improved details of their approach. Thus, irrespective of the initial ideation outcome, quickly iterating prototype tests seem an excellent means to achieve high solution effectiveness. This supports the view that ideation need not target immediately effective ideas, since ideation outcomes can easily be rendered more effective in subsequent process phases.

At present, design thinking education conveys straightforward messages about originality and effectiveness as important idea dimensions. Explicitly students are prompted to produce original outcomes in all process phases up to ideation. In the understand and observe phases they shall gain new insights about user needs, which go beyond the explicit knowledge of humanity at the project outset. The teams shall discern truly existing need-patterns in the project domain that no one could see or explicitly describe at the project outset – neither the team members, nor domain experts, nor the users. Then design thinking teams are expected to specify their point of view in a single sentence, describing what the user needs based on a key observation insight (d.school 2010, p. 21). Design thinking students often get to hear that their point-of-view-statement should be "a sentence no one else has ever thought before". Afterwards, in the ideation phase, teams are told to head for "wild" ideas, which means that they shall try to produce original ideas, not shying away from suggestions that may sound crazy or unrealistic when taken literally.

On behalf of effectiveness, students learn both explicitly and implicitly that this is a matter of addressing basic user needs. Consistently, in terms of explicit and implicit messages, students also learn to not choose ideas based on expectations of immediate effectiveness in the ideation stage. Wild-sounding ideas can be rendered more effective by means of testing and iterating prototypes in later project stages.

5.2.4 Study Hypotheses: From Static to Dynamic Assessment Styles

Definitions of creativity in terms of original and effective outcomes court a static view on creativity (cf. Corazza 2016a). Yet, creative processes can be better understood and supported from a dynamic perspective, as for most of the time original and effective ideas are sought, but they have not yet materialized.

When a static assessment style is endorsed, originality and effectiveness matter invariably, regardless of the stage a creative project is in. By contrast, dynamic assessment styles allow a careful orchestration of idea evaluations over time. Estimators can emphasize or de-emphasize assessment dimensions depending on the process stage.

Both static and dynamic assessment styles may exist in different versions. Design thinking is typically used in product-developing contexts. Such an environment is likely different from, e.g., the realm of art where by default originality likely plays a greater role.

In product-developing contexts "breakthrough innovation" may be an ideal, but most importantly novel outcomes shall be effective. In everyday business, radical change is rare. Incremental change is more common. When new products are developed, originality is often not even pursued as a self-standing goal, only increased effectiveness counts as progress.

We expect participants in our longitudinal study to initially display a static evaluation style, adhering to the typical values in product-developing contexts. Thus, even in the middle of the creative process – when considering ideation outcomes – we expect participants to react as though they were evaluating final products, assessing primarily the immediate effectiveness of ideas. After the training, we expect participants to have developed a dynamic assessment style attuned to design thinking practices and values.

5.3 When Estimators Undergo Training: A Longitudinal Study of Idea Assessment Styles

To illuminate how people evaluate ideas in creative processes and how their evaluative style changes over time we developed *Idea Assessment Probes* (Sect. 5.3.1). After introducing this assessment methodology, we will describe the sample of study participants (Sect. 5.3.2) and the study procedure (Sect. 5.3.3).

5.3.1 Measuring Evaluation Styles with Idea Assessment Probes

The assessment methodology for this longitudinal study was developed in light of two constraints. First, the method should allow non-conflated, quantitative analyses regarding idea characteristics that impact value-judgements of single estimators. As discussed above (Sect. 5.2.3), in natural settings evaluative dimensions are often conflated. In particular, ideas that are more original typically show less immediate effectiveness. As Blair and Mumford (2007) would emphasise, the social benefits of original solutions also tend to be less clear. Forecasts are more difficult; both positive and negative consequences could obtain. Against this background, our assessment approach should render it possible to calculate the impact of single idea characteristics on value-judgements of estimators in non-conflated ways. In particular, it should be possible to assess the impact of idea originality on judgements of idea value without spurious correlations; high idea originality should not go along with reduced immediate effectiveness or reduced social benefits / less gratification of user needs. As a second requirement, assessments should be time-efficient. Study participants should not have to invest more than 10–12 min to fill out the questionnaire.

In light of these constraints, we developed *Idea Assessment Probes (IAPs)* as a measurement approach. Questionnaire items refer to ideas, which vary systematically on the dimensions of interest in dichotomizing ways. E.g., the ideas to be evaluated by the participants are either clearly original or clearly unoriginal. Since our study concerns four idea dimensions, we had to generate $4^2 = 16$ ideas (see Fig. 5.4) to cover all possible combinations.

We created two *IAPs* altogether, one idea set for the pre-test and another idea set for the post-test. Each questionnaire consists of an instruction sheet with a short scenario description and 16 idea cards. The scenario suggests a situation right after ideation, thus in the middle rather than at the end of the creative process. This should

5 Estimator Socialization in Design Thinking: The Dynamic Process of Learning…   81

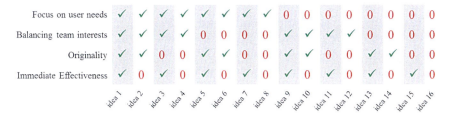

Fig. 5.4 Ideas in the questionnaire vary systematically on the dimensions (i) focus on user needs, (ii) balancing team interests, (iii) originality and (iv) immediate effectiveness

be a highly time-efficient method to distinguish between static and dynamic assessment styles of study participants.

To assess how strongly the value judgements of study participants are informed by design thinking practices and values, our scenario describes a persona (the indented user) and mentions diverging team interests. For instance, in the pre-test the following scenario is used.

You work as a design thinking coach. Your team has come up with persona Fritz Freundlich. Fritz is a 30-year old passionate farmer, who often suffers from back pain after harvesting asparagus, and who feels a bit lonely in his job. Your team has different preferences as to how the challenge should be tackled. Some team members want to concentrate on psychological wellbeing, while other team members want to concentrate on physical wellbeing.

To generate idea probes for the study participants to evaluate, we brainstormed about three times as many items as we finally included in the questionnaire. Two design thinking experts coded each idea on the four dimensions of interest. Only those ideas were considered for the questionnaire where the coding displayed perfect inter-rater-agreement. Among all remaining items, ideas were selected such as to avoid duplications of similar solution approaches, favouring instead a variety of differing solution ideas.

We used the following specifications to clarify the meaning of terms.

- *Focus on user needs*: The idea attempts to satisfy one or more persona needs; it does not conflict with persona interests.
- *Balancing team interests*: The idea addresses multiple needs; it accommodates the varying interests of different team members.
- *Originality*: The idea is novel. No product or service like this currently exists, nor is the idea familiar from fiction novels or movies.
- *Immediate Effectiveness*: The approach seems realizable without major hurdles. It is very likely to produce the intended effect – specified in brackets on each idea card – rather quickly.

One sample idea (# 4) is the following:

The farmer publishes an ad in a magazine to find a marriage partner. She can help him at work (so he has less back pain and is also less lonely).

This idea focuses on user needs because it attempts to satisfy the specific needs of Fritz Freundlich. The approach balances team interests because it pursues both the user's physical and emotional well-being, which is what different team members want to do. The solution is unoriginal because publishing ads to seek marriage partners is not a novel thing to do. Furthermore, the plan of relieving Fritz from back pain and loneliness by finding a spouse via ads is unlikely to work out quickly and smoothly, so the idea is not immediately effective.

On each card the test-takers read about one idea and shall answer two questions.

- *How do you find this idea?* Answers can be provided on a five-point scale ranging from "terrible" to "excellent". Later answers are coded on a scale from −2 (terrible) to +2 (excellent), so that positive values indicate approval while negative values indicate disapproval.
- *If the team wants to pursue this idea as their only prototype, do you want to intervene?* Here, answers can be provided on a five-point scale ranging from "not at all" to "absolutely". Answers are then coded on a scale from −2 (not at all) to +2 (absolutely), so that positive values indicate the coaches' wish to intervene. Negative values indicate that the team shall proceed without coaching intervention.

Notably, this assessment strategy splits the creativity criterion of *effectiveness* in different aspects:

- *Subjective value* is operationalized via the question "How do you find this idea?" to be answered individually by each study participant.
- *Immediate effectiveness* is operationalized as the consensus expectancy of design thinking experts that a solution approach will produce the intended effect rather quickly and smoothly.
- *Long-term effectiveness* of solution ideas could allude to the realisability of the intended effect by means of a prolonged process, in which hurdles may have to be overcome. Yet, this aspect is not assessed in our present study.
- Furthermore, ideas may have *serendipitous value:* They can bring about additional benefits beyond the originally indented effects. This aspect is also not assessed in our study.

Figure 5.5 shows the complete item set of one test-taker.

We created questionnaire versions in German and English, which are the two most frequently spoken languages in the *Certification Program for Coaches* at the HPI Potsdam. Idea cards were cut out and hand-mixed to ensure that test-takers view them in a random order. The complete *Idea Assessment Probes* from our pre- and post-test as well as a discussion of their psychometric properties are provided by von Thienen et al. (forthcoming-b).

5 Estimator Socialization in Design Thinking: The Dynamic Process of Learning… 83

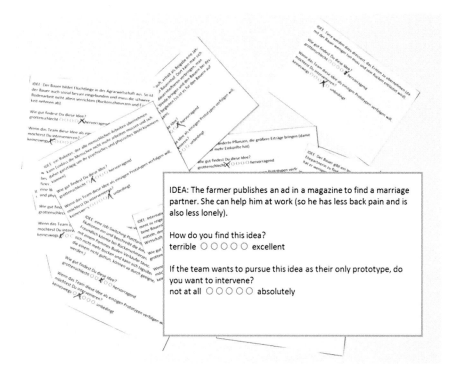

Fig. 5.5 The *Idea Assessment Probes* come in the form of 16 idea cards. One sample card is zoomed in

5.3.2 Study Participants

Each semester 25 coaches can participate in the *Certification Program for Coaches* at the HPI Potsdam. At our first assessment session 24 persons were present and thus included in the study, 16 males, 8 females. Their age ranged from 28 to 51, averaging on 39. Most participants were rather inexperienced with the design thinking approach and even fewer participants had prior coaching experiences (see Fig. 5.6).

5.3.3 Assessment Procedure

Design thinking sessions begin with warm-up exercises that specifically serve the purpose of advancing specific moods and cognitive styles, which are considered favourable for subsequent design thinking objectives. Therefore, care had to be taken to avoid conflated measurements in the pre-test. When the semester's *Certification Program* started, the program head briefly welcomed all participants

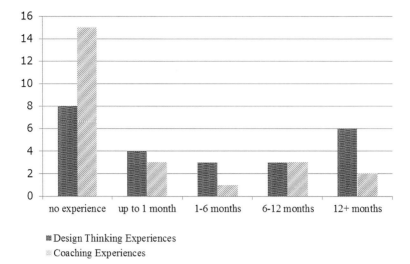

Fig. 5.6 Upon entering the *Certification Program*, the study participants are rather inexperienced in design thinking and coaching

for about 2 min, then immediately invited the attendees to take part in our study and questionnaires were given out. Participants could choose between German and English versions. A number of participants expressed their convenience with either language; they simply picked the physically closest version. In the pre-test, 14 participants filled out German questionnaires, 10 worked on English versions. All participants filled out the questionnaires completely, without producing invalid or missing answers. The assessment procedure took about 12 min.

The post-test was carried out in the final week of the *Certification Program*, following an analogous routine. Participants were welcomed in the morning by the head of the program for about 2 min. Then questionnaires were offered in two languages. In the post-test, 17 participants filled out German questionnaires and 7 attendees worked on English versions. Again, the participants provided valid answers on all questionnaire items.

To avoid redundancy we will not report the N (number of cases) in statistical analyses below, since it is always the same N = 24, the number of persons included in the study.

5.4 Results

Each questionnaire comprises 32 items: 16 ideas are provided and two questions asked about each of them.

In the pre- and post-training assessments different ideas were presented for evaluation, resulting in 64 items altogether being processed by the participants in the course of the whole study. Since the participants could choose between English and

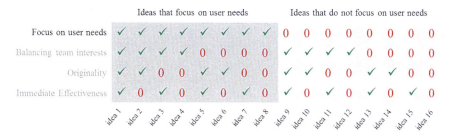

Fig. 5.7 On the four dimension of interest, group means are compared that draw on eight items each. To assess whether the idea characteristic "focus on user needs" impacts the coaches' responses, mean response values on items 1–8 are compared to mean response values on items 9–16

German questionnaire versions, we first assessed whether all answers would be comparable or whether the chosen language would impact participant responses. No statistically significant difference of answer-values was found on any of the 64 questionnaire items, which indicates a sound degree of test reliability.

We then pursued two major lines of data analysis. First, we calculated paired sample t-tests to see whether the four idea characteristics of interest (focus on user needs, balancing team interests, originality and immediate effectiveness) would impact the perception of idea value and the coaches' inclinations to intervene. For each t-test, the questionnaire's 16 idea items were split up in two groups to calculate means (see Fig. 5.7).

Furthermore, we calculated linear regression models, predicting the coaches' perception of idea value based on the four idea characteristics.

5.4.1 Focus on User Needs

At the beginning of the coaches training, the participants do not attend to the factor "focus on user needs". They value ideas that focus on user needs as much as they value other ideas (see Table 5.1, results at t_0).

By contrast, after the training, ideas that focus on user needs are clearly preferred (see Table 5.1, results at t_1). The difference of value-judgements is statistically highly significant at a level of $p \leq .01$. This difference is established both by an increased valuation of ideas that address user-needs (here the mean valuation moves up from 0.34 in the pre-test to 0.47 in the post-test) and by a decreased valuation of ideas that would not help the pre-defined target user (average ratings drop from 0.22 in the pre-test to −0.03 in the post-test).

Regarding inclinations to intervene, a similar picture obtains (see Table 5.2). At first, the existing or lacking focus on user needs does not inform the coaches' inclination to intervene in their team's creative process. After the training, the coaches feel more inclined to intervene when their team lacks a focus on user needs

Table 5.1 Perceived value of ideas with vs. without focus on user needs

	Value judgements when ideas	Mean	Std. dev.	t	Sig. (2-tailed)
t_0	Focus on user needs	0.34	0.60	0.88	0.39
	Don't focus on user needs	0.22	0.49		
t_1	Focus on user needs	0.47	0.49	4.29	0.00**
	Don't focus on user needs	−0.03	0.52		

t_0 pre-training assessment, t_1 post-training assessment, *std. dev.* standard deviation, *sig.* level of significance, t-values of a paired-samples t-test, ** result statistically significant at a level of $p \leq .01$

Table 5.2 Wish to intervene when ideas focus vs. do not focus on user needs

	Wish to intervene when ideas	Mean	Std. dev.	t	Sig. (2-tailed)
t_0	Focus on user needs	−0.01	0.87	0.04	0.97
	Don't focus on user needs	−0.01	0.79		
t_1	Focus on user needs	−0.06	0.62	−1.58	0.13
	Don't focus on user needs	0.13	0.68		

(the intervention mean is positive with a value of 0.13, indicating that on average the coaches want to intervene). Conversely, ideas that attend to user needs incline the coaches to let their teams proceed incessantly, without interventions (here the intervention mean is negative with a mean value of −0.06, indicating that on average the coaches feel rather inclined to not-intervene). However, this difference does not quite reach statistical significance.

Generally, a pattern crystallises that can be observed on all four idea dimensions. To avoid repetitions we will only discuss it once, here pertaining to the focus on user needs. The participants show considerable consensus when providing value estimates for ideas. Standard deviations on value items are comparatively small, even prior to the training. In this case, they amount to .60 and .49 (see t_0 in Table 5.1). By contrast, regarding the question whether or not to intervene in the team's creative process the coaches initially articulate strongly diverging intuitions. In the pre-training assessment, standard deviations on intervention items are rather large (.87 and .79). However, from pre- to post-training the coaches develop more homogeneous intuitions as to when they should intervene. At t_1, standard deviations on intervention items have dropped to .62 and .68.

5.4.2 Balancing Team Interests

Prior to their training, the coaches strongly attend to the factor of team member interests. They significantly prefer ideas, which accommodate the interests of all team members. This preference is statistically highly significant at a level of $p \leq .01$ (see Table 5.3, results at t_0). After their training, the coaches still prefer ideas that balance team interests. However, the impact of this factor has declined; the

Table 5.3 Perceived value of ideas that balance vs. do not balance team interests

	Value judgements when ideas	Mean	Std. dev.	t	Sig. (2-tailed)
t_0	Balance team interests	0.50	0.48	3.46	0.00**
	Don't balance team interests	0.06	0.61		
t_1	Balance team interests	0.30	0.51	1.26	0.22
	Don't balance team interests	0.15	0.52		

Table 5.4 Wish to intervene when ideas balance vs. do not balance team interests

	Wish to intervene when ideas	Mean	Std. dev.	t	Sig. (2-tailed)
t_0	Balance team interests	−0.16	0.91	−2.33	0.03*
	Don't balance team interests	0.18	0.81		
t_1	Balance team interests	−0.06	0.68	−1.26	0.22
	Don't balance team interests	0.10	0.71		

*Result statistically significant at a level of p≤.05.

difference of value-judgements is not statistically significant any more (see Table 5.3, results at t_1).

In the pre-test the intuitions of the coaches as to whether or not they should intervene are also clearly attuned to interests of design team members (see Table 5.4, results at t_0). When solution ideas fail to pick up on some team members' interests the coaches feel inclined to intervene (with a mean of 0.18 tending positively towards interventions). Conversely, the coaches do not intervene but let teams proceed when the pursued solution idea accommodates differing team member interests (in that case, the inclination-mean figures in the negative realm at −0.16).

After the training, coaching strategies are still somewhat attuned to the balancing of team interests, but the factor is less important than it was in the beginning (see Table 5.4, results at t_1). It does not make a statistically significant difference any more whether ideas balance or do not balance team interests.

5.4.3 Originality

Before the training, the coaches do not attend to the factor "originality". The average perceived idea value is the same (.28 and .28, see t_0 in Table 5.5), irrespective of whether ideas are original or unoriginal. After the training, the coaches have become highly sensitive to the originality-dimension of ideas. However, contrary to our hypotheses, the coaches strongly prefer unoriginal ideas (see t_1 in Table 5.5). The average value-estimate of original ideas now figures in the negative realm at −.02, while the average value-rating for unoriginal ideas is even increased compared to the pre-test and now amounts to .46.

The repudiation of originality after the training is in fact a consistent pattern that obtains even on a more fine-grained level of analysis. About the same value-difference in favour of non-originality is found when groups of immediately

Table 5.5 Perceived value of original vs. unoriginal ideas

	Value judgements when ideas	Mean	Std. dev.	t	Sig. (2-tailed)
t_0	Are original	0.28	0.56	0.03	0.98
	Are unoriginal	0.28	0.45		
t_1	Are original	−0.02	0.55	−4.92	0.00**
	Are unoriginal	0.46	0.41		

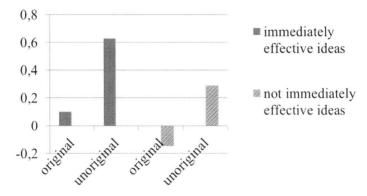

Fig. 5.8 In the post-training assessment, coaches consistently prefer unoriginal ideas. This pattern holds both when they evaluate immediately effective ideas (which on average are attributed greater values, cf. means of .10 and .63) and when they assess not immediately effective ideas (which on average are attributed lesser value, cf. means of −.15 and .29)

Table 5.6 Wish to intervene when ideas are original vs. unoriginal

	Wish to intervene when ideas	Mean	Std. dev.	t	Sig. (2-tailed)
t_0	Are original	−0.01	0.90	−0.04	0.97
	Are unoriginal	−0.01	0.75		
t_1	Are original	0.20	0.66	2.73	0.01**
	Are unoriginal	−0.14	0.66		

effective vs. not immediately effective ideas are analysed separately (see Fig. 5.8). In the discussion we will return to this issue.

As the coaches demonstrate no "antennas" for originality in the pre-test they also disregard this aspect in their coaching at first. The average inclination to intervene is the same (−.01 and − .01, see t_0 in Table 5.6), irrespective of whether teams pursue original or unoriginal ideas. After the training, the coaches have developed highly sensitive antennas for originality and in fact appear to censor ideas with this characteristic. As the positive value of .20 indicates, the coaches want to intervene when their teams pursue original ideas (see t_1 in Table 5.6). By contrast, the negative value of −.14 indicates that teams are left to proceed incessantly when unoriginal ideas are pursued.

/ Estimator Socialization in Design Thinking: The Dynamic Process of Learning…

Table 5.7 Perceived value of immediately effective vs. not immediately effective ideas

	Value judgements when ideas	Mean	Std. dev.	t	Sig. (2-tailed)
t_0	Are immediately effective	0.71	0.61	6.65	0.00**
	Are not immediately effective	−0.15	0.49		
t_1	Are immediately effective	0.37	0.47	2.90	0.01**
	Are not immediately effective	0.07	0.51		

Table 5.8 Wish to intervene when ideas are immediately effective vs. not immediately effective

	Wish to intervene when ideas	Mean	Std. dev.	t	Sig. (2-tailed)
t_0	Are immediately effective	−0.14	1.02	−1.20	0.24
	Are not immediately effective	0.12	0.84		
t_1	Are immediately effective	−0.05	0.69	−1.17	0.26
	Are not immediately effective	0.11	0.66		

5.4.4 Immediate Effectiveness

Prior to the training, the coaches base their value-judgements clearly on the dimension of immediate effectiveness (see t_0 in Table 5.7). Ideas that lack immediate effectiveness receive a negative average rating of −.15. By contrast, the mean rating of immediately effective ideas is strikingly positive at a value of .71. After the training, immediately effective ideas are still preferred, but the difference is not as large any more (.37 vs. .07 at t_1).

The inclinations to intervene tend to mirror the coaches' preference for immediately effective ideas. The coaches rather want to intervene when teams pursue not-immediately effective solutions (with a mean of .12 at t_0 and .11 at t_1, see Table 5.8). Conversely, the coaches rather refrain from interventions on their team's solution trajectory when the pursued idea seems immediately effective (−.14 at t_0 and − .05 at t_1). However, coaching inclinations do not differ to a statistically significant degree, neither in the pre- nor in the post-test. Thus, a noteworthy discrepancy obtains between the clarity of personal preferences for immediately effective ideas on the one hand and rather indifferent coaching approaches on the other. We will return to this issue in the discussion.

5.4.5 Predicting Value-Attribution Based On Idea Characteristics

Linear regression models are computed to estimate the impact of each factor (focus on user needs, balancing team interests, originality, immediate effectiveness) on the coaches' attribution of value to ideas. We permitted no computation of a regression constant to render the beta weights of the four idea dimensions more easily comparable.

Table 5.9 A linear regression model predicting perceived idea value, before the training

	Unstand. Beta	Standard. Beta	t	sig.
Focus on user needs	−.07	−.04	−.60	.55
Balancing team interests	.27	.15	2.45	.02
Originality	−.17	−.09	−1.53	.13
Immediate effectiveness	.70	.38	6.34	.00

unstand. Beta unstandardized beta coefficient, *standard. Beta* standardized beta coefficient

The two regression models for the pre- and post-test data both explain only a limited amount of variance (R = .41 in the pre-test model and .35 in the post-test model; both models are statistically highly significant at a level of $p \leq .001$). This is in line with prior expectations, since differing personal perspectives on ideas are considered a resource in creative communities and trainings do not serve the purpose of creating uniform responses.

The pattern of significant vs. insignificant beta weights in the regression models mostly accords with the study hypotheses.

When the pre-training data is analysed, the standardized beta coefficient of the factor "focus on user needs" is close to zero and not statistically significant (see Table 5.9). This, again, suggests that the coaches do not attend to this dimension prior to their training.

"Balancing team interests" is the second best predictor for value-ratings of the coaches. The standardized beta weight of this factor amounts to .15, which is statistically significant at a level of $p \leq .05$. This idea dimension clearly informs value-ratings of the coaches.

The beta weight of "originality" is not statistically significant. Prior to their training, the coaches obviously do not screen this idea characteristic systematically in the process of estimating idea value.

"Immediate effectiveness" is the best predictor for value-ratings. The standardized beta weight of .38 is the largest in the whole model, reflecting a strong increase in perceived idea value when ideas are immediately effective. This beta weight is statistically significant at a level of $p \leq .01$.

After the training, the factor "focus on user need" has become the most important predictor for value-judgments (see Table 5.10). Its standardized beta weight of .28 is statistically significant at a level of $p \leq .01$.

The impact of the factor "balancing team interests" has considerably declined. Its beta weight of .08 is not statistically significant any more.

The factor "originality" has become the second best predictor for value estimates. However, the standardized beta weight is negative at a value of −.27, which is statistically highly significant at a level of $p \leq .01$. Thus, increases in idea originality predict reduced value-attributions by the coaches.

The impact of the factor "immediate effectiveness" has dropped considerably. The beta weight now amounts to .16 (compared to .38 in the pre-test), which is, however, still statistically significant on a level of $p \leq .01$. Figure 5.9 summarises the outcomes on behalf of all study hypotheses.

5 Estimator Socialization in Design Thinking: The Dynamic Process of Learning...

Table 5.10 A linear regression model predicting perceived idea value, after the training

	Unstand. Beta	Standard. Beta	t	sig.
Focus on user needs	.50	.28	4.51	.00
Balancing team interests	.15	.08	1.32	.19
Originality	−.49	−.27	−4.42	.00
Immediate effectivity	.29	.16	2.64	.01

	Before the training	
H1	The factor *"focus on user needs"* does not impact value-judgments.	✓
H2a	*Balancing team interests* increases the value attributed to ideas.	✓
H2b	The factor *"balancing team interests"* is the second best predictor for value-judgements (this factor has the second most impactful beta weight in the regression model).	✓
H3	The factor *"originality"* does not impact value-judgments.	✓
H4a	*Immediate effectiveness* increases the value attributed to ideas.	✓
H4b	The factor *"immediate effectiveness"* is the best predictor for value-judgements (this factor has the most impactful beta weight in the regression model).	✓
H5	The coaches pursue strongly varying *intervention strategies* (as indicated by large standard deviations on intervention items).	✓

	After the training	
H6a	*Focusing on user needs* increases the value attributed to ideas.	✓
H6b	The factor *"focus on user needs"* is the best predictor for value-judgements (this factor has the most impactful beta weight in the regression model).	✓
H7a	*Balancing team interests* increases the value attributed to ideas.	✓
H7b	The impact of this factor is decreased compared to the pre-test.	✓
H8a	*Originality* increases the value attributed to ideas.	✗!
H8b	The factor *"originality"* is the second best predictor for value-judgements (this factor has the second most impactful beta weight in the regression model).	✓
H9a	*Immediate effectiveness* increases the value attributed to ideas.	✓
H9b	The impact of this factor is decreased compared to the pre-test.	✓
H10	The coaches pursue more homogeneous *intervention strategies* (standard deviations on intervention items drop from pre- to post-test).	✓

Fig. 5.9 Overview of study hypotheses and respective findings

5.5 Discussion

The evaluation style of coaches who attend the *Design Thinking Certification Program* clearly changes over time.

Prior to their training, the coaches display a static assessment style, evaluating ideas in the middle of the process as though they were facing final products. All ideas should be immediately effective, else wise they are considered poor. Furthermore, design thinking values such as the focus on user needs do not inform idea perceptions of the coaches. Ways of incorporating team-dynamics in the process are also not aligned to design thinking practices.

After the training, the coaches have adopted a dynamic assessment style, de-emphasizing the importance of "immediate effectiveness" in the ideation phase. Their value-set has changed mostly in accordance with design thinking teachings. In particular, coaches now favour ideas that focus on user needs. This factor has become the most important predictor for value judgements. In addition, team-dynamics are still attended, but do not lead to an overly rigorous constriction of the solution space; teams are not expected any more to gratify multiple user needs with their solution simply to accommodate differing team member interests. Finally, the coaches have become highly sensitive to the dimension of idea originality. However, this idea characteristic factors in negatively in the coaches' estimation of idea value, which is contrary to design thinking teachings and a highly surprising result.

As an overall finding, this study shows that idea assessment styles are not fixed. They are no unalterable personality characteristics. People can learn to perceive ideas in novel ways due to creativity education. Moreover, methodologically it is possible to measure the idea assessment styles of single estimators and groups, and to trace changes in their evaluation styles in the course of creativity trainings.

While the overall results are certainly multi-facetted, we shall confine further discussions to two issues only, which are likely to stimulate further research. One issue concerns a deeper understanding of valuation processes, the other bears on the handling of idea originality.

1. How do emotional and cognitive aspects figure in value estimations, and how do they influence coaching/teaching behaviours?

To assess the attribution of value to ideas, in our study the participants were asked a general question: "How do you find this idea?" Notably, answers to such a general question can reflect both emotional and cognitive aspects of valuation. When a coach states "I find this idea terrible", she may sense a strong emotional aversion while cognitively believing that the idea would work for other people. Or she might consider the idea futile on a cognitive level, while not feeling much about the subject at all. Of course, mixed cases can occur just as well.

One might assume that coaches translate their perceptions of idea value more readily into coaching behaviour when the valuation accords with cognitive reasoning. In our pre-training assessment two strikingly different patterns crystallise on behalf of the factors "balancing team interests" and "immediate effectiveness". In the pre-training assessment both dimensions strongly inform the coaches' attribution of value to ideas. However, only the factor "balancing team interests" has a significant impact on coaching interventions. This pattern makes sense if "balancing team interests" is cognitively construed as advantageous. After all, literature on social competence is often taken to suggest that the balancing of team interests be important and favourable. By contrast, "immediate effectiveness" could be a characteristic the coaches prefer emotionally, but not necessarily on a cognitive level. Probably it feels good when team ideas are expected to work out quickly and smoothly. At the same time, cognitively the coaches might still believe that innovation projects should be open to ideas that lack immediate effectiveness. After all, satellites, GPS and mobile phones – to name just a few examples – certainly did not achieve immediate effectiveness right after the ideas were first conceived. Such a discrepancy between emotional and cognitive appraisals could explain why the coaches value immediately effective ideas more highly, but do not base their coaching strategies consistently on this preference.

If this were true, the *Certification Program* was likely beneficial in helping the coaches emotionally handle ideation outcomes that lack immediate effectiveness. After the training, the coaches' preference for immediately effective ideas is greatly reduced, while the respective coaching strategy remains almost unchanged. This would be an excellent emotional learning outcome for coaches in innovation projects, where having to handle highly original, but not immediately effective ideas may be everyday business.

In any case, emotional and cognitive aspects of idea valuation can be a fruitful subject for creativity research, well-beyond the training of design thinking coaches. In creativity education, or even education quite generally, teachers have to react – often spontaneously – to student ideas. To support teachers (or design thinking coaches) in this difficult task, a better understanding of the underlying estimation processes would seem very helpful. Research could, for instance, focus on the following set of questions:

- What immediate feelings do specific types of student ideas (e.g., original vs. unoriginal) elicit in teachers/coaches?
- What cognitive rationales do teachers/coaches follow when they decide about behavioural reactions to student ideas?
- What heuristics should teachers/coaches follow when they react to student ideas (e.g., in order to help students develop creative mindsets)?
- How can we train teachers/coaches, so that their immediate emotional reactions to student ideas facilitate favourable behavioural reactions?

Studies bearing on these or related issues have already been undertaken in different contexts and much progress can be expected from a knowledge synthesis across different domains (e.g., Zajonc 2001; Oreg 2006; Beghetto 2016; Corazza 2017). We are curious what the community of creativity researchers will jointly bring to light over time.

The second study finding to be discussed in more detail concerns specifically the handling of originality.

2. *Why do the study participants develop disdain for original ideas?*

In our longitudinal study, coaches strongly repudiate original ideas in the post-training assessment. This is an unexpected, yet statistically highly significant outcome. We shall consider a number of potential explanations in turn.

As has been noted above (in Sect. 5.2.3), original ideas often necessitate prolonged periods of refinement to render them effective. Might the coaches have sensed a conflict between the higher resource demand in the case of original ideas and limited available project resources, such as remaining time? That could explain why they would prefer unoriginal ideas. However, for several reasons this explanation does not seem to work in the case of the present study. First, the coaches answered questions on behalf of a purely hypothetical scenario where no information was even mentioned about available project resources. Second, the ideas had been artificially generated so as to not entail different resource demands. On average the original ideas were just as immediately effective (easy to implement and likely to produce the intended effects, judged by two expert raters) as were the unoriginal ideas. Thirdly, if the study participants had sensed a conflict between idea originality and available project resources, this conflict should have existed in the pre- and the post-test alike. Yet, only in the post-test did the coaches display a significant preference for unoriginal ideas. Finally, even if we assume that the coaches saw conflicts between idea originality and available project resources in the post-test only, they could still have personally liked the original ideas. In that case, they might have stated in the questionnaire that they personally found the original ideas excellent, while at the same time they would have launched coaching interventions against them in light of limited project resources. However, this pattern was not observed, quite to the contrary. The coaches were much clearer in devaluing original ideas (t = −4,92) than they were in launching coaching interventions when faced with original ideas (t = 2.73). Here t-values that diverge more greatly from zero indicate stronger differences between original and unoriginal ideas.

Considering further explanations proposed in the literature for why people might prefer unoriginal ideas, we can also return to Blair and Mumford (2007). They emphasize how it is more difficult for audiences to forecast the effects of original ideas, since these are unprecedented. Hurdles might emerge in the implementation phase and social benefits might be less foreseeable. Again, however, in our study the ideas were artificially designed to avoid spurious correlations between idea originality and (unclear) implementation difficulties or (unclear) social benefits. On average, the original and unoriginal ideas did not differ in their immediate effectiveness or their social favourability/serviceability to user needs. Notably, it is also quite easy to come up with unoriginal ideas that entail great forecasting difficulties. For instance, in the case of the unoriginal idea mentioned in Sect. 5.3.1, the plan is to make a farmer happy by finding a spouse for him via a partnership ad. It is hard to foretell what hurdles will arise given this solution strategy and how the social benefits or misfortunes will balance out in the end. Different women answering the ad could affect the farmer's happiness in various ways. It is unclear whether a person who publishes a partnership ad will ever find a spouse, let alone one who makes him happy and helps him at work. This is not to deny that particularly great forecasting difficulties can explain the disdain for original ideas in some contexts, but for the present study results a different explanation seems needed.

Barron's (1955) research suggests that people display dispositions towards originality: Some people favour the original, other people favour the conventional consistently across different situations. For Barron, these dispositions develop throughout childhood and they become so stable that they can be addressed as personality traits in adult populations. We only reported group results above. They did, however, also indicate something in the direction of cross-situational dispositions. The coaches consistently favour unoriginal ideas in the post-training assessment. More specifically, this preference becomes evident in two different situations, namely when the assessed ideas are immediately effective and when the ideas lack immediate effectiveness (cf. Fig. 5.8). Notably, though, these cross-situational dispositions to prefer the unoriginal are not carved in stone. Preference patterns change from the pre- to the post-test. Thus, our study results are compatible with the belief that people develop particular dispositions to either prefer the original or the conventional across different situations. Importantly, though, these dispositions do not seem to be unalterable personality traits. They can change in the course of creativity trainings. While in the case of our study the coaches, unexpectedly and against the trainers' intentions, developed a disposition to favour the conventional, an important point is that the dispositions did change.

The question remains why the participants in our study developed disdain for original ideas. Some qualitative feedback provided by the study participants after their training gave hints to make sense of the findings. As a number of coaches indicated in personal conversations about the study outcomes, they had picked up the importance design thinking experts attributed to originality in the course of their training, as for instance the motto "encourage wild ideas" was placed centre-stage in ideation sessions. Still, the coaches were not convinced that wild ideas would eventually entail better project results. Some coaches also indicated that they found "crazy-sounding ideas unsuitable and not feasible in the more serious work contexts" where they lead innovation teams. Follow-up qualitative research needs to clarify these issues more systematically. Nonetheless, an important objective for creativity educators becomes apparent, which is likely relevant beyond design thinking trainings: *Creativity education needs to show how originality leads to something better, not just something different.*

Indeed, even in our test scenario originality was not associated with *better* ideation outcomes. As our questionnaire had been designed like this, original ideas were not associated with greater immediate effectiveness or clearer social benefits/more gratification of user needs. Had the coaches preferred original ideas, they would have preferred originality for its own sake, as an idle idea characteristic, unrelated to idea effectiveness. The coaches did not appreciate originality for its own sake, and there may even be good reasons for such a stance as long as "radical innovation" or "creativity" are no self-standing goals. After all, in real-world challenges original ideas often do necessitate a greater investment of resources later on, e.g., more time is required to refine the idea, eliminate bugs and make the approach work (cf. Sect. 5.2.3). Moreover, as Blair and Mumford (2007) point out, potential positive or negative effects of unprecedented, original ideas can be difficult to anticipate.

All in all, the handling of originality appears to be a particularly delicate learning and teaching objective. In our study everything else seemed easier. The coaches readily de-creased their preference for immediately effective solutions. They readily attended to a novel characteristic, the focus on user needs, making it their primary criterion for idea value. They readily changed the handling of team dynamics. However, the coaches did not readily accept standard teachings on how to handle originality.

Yet, originality is a defining characteristic of creative achievements. Therefore, it seems an important objective for creativity education to help learners develop proficiency in the handling of original ideas. A consistent experience of disdain for original ideas is likely to be a major creativity block that research and education need to tackle. Against this background, we will close this chapter with considerations how the handling of originality might be better facilitated in the future.

5.6 Outlook: How to Facilitate the Acceptance of Originality?

A creative mindset must include some openness to original ideas. While it may be unnecessary (or even unfavourable) that people prefer all novel ideas simply for the sake of originality, people who aspire to be creative, or who want to lead innovation teams, must be ready to embrace at least some (promising) novel ideas. Otherwise their projects remain tied to the realm of the conventional and they cannot possibly succeed.

Especially in educational contexts it has already been noted how unconstrained originality – permitting all kinds of novelty – is perceived as daunting and something to be carefully avoided (Beghetto 2016). A likely follow-up question is how originality can be directed along task-appropriate lines. Creativity researchers could advance theories and methods to help learners explain, predict and control the development of creative potential in their projects, based on how they make use of originality in the process. In this context, it seems promising to elucidate the varying roles of originality in different project stages. Moreover, explanations can be sought as to why some original contributions seem much more promising than others in each project stage.

Clearly there are many ways to incorporate originality in a creative process, and not all of them seem equally helpful to build up creative potential. In design thinking projects, as probably in many other creative endeavours, people start by understanding and observing a subject domain. This is already the first phase in which a creative project can be imbued with more or less originality. In this phase, originality could be intentionally induced (i) by means of random imaginings about the field, (ii) by building on any arbitrary observation or (iii) by attending to a surprising, unexpected observation in the field. With these three approaches, the same level of originality might be achieved, but the creative potential that is added to the project does not seem the same. Similar things can be said basically about all steps and means of creative work.

To consider one more sample project phase, we can turn to ideation, i.e. the stage of thinking up ideas and selecting one or more of them to be further pursued. In this phase, not all original ("wild") ideas seem similarly promising. A well-known positive example of "wild ideas" benefitted Polaroid developments. When Edwin Land of Polaroid Corporation first imagined a printed colour picture that would be available within a few seconds after a camera had captured the image, his idea seemed "wild" to the contemporaries: original, bold, almost unrealistic. Land had to work for many years on his project to render the idea effective. Yet, eventually this idea helped to expand the realm of what humanity could do (Arnold 1959/2016). His wild idea had endowed Land's project with a great creative potential. In other cases, wild ideas may be truly impossible to realise. They could still be helpful, e.g., as metaphors that guide the search for feasible solutions. By contrast, other original/wild ideas may do very little in terms of adding creative potential. It is not the wildness of ideas per se that gets a project far. In design thinking, examples of original/

wild ideas that do not seem particularly promising can be easily generated by imagining a new, unrealizable solution that would not even make the user happy if it could be implemented.

When estimators dislike originality because they do not see how it improves overall project outcomes, they have a point to make. Not all originality is necessarily productive. Moreover, we know that originality often comes at a cost. However, when creativity educators can explain and demonstrate how to use originality in beneficial ways, the estimators we train have no reason to feel badly about it in lump-sum ways.

We submit the following questions for further discussions:

- How do learners experience the role of originality in their processes? Do they experience originality as a route to something better, or merely as a route to something different? How are potential negative effects of originality construed (such as increased resource demands)?
- What techniques of producing and handling originality help to amplify a project's creative potential? Are different techniques required in different work stages?
- What distinguishes helpful original contributions in a creative process from less helpful ones? Or can all original contributions endow projects with a high creative potential if only the original elements are processed in a particular way?
- How does original information build up in the course of creative work? (E.g., what is the relationship between original notes about a research domain, developments of original problem views, novel solution ideas etc.?)
- How do imagination abilities impact the acceptance of original ideas? Can people picture conventional solutions better than original ones? Might people simply prefer solutions they can easily imagine?[1]
- Extensive literature treats the subject of resistance to innovation and change (e.g., Oreg 2006; Talke and Heidenreich 2013). To what extent do the phenomena of people repudiating change/innovation and people repudiating originality overlap or differ from one another?
- How does the acceptance of original ideas differ in cases when they have been (a) thought up by oneself, (b) developed in one's own creative team, (c) proposed by a friend or (d) by someone else?

All in all, it seems the process of learning how to judge creative work is dynamic in a double sense. Single estimators learn novel assessment styles in the course of creativity trainings. At the same time, creativity experts are still in the process of finding out which assessment styles to recommend and how to convey them. In any case, people's intuitions concerning idea value do not seem to be carved in stone. They rather appear to be readily changeable by means of trainings. This, of course, entails great responsibilities on the part of creativity researchers, whose views of the creative process impact the way in which teachers and coaches assess student ideas.

---

[1] These research questions were suggested to us by Axel Menning.

Acknowledgements We thank Ronald Beghetto and Giovanni Emanuele Corazza for inviting this research to be part of their comprehensive project on dynamic perspectives in creativity education and helpful feedback on our first draft. We thank the participants of the *Certification Program for Design Thinking Coaches* in the summer semester of 2017 at the *HPI Potsdam* for taking part in our survey and for their openness to subsequent individual discussions of study results. We thank Toni Mattis for the permission to print his picture.

References

Agnoli, S., Mastria, S., Kirsch, C., & Corazza G. E. (under review). *Creativity in the advertisement domain: The mediating role of experience on creative achievement.*

Arnold, J. E. (2016). Creative engineering. In W. J. Clancey (Ed.) *Creative engineering: Promoting innovation by thinking differently* (pp. 59–150). Stanford : Stanford Digital Repository. Original manuscript 1959. http://purl.stanford.edu/jb100vs5745. Accessed 13 June 2017.

Barron, F. (1955). The disposition toward originality. *Journal of Abnormal and Social Psychology, 51*(3), 478–485.

Beaney, M. (2005). *Imagination and creativity*. Milton Keynes: Open University.

Beghetto, R. A. (2007). Does creativity have a place in classroom discussions? Prospective teachers' response preferences. *Thinking Skills and Creativity, 2*(1), 1–9.

Beghetto, R. A. (2010). Creativity in the classroom. In J. C. Kaufman & R. J. Sternberg (Eds.), *Cambridge handbook of creativity*. New York: Cambridge University Press.

Beghetto, R. A. (2013). Nurturing creativity in the micro-moments of the classroom. In K. H. Kim, J. C. Kaufman, J. Baer, & B. Sriraman (Eds.), *Creatively gifted students are not like other gifted students. Advances in creativity and giftedness* (Vol. 5). Rotterdam: Sense Publishers.

Beghetto, R. A. (2016). Learning as a creative act. In T. Kettler (Ed.), *Modern curriculum for gifted and advanced learners* (pp. 111–127). New York: Routledge.

Blair, C. S., & Mumford, M. D. (2007). Errors in idea evaluation: Preference for the unoriginal? *Journal of Creative Behavior, 41*(3), 197–222.

Brown, T., & Katz, B. (2009). *Change by design: How design thinking transforms organizations and inspires innovation*. New York: Harper Collins.

Carleton, T., & Leifer, L. (2009). Stanford's ME310 course as an evolution of engineering design. In R. Roy & E. Shehab (Eds.), *Proceedings of the 19th CIRP design conference – Competitive design* (pp. 547–554). Cranfield: Cranfield University.

Cojuharenco, I., Cornelissen, G., & Karelaia, N. (2016). Yes, I can: Feeling connected to others increases perceived effectiveness and socially responsible behavior. *Journal of Environmental Psychology, 48*, 75–86.

Corazza, G. E. (2015). *Impresa e creatività*. Online lecture. https://www.youtube.com/watch?v=mfR8qJWtpfs. Accessed 14 Sept 2017.

Corazza, G. E. (2016a). Potential originality and effectiveness: The dynamic definition of creativity. *Creativity Research Journal, 28*(3), 258–267.

Corazza, G. E. (2016b). *Creativity: A dynamic definition*. Keynote speech at the MIC Conference 2016: From creative brains to creative societies, Università di Bologna, Bologna, 14–16 September 2016.

Corazza, G. E. (2017). *Creativity in education: a recursive exercise in estimation ability*. Keynote speech at the Utrecht platform for creativity in education, Ut-recht University, Utrecht, 30–31 March 2017. https://platformcreativity.sites.uu.nl/wp-content/uploads/sites/145/2017/04/2017-UPCE-Giovanni-E.-Corazza.pdf. Accessed 14 Oct 2017.

d.school. (2010). *Bootcamp bootleg*. http://dschool.stanford.edu/wp-content/uploads/2011/03/BootcampBootleg2010v2SLIM.pdf. Accessed 6 Mar 2017.

Dow, S. P., & Klemmer, S. R. (2011). The efficacy of prototyping under time constraints. In H. Plattner, C. Meinel, & L. Leifer (Eds.), *Design thinking research. Understand – improve – apply* (pp. 111–128). Heidelberg: Springer.

Gaut, B. (2010). The philosophy of creativity. *Philosophy Compass, 5*(12), 1034–1046.

Greenberg, R. (2003). The role of neophobia and neophilia in the development of innovative behaviour of birds. In S. M. Reader & K. N. Laland (Eds.), *Animal innovation* (pp. 175–196). Oxford: Oxford University Press.

Hasso Plattner Institute for Digital Engineering. (2017). *This is design thinking: A collection of case stories.* http://thisisdesignthinking.net. Accessed 29 Oct 2017.

Kaufman, A. B., & Kaufman, J. C. (2014). Applying theoretical models on human creativity to animal studies. *Animal Behavior and Cognition, 1*(1), 78–90.

Kelley, T., & Kelley, D. (2013). *Creative confidence*. London: Harper Collins.

McKim, R. H. (1972). *Experiences in visual thinking*. Belmont: Wadsworth Publishing.

McKim, R. H. (2016). Designing for the whole man. In W. J. Clancey (Ed.) *Creative engineering: Promoting innovation by thinking differently* (pp. 198–217). Stanford: Stanford Digital Repository. Original manuscript 1959. http://purl.stanford.edu/jb100vs5745. Accessed 13 June 2017.

Ney, S. (2016). *Manual for design thinking coaches*. Potsdam: HPI School of Design Thinking.

Oreg, S. (2006). Personality, context and resistance to organizational change. *European Journal of Work and Organizational Psychology, 15*(1), 73–101.

Roth, B. (2015). *The achievement habit*. New York: Harper Collins.

Runco, M. A., & Jaeger, G. J. (2012). The standard definition of creativity. *Creativity Research Journal, 24*(1), 92–96.

Talke, K., & Heidenreich, S. (2013). How to overcome pro-change bias: Incorporating passive and active innovation resistance in innovation decision models. *Journal of Product Innovation Management, 31*(5), 894–907.

von Thienen, J. P. A., Noweski, C., Meinel, C., & Rauth, I. (2011). The co-evolution of theory and practice in design thinking – or – "mind the oddness trap!". In H. Plattner, C. Meinel, & L. Leifer (Eds.), *Design thinking research. Understand – improve – apply* (pp. 81–99). Heidelberg: Springer.

von Thienen, J. P. A., Royalty, A., & Meinel, C. (2016). Design thinking in higher education: How students become dedicated creative problem solvers. In C. Zhou (Ed.), *Handbook of research on creative problem-solving skill development in higher education* (pp. 306–328). Hershey: IGI Global.

von Thienen, J. P. A., Clancey, W. J., Corazza, G. E., & Meinel, C. (2017a). Theoretical foundations of design thinking. Part I: John E. Arnold's creative thinking theories. In H. Plattner, C. Meinel, & L. Leifer (Eds.), *Design thinking research. Making distinctions: Collaboration versus cooperation* (pp. 13–40). Cham: Springer.

von Thienen, J. P. A., Paladini, C., & Meinel, C. (2017b). *Do creative ideas give rise to unique private-mind or private-language problems?* Paper presented at the 25th annual conference of the European Society for Philosophy and Psychology, University of Hertfordshire, Hertfordshire, 14–17August 2017.

von Thienen, J. P. A., Clancey, W. J., & Meinel, C. (forthcoming-a). Theoretical foundations of design thinking. Part II: Robert McKim's need based design theory. In H. Plattner, C. Meinel, & L. Leifer (Eds.), *Design thinking research*. Cham: Springer.

von Thienen, J. P. A, Ney S., Meinel C. (forthcoming-b). *Idea Assessment Probes. Questionnaires to measure the idea assessment style of estimators in creative projects*. Electronic Colloquium on Design Thinking Research.

Zajonc, R. B. (2001). Mere exposure: A gateway to the subliminal. *Current Directions in Psychological Science, 10*(6), 224–228.

Chapter 6
Exploration as a Dynamic Strategy of Research-Education for Creativity in Schools

Monica Guerra and Federica Valeria Villa

Abstract Creativity, due to its very nature as polymorphous, cannot be considered a static concept, but a laborious process, activated by several factors strongly interconnected with the environment and the situation of reference. Each of these is also the object of important reflections in education, put as the objective for the development of the individual in learning, allowing us to make a parallelism between the creative process and the teaching-learning process. These processes have important subjective variables, but also constant elements which are discussed here in a dimension of dynamic and parallel references. The teacher, as a key figure and mediator with society, is considered explorer of contexts, strategies, skills, activities and ideas which become fundamental for his/her training and for that of others. The intrinsically dynamic nature of both processes brings them closer, tracing the possibility of including creativity as an indispensable and transversal skill in daily didactics. In this perspective, the exploratory appears a coherent way as a dynamic methodology of schooling. Exploring becomes a dynamic creative path, which has seen different applications in the area of research-education with teachers, but also research-action at school with children.

6.1 Introduction

Creativity, probably due to its very nature as polymorphous, cannot be considered a static and rigid concept, but a laborious process, activated by several factors – "cognitive, emotional, motivational and personality traits" (Barbot et al. 2011,

---

This contribution is the result of a collective work. For academic purposes please note that Monica Guerra has authored sections 6.1, 6.3 and 6.4; Federica Valeria Villa has authored sections from 6.1.1 to 6.1.5 and 6.2.

M. Guerra (✉) · F. V. Villa
Department of Human Sciences and Education "Riccardo Massa",
University of Milano-Bicocca, Milan, Italy
e-mail: monica.guerra@unimib.it

p. 59) – strongly interconnected with the environment and the situation of reference. Each of these is also the object of important reflections in the world of education, put as the objective of reference for the development of the individual in learning, allowing us to make an immediate parallelism between the creative process and the teaching-learning process.

The multiple variables involved in both processes are often unexpected, not controllable and differ from one subject to another and from one situation to another, but there are just as many factors that are constant and therefore the object of investigation in greater depth. It can therefore be said that it is the way in which these are related and entwined with one another that creates that cocktail of personal and contextual elements, unique to each one. The creative process or product of a subject is something new – for the person, the community or the whole of society – and useful, suitable for meeting the initial stimulus; just as learning, all new information – or creation – is integrated and acquired by each person in a different way, reorganizes old beliefs, or takes a place next to them. The way these processes take place has important subjective variables, but at the same time they present constant elements which it is worthwhile discussing here in a dimension of dynamic and parallel references.

6.1.1 Cognitive Factors

The processing of information and thoughts is the faculty of the cognition, understood as the ability to interpret and attribute meaning to the data perceived. The creative process takes advantage of this human skill by soliciting sub-faculties, mechanisms of production and management of incoming ideas or that have already been controlled. The process starts through the identification, by the subject, of a situation defined "problem", in which an obstacle or a desired objective is recognized. This activates a consequent production of a broad spectrum of ideas, aimed at seeking a solution (which can be defined as divergent thought), to be reduced to a temporary conclusion in the choice of the most suitable and appropriate one for the situation in question – convergent thought (Hadani 2015). This pattern outlines a macro level creative process, which is even excessively simplistic and linear, as going into detail, both divergent thought and convergent thought have their respective characterizing factors.

The cognitive faculty of divergence effectively implies flexibility of thought – understood as the ability to consider the problem from different perspectives, going through different conceptual categories, experimenting different styles and strategies –, fluidity of ideas – proposing a wide number of ideas and solutions referring to a problem –, originality – building up something different or that others would not have tried to do that is unusual and unique (Runco 2015). In addition to these classic characteristics of divergent thought (e.g. Guilford 1950; Torrance 1974) others can be found, such as the ability to think by combinations and systems, as continuous redefinition and combinations of different solutions to create new insights (*ibid.*), or the elaboration, the ability to make associations or also to completely restructure the problem (e.g. Hocevar 1980; Runco and Pritzker 1999; Giorgetti et al. 2009; Cropley and Cropley 2012).

The converging counterpart, on the other hand, comes at the time which moves towards the conclusion/resolution of the creative macro-process seen earlier, in which the decision-making process is activated, where the subject, from the many options and opportunities thought of and proposed, selects one – or a combination of several – pertinent to that specific situation-problem and which, to be creative, does not adapt to conventions: original and valid. It is a path characterized by continual references between divergent and convergent thought that is characterized by being cyclical (Hadani 2015), where one does not exclude the other but is constantly dependent on it.

The teaching-learning process is, in the same way, completely based on and structured by the cognitive faculties. The processes of thought, conceptualization, reasoning, memorization etc. are involved actively and continuously in the educational field. "The characteristics underlying this behaviour of the mind are of an abstract nature, of involvement of symbolic processes, of intuition, expectation, of the use of complex rules, of problem-solving, etc." (Stella 2001–2003, p. 1). An attitude of restructuring knowledge through the reception and interpretation of the multiple inputs both from the exterior and the interior is constant. Learning is the result of a process which follows and interprets new experiences in the light of the preceding ones (Donovan and Bransford 2005; Beghetto 2016) which, if it transforms and modifies the subject (Antonietti and Cantoia 2010, p. VIII), activates the perception and the definition of the real in a new way. Cognitive restructuring understood this way takes on sense becoming a combinatory and creative process, on which leverage can be used in education to reach personally significant learnings.

Cognitive style (Gardner 1983) is also talked of, as the individual variation in the way of perceiving, remembering, thinking, learning, storing, transforming and using information (Kogan 1971), which is connected in turn to the style of learning understood as a "set of operations and procedures that the student can use to acquire, retain and recover different types of knowledge and performance" (Kigney in Antonello 2002, p. 72). It is a personal style of managing and organizing one's cognitive faculties and using them in learning, in teaching – we will now speak of educational style –, but also in the creative process.

6.1.2 Emotional Factors and Motivational Drives

"Communicating to others one's perspective, resolution or idea plays a vital role in creativity as it allows expressing one's feelings and desires" (Hadani 2015, p. 29). For some time now, research in psychology has maintained that the positive emotions have a role of exhorting creativity as "amplifiers of the mind" while negative ones were damaging as they were aimed at narrowing the view in a convergent way to only one perspective. New research (e.g. Gable and Harmon-Jones 2008, 2011; Akbari Chermahini and Hommel 2012) supports a new theory, suggesting that the critical variable that influences the focus on reaching a purpose "is not the emotional value (i.e. the dichotomy between positive emotions and negative emotions) but the intensity of the motivation to reach an objective" (Kaufman 2015). Emotions and motivation thus become closely interconnected and dependent variables, which involve one sphere of the individual which goes beyond the rational and definable, and which cannot be discussed separately.

In education, as in the creative process, "motivation is at the heart of the experience of development and inspires the subject to explore, to seek satisfaction for their curiosity" (Hadani 2015, p. 34). It inspires teachers in planning and in the passion of what they want to convey to the children, in the search for meaning of their acting; but it is also an element that allows learners to pay attention, to be involved and to keep their hunger for curiosity alive.

Motivation, as a container of the emotions adjoined to it, can also be understood in unconsciously negative terms; if resistance is opposed to an activity, or when a path is avoided. It is energy that supports acting in any field, but it requires a supportive and guiding environment. According to Moè (2001), motivation has deep roots that can be traced back to categories of power, success and affiliation, where each one has respectively an implication a fear (of losing, of failing, of being rejected). Our emotions intervene by revealing, at times, which of these motivations comes into play, through the classic dichotomy "avoid – confront" (as in the *fight or flight* theory of Cannon 1929). This strategy is fully part of the educational process as well as of the creative one because both can be defined as situations-problem to be avoided or confronted.

A further classification, also deemed valid for both the processes in question, concerns extrinsic and intrinsic motivation. The former is bound to external influences, more interested in the benefit given by the finished product, while the latter is guided by the individual's own interests, leading to autonomous control of the situation, to involvement and to the consequent learning (Hadani 2015), which can be interpreted here as real motivation. This motivation which comes from the interior, emerged as a drive (Bragby et al. 2012, p. 33) acts without the promise of a reward, without an interest finalized to the product alone, but to satisfy a curiosity, a need for knowledge, seeking a meaning (*ibid.*) leading to a greater inclination to creativity, learning or teaching, as there is a real reason by the subject to invest time and energy. Real motivation drives a real involvement which intertwines with the previously identified elements, triggering off a chain of relations which is enclosed in the macrosystem (Bronfenbrenner 1979) in which the individual is placed.

6.1.3 Personality

Abundant literature deals with the subject of the personality of the creative student, identifiable through standard characteristics which can be observed by teachers and researchers (e.g. Aljughaiman and Mowrer Reynolds 2005; Glăveanu and Tanggaard 2014; Gralewski and Karwowski 2016), often related to the recognition of particular attitudes, motivations and/or cognitive factors.

We limit ourselves here to highlighting how the personality is a fluctuating variable, a bubble containing all those aspects characterizing the individual, and how this differs with the varying of contexts and relations.

In the educational field, the co-presence of several players means that each one intervenes, with a different personality, in building the teaching-learning process. The way of presenting oneself in the educational relationship, the teaching style and the pedagogical school/s of thought, like the cognitive style of the learner, make the dimension in which these dynamics take place unique and personal. In the same way, the creative process, as mentioned earlier, becomes personalized according to the subject who has activated it and the context of reference: the same essential conditions as the educational process.

"Numerous studies have found that some traits of the personality can be directly connected with creativity, such as the desire to overcome obstacles, to take risks, to tolerate ambiguity" (Sternberg 2006, p. 89). At a more visible level, the observations of individuals deemed creative have characteristics of shyness, domination, seriousness, little or no attention to rules, sensitivity and autonomy (Guastello 2009; Runco 2007). These are again qualities which cannot be static or fixed; "Csikszentmihalyi (1996), in his interviews, meets subjects who seem to be at the same time logical and naïve, disciplined but jokey, introvert and extrovert, realistic but imaginative, objective and passionate…" (Lin et al. 2012, p. 114), where ambiguity, in the positive pragmatic sense of containment of dualism seems to reign in them.

Learning implies checking "behavioural changes as the result of experience" (Taylor and MacKenney 2008, p. 2), that lasts in time. The method consists of the use of strategies, called learning styles, which vary from one subject to another and from one situation to another. The personality traits and the learning styles are interconnected dimensions, where the personality forms an important aspect of learning. The learning strategies do not work autonomously, but are directly dependent on the personal variables (e.g. Cohen 1996; Sadeghi et al. 2012; Ibrahimoglu et al. 2013, p. 97), and vice versa.

6.1.4 *Context*

The context, "co-presence of spatial-temporal dynamics and psychological phenomena" (Glăveanu 2014, p. 382), is a place for meeting, exchange and sharing; a complex of circumstances within which an event, a matrix of meanings, is born and developed (Bateson 1972).

Barbot et al. (2011), in their definition of creativity, attribute to the context the power to stimulate or inhibit the expression of the creative potential (see also Besançon and Lubart 2008). It is, however, the subject that defines this relation; their exploration allows them to be overcome – inhibiting their potential – or to dominate the context (Sternberg 2006) – in terms of management and organization.

Like the subjective differences, the differences of setting also influence creativity, creating a *person-environment interaction* "that can explain the reasons why certain factors can stimulate the creative efforts of one person and freeze those of others" (Runco 2014, p. 153). For Runco and other researchers, the key element is perception, a variable based on expectation and interpretation (Carson and Runco 1999; Millward and Freeman 2002; Nicol and Long 1996; Runco 2012), which intervenes in the analysis of the situation, of the context and therefore in the consequent reaction of the subject.

This is a dynamic conception and one of continuous references between physical situation – which entails the presence of a problem to solve, activating a creative process – and psychology of the individual, which can be observed to the same extent in educational contexts as well, based wholly on the relation between subject-subjects, subjects-objects, subjects-environment and objects-environment, in continuous change and reciprocal adaptation. The importance of the "preparation of the context, as rich and motivating" (Malaguzzi 1983, p. 74), can accompany the subject in the discovery, in the exploration and therefore in the view of supporting their creative process. Vygotskij (1972) also believed that the principle of freedom was essential as a presupposition of the creative act, considered in broad and free environments to allow combinations, associations and syntheses.

In addition to the physical space, there is also the social, psychological and personal space that analyse and contain all those complex connections that only the interaction between several individuals with the environment can have. Being in an educational context implies being inside this close-knit network, here described briefly, of meanings, values and actions which make the educational experience significant and rich. Observing the context at school is necessary to be included in its specificity and in its implicit dynamism, which is also essential in the actions where flexibility is the essential requisite of the figure of the teacher.

6.1.5 Creative Democracy

The continuous reference between these two processes, the creative one and that of learning, tracing their connections and potential, underlines and consolidates what has already been maintained and confirmed for some time now by several researchers (e.g. Runco 2004; Hadani 2015; Robinson 2015; Craft 2001a), as a basic presupposition which supports all our claims: everyone has creative potential, as every person is naturally gifted with the implied factors. We can therefore talk of creative sharing, in broad terms of a common "characteristic", way of thinking, of coping with problems and situations in a different way. Creativity is exploration of possibilities, alternatives, solutions and feedback that are then shared to be given meaning and sense, leaving the intrapsychological sphere to explore the interpsychological one (Beghetto 2016). Creativity would be meaningless without a social dimension, as if it remained that of the individual, all their discoveries would potentially be a creative revolution; this brings us back to the importance of the context, as a social group in which the creative process takes on value and sense. "According to this perspective, creativity becomes a democratic construct as we can all be creative" (Gariboldi and Cardarello 2012, p. 66). An anti-elitist concept of creativity, referred to everyday life (Banaji et al. 2010) – also called "little-c" or "mini-c" (e.g. Craft 2001b; Craft 2005; Kaufman and Beghetto 2009; Simonton 2017) –, with a social and essentially a diffused, shared and common meaning. In these terms, creativity becomes everyone's, of children as much as of adults, and today, more than ever necessary in a constantly evolving society. The democratic dimension puts it "within reach", more easily usable and equally requested at all levels. "Its dimension expressed in terms of a complex process would seem to complicate the school curriculum but in actual fact it acts to its advantage: instead of focusing on a single process or a single skill, it allows supporting many and different behaviours and attitudes; instead of making the children adapt to a single attitude, "signs of creativity" can be observed in many activities and in many contents" (Runco 2015, p. 4; Guerra and Villa 2017a).

The teacher, as a key figure and mediator with society, now requires attention as the explorer of contexts, strategies, skills, activities and ideas which become fundamental for their training and for that of others. It is a dynamic trend of doing and discovering, of return journeys, of experiences and feedback.

6.2 Dynamisms

'Dynamic', from the Greek *dynamikós*, means strength associated with movement, as opposed to the term 'static'. In painting or sculpture, for example, a canvas or a statue are dynamic if they can transmit an idea of movement, even in their static matter, inducing in the observer an action during their fulfilment, a process. Therefore, in a classic transitive reaction, if creativity is process, and process is movement as the activation of several elements together, therefore dynamism, creativity is also dynamism.

The composition of the factors involved in the creative process, as mentioned, is different in each individual and as the situation varies: movement is already observed here, in the change of perspective, in considering positively different each process in each individual in the most widely varying contexts. Education is also dynamic due to its continuous entwining of a multitude of elements, unfolding into an unforeseeable chain of references between the suggestions and the feedback.

Education and creativity are therefore increasingly becoming closely linked topics which it is worthwhile discussing in connection where one – the educational context – becomes the ideal underlying base of support and field of action for the creative potential of the subjects involved.

The intrinsically dynamic nature of both processes brings them closer together, now tracing the possibility of including creativity as an indispensable and transversal skill in daily didactics (Guerra and Villa 2017b, c; Villa 2017). In detail, the dynamism intrinsic to creativity can be traced back to several levels: (1) individual but also (2) extra-individual. The first embodies the expression of all the previously stated factors; the ability to process internal and external information, the personality, the motivation and the emotivity of the individual are combined in a unique way in the subject, who creates a dynamic relationship with the context. It appears as a useful metaphor of comparison, the first theorization of the multiple intelligences suggested by Gardner (1983), which can be interpreted here as the theory 'of glasses' – for the sole explanatory and not reductive purpose. If, as maintained by the author, the concept of intelligence is considered as non-unitary, but broken down into different areas linked to different styles and types of knowledge, these can be represented as several glasses containing different quantities of liquid. Each individual has all the glasses, but the level of liquid in each one will be different; a personal mix will be obtained from them all which determines the individual profile of knowledge (Gardner 1982). At first, Gardner does not distinguish an artistic-creative intelligence as he believed that each one of those shown could be interpreted in those terms. The creative process can thus be interpreted in a similar way, in the idea that the different elements involved in the final mix are dependent on the set of individual variables and the relative relationship with the context. Going further into his research, Gardner effectively inserted creativity in an interactive dimension as the relationship between the person, the field or the discipline and the environment (Gardner 1989, 1993), making it subsequently important to the point of being contemplated in the five keys for the future (Gardner 2007), useful for the citizens of the future who will have to cope with the complexity of the world. He highlights how it is necessary to make this dimension explicit, as a fundamental element in the individual, focusing attention on a mind that cultivates new ideas and skills, that is always asking new questions to discover new problems and methods (Gardner in EduSkills OECD 2012).

In both representations, the relationship with the context seems to remain the indispensable indicator, especially as it is extremely dynamic, never fixed or perpetual. From the point of view of teaching-learning processes, this means paying particular attention to the arrangement and organization of the educational space, with the aim of fostering different forms of communication and strategies, such as to allow both processes, educational and creative, to take place.

The physical space, like the methodological-operative one as well, outline the background against which the actions take place, becoming a characterizing element of the extra-individual level (2). The reference to the social dimension of creativity and to some questions concerning the context of reference within which a process or a product are considered creative is immediate.

In educational experience and practice, the social dimension means sharing, collaboration, comparison and discussion. The Other is too important not to be considered, especially if it is a group, in the awareness that through an encounter we become mature and achieve knowledge of a higher level than can normally be reached individually, as it is built up, integrated and discussed: "groups may discuss a wider range of topics and emphasize marketability" (McMahon et al. 2016, p. 254).

The sociality of creativity gravitates around the concept of sharing the idea because exposure to the thought of others contributes to cognitive stimulation

(Dugosh et al. 2000; Paulus and Yang 2000) and therefore, to a consequent greater production and activation of the creative process, creating a continuous flow. This refers back to an umpteenth and strong dynamism between stimuli that are external and internal to the individual, where one set influences the other and vice versa and where both are indispensable for a *learning-in-creativity* (Beghetto 2016).

The idea is certainly the hinge on which the creative potential takes shape, understood as the visible and directly usable moment; a large part of an even larger complex process. However, we believe that the start of the whole process can be traced back to something less explicit and spectacular like the phase of idea generation, but definitely fundamental: a problem. The problem here is to be understood as a situation – social, relational, contextual – a stimulus that can trigger a series of new questions which in turn activates a procedure and an attitude of research in the person involved.

One question now remains suspended on how it is possible to identify positively problematic situations in everyday life and in the educational field, capable, that is, of activating processes of research which are creative and of learning at one and the same time. The adequate approach is, for us, of the exploratory type, which allows the subject to be in an attitude of constant material and contextual research, to have eyes attentive to the world. Exploring becomes the matrix and frame within which the whole creative process is activated: an attitude that is the container of all its dynamism.

6.3 Acts of Exploration

If creativity is per se a dynamic concept due to the co-presence of various factors related to the personality and its relationship with the context, we can maintain that its dynamism can be increased by educational methodologies which widen the field of the possibilities of response to a given problem. In this sense, educational and didactic project development can be usefully engaged in supporting creativity as a cross–curricular objective, which means in the first place accepting its manifestations at the time they emerge. What is prefigured is a frame within which the strategies, the methodologies and the opportunities made available to children allow them to build up their own paths of learning in an original way.

In this perspective, a way of proceeding which appears coherent as a dynamic methodology of schooling is the exploratory one, which takes its cue from the work of the Canadian artist Keri Smith and her "explorations of the world", first presented in her book "How to be an explorer of the world" (2008) and continued in many others (2007a, b, 2010, 2011, 2014, 2016).

In its educational variation (Guerra 2013a), each exploration can be described as an open question, which asks for the study of an element of or a situation, first observing it and then documenting it. This is a procedure which makes some specific requests of the subject but which explicitly leaves room for individual interpretation, so that each person can approach the instruction in personal ways

(Guerra 2016). This openness, placed in a methodology which is offered as a frame for the action, is what immediately connects the exploratory approach with an educational and didactic project development concerned with supporting the expression of creativity: the multiplicity of the possible answers to the same instruction, just as the structuring of paths to answer it, represent ways through which different and even diverging answers find room, which leave space for original possibilities of proceeding.

Moreover, the roots of Keri Smith's original proposal seem to lie in the beginnings of her biography of a child bored by school which offered – and required – repetitive and anonymous tasks: precisely to flee that routine which suffocated her creative inclination, Ms. Smith hypothesized becoming a "creative" child as a response to a request of productivity but above all of uniformity. That response takes shape in the exploration of unusual materials (Guerra 2013b), which she used to construct, transform and create which, along a path which was not linear or painless, led her to an artistic research, offering her the occasion to legitimize her particular perspective, along a path which does not fear disorientation or chaos. Following this path, her training was nourished by heterogeneous references which often refer to other "rebels", underlining how personal expression – of Ms. Smith but of many other students besides her – often finds space as divergence from the status quo, from what is conventionally requested. In the first place by school. Her artistic experimentation then takes on as presuppositions the legitimacy of error against the slavish respect for the rule, understood as conformity and standardization. Her production, in particular as a writer, has its origin in the desire supported by creative thinking, of sharing a thirst for knowledge, understood as an original interpretation of the world. This is why, the use of articulated and heterogeneous methods of investigation, in turn interested in bringing out multiple ways of seeing, find a place in her work, as in evidence for example in *Finish this book* (2011): here the reader is accompanied in structured training on the methods of observation and documentation and then introduced to techniques of analysis of the objects found. In parallel, her proposal insists not only on practising how to investigate the world, but to act on it to transform it, as for example in *The Guerilla Art Kit* (2007a), and then increasingly in *The imaginary world of …* (2014) or *The Wander Society* (2016).

These presuppositions help to better understand the origin and peculiarity of Keri Smith's proposal, including in its pedagogical and didactic translation (Guerra 2013a, 2016). It includes the possibility of thinking and planning educational and learning experiences of children and youngsters as occasions that the adult offers, so that they can be seized, interpreted and structured in a personal way. Through this methodology, there is practice in observing, connecting, documenting, remaining open to the unexpected and accepting error as an occasion for discovery, all of which are actions that support the exercise of creativity.

The exploratory methodology forms a possibility of interrogating the world (Guerra 2015) through the intelligences of each person: it is an encounter that is simultaneously material and reflective, which comes into being from the experimentation of the matter, because each instruction starts from a question of investigation around objects, situations, concrete contexts that belong to the inhabited contexts. This moment is however accompanied by a constant reflection, which arises from the interrogation of materials and the objects investigated and above all by the possible connections between them. This close-knit work, starting from a "material" starting base (Guerra 2017), i.e. which requires measuring up to the physical nature of the environment observed and described, supports the continuous search for connections between objects and contexts and, with them, the multiplication of levels of interpretation, making room for divergence.

Exploring this becomes a dynamic creative path, which has seen different applications in the area of research-education with teachers, but also research-action at school with children.

The proposal of an exploratory approach in the educational and scholastic field has effectively been experimented in the training of educators and teachers, allowing the collection of over two thousand explorations inspired by *How to become an explorer of the world*, the analysis of which shows how this practice – understood as the possibility of experiencing research around an object, documenting it and then rethinking in in an educational way – allows bringing out some problems relative to methodological strategies which can foster approaches attentive to the inclinations of each person, but also to discover creative potential in the way of presenting oneself educators and teachers, recognizing in oneself abilities that had not previously been identified. This appears particularly in line with the dynamism that mainly regards the work of the teacher: it changes continuously, in the constant need to restructure knowledge and situations, but also to take decisions on the spot (e.g. Mortari 2009).

In parallel, the use of this approach directly offered to children appears a strategy that allows generating questions that allow going into depth, in the world and in knowledge (Antonacci and Guerra 2015). Transposing the exploratory approach into education puts the children into the condition of researchers, "scientists" interested in getting to know themselves, the world and things with an open and curious approach, oriented towards learning the mechanisms of what surrounds them. In this sense, the project of scholastic innovation called "Una scuola" has found one of its cornerstones.

The project originated with two educationalists, researchers in the Department of Education of the University of Milano-Bicocca, active in research and education in the field, with the aim of giving shape to a possibility of school that many good practices, in Italy and abroad, show is feasible and concerns schools for children aged from 3 to 13, therefore pre-school, primary school and middle school. The project rereads and reinterprets some crucial and structural elements of school, varying them in the light of the most recent research in education and didactics. The central aspects include: the group, heterogeneous to take best advantage of the possibilities offered by different skills, but also fluid to allow organization that respect time, ways and interests; the learning context, organized instead of in classrooms through diversified but interrelated areas of experience, equipped with materials and instruments that support autonomous research; languages, mainly on the subjects and present without hierarchical logics; assessment, understood as a moment of reflection rather than judgement. Alongside these, the educational and didactic orientation identifies in questions the privileged form of learning and, in this sense, addresses the construction of questions of exploration (Smith 2011; Guerra 2013a, b), understood as the authentic questioning of contexts, oriented at supporting multiple paths of enquiry and shunning univocal answers. The use of exploratory instructions is oriented in the first place to building up a habitus interested in the discovery of knowledge. Their construction in the form of open questions of research allows each child to go through them starting from their own skills, but also to investigate those skills and challenge them. In this approach, knowledge is built up through the act of exploring at a material and contextual, individual and collective, personal and social level and this fosters the exercise of creativity, as it allows each one to create paths, conceive of possibilities and build up knowledge.

6.4 Conclusions

The exploratory approach, inspired by the work of Keri Smith but reinterpreted as a pedagogical and didactic methodology of interrogating the world to try to know its meaning and functioning personally and therefore originally, appears a coherent way with a proposal of school that wishes to foster and encourage the expression and exercise of creativity. Exploration appears as a constitutive dimension of the educational experience, which solicits attitudes of research oriented towards bringing out questions through constant dialogue with the contexts and with others. The suggestions made by Smith have many nuances which allow articulated directions: by making for example reference to "How to become an explorer of the world", any exploration starting from the initials, like number 5 – which suggests "start[ing] a collection based on the first found object you see on your walk, whatever that is. You decide what the connection between the objects is (can be based on shape, colour, size, etc.) – is an invitation to investigate the world in a way that is not linear but reticular and highlights an inclination to research which is far removed from the disciplinary fragmentation at school. Every exploratory question goes in this direction and can be treated in infinite combinations: using them thinking of them inside the educational and scholastic experience can be a useful strategy but above all its can indicate a fertile path to build and ask good questions again. The suggestion proposed. i.e. is not necessarily that of referring to the explorations imagined by Smith which, moreover and curiously, do not come into being for educational or scholastic purposes, but of being a reference as an exercise to recognize and cultivate productive questions for the construction of knowledge and the promotion of creative thinking. This means, on the one hand, learning to recognize the questions of meaning, relation and correlation that children and youngsters ask themselves, giving value to them and offering space and time to consider them in depth, even if they are not the ones that the teachers would have proposed: their coming into being from the field, from experience and from curiosity makes them an intriguing opportunity not to be missed and to investigate. On the other hand, it teachers translate it into looking for questions that are neither rhetorical or univocally oriented to acquiring predetermined contents, but privileging questions – exploratory, precisely – which invite looking at the objects investigations from several points of view, whatever they are, to find connections between what emerges in progress, to make suppositions based on the research.

The attitude to research which the approach which we define exploratory supports, allow reinforcing/consolidating the skills oriented towards learning to learn, understood here as a permanent way of investigation interested in building up questions from the context but also soliciting connections between the elements making it up and between the subjects and these elements. Above all, this exercise of continually connecting the parts with one another and with the context allows stimulating the skill of reading the relationships between things, but also reorganizing them according to personal inclinations and interest. This constant solicitation to think and redefine relations and connections seems particularly promising for the purpose of cultivating creative skills, which can appear from this interpretation of the existing world which is always new and original.

References

Akbari Chermahini, S., & Hommel, B. (2012). More creative through positive mood? Not everyone! *Frontiers in Human Neuroscience, 6*, 319.

Aljughaiman, A., & Mowrer Reynolds, E. (2005). Teachers' conceptions of creativity and creative students. *The Journal of Creative Behaviour, 39*(1), 17–34.

Antonacci, F., & Guerra, M. (2015). *Manifesto per Una scuola*. Retrieved from: http://unascuola.blogspot.it/2015/07/manifesto-per-una-scuola.htm.

Antonello, D. (2002). Stili cognitivi e forme di intelligenza: lo stato attuale della ricerca. In M.R. Zanchin (Ed.), *I processi di apprendimento nella scuola dell'autonomia*. Roma: Armando editore.

Antonietti, A., & Cantoia, M. (2010). *Come si impara. Teorie, costrutti e procedure nella psicologia dell'apprendimento*. Milano: Mondadori.

Banaji, S., Burn, A., & Buckingham, D. (2010). *The rhetorics of creativity: A literature review*. Newcastle: Creativity, Culture and Education.

Barbot, B., Besançon, M., & Lubart, T. I. (2011). Assessing creativity in the classroom. *The Open Education Journal, 4*(1), 58–66.

Bateson, G. (1972). *Steps to an ecology of mind: Collected essays in anthropology, psychiatry, evolution, and epistemology*. Chicago: University of Chicago Press.

Beghetto, R. A. (2016). Creative learning: A fresh look. *Journal of Cognitive Education and Psychology, 15*(1), 1–15.

Besançon, M., & Lubart, T. (2008). Differences in the development of creative competencies in children schooled in diverse learning environments. *Learning and Individual Differences, 18*(4), 381–389.

Bragby, K., Söderhäll, B., & Vilhelmson, P. (Eds.). (2012). *Panorama mentale interno e panorama esterno: Radicare una Cultura di Intraprendenza e Creatività nel piano formativo*. Gävle: ECECC.

Bronfenbrenner, U. (1979). *The ecology of human development: Experiments by design and nature*. Cambridge: Harvard University Press.

Cannon, W. B. (1929). *Bodily changes in pain, hunger, fear and rage*. New York/London: D. Appleton and Company.

Carson, D. K., & Runco, M. A. (1999). Creative problem solving and problem finding in young adults: Interconnections with stress, hassles, and coping abilities. *The Journal of Creative Behaviour, 33*(3), 167–188.

Cohen, A. D. (1996). Second language learning and use strategies: Clarifying the issues. In *Symposium on strategies of language learning and use*. Spain: Seville.

Craft, A. (2001a). *An analysis of research and literature on creativity in education measurement*. Report for the Qualifications and Curriculum Authority, UK. pp. 1–37.

Craft, A. (2001b). Little c creativity. In A. Craft, R. Jeffrey, & M. Leibling (Eds.), *Creativity in education* (pp. 45–61). London/New York: Continuum.

Craft, A. (2005). *Creativity in schools. Tensions and dilemmas*. New York: Routledge.

Cropley, D., & Cropley, A. (2012). A psychological taxonomy of organizational innovation: Resolving the paradoxes. *Creativity Research Journal, 24*, 29–40.

Csikszentmihalyi, M. (1996). *Creativity: Flow and the psychology of discovery and invention*. New York: Harper Collins.

Donovan, S. M., & Bransford, J. D. (Eds.). (2005). *How students learn: History, mathematics, and science in the classroom*. Washington, DC: National Academies Press.

Dugosh, K. L., Paulus, P. B., Roland, E. J., & Yang, H. C. (2000). Cognitive stimulation in brainstorming. *Journal of Personality and Social Psychology, 79*(5), 722–735.

Gable, P. A., & Harmon-Jones, E. (2008). Approach-motivated positive affect reduces breadth of attention. *Psychological Science, 19*, 476–482.

Gable, P. A., & Harmon-Jones, E. (2011). Attentional consequences of pre-goal and post-goal positive affects. *Emotion, 11*(6), 1358.

Gardner, H. (1982). *Art, mind, and brain: A cognitive approach to creativity*. New York: Basic Books.

Gardner, H. (1983). *Frames of mind: The theory of multiple intelligences*. New York: Basic Books.

Gardner, H. (1989). *To open minds*. New York: Basic Books.

Gardner, H. (1993). *Creating minds: An anatomy of creativity seen through the lives of Freud, Einstein, Picasso, Stravinsky, Eliot, Graham, and Gandhi*. New York: Basic Books.

Gardner, H. (2007). *Five Minds for the future*. Boston: Harvard Business School Press.

Gardner, H. (2012). *Conversation with Howard Gardner*. EduSkills OECD [video] Available at: https://tinyurl.com/ydfsmsfm. Accessed 13 Oct 2017.

Gariboldi, A., & Cardarello, R. (2012). *Pensare la creatività. Ricerche nei contesti educativi per l'infanzia*. Reggio Emilia: Edizioni Junior.

Giorgetti, M., Pizzingrilli, P., & Antonietti, A. (2009). Creatività: come promuoverla a scuola? *Psicologia e scuola*, 42–48.

Glăveanu, V. P. (2014). Theorising context in psychology: The case of creativity. *Theory & Psychology, 24*(3), 382–398.

Glăveanu, V. P., & Tanggaard, L. (2014). Creativity, identity, and representation: Towards a sociocultural theory of creative identity. *New Ideas in Psychology, 34*, 12–21.

Gralewski, J., & Karwowski, M. (2016). Are teachers' implicit theories of creativity related to the recognition of their students' creativity? *The Journal of Creative Behaviour, 32*(10), 1–17.

Guastello, S. J. (2009). Creativity and personality. In T. Rickards, M. A. Runco, & S. Moger (Eds.), *Routledge companions. The Routledge companion to creativity* (pp. 267–278). New York: Routledge/Taylor & Francis Group.

Guerra, M. (2013a). *Progettare esperienze e relazioni*. Parma: Edizioni Junior-Spaggiari.

Guerra, M. (2013b). Materiali non convenzionali a scuola: esperienze didattiche e potenzialità formative. *Reladei, 2*(1), 105–120.

Guerra, M. (A cura di). (2015). *Fuori. Suggestioni nell'incontro tra educazione e natura*. Milano: FrancoAngeli.

Guerra, M. (2016). Tracce di mondo per esploratori bambini. In F. Antonacci & E. Rossoni (Eds.), *Intrecci d'infanzia*. Milano: FrancoAngeli.

Guerra, M. (A cura di) (2017). *Materie intelligenti. Il ruolo dei materiali non strutturati naturali e artificiali negli apprendimenti di bambine e bambini*. Parma: Edizioni Junior-Spaggiari.

Guerra, M., & Villa, F. V. (2017a). Creative Research in Schools: a Methodology for Teacher-Researcher. In *Proceedings of EDULEARN17 Conference 3rd-5th July 2017* (pp. 3464–3468). Barcelona, Spain.

Guerra, M., & Villa, F. V. (2017b). La figura docente fra creatività e competenze / The teaching figure between creativity and competences. *MeTis Progredit, 7*(1).

Guerra, M., & Villa, F. V. (2017c). Open educational methods and divergent thinking (DT): A preliminary study in an italian primary school. *The International Journal of Creativity & Problem Solving, 27*(1), 73–89.

Guilford, J. P. (1950). Creativity. *American Psychologist, 5*(9), 444–454.

Hadani, H. (2015). *Inspiring a generation to create: Critical components of creativity in children*. Sausalito: Center for Childhood Creativity.

Hocevar, D. (1980). Intelligence, divergent thinking, and creativity. *Intelligence, 4*, 25–40.

Ibrahimoglu, N., Unaldi, I., Samancioglu, M., & Baglibel, M. (2013). The relationship between personality traits and learning styles: A cluster analysis. *Asian Journal of Management Sciences and Education, 2*(3), 93–108.

Kaufman, S. B. (2015). The emotions that make us more creative. *Harvard Business Review*. Available at: https://hbr.org/2015/08/the-emotions-that-make-us-more-creative.

Kaufman, J. C., & Beghetto, R. A. (2009). Beyond big and little: The four c model of creativity. *Review of General Psychology, 13*(1), 1–12.

Kogan, N. (1971). Educational implications of cognitive styles. In G. S. Lesser (Ed.), *Psychology and educational practice*. Glenview: Scott & Foresman.

Lin, W.-L., Hsu, K.-Y., Chen, H.-C., & Wang, J.-W. (2012). The relations of gender and personality traits on different creativities: A dual-process theory account. *Psychology of Aesthetics, Creativity, and the Arts, 6*(2), 112–123.

Malaguzzi, L. (1983). "Che posto c'è per Rodari?". In C. De Luca (a cura di). Se la fantasia cavalca con la ragione. prolungamenti degli itinerari suggeriti dall'opera di Gianni Rodari, Juvenilia, Bergamo. In A. Gariboldi & R. Cardarello (2012). *Pensare la creatività. Ricerche nei contesti educativi per l'infanzia*. Edizioni Junior.

McMahon, K., Ruggeri, A., Kämmer, J. E., & Katsikopoulos, K. V. (2016). Beyond idea GENERATION: The power of groups in developing ideas. *Creativity Research Journal, 28*(3), 247–257.

Millward, L. J., & Freeman, H. (2002). Role expectations as constraints to innovation: The case of female managers. *Communication Research Journal, 14*(1), 93–109.

Moè, A. (2001). *Motivati si nasce o si diventa?* Bari: Laterza.

Mortari, L. (2009). *Ricercare e riflettere. La formazione del docente professionista*. Roma: Carocci.

Nicol, J. J., & Long, B. C. (1996). Creativity and perceived stress of female music therapists and hobbyists. *Creativity Research Journal, 9*(1), 1–10.

Paulus, P. B., & Yang, H.-C. (2000). Idea generation in groups: A basis for creativity in organizations. *Organizational Behaviour and Human Decision Processes, 82*(1), 76–87.

Robinson, K. (2015). *Fuori di testa. Perché la scuola uccide la creatività*. Trento: Edizioni Centro Studi Erickson (Original work published 2001).

Runco, M. A. (2004). Everyone has creative potential. In R. J. Sternberg, E. L. Grigorenko, & J. L. Singer (Eds.), *Creativity: From potential to realization* (pp. 21–30). Washington, DC: American Psychological Association.

Runco, M. A. (2007). *Creativity: Theories and themes: Research, development and practice*. London: Elsevier Academic Press.

Runco, M. A. (2012). Creativity, stress, and suicide. In M. A. Runco (Ed.), *Creativity research handbook* (Vol. Vol. 3, pp. 163–192). Cresskill: Hampton Press.

Runco, M. A. (2014). *Creativity: Theories and themes: Research, development, and practice*. San Diego: Elsevier.

Runco, M. A. (2015). *Assessing student creativity*. LEGO Education.

Runco, M. A. & Pritzker, S. R. (1999). *Encyclopedia of creativity*. San Diego: Academic Press.

Sadeghi, N., Kasim, Z. M., Tan, B. H., & Abdullah, F. S. (2012). Learning styles, personality types and reading comprehension performance. *English Language Teaching, 5*(4), 116–123.

Simonton, D. K. (2017). Big-C versus little-c creativity: Definitions, implications, and inherent educational contradictions. In *Creative contradictions in education* (pp. 3–19). Cham: Springer.

Smith, K. (2007a). *The guerilla art kit*. New York: Princeton Architectural Press.

Smith, K. (2007b). *Wreck this journal*. London: Penguin.

Smith, K. (2008). *How to Be an Explorer of the World: Portable Art Life Museum*. London: Penguin.

Smith, K. (2010). *Mess. The manual of accidents and mistakes.* London: Penguin.

Smith, K. (2011). *Finish this book*. London: Penguin.

Smith, K. (2014). *The imaginary world of...* . USA: Penguin

Smith, K. (2016). *The wander society*. USA: Penguin.

Stella, G. (2001–2003). 1. Lo sviluppo cognitivo. Cenni sull'evoluzione normale delle funzioni intellettive. *Master per operatori nel campo della prevenzione della riduzione del disagio scolastico ed extrascolastico nelle età preadolescenziali*. Repubblica di San Marino: Università degli Studi della Repubblica di San Marino. Dipartimento della Formazione. Retrieved from: http://web.unirsm.sm/masterdisagio2/Moduli/Download/Stella/Liv1/mod1aStella.pdf

Sternberg, R. J. (2006). The nature of creativity. *Creativity Research Journal, 18*(1), 87–98.

Taylor, G. R., & MacKenney, L. (2008). *Improving human learning in the classroom: Theories and teaching practices*. Lanham: R&L Education.

Torrance, E. P. (1974). *The torrance test of creative thinking: Norms – Technical manual*. Bensenville: Scholastic Testing Service.

Villa, F. V. (2017). Strategie creative – educative. *Bambini, 3*, 23–26.

Vygotskij, L. S. (1972). *Immaginazione e creatività nell'età infantile*. Roma: Editori Riuniti.

Chapter 7
Educational Implications of the 'Self-Made Worldview' Concept

Alexandra Maland and Liane Gabora

Abstract Immersion in a creative task can be an intimate experience. It can feel like a mystery: intangible, inexplicable, and beyond the reach of science. However, science is making exciting headway into understanding creativity. While the mind of a highly uncreative individual consists of a collection of items accumulated through direct experience and enculturation, the mind of a creative individual is self-organizing and self-mending; thus, experiences and items of cultural knowledge are thought through from different perspectives such that they cohere together into a loosely integrated whole. The reweaving of items in memory is elicited by perturbations: experiences that increase psychological entropy because they are inconsistent with one's web of understandings. The process of responding to one perturbation often leads to other perturbations, i.e., other inconsistencies in one's web of understandings. Creative thinking often requires the capacity to shift between divergent and convergent modes of thought in response to the ever-changing demands of the creative task. Since uncreative individuals can reap the benefits of creativity by imitating creators, using their inventions, or purchasing their artworks, it is not necessary that everyone be creative. Agent based computer models of cultural evolution suggest that society functions best with a mixture of creative and uncreative individuals. The ideal ratio of creativity to imitation increases in times of change, such as we are experiencing now. Therefore it is important to educate the next generation in ways that foster creativity. The chapter concludes with suggestions for how educational systems can cultivate creativity.

A. Maland · L. Gabora (✉)
Department of Psychology, Fipke Centre for Innovative Research,
Kelowna, BC, Canada
e-mail: liane.gabora@ubc.ca

7.1 Introduction

Immersion in a creative task can be an intimate experience. It can feel like a mystery: intangible, inexplicable, and beyond the reach of science. However, science is now making exciting headway into understanding creativity. This chapter examines factors involved in the making of a creative mind, with the ultimate aim of helping educational systems to *cultivate* creative thinking. We believe the time for this is ripe, as our world is changing quickly, yielding new opportunities to be mined, new challenges to be met, and new problems to be solved. Thus, innovative thinkers are needed, perhaps more than ever before.

7.2 The 'Self-Made' Worldview (SMW)

We will use the term *worldview* to refer to a mind as it is experienced subjectively, from the inside. It is a way of *seeing* the world and *being in* the world that emerges as a result of the structure of ones' web of understandings, beliefs, and attitudes. A worldview reveals itself through behaviour, expression, and responses to situations (Gabora 2017a).

The worldviews of people who would be considered relatively *uncreative* consist largely of knowledge, social rules, and norms they've picked up from others through imitation and other *social learning* processes (i.e., process that involve learning from others). There is evidence that uncreative people tend on the whole to be pleasant, reliable, and uncomplicated (Feist 1998). Their worldviews are largely compilations of the knowledge, rules, and norms they've picked up from the world around them. If you were to envision the worldview of a very uncreative person, it might look like a stack of discrete and separate cards, with each card representing something they've seen, heard, or been told. In the classroom this type of student may be a teacher's dream, reproducing knowledge as expected in an obedient and passive manner. Thus, teachers may consciously or subconsciously, try to cast students into this mold. This may not, however, be what it takes to nurture a future innovator.

The worldview of a *creative* person might be envisioned as a stack of cards set on fire, edges ruffling. They are in a state of frenzy, becoming increasingly less separate and distinct; turning into something quite different from what they were previously. Despite the diversity of creative people, they tend to exhibit certain personality traits, such as curiosity, openness, high energy, confidence, lack of reliability, rebelliousness, and a tendency to deeply immerse themselves in projects they feel passionate about, often to the exclusion of everything else (Feist 1998).

Of course, in reality, almost everyone falls somewhere in between these two extremes. However, for simplicity, we refer to the worldview of an uncreative person as a *socially-made worldview* and the worldview of a creative person as a *self-made worldview,* or SMW for short. In what follows, we explain the rationale for connecting creativity with the degree to which one's worldview is self-made.

7.2.1 The Making of a Self-Made Worldview

The above-mentioned process of social learning is sometimes contrasted with *individual learning*, which involves learning outside a social context and which unfolds through direct experience in the world. It is sometimes assumed that individual learning encompasses creativity, but while individual learning culminates in the *discovery* of something that already exists in the world, creativity culminates in the *generation* of something that did not previously exist. Moreover, creativity can take place independent of direct experience in the world; it can be wholly or partially internal as opposed to external, and unlike individual learning it can occur in a social context. Thus, creative people venture beyond both social and individual learning; they rehash and reflect upon learned information, put their own spin on it, and make it their own (Feinstein 2006). This happens through processes that Piaget (2013) referred to as *assimilation*—fitting new information into one's existing web of understandings—and *accommodation*—the complementary process of restructuring one's existing web of understandings to make sense of the new information.

In short, while an uncreative worldview reflects *what the individual has been told*, the structure of a creative worldview reflects *what the individual has done with what he or she has been told:* their imaginative spin, as well as symbol manipulation and deductive, inductive, and abductive processes. An 'uncreative' student might fit well in a traditional education system wherein fact reproduction and rote memorization make for structured classrooms and efficient evaluations. A 'creative' student, however, is more likely to thrive in an environment that allows for more open-ended teaching methods. (A concrete example of an open-ended assignment will be provided at the end of this chapter.)

A worldview—and particularly a SMW—is *self-organizing* and *self-mending* (Gabora and Merrifield 2012; see also Osgood and Tannenbaum 1955). SMWs explore and play with previously encoded knowledge and experiences, looking at them from different perspectives. As such, over time, items in memory tend to weave into a coherent web and take a form that may be unrecognizable to the original. In response to *perturbations*—i.e., external stimuli or internal realizations that are found to be disturbing or inconsistent with deep-seated beliefs—the SMW reconfigures itself through local interactions amongst its components, and thereby maintains a more or less orderly structure. The SMW explores relationships amongst its contents to establish internal consistency, and does so spontaneously. If something surprises us, or someone does something that seems inconsistent with how they normally behave, we cannot stop ourselves from trying to figure out *how* and *why*. Our worldview attempts to mend itself, just as does a body when injured; thus, we are inclined to explore possibilities and modify our interpretations of situations in order to restore our sense of consistency and integrity (Greenwald et al. 2002).

The greater the tendency of a worldview to self-organize, the more likely it comes to deviate from the status quo. However, since the internal upheaval that comes with self-organized restructuring can be cognitively and emotionally demanding, the SMW individual may be more likely to been seen as unusual (Feist 1998), or even diagnosed with an affective disorder (Andreasen 1987). On the plus side though, they have greater potential to produce something—be it an idea, artifact, or class project—that others will regard as creative.

7.2.2 The Trade-Off Between Creating and Copying

It isn't actually necessary for everyone to be creative for the benefits of creativity to be felt by all. We can reap the rewards of a creative person's ideas by copying them, buying from them, or simply admiring them. Few of us can design a skyscraper or compose an opera, but they are nevertheless ours to use and enjoy.

As in any kind of evolutionary process, novelty must be balanced with preservation. In cultural evolution, the novelty-generating component is creativity, and the novelty-preserving components include imitation and other forms of social learning (Gabora 2013). The relative contributions of creativity versus imitation to cultural 'fitness' and diversity can be studied using an agent-based computational model of cultural evolution (Gabora 1995). In an experiment conducted using a variant of this agent-based architecture, in which artificial neural network-based agents invent and imitate ideas, the society's ideas evolve most quickly when there is a good mix of creative "inventors" and conforming "imitators" (Gabora and Tseng 2017). Of course, if there are no creative agents, then there are no novel ideas or outputs to preserve in society. But, if the frequency of creative agents is too high, the collective suffers by never implementing or sharing their fittest ideas. Thus, a society thrives when some individuals create and others preserve their best outputs.

So, there is a trade-off to peppering the world with creative minds. However, we should not avoid trying to enhance creativity in society—beginning with the classroom—because the pace of cultural change is accelerating more quickly than ever before. In some biological systems, when the environment is changing quickly, the mutation rate goes up. Similarly, in order to generate the innovative ideas that will keep us afloat during times of societal change, we can all benefit if we encourage students to explore their creative musings.

7.2.3 'Minding the Gap'

It is often the case that as soon as you clean one part of your house, such as the kitchen countertops, you notice how dirty other parts are, such as the floors and cupboards. The same principle holds true for your internal world; once you restructure one part of your worldview (e.g., from making a new friend who challenges a stereotype you hold), you glimpse the need to revise other parts as well (such as your judgement of others previously labeled with this stereotype). Similarly, it is widely known amongst scientists that answering one question, or solving one problem, often leads to others. So, ironically, though a SMW spends more time 'fixing' itself, it nevertheless still feels more in need of fixing. Whereas the uncreative worldview may not restructure itself until it experiences an *external* perturbation—i.e., a disturbance in the outside world—the SWM continuously reevaluates its own structure by seeking, or even *generating*, perturbations.

Thus, someone with a SMW is particularly inclined to experience the kind of question, problem, sense of incompletion or disconnect, feeling of curiosity, or need for self-expression that Feinstein (2006) notes tends to precede creativity. It may arise suddenly, or slowly over the course of years, and be either inconsequential or of far-reaching importance, and it has been described as a relatively chaotic cognitive state (Guastello 2002).

This state of mind can be framed in terms of the concept of *entropy*, a term that comes from thermodynamics and information theory, and refers to the amount of uncertainty and disorder in a system. As self-organizing systems, worldviews minimize internal entropy by continually interacting with and adapting to their environments. As open systems, worldviews capture energy (i.e., knowledge or information) from their environment, use it to maintain partially-stable states, and keep their own entropy low by displacing it into the outside world. Hirsh et al. (2012) use the term *psychological entropy* to refer to anxiety-provoking uncertainty, which they claim humans attempt to keep at a manageable level. However, uncertainty can also be experienced positively, as a wellspring for creativity; not just negatively, as anxiety. (It can also be experienced as some combination of the two.) Accordingly, the concept of psychological entropy has been redefined in terms of *arousal* rather than anxiety, i.e., as arousal-provoking uncertainty rather than anxiety-provoking uncertainty (Gabora 2017a, b).

Our attention is often pulled toward arenas of life where there is conflict, confusion, or uncertainty, because they are an arousing source of psychological entropy, and the creative process restructures this high entropy material so as to make it more acceptable. Since SMWs are continuously reorganizing and re-assessing themselves, they are more inclined to detect psychological entropy and engage in self-organized restructuring.

7.2.4 The Chaining of Thoughts and Actions

How does a mind self-organize? It has been proposed that the extraordinary creativity of the human mind was due to the onset of two exclusively human cognitive abilities. The first, which evolved following an increase in cranial capacity (skull size) approximately two million years ago, was the onset of the *self-triggered recall and rehearsal loop* (Donald 1991). This 'loop' marked the capacity for one thought to trigger another thought and enabled our early ancestors to rehearse and refine skills, recall and reflect upon the past, and fantasize about the future. It has also been referred to as *chaining* (Gabora and Tseng 2017), as it enables the chaining of thoughts and actions into streams of free-association, critical reflection, or complex behavioral sequences. Chaining enabled our ancestors to minimize arousal by repeatedly considering high psychological entropy material from new contexts until it was amply reorganized, and a new idea or perspective was achieved.

Chaining concepts begins by connecting items in memory that were previously assumed to be unrelated. The onset of the capacity for chaining enabled our ancestors to respond flexibly to stimuli and then reflect on their responses. The hypothesis that the onset of the capacity for chaining made cultural evolution possible can be demonstrated by an agent-based computer model of cultural evolution, called EVOC (for EVOlution of Culture). In EVOC, chaining increases the mean fitness and diversity of cultural outputs, which supports the hypothesis that chaining is what transformed a culturally stagnant society into one characterized by open-ended novelty (Gabora et al. 2013; Gabora and Smith in press).

Although the ability to chain began long ago, it is probably not the case that all modern people are equally inclined to engage in it. The greater the extent to which one chains thoughts and ideas together, the more likely one is to end up with a worldview that deviates from the status quo. Conversely, those with a SMW are more likely to engage in chaining, weaving stories about the past, or fantasizing about the future. This is consistent with the notion of an absent-minded professor or a daydreaming student; such an individual tends to be 'lost in thought' as opposed to living in the present moment. However, if something *does* manage to pull their attention, it tends to be more thoroughly honed before they settle into a particular understanding of it.

7.2.5 Shifting Between Analytic and Associative Modes of Thought: Contextual Focus

The second uniquely human cognitive ability is posited to have given rise to the 'big bang' of human creativity (Mithen 1998) approximately 50,000 years ago. It is referred to as *contextual focus* (CF) because it involves the capacity to adapt ones' mode of thought to the context by focusing or defocusing attention (Gabora 2003; Chrusch and Gabora 2014). CF enabled our ancestors to spontaneously shift between a *convergent* or *analytic* mode of thought and a *divergent* or *associative* mode of thought, wherein the interconnections between concepts and ideas become more fluid and malleable. Convergent or analytic thought is conducive to mentally demanding analytic tasks; it stifles associations, and reserves mental effort for symbol manipulation and detecting relationships of *causation*. Divergent or associative thought, on the other hand, is conducive to mind-wandering, forging new associations when stuck in a rut, and detecting relationships of *correlation*.

While chaining enabled the connecting of *closely* related items in memory, CF enabled the forging of *distant* connections. Divergent thought allowed these connections to be glimpsed, and convergent thought enabled them to be polished into their final form.

It is interesting to view these forms of thought not just in terms of what they're good for but in terms of how they process information at the conceptual level, i.e., the level of concepts. While convergent thought involves using concepts in their most stereotypical, undifferentiated form, i.e., *sticking to their most conventional contexts*, divergent thought is characterized by exploring the broader 'halo' of *potentiality* surrounding concepts, *i.e., the new meanings or feelings that arise when concepts are conceived of in particular, often unconventional, contexts* (Gabora 2018). Divergent thought is a matter of making broad use of contextual information to make associations in *constrained* (though potentially obscure) ways, rather than *loosely* expanding ones' sphere of associations in a generic sense. Thus, while in a convergent mode of thought you might think of a toothbrush only in terms of its role in brushing teeth, but while puzzling over how to clean a narrow bottle, in a divergent mode of thought you might conceive of a toothbrush as a possible bottle cleaner.

CF, like chaining, contributes to the making of a SMW, and does so through the forging of strange and often personal associations. The formation of a SMW entails the ability to not just *use* both modes of thought, but apply them when needed. As the SMW individual experiences more psychological entropy, there is a greater perceived need for restructuring, and thus a need for CF. When psychological entropy is experienced, creative individuals often attempt to mend their fractured worldviews by making use of divergent thought, which can forge new connections and come up with ideas. However, since new ideas are born in a divergent mode of thought, they are not likely to be immediately implementable, or even intelligible. Novel ideas and discoveries must be reflected upon or honed from different perspectives in a more clear-headed, convergent mode of thought. In short, the SMW is able to place what is discovered in one mode of thought 'into the hands of' the other, thereby achieving a more nuanced web of associations.

Like chaining, CF has also been modeled using EVOC (Gabora et al. 2013; Gabora and Smith in press). The mean fitness of actions across EVOC's artificial society increased with CF, and CF was also particularly effective when the fitness function changed. These findings support CF's hypothesized usefulness in breaking out of a rut, adapting to new or changing environments, and generating insight.

7.2.6 *From Task or Problem, to 'Half-Baked' Idea, to Creative Output*

Honing is the process of putting chaining and CF to work on a particular creative task until psychological entropy reaches an adequately low level. Honing involves viewing something in a new context, which leads to a new take on it, which suggests another new context to consider it from, and so forth, until the 'gap' is filled, and the worldview is less fragmented (Gabora 2017a). A more stable image of the world, and one's own relation to it, comes into focus through immersion in a creative task (Pelaprat and Cole 2011). Honing may also utilize *imagination:* the ability to form internal images or ideas by combining previous knowledge and experience.

A SMW is likely to experience cognitive states that feel unclear, ill-defined, and in need of honing, because it is in a process of constant renewal. When a problem (or task or concept) is considered in a new way for the first time, it is not always clear how the problem and context fit together. The phrase *half-baked idea* epitomizes how a creator may not even be able to comprehend their own newly hatched idea. Even so, since the SMW is more likely to *have* half-baked ideas in the first place, it is more likely to *hone* them into a state in which they are able to manifest, or take on a life in the outside world.

Our minds gain a deeper understanding of something, such as a half-baked idea, by looking at it from different perspectives. It is this kind of deep processing and the resulting integrated webs of understanding that make the crucial connections that lead to important advances and innovations (Gabora 2017a). Encouraging individuals to engage in deeper reflection and understanding is vital to creative thinking, and is particularly important in our society's distracting, high-stimulation environment. Youth spend so much time processing new stimuli that there is less time to venture deep into stimuli they've already encountered. With smartphones in hand and a continuous inflow of new content to consume, there is less time devoted to thinking about ideas and situations from different perspectives such that ideas are honed and worldviews become more integrated.

7.2.7 Insight as Self-Organized Criticality

Insight can be experienced as an '*aha!*' moment, and defined as a sudden new representation of a task or a realization of how to go about it (Mayer 1995). It is a deliberate cognitive reorganization that concludes in a new and useful interpretation or understanding that is non-obvious, or even peculiar (Kounios and Beeman 2009, 2014).

Insight marks a cognitive phase transition (Stephen et al. 2009) arising due to *self-organized criticality*, or SOC (Gabora 1998). SOC is a phenomenon wherein, through simple local interactions, complex systems tend to find a critical state—at the cusp of a transition between order and chaos—from which a single minor agitation sometimes exerts a disproportionately large effect (Bak et al. 1988). The signature of SOC is an inverse power law relationship in which most perturbations have little effect, but the occasional perturbation has a dramatic effect. For example, most of our moment-to-moment thoughts are inconsequential, but once in a while one thought triggers another, which triggers another, causing an 'avalanche' of reconceptualizations, concluding in a noticeably altered understanding of a concept, i.e., a moment of insight.

Like other SOC systems, a creative mind may function within a system midway between order (involving the systematic progression of thoughts), and chaos (wherein everything reminds you of everything else) (Gabora 1998). The SMW may make use of CF to *stay* in this regime, by utilizing systematic analysis when life gets complicated, and letting the mind wander when things get dull. As such, when our learning environments are designed to offer learning opportunies at multiple scales, i.e., at different levels of complexity and difficulty, they foster mastery of CF, and provide opportunities for the mental exercise that can culminate in a SMW.

Some attribute the unpredictability of insight to a blind, sequential, trial-and-error process of idea generation, but in our view insight arises through SOC due to the dynamical process of constant change and interaction in SOC systems. This is consistent with several lines of evidence. Firstly, the 'insight as SOC' hypothesis corroborates with the fact that worldviews rapidly reconfigure in response to external inputs, and findings that a series of small conceptual changes is often followed by large-scale creative conceptual change (Ward et al. 1997). It is also consistent with findings that insight tends to come suddenly (Gick and Lockhart 1995), and with ease (Topolinski and Reber 2010), despite extensive unsuccessful prior intense effort. Evidence that power laws are applicable to novelty transmission is another indication of SOC (Jacobsen and Guastello 2011). Further, there is evidence of SOC in the human brain (Kitzbichler et al. 2009). Moreover, at the cognitive level, word association studies have shown that concepts are clustered and sparsely connected, with some having many associates and others few (Nelson et al. 2004). Semantic networks exhibit the sparse connectivity, short average path lengths, and strong local clustering that are typical of SOC structures (Steyvers and Tenenbaum 2005).

7.3 A Micro-level View of The Self-Made Worldview

Having introduced the concept of a SMW as it manifests at the macro-level of everyday life, let us now briefly examine how a SMW is structured at the micro-level of neuron assemblies.

7.3.1 The Birthplace of Creativity

The notion of a SMW can be grounded in the brain's architecture by examining some key attributes of associative memory. First, our memory encoding is *sparse* (Kanerva 1988). This means that the number of possible items that can be encoded is far greater than the number of neurons in the human brain.

Second, human memories exhibit *coarse coding* (Sutton 1996): they are encoded in neurons that are sensitive to ranges of microfeatures. When memory organization follows coarse coding, a neuron responds maximally to a particular microfeature, and responds to a lesser extent to similar microfeatures. For example, neuron *A* may respond preferentially to a certain color (e.g., pink), while its neighbor *B* responds preferentially to a slightly different color (e.g., magenta), and so forth. However, although *A* may respond maximally to pink, it still responds, to a lesser degree, to magenta (or another similar color).

The upshot of coarse coding is that an item in memory is *distributed* across a cell assembly of neurons that are sensitive to particular properties. This means that a given experience activates not just one neuron, nor every neuron to an equal degree, but spreads across an assembly. Thus, the content of an item in memory doesn't arise due to the activation of any single neuron, but an overall pattern of activation, wherein the same neurons are used and re-used in different capacities (McClelland et al. 2003; Edelman 1987). Distribution guarantees the possibility of forging associations amongst items (Josselyn et al. 2015)—whether closely or distantly related—in a potentially new and useful, even surprising, way.

Human memory is also *content addressable*: there is a systematic relationship between stimulus content and the cell assemblies that encode it (Kanerva 1988). This enables the brain to take what is being experienced (i.e., context), and then naturally bring items to mind that are related, in either obvious or unexpected ways. Content addressability ensures that memory items are awakened by stimuli that are similar, or that resonate with one another (Hebb 1949). It is often the case that in moments of insight, the correlation between items has never been explicitly noticed, and their overlapping distribution is what awakened this new connection.

It is because of these features of memory that we can generate a new concept, or draw a new connection, that is more appropriate to the situation than anything our brain has ever been fed as input (McClelland et al. 2003). If memory were not sparse, and all neurons were packed like sardines within a small region, then we would not be able to make distinctions across the vast range of stimulus qualities that we can. Without distribution and coarse coding, there would be no overlap between items that share microfeatures, and thus no means of forging associations between them. Without content addressability, these associations would not be appropriate or significant; we would be wandering blindfolded through memory (McClelland et al. 2003). This cognitive architecture, as well as the compulsion of a SMW to self-organize in response to psychological entropy, is in our view the key to our creativity.

Lastly, items in memory are never re-experienced in exactly the same form as when first encoded, because the meanings of items are not stored in seclusion, and are in part derived from the meanings of other representations that excite associated groups of neurons. Thus, retrieving a specific, singular memory is essentially impossible, and memory does not work through a verbatim retrieval process. Recalled items are inevitably shaped by experiences the individual has had since encoding (Paterson et al. 2009; Schacter 2001), because the strength and pattern of connections amongst neurons are always changing (McClelland 2011). Changing patterns also means that items can spontaneously re-assemble in a way that relates to the task at hand. In this way, a worldview gets restructured.

7.3.2 How Chaining Is Implemented at the Neural Level

At the neural level, the onset of chaining meant that more features of any particular experience were encoded in memory, because more microfeature-specific neurons participated. It follows that the proclivity for a SMW may stem from the tendency to encode items in greater detail. Since more details lead to more distinctions, which enable more routes by which one thought can evoke another, this ultimately leads to more possibilities for connecting the dots between past and present experiences. Altogether, chaining and detailed encoding produce a more nuanced worldview. This is why our modern, high-stimulation world, in which teachers expect efficient, rehearsed answers, may be at a disservice to creative minds—which are born out of prolonged, detailed investigation.

7.3.3 How Contextual Focus Is Implemented at the Neural Level

Recall, CF is the capacity to effectively tailor one's mode of the thought to the current situation or context by focusing or defocusing attention (Gabora 2003). Analytic thought involves focusing attention and constraining activation such that items are considered in a compact form that is amenable to complex mental operations. Associative thought involves defocusing attention such that obscure, though potentially relevant, aspects of a situation to come into play, and the set of possible associations expands.

It has been proposed that the 'shift' experienced in CF is carried out through the recruitment and decruitment of *neurds* (Gabora 2010, 2018; Gabora and Ranjan 2013): the neural assemblies that are *not* activated in analytic thought, but *are* in associative thought (Gabora 2010; see also Ellamil et al. 2012; Yoruk and Runco 2014). Neurds respond to properties that are of minimal relevance to the current thought, and thus more distantly associated. The subset of cell assemblies that count as neurds shifts depending on the situation, such that they do not reside in any particular region of memory. Every different perspective one takes on a particular idea or concept recruits a different set of neurds.

In associative thought, diffuse activation recruits more cell assemblies, including neurds, which enables one thought to stray far from another, while still retaining a thread continuity. Insight occurs when concepts previously assumed to be unrelated are united and sufficiently activated to cross into conscious awareness (Salvi et al. 2016). Following insight, an idea must be honed to completion, which necessitates the shift to an analytic mode of thought. This analytic shift is accomplished by dismissing the cell assemblies that are active during associative thought, i.e., the *decruitment* of neurds.

An individual is more likely to have a SMW if they utilize CF to tailor their mode of thought to the current situation to a greater extent. Although engagement in associative thought navigates memory both deeply and quickly, the ability to reign it in is as important as the ability to initiate it. If everything always reminds you of everything else all the time, then the ability to draw connections becomes counterproductive. The ability to shift between, and control, both associative and analytic thought enables the structure of one's worldview to capture not only the contents acquired through social and individual learning, but also how they are all related. These relationships include not only basic-level connections, but relationships with respect to different contexts, and at different levels of abstraction.

7.3.4 The Ancestral Origins of New Ideas

The fact that associations come to mind spontaneously as a result of representational overlap and shared features means there is no need for memory to be randomly searched to make creative associations (Gabora 2010). The more detail with which stimuli and experiences are encoded, the greater their distributed representations overlap, and the more potential routes by which they can act as contexts for one another and combine.

Let us consider a concrete example. One morning, one of the authors of this chapter awoke from a dream in which she opened a small business basically hauling people around in a bus, and had come up with the slogan, "We put the Bus in Business". Where on earth did *that* come from, she wondered. It was obvious, though. It came from a combination of the Sense8 Netflix series she'd been binge-watching in which one of the heros hauls people around in a bus, and sayings like "We put the Fun in Fundraiser".

You may now have some idea of what caused her mind to pull these things together to generate this weird, new slogan. In the context of wanting to invent a slogan about a 'bus business' her dreaming brain didn't randomly mutate BUSINESS to get, say, "we put the harness in business"; it immediately hit on something that, albeit silly, is at least relevant (even when dreaming). This is consistent with the distributed and content-addressable architecture of memory; as a result, associations are forged by way of shared structure. The first author's dreaming mind connected BUS and BUSINESS on the basis of the shared syllable BUS, because they both activate neurds that are tuned to respond to the features of this syllable.

Having examined how new ideas emerge in associative memory, it is clear that they do not 'arise out of the blue'; they bear some relationship to knowledge and experiences encoded in memory before the creative act took place. Thus, due to the organization of memory, insight is not simply a matter of chance or expertise, but of becoming newly aware of the shared features between memories and concepts.

7.4 The Evolution of Creative Worldviews

To fully understand creativity, we must assess where creativity fits into the 'big picture' of humanity. Humans uniquely participate in two evolutionary processes: biological and cultural. Within this second cultural evolutionary process, creativity is the driving force that enables cultural outputs to proliferate in an open-ended fashion, i.e., without limit (Gabora 1997).

Although it may at first seem possible that culture, like biological organisms, could evolve through a Darwinian process (of natural selection or 'survival of the fittest'), there is abundant theoretical and empirical evidence against a Darwinian framework for culture (Gabora 2004, 2006, 2011, 2013). Even very early life itself went through a stage where it evolved—i.e., exhibited cumulative, adaptive, open-ended change—through a process that functioned rather differently from natural selection. What made early *biological* evolution possible was the emergence of *protocells*: simple cell-like structures that were self-organizing, self-mending, communally interacting, and self-reproducing (Hordijk et al. 2010; Kauffman 1993). It has been shown that these protocells evolved through a more haphazard process that can be referred to as *self-other organization* (SOR) *communal exchange*, which involves interactions not just within but amongst these self-organizing structures (Vetsigian et al. 2006).

It has been proposed that what made *cultural* evolution possible is the emergence of a *mind or worldview* that is self-organizing, self-mending, communally interacting, and self-reproducing (Gabora 2013). In short, the worldview is to cultural evolution what the protocell is to biological evolution. The internal state of a worldview changes dynamically due to a communal exchange of information with the external world, just like the earliest forms of life. By sharing experiences, ideas, and attitudes with others, individuals influence the process by which other peoples' worldview form and transform. One of the earliest environments that expose us to sharing through both internal restructuring and self-organization of thoughts and ideas, and communal exchange of thoughts and ideas with others, is the classroom. If teaching methods follow strict, traditional guidelines, peer interaction and questioning what the teacher says may be discouraged, thus stifling processes that play a role in the development of SMWs.

When people directly or indirectly interact with one another, elements of their worldview can be passed on and imperfectly reconstituted in each other. For example, students may assimilate fragments of their parent's or teacher's worldview and expose these fragments to the student's own unique experiences and physical limitations. In so doing, they forge unique internal models of the relationship between self and world. Thus, worldviews are not just communally interacting, but also self-regenerating. Unlike the case in modern-day biological evolution, in the cultural evolution of human worldviews, there is no universal 'self-assembly code' (e.g., DNA) ensuring the reliability of the replication. Consequently, particular beliefs or ideas may take on a different role within different people's worldviews as a result of their unique experiences and unique ways of structuring their knowledge.

A worldview evolves by interweaving both (1) internal interactions amongst its parts, and (2) external interactions with others. A worldview is more likely to become a SMW if it is exposed to more social and environmental interactions and experiences, thus encoding more information and having more potential configurations. When creativity is viewed in light of its role in fueling cultural evolution, the proposal of insight as self-organized criticality (SOC) fits into a broader conceptual framework. According to the *theory of punctuated equilibrium*, for which there is substantial well-documented evidence, changes in biological species are restricted to rare, rapid events interspersed amongst prolonged periods of stasis (Eldridge and Gould 1972). Punctuated equilibrium is perhaps the best-known example of SOC in nature, and it has been suggested that cultural evolution, like biological evolution, exhibits punctuated equilibrium (Orsucci 2008). Insight may play the role in cultural evolution that punctuated equilibrium plays in biological evolution, fueling the reorganization of, not species in an ecosystem, but concepts and ideas in an 'ecology of mind'.

One of the more prominent implications of applying the SOR or communal exchange theory to cultural evolution is that it is not the creative artifacts or ideas that are evolving, but the worldviews that produce them (Gabora 2004). Creative outputs are the byproducts of evolving worldviews. Since a worldview cannot be seen, it reveals itself through behavioural consistencies in social interaction and through generating creative outputs (Gabora 2017a). For example, when students debate about politics, or present their art projects to each other, these interactions and outputs are what allow worldviews to view and shape one another.

7.4.1 The Role of Education

Just as the cumulative creativity of biological evolution completely transformed our planet, so too has the cumulative creativity of cultural evolution. Although the creative processes underlying cultural evolution may be more strategic—i.e., less random—than biological evolution, we still cannot predict where its headed. While we have made considerable headway in understanding how the creative process works, we are no better able to predict the next new gadget that will captivate us nor the next novel that will move us to tears. Thus, we cannot predict the world that today's students will have to navigate once they graduate.

We *can*, however, educate them to be, not compilations of knowledge and social rules, but SMWs, able to weave what they are told into a unique cognitive structure of their own making that reflects their unique proclivities and experiences. This means that providing opportunities not just to learn but to *explore* how what they are learning could relate to personal experiences and knowledge in other domains. This will foster the ability to creatively respond to perturbations and cope with the unexpected.

Although teachers claim to value creativity, many hold negative attitudes toward the attributes associated with it, as many fear that encouraging creativity in the classroom could be disruptive (Beghetto 2007). Teachers tend to emphasize correct responses and the regurgitation of knowledge at the expense of creativity, as such a framework allows for more straightforward evaluation. Creative projects and testing, on the other hand, take considerable effort, and result in minimal benefits to standardized testing. When efforts are made to encourage creativity within an educational setting, neither teacher nor students often knows what the expectations are. However, despite the risks of encouraging creative classrooms, such an investment is potentially rewarding.

Each student can be seen as a unique wellspring of creative potentiality, which the teacher can help actualize, or bring to fruition. Allowing the full-ranging exploration of a student's potentiality may result in new emergent ideas and outcomes that could not be predicted in a straightforward logical way from knowledge of the teacher, student, or lesson plan (Ranjan and Gabora 2012).

7.4.2 Cultivating Creativity in the Classroom

An obvious final question to address is: how can creativity be nurtured in an educational setting? Incorporating creativity into the classroom may appear challenging and counterproductive, given that the current system is rooted in a certain structure, but there are a multitude of ways to do so (see Gregerson et al. 2013). The following section outlines three key ways in which teachers can begin to incorporate creativity (Gabora 2017b).

A first suggestion is to focus less on the reproduction of information, and more on critical thinking and problem solving. This allows students to build the necessary skills to engage in CF, wherein associative thought processes allow them to traverse their minds for ideas, and then analytic thought refines what is found. Incorporating this is as simple as using open-ended written questions as opposed to multiple choice questions on exams, or at least having a mixture. For example, presenting a real-world scenario and then following up with a question that requires using knowledge learned in class, as well as critical thinking and reflective skills.

Second, teachers can curate activities that transcend traditional disciplinary boundaries, such as by painting murals that depict biological food chains, or acting out plays about historical events, or writing poems about the cosmos. After all, the world doesn't come carved up into different subject areas. If our culture and classrooms tell students that these disciplinary boundaries are real, then their thinking becomes trapped in them. In reality, harsh lines do not exist between various domains in life. A worldview that is dynamic and creative may be reflected in a student who is capable of both building a beautiful diorama of a cell body and correctly labelling all of the parts.

Third, by posing questions and challenges, and then following up with opportunities for solitude and reflection, teachers can provide time and space for more detailed contemplation. In the current high-stimulation environment that students are exposed to daily, classrooms have the potential to offer a place for deeper reflection and understanding. Reflecting upon what is learned or asked fosters the forging of new connections that is so vital to creativity. While time-constraints may lead students to produce uncreative answers that reflect what they've been told, allowing time for information to 'incubate' may cultivate more creative outputs that showcase what students have done with what they've been told. It may be especially helpful for teachers or professors to view their students as entities that are able to rehash and reflect upon learned information, put their own spin on it, and later, do something novel with it.

7.4.3 A Creative Assignment in Practice

To make the above suggestions more concrete, let us examine a particular example of a university classroom assignment (from Ranjan and Gabora 2012)—aspects of which could be made to suit a younger group, as well. At the beginning of the term, students are asked to choose to complete a presentation, essay, or project, which is due at the end of the term. Students may choose their own topic, but it must pertain to a major theme or subject of the course. By giving students a choice of format and topic, plus the entire term to work on it, they can discover and explore their own interests and talents in-depth, and mull over the assignment from day one. Although it may be difficult to initially generate a topic, the time allowance means that a student can engage in associative thought and connect their own curiosity and abilities with what has been learned in class. In this associate stage of idea-generation, one thought is able to stray far from the next, yet a thread continuity is still retained by the subject or topic (e.g., politics or biology), keeping even far-reaching ideas somewhat relevant to the assignment. Once an idea is conjured up, analytic thought constrains the student's flight of ideas so that they can refine it to produce a learning experience tailored to the students' interests. Students thereby learn to engage in CF and use it to their advantage.

Since creativity thrives in situations where both freedom and constraint coexist, for an open-ended task such as this, instructors can ensure that students have clear expectations by both providing examples and breaking up the assignment into multiple steps. For example, they could be asked to submit just the title, one sentence, and one reference 2 weeks after the start of class, then submit one paragraph 1 month after the start of class, (and so forth), with feedback provided at each stage. In this way, students have abundant opportunity to hone and revise their ideas, and fulfill their creative potential.

This assignment incorporates (1) focusing on critical thinking and problem solving, (2) posing questions and challenges followed by opportunities for solitude, reflection, and detailed contemplation. It could also potentially incorporate (3) activities that transcend traditional disciplinary boundaries; for example, students might respond to this kind of open-ended assignment by creating a video game that explores the laws of physics, or by writing a short story about someone with a psychological disorder.

Studies on conceptual combinations suggest that because more ambiguous tasks such as this offer more opportunities to for students to connect dissimilar concepts, they may result in more creative outputs (Wilkenfeld and Ward 2001). When students choose their own topics, they are more likely to be intrinsically motivated, and to find personal meaning in what they are learning. Giving them several months to carry out the assignment, and staggering it into sub-goals, encourages students to put more of themselves into their work, which, and provides sufficient time for half-baked ideas to crystallize into final creative products that students can feel proud of. Although some skills may be specific to particular domains (e.g., multiplication ability is more specific to math than literature), creative processes of the kind that may be engendered by such open-ended assignments may catalyze internal transformation that transcends such boundaries.

7.5 Conclusion

Although educators claim to value creativity, a disconnect exists between this claim and what actually happens in school. This is likely because traditional misconceptions and assumptions about creativity keep educators from effectively incorporating it in their syllabi. Thus, the aim of this chapter was to introduce a new conception of the creative mind as a complex, dynamical system that begins with worldviews. The ideas proposed here paint creativity as not being domain-specific, and as not measurable by tangible creative outputs. The real transformation that takes place is internal. We believe that no other investment in education could be more important and potentially rewarding than encouraging this understanding and thus encouraging creative classrooms. By nurturing the skills and attributes characteristic of creative minds, education systems have the potential to cultivate the kinds of people that society needs.

Acknowledgments This work was supported by a grant (62R06523) from the Natural Sciences and Engineering Research Council of Canada.

References

Andreasen, N. C. (1987). Creativity and mental illness: Prevalence rates in writers and their first-degree relatives. *American Journal of Psychiatry, 144*, 1288–1292.

Bak, P., Tang, C., & Weisenfeld, K. (1988). Self-organized criticality. *Physical Review A, 38*, 364.

Beghetto, R. A. (2007). Ideational code-switching: Walking the talk about supporting student creativity in the classroom. *Roeper Review, 29*, 265–270.

Beghetto, R. A. (2013). *Killing ideas softly?: The promise and perils of creativity in the classroom.* Charlotte: Information Age Publishing.

Chrusch, C., & Gabora, L. (2014). A tentative role for FOXP2 in the evolution of dual processing modes and generative abilities. In P. Bello, M. Guarini, M. McShane, & B. Scassellati (Eds.), *Proceedings of 36th annual meeting of cognitive science society* (pp. 499–504). Austin: Cognitive Science Society.

Donald, M. (1991). *Origins of the modern mind: Three stages in the evolution of culture and cognition.* Cambridge, MA: Harvard University Press.

Edelman, G. (1987). *Neural Darwinism: The theory of neuronal group selection.* New York: Basic Books.

Eldridge, N., & Gould, S. J. (1972). Punctuated equilibria: An alternative to phyletic gradualism. In T. Schopf (Ed.), *Models in paleobiology* (pp. 82–115). New York: Freeman, Cooper &.

Ellamil, M., Dobson, C., Beeman, M., & Christoff, K. (2012). Evaluative and generative modes of thought during the creative process. *NeuroImage, 59*, 1783–1794.

Feinstein, J. S. (2006). *The nature of creative development.* Stanford: Stanford University Press.

Feist, G. J. (1998). A meta-analysis of personality in scientific and artistic creativity. *Personality and Social Psychology Review, 2*(4), 290–309.

Gabora, L. (1995). Meme and Variations: A computer model of cultural evolution. In L. Nadel & D. L. Stein (Eds.), *1993 lectures in complex systems* (pp. 471–486). Boston: Addison Wesley.

Gabora, L. (1997). The origin and evolution of culture and creativity. *Journal of Memetics: Evolutionary Models of Information Transmission, 1*(1). http://cfpm.org/jom-emit/1997/vol1/gabora_l.html

Gabora, L. (1998). Weaving, bending, patching, mending the fabric of reality: A cognitive science perspective on worldview inconsistency. *Foundations of Science, 3*(2), 395–428.

Gabora, L. (2003). Contextual focus: A cognitive explanation for the cultural transition of the middle/upper paleolithic. In R. Alterman & D. Hirsch (Eds.), *Proceedings of 25th annual meeting of cognitive science society* (pp. 432–437). Hillsdale: Lawrence Erlbaum Associates.

Gabora, L. (2004). Ideas are not replicators but minds are. *Biology and Philosophy, 19*(1), 127–143.

Gabora, L. (2006). Self-other organization: Why early life did not evolve through natural selection. *Journal of Theoretical Biology, 241*, 443–450.

Gabora, L. (2010). Revenge of the 'neurds': Characterizing creative thought in terms of the structure and dynamics of human memory. *Creativity Research Journal, 22*, 1–13.

Gabora, L. (2011). Five clarifications about cultural evolution. *Journal of Cognition and Culture, 11*, 61–83.

Gabora, L. (2013). An evolutionary framework for culture: Selectionism versus communal exchange. *Physics of Life Reviews, 10*(2), 117–145.

Gabora, L. (2017a). Honing theory: A complex systems framework for creativity. *Nonlinear Dynamics, Psychology, and Life Sciences, 21*(1), 35–88.

Gabora, L. (2017b, August 30). What creativity really is – and why schools need it. *The Conversation*. Retrieved from https://theconversation.com/what-creativity-really-is-and-why-schools-need-it-81889

Gabora, L. (2018). The neural basis and evolution of divergent and convergent thought. In O. Vartanian & R. Jung (Eds.), *The Cambridge handbook of the neuroscience of creativity*. Cambridge, MA: Cambridge University Press.

Gabora, L., & Merrifield, M. (2012). Dynamical disequilibrium, transformation, and the evolution and development of sustainable worldviews. In F. Orsucci & N. Sala (Eds.), *Complexity science, living systems, and reflexing interfaces* (pp. 69–77). Hershey: IGI Global.

Gabora, L., & Ranjan, A. (2013). How insight emerges in distributed, content-addressable memory. In A. Bristol, O. Vartanian, & J. Kaufman (Eds.), *The neuroscience of creativity* (pp. 19–43). Cambridge, MA: MIT Press.

Gabora, L., & Smith, C. (in press). Two cognitive transitions underlying the capacity for cultural evolution. Journal of Anthropological Sciences.

Gabora, L., & Tseng, S. (2017). The social benefits of balancing creativity and imitation: Evidence from an agent-based model. *Psychology of Aesthetics, Creativity, and the Arts, 11*(4), 457–473.

Gabora, L., Chia, W. W., & Firouzi, H. (2013). A computational model of two cognitive transitions underlying cultural evolution. In M. Knauff, M. Pauen, N. Sebanz, & I. Wachsmuth (Eds.), *Proceedings of 35th annual meeting of cognitive science society* (pp. 2344–2349). Austin: Cognitive Science Society.

Gick, M. L., & Lockhart, R. S. (1995). Creative insight and preventive forms. In R. J. Sternberg & J. E. Davidson (Eds.), *The nature of insight*. Cambridge: MIT Press.

Greenwald, A., Banaji, M., Rudman, L. A., Farnham, S., Nosek, B., & Mellott, D. (2002). A unified theory of implicit attitudes, stereotypes, self-esteem, and self-concept. *Psychological Review, 109*, 3–25.

Gregerson, M., Kaufman, J., & Snyder, H. (Eds.). (2013). *Teaching creatively and teaching creativity*. New York: Springer.

Guastello, S. J. (2002). *Managing emergent phenomena: Nonlinear dynamics in work organizations*. Mahwah: Lawrence Erlbaum Associates.

Hebb, D. (1949). *The organization of behavior*. New York: Wiley.

Hirsh, J., Mar, R., & Peterson, J. (2012). Psychological entropy: A framework for understanding uncertainty-related anxiety. *Psychological Review, 119*, 304–320.

Hordijk, W., Hein, J., & Steel, M. (2010). Autocatalytic sets and the origin of life. *Entropy, 12*, 1733–1742.

Jacobsen, J. J., & Guastello, S. J. (2011). Diffusion models for innovation: S-curves, networks, power laws, catastrophes, and entropy. *Nonlinear Dynamics, Psychology, and Life Sciences, 15*, 307–333.

Josselyn, S., et al. (2015). Finding the engram. *Nature Reviews Neuroscience, 16*(9), 521–534.

Kanerva, P. (1988). *Sparse distributed memory*. Cambridge: MIT Press.

Kauffman, S. (1993). *Origins of order*. New York: Oxford University Press.

Kitzbichler, M. G., Smith, M. L., Christensen, S. R., & Bullmore, E. (2009). Broadband criticality of human brain network synchronization. *PLoS Computational Biology, 5*, e1000314.

Kounios, J., & Beeman, M. (2009). The "Aha!" moment: The cognitive neuroscience of insight. *Current Directions in Psychological Science, 18*, 210–216.

Kounios, J., & Beeman, M. (2014). The cognitive neuroscience of insight. *Annual Review of Psychology, 65*, 71–93.

Mayer, R. E. (1995). The search for insight: Grappling with gestalt psychology's unanswered questions. In R. J. Sternberg & J. E. Davidson (Eds.), *The nature of insight*. Cambridge, MA: MIT Press.

McClelland, J. L. (2011). Memory as a constructive process: The parallel distributed processing approach. In S. Nalbantian, P. M. Matthews, J. L. McClelland, S. Nalbantian, P. M. Matthews, & J. L. McClelland (Eds.), *The memory process: Neuroscientific and humanistic perspectives* (pp. 129–155). Cambridge, MA: MIT Press.

McClelland, J. L., Rumelhart, D. E., & Hinton, G. E. (2003). Parallel distributed processing: Explorations in the microstructure of cognition. In M. P. Munger (Ed.), *The history of psychology: Fundamental questions* (pp. 478–492). New York: Oxford University Press.

Mithen, S. (1998). *Creativity in human evolution and prehistory*. London: Routledge.

Nelson, D. L., McEvoy, C. L., & Schreiber, T. A. (2004). The University of South Florida word association, rhyme and word fragment norms. *Behavior Research Methods, Instruments, & Computers, 36*, 408–420.

Orsucci, F. (2008). *Reflexing interfaces: The complex coevolution of information technology ecosystems*. Hershey: Idea Books.

Osgood, C. E., & Tannenbaum, P. H. (1955). The principle of congruity in the prediction of attitude change. *Psychological Review, 62*, 42–55.

Paterson, H. M., Kemp, R. I., & Forgas, J. P. (2009). Co-witnesses, confederates, and conformity: The effects of discussion and delay on eyewitness memory. *Psychiatry, Psychology and Law, 16*(1), S112–S124.

Pelaprat, E., & Cole, M. (2011). "Minding the gap": Imagination, creativity and human cognition. *Integrative Psychological and Behavioral Science, 45*(4), 397–418. https://doi.org/10.1007/s12124-011-9176-5.

Piaget, J. (2013). *The construction of reality in the child* (Vol. 82). London: Routledge.

Ranjan, A., & Gabora, L. (2012). Creative ideas for actualizing student potential. In H. Snyder, M. Gregerson, & J. Kaufman (Eds.), *Teaching creatively* (pp. 119–132). Berlin: Springer.

Salvi, C., Bricolo, E., Kounios, J., Bowden, E., & Beeman, M. (2016). Insight solutions are correct more often than analytic solutions. *Thinking & Reasoning, 22*, 443–460. https://doi.org/10.1080/13546783.2016.1141798.

Schacter, D. L. (2001). *The seven sins of memory: How the mind forgets and remembers*. Reading: Houghton Mifflin.

Stephen, D. G., Boncoddo, R. A., Magnuson, J. S., & Dixon, J. (2009). The dynamics of insight: Mathematical discovery as a phase transition. *Memory & Cognition, 37*, 1132–1149.

Steyvers, M., & Tenenbaum, J. B. (2005). The large-scale structure of semantic networks: Statistical analyses and a model of semantic growth. *Cognitive Science, 29*, 41–78.

Sutton, R. S. (1996). Generalization in reinforcement learning: Successful examples using sparse coarse coding. In *Advances in neural information processing systems* (pp. 1038–1044). Cambridge: MIT Press.

Topolinski, S., & Reber, R. (2010). Gaining insight into the "Aha" experience. *Current Directions in Psychological Science, 19*, 402–402.

Vetsigian, K., Woese, C., & Goldenfeld, N. (2006). Collective evolution and the genetic code. *Proceedings of the National Academy of Science, 103*, 10696–10701.

Ward, T., Smith, S., & Vaid, J. (1997). Conceptual structures and processes in creative thought. In T. Ward, S. Smith, & J. Vaid (Eds.), *Creative thought: An investigation of conceptual structures and processes* (pp. 1–27). Washington, DC: American Psychological Association.

Wilkenfeld, M. J., & Ward, T. B. (2001). Similarity and emergence in conceptual combination. *Journal of Memory and Cognition, 45*, 21–38.

Yoruk, S., & Runco, M. A. (2014). The neuroscience of divergent thinking. *Activitas Nervosa Superior, 56*, 1–16.

Chapter 8
Dynamic Creativity: Influential Theory, Public Discourse, and Generative Possibility

Carol A. Mullen

Abstract This conceptual essay introduces dynamic creativity, bridging with influential theory, public discourse, and generative possibility. The concept of dynamic creativity grows out of literature referring to dynamics of creativity—both educational and cultural. Creative rhetoric in public discourse is also taken up for its global reach and especially because it assigns internationally competitive and economic functions to creativity. Discussion moves to select influential creativity theories—Beghetto and Kaufman's 4-C Model of Creativity and Csikszentmihalyi's systems model of creativity. A creative synthesis is ventured of these theories, foregrounding their dynamic possibilities, with graphical representation. A fifth C—Hidden-c—extends the theorizing about creativity with particular reference to Corazza's theory of dynamic creativity while demonstrating dynamic creativity in a Chinese learning context. Illustrations of creativity reveal Canada and China's different ways of relating to the high-stakes testing ethos and pressure to dominate on the world stage as creative innovators. The role of adopter and shaper of creativity models informs the author's approach to this eclectic, layered work. Implications for continuing the conversation about dynamic creativity end this writing.

8.1 Introduction

How might dynamic creativity apply to influential theory, public discourse, and generative possibility? This speculative question—at the heart of this literature-informed conceptual essay—is itself a response to creativity researchers' call. To quote Beghetto (2016), "As our understanding of the phenomenon of creativity continues to grow, it is becoming more and more evident that researchers need new ways of conceptualizing, identifying and studying creativity in the midst of social practices" (p. 270). Tan (2013) also states, "The increasing interest in nurturing creativity

---

C. A. Mullen (✉)
Virginia Tech, Blacksburg, VA, USA
e-mail: camullen@vt.edu

around the world calls for a timely reflective analysis on knowledge of creativity and cultivating creativity" (p. 27). Adding to this dialogue, I consider dynamic creativity in relationship to influential creativity theories as well as public discourse.

To discover ways of seeing dynamic creativity that are educational and cultural in nature while identifying political overtones, I engage two highly recognized academic creativity theories: Kaufman and Beghetto (2009) 4-C Model of Creativity and Csikszentmihalyi's (1996, 1999) systems model of creativity. A fresh perspective is being attempted from the vantage point of dynamic creativity and a creative synthesis foregrounding generative possibilities. I also integrate into my theory-building the unique contribution of Corazza's (2016) theory of dynamic creativity for which my new idea of Hidden-c is being introduced.

Regarding public discourse about creativity, I wonder, how do entities outside academia take up the topic of creativity? What educational and cultural meanings of creativity does nonacademic public discourse generate, support, and circulate?

8.2 Literature Review Methods

This writing's conceptual methodology aims to identify, discuss, and conceptualize select scholarship of contemporary influence in the area of creativity. Another goal is to examine how creativity might be viewed within the public discourse sampled.

8.2.1 Identifying Creativity Scholarship as Primary Purpose

Sought in the published canon were scholars' creativity theories in psychology and education. Methodological support for theory building particularly came from Kaufman and Beghetto's (2009) and Csikszentmihalyi's (1996) creativity models. A synthesis of these frameworks is displayed, with discussion of possible overlap and interplay.

Another step involved reviewing the academic literature on creativity in high-impact journals and (hand)books spanning 1996 to 2017. Cambridge University Press and Springer are among the sponsoring publishers. Online databases searched included the full text holdings of publishers and my home university's library. ERIC from WorldCat and Education Research Complete from EBSCOhost yielded relevant articles from academic journals and pertinent books. Documents were also accessed via Google Scholar.

Discourse about creativity appeared in diverse sources: academic journals devoted to the topic of creativity (e.g., *Creativity Research Journal*), book series (e.g., Creativity Theory and Action in Education, published by Springer), and edited books (e.g., Kaufman and Sternberg 2010). Within these parameters, influential theoretical and empirical sources were located using the search term *creativity* in association with *culture*, *education*, *educational psychology*, and *theory*.

Inan earlier literature review of creativity frameworks (Mullen 2017a; current to 2016), I found that educational psychology was particularly well represented among the academic disciplines as a prolific contributor to the creativity paradigm. Moreover, educational psychology is multidisciplinary and transdisciplinary (as opposed to insular) in both the conception and treatment of creativity. About disciplinary border crossing, Tan (2013) confirms, "There have been efforts to explore new paradigms of creativity" (p. 27). Csikszentmihalyi (1996) describes creativity itself as "crossing the boundaries of domains" (p. 9)—boundary crossing is what many creativity researchers do.

Relevant are the pedagogically-oriented research questions from my completed study (Mullen 2017a). To paraphrase, what examples of Mini-c, Little-c, Pro-C, and Big-C might Chinese students identify when prompted? What types of experiences might test-weary students have from being exposed to open-ended creativity?

I found the select creativity frameworks to be amenable to the creative development of Chinese preservice teachers (as illustrated later). Crossing the disciplinary boundary as such into teacher education is not new for educational psychologists. Border crossing has created forays into early childhood education (Craft et al. 2012a, b), cultural studies (e.g., Sternberg 2006), systems thinking/science and sociology (Csikszentmihalyi 1996, 1999), and more. Thus, *educational psychology* served as a baseline descriptor for searching databases and taking my analysis into other disciplines.

Reviewing the creativity research, I settled on four criteria arising from evidence pointing to the salience of Kaufman and Beghetto's (2009) and Csikszentmihalyi's (1996) models.

1. Communities of creativity researchers worldwide cite and describe the recognized theory, using it as point of reference for contributing to the conversation about creativity within the field (e.g., Neber and Neuhaus 2013).
2. The recognized theory advances the author's knowledge building about creativity, such as by using systems theory (e.g., Tan 2013).
3. Application to pedagogical and learning contexts extends the recognized theory's influence and value in such areas as the nurturing of creativity within classrooms subjected to high-stakes testing (Collard and Looney 2014).
4. The recognized theory is central to the ongoing debate around complexities involved in the individual creator's (creative self) relationship to, and interplay with, impactful cultural and environmental forces (e.g., Glăveanu and Tanggaard 2014).

To clarify, creativity researchers have described, analyzed, applied, or in some other way highlighted and thereby validated these select theories. Thus, I give weighted attention to Kaufman and Beghetto's and Csikszentmihalyi's creativity theories as recognized by experts.

8.2.2 Targeting Public Discourse as Secondary Purpose

Methodological follow-through pertained to how entities (e.g., governments) conceptualize creativity, and to what end and in what contexts. An a priori assumption is that powerful bodies potentially influence society, with implications for change within academies around the study of creativity. Within the public sphere, to uncover trends with embedded perspectives on creativity, I followed the steps already outlined. Google searches used the descriptor *creativity* in association with *business, corporation, culture, economics, education, global, government,* and *international*. Reports from nonacademic entities and news stories from the global press resulted; current and informative information was selected for commentary.

8.3 Definitions of Key Terms and Concepts

Creativity, culture, and systems all constitute complex, changing domains of knowledge in academia. Numerous definitions and multiple conceptualizations exist. As conceived for this writing, each is anchored to the concept of dynamic creativity.

8.3.1 Creativity

Creativity refers to generating something new and valuable that is tangible (e.g., an invention or literary work) or intangible (e.g., an idea or theory) (Mumford 2003). It encompasses the collaborative process of arriving at creative (re)solutions to complex problems and performances, for example (Sawyer 2012). In such group situations, the "collective social product" cannot be attributed to individual contributors (Sawyer, p. 67). Original work and transformation of thoughts or things into something not preexisting is a dynamic creative process as is the recreation or reinvention of that which exists. Knowledge building can also be creative (Tan 2013), as can applying knowledge in practical pedagogic contexts (Beghetto 2006) and thoughtfully appraising knowledge (Robinson 2015). Open-ended questions invoke creativity, and complex problem identification and problem-solving enhance it. These approaches to creativity contrast with constraints in such forms as problems already posed through direct instruction and testing (Eisner 2004) and autocratic leadership and leading (Sawyer 2012).

8.3.2 Culture

Culture is the "act of developing the intellectual and moral faculties especially by education," as well as the "pattern of human knowledge, belief, and behavior that [relies on] the capacity for learning and transmitting knowledge to succeeding generations" ("Culture" 2017). Besides educational value, the arts, creativity, and other self-expressions are collectively regarded as integral to culture. Culture takes into account "the totality of a person's learned, accumulated experience" (Zimmermann 2015).

To have cultural impact, a creative idea "must be included in the cultural domain to which it belongs" (Csikszentmihalyi 1996, p. 27). Influential creative works can come from radically different cultures and worldviews (Kaufman and Beghetto 2009), supporting the claim that dynamic creativity occurs worldwide.

8.3.3 Systems

Systems thinking, a highly influential way of framing creativity, recognizes that creative processes are emergent. Sawyer (2012) attributes to Csikszentmihalyi (1988), albeit not exclusively, the development of the systems model for which analysts of creativity seek to explain the micro (creative individual's psychology) and macro (social system) interrelationship. Keller-Mathers and Murdock (1999) similarly describe Csikszentmihalyi's (1996) systems approach to creativity theory. They reason that creators must navigate a system (e.g., organization, field, domain, culture, community, etc.) and its levels and domains to succeed. Sawyer sees the navigational process as a creative collaborative phenomenon involving social groups. Expertise allows one to progress through these levels, coming to understand how to create novelty and hopefully contribute to the targeted domain of shared knowledge (Csikszentmihalyi 1988, 1996, 1999).

Viewing creativity as a system, as Csikszentmihalyi (1988, 1996, 1999) does, recognizes "interrelated forces operating at multiple levels" (Hennessey 2013, p. viii). Moreover, "an individual is regarded as a system" with psychological and other "subsystems" that have "to function well to regulate efficiently" (pp. 30–31). Evocatively, Tan (2013) also states that attempts to cultivate creativity "can assimilate strengths of [ecological and other] life systems" (p. 30).

8.3.4 Dynamic Creativity

To present a working definition of *dynamic creativity*, I borrow from key sources that resonate with my intended meanings: Corazza's (2016) notion of dynamic creativity as a phenomenon that extends well beyond "static creative achievement" (p. 261) and Glăveanu and Tanggaard's (2014) description of creative identity as always changing, making identity a protean reality and generative process. *Dynamic creativity*, then, refers to creativity that has "inconclusive outcomes" for people engaging in, and persisting with, creativity, according to Corazza who explains,

> The fundamental element that should be at the core of the definition of creativity is … the search for potential originality and effectiveness, much before any attribution of creative achievement (or inconclusiveness) has materialized. This is extremely important both to reflect the overall experiential evidence of the phenomenon … and to effectively educate new innovators in their approach to the process… (p. 261)

Dynamic's etymology comes from ancient Greek to denote power/full and able ("Dynamic" 2017). Complex, dynamic interplays among individuals, systems, and cultures stimulate change or progress within a system ("Dynamic" 2017). Conceived dynamically, creativity involves constant activity, change, or progress. Intrinsic to the dynamic process of creativity and outcomes are "subjectivity and the imagination," which can incite greater disagreement among stakeholders (e.g., experts) where original outcomes question or especially violate norms and paradigms (Corazza 2016, p. 262).

In contrast, *stasis* blocks action and progress. Connoting stasis are narrow definitions of creativity that focus on successful outcomes and productivity in the realm of creative achievement, in effect shortchanging a multitude of dynamics involved in creators' generative process (e.g., "search[ing] original ideas" and "explor[ing] multiple alternatives") (Corazza 2016, p. 261). From this perspective, complexities and unknowns are integral to the process of being actively engaged and should thus be recognized as having creative value. A richer definition of creativity incorporates the word "potential" in the standard definition: "Creativity requires potential originality and effectiveness" (Corazza, p. 262). The inclusion of this one word (potential) arguably invokes a different perspective—creativity's dynamism depends upon exploration and involves uncertainty and indetermination in the process.

Instead, complexities and unknowns of creativity are reduced to several factors and components ("Stasis" 2017). A less dichotomized, more nuanced possibility is that human dynamics can emerge from systems that themselves are stable, as in motionless yet paradoxically perpetuating tradition or the status quo ("Stasis" 2017). In fact, "Disequilibrium may spur creative processes," given a study finding that "learners (including teachers) were most likely to benefit from creative processes that addressed significant problems or … that challenged their previous conceptions" (Collard and Looney 2014, p. 350).

Dynamic creativity depends on an attitude of possibility. Craft (e.g., Craft et al. 2012a) has long described creativity as possibility thinking, driven by "what-if" formulations. She even forwarded possibility thinking as an evidence-based concept driving creativity. With everyone being capable of questioning and imagining, as children do through "self-initiated play" (Craft et al. 2012b), this is a creative breakthrough that may effect change within systems.

From the life science discipline, systems theorist Wheatley (1992) also asserts that a "what-if" mindset disrupts a "fix-it" mentality. To her, the possibility attitude is a catalyst for change and renewal of organizational systems. If possibility is conducive to change, as Ferdig and Ludema (2005) also contend, then it stands to reason that generative possibility fuels the existence of dynamic creativity.

8.4 Creativity Within Public Discourse

The context-setting question for this section is, what creativity terms or expressions are used in the public discourse of governments, corporations, and sponsored individuals and bodies (collectively conceived as *entities*)? A related query probes dominant lenses and any patterns that may be discernible. A guiding question is how outside-in influential sources (i.e., analogously, the neighborhood) conceptualize, describe, and potentially shape the modern age and what is possible. The descriptors that follow overlap to some extent, as do the examples; for the sake of clarification, I make differentiations.

8.4.1 Modern Creativity Era

Modern creativity era or *creativity era* is implied in many contemporary sources, as in: "We've entered a new era. Call it the age of … creativity … Creativity, mental flexibility, and collaboration have displaced one-dimensional intelligence" (Hunter 2013, p. 6). Here, the words *creativity* and *era* (as well as *age*) are both used, even though *era* is not a moniker per se.

Erupting into being 6 decades ago, *modern creativity era* is popular in the public discourse (see Cropley and Cropley 2010). The year 1957 turned out to be historic for the United States, with the former Soviet Union's launching of *Sputnik*, the first artificial Earth satellite. Following this cultural jolt for American society, global competitiveness escalated, placing a premium on innovation. However, interest was uppermost in "functional creativity"—practical developments and machines (products), many designed for wartime use (Cropley and Cropley 2010).

Consequently, the value of tangible, concrete products of creativity has likely cast creativity's entanglements with innovation and invention. On the one hand, for thinkers like curriculum theorist Schwab (2004), *creativity* is interchangeable with *innovation* and *invention*: "Creativity implies some measure of invention" (p. 114). On the other hand, Hunter (2013) is among those who distinguish creativity from these other types: *Creativity* is the "capability/act of conceiving something original or unusual," *innovation* is the "implementation of something new," and *invention* is the "creation of something that has never been made before" (p. 9). An implication is that creativity has a lesser purpose and status, in effect only serving as the catalyst for innovations and inventions.

Alternatively, Tan (2013) describes something other than a creativity-innovation-invention hierarchy. Conceived as a continuum relative to its dynamic role, creativity "includes actions and interactions that lead to human development, innovations, civilizations, inventions, breakthroughs, discoveries, revolutions, and evolutions" (p. 28). Specifically, creativity can be a discovery or adaptation: "*Breakthrough* creativity" involves the "search for new ideas," whereas "*adaptive* creativity is the result of responding creatively to breakthroughs [such as] to transform them for applications in everyday life" (p. 28; italics are in the original). Further, "discovery, invention, and innovation in varying degrees are related to creativity" (p. 28).

Perhaps having inspired such conceptualizations, Bandura (1997) affirms creativity and its relationship to innovation. He asserts that "creativity constitutes one of the highest forms of human expression," subtly differentiating it from innovation while casting it as somehow integral to creativity. To further quote, "Innovativeness largely involves restructuring and synthesizing knowledge into new ways of thinking and of doing things," which importantly depends on "cognitive facility [in the exploration of] novel ideas and search for new knowledge" (p. 239).

8.4.2 Knowledge Economy/Era

Yet another framing of modern civilization is *knowledge economy*. Boily et al. (2014) see this descriptor as belonging to the past: "Just as the knowledge economy shaped economic development through the second half of the 20th century, the creative economy has become a dominant force in today's world economy" (p. 12).

Nonetheless, *knowledge economy* (and the variations *knowledge-based, global economy* and *knowledge civilization age*) also describes the twenty-first century. This surpasses the descriptor *modern creativity era* but not *creative economy*, likely the more popular coinage.

Knowledge economy got its start as a descriptive term around 1980, when economic pressures demanded knowledge of creativity and innovation. As Wierzbicki and Nakamori (2006) explain, emergent understandings of the world (e.g., dynamic and chaotic) targeted qualitative explorations of "new properties of complex systems" (p. 12). Before 1980, creativity was more associated with a quantitative mindset. Compartmentalizing creativity's properties as knowable, predictable, and organized was the norm. Fallout from a positivistic worldview of creativity in the knowledge economy could driven Tan's (2013) decision to make a creative contribution by "examin[ing] the existence of creativity," not only its "presence" (p. 27).

8.4.3 Global Economy/Era

More popular than the knowledge economy/era usage is *global era*, described as a process of globalization. Historian Hunt (2014) explains that the global age expressed a new perception of the world, owing to the spread of the Internet in the 1990s. However, she points out that this view of contemporary life in and across societies is debatable. For, to some academicians, globalization has been a historical development from the beginning of time, whereas for others it resulted from European discoveries and conquests. The debate over *globalization* hints at complexity.

Globally important, creativity is typically seen as a catalyst for innovation and invention. Nations fixate on economic prosperity, assuming that "innovation is a key driver of productivity" (Boily et al. 2014, p. 1). However, dynamics of cultural tolerance in service of creative productivity and ultimately global competitiveness are rarely acknowledged, except in passing, as in: "Cultural diversity is an important driver of the creative economy [that] contributes to our national competitiveness…. Canada is … a culturally diverse, prosperous society [of] newcomers from over 200 countries (Conference Board of Canada 2008, p. 2).

Three national priorities for countries around the globe—competitiveness, creativity, and tolerance—may appear unrelated or contradictory. Sources favor one of these perspectives to arrive at a dynamic understanding of creativity. For example, linking creative and innovative production only to global competitiveness, Canadian reports claim a national crisis over being "in the bottom quartile for innovation" … and behind "competitors in innovation and productivity" (Boily et al. 2014, p. 1). Despite 30 years of "public polic[ies] and incentive programs," Canada's productivity growth is 20% less than the United States' (Boily et al. p. 1).

Yet competitiveness, creativity, and tolerance are interrelated dynamics of creativity. One way of unpacking tolerance is to think of Canada's increasing capacity for global competitiveness as having occurred *despite* its tolerance of cultural diversity. Another way of considering this notion is to think of the spike in education competitiveness, leading to its newly bestowed title of "education superpower," as largely *owing to Canada's capacity for tolerance.* Canada has the ability to turn tolerance into socioeconomic capital, without draining resources.

To explain, some of Canada's international test-takers were migrant teenagers, many from the Asia Pacific (BBC 2017). Yet it was reported that these migrant children "seem to integrate rapidly enough to perform at the same high level as their classmates" (pp. 1–2). Accountability officials and education professors alike have asserted that "Canada's 'big uniting theme is equity,'" and despite provincial policy differences, "there is a common commitment to an equal chance in school" (p. 2). The "narrow socio-economic gap in school results" (p. 2) means that Canada "does not have a tail of underachievement, often related to poverty" (p. 3). High immigration levels are integral to Canada's "success story" (p. 3).

In the global economy/era, it may not be enough to aim for tolerance, given that cultural diversity can be tolerated or actively accepted (Jacobs 2006). Understanding that crucial differences exist among tolerance, acceptance, and active acceptance could influence how nations and schools approach creativity. Moreover, might creativity be imagined as an axis, such as tolerant–globally uncompetitive (Canada's former global status), tolerant–globally competitive (Canada's current global status), and intolerant–globally competitive (some other countries)?

An attitude of receptivity enables Canada to shine as a diversity powerhouse alongside Asian and Nordic populations on the high-stakes international tests (BBC 2017). While Canadian journalist sources and, importantly, some political leaders document these changes, many Canadian officials and sponsored entities (such as Boily et al. 2014) overlook the crucial role of cultural tolerance in creativity for aiding global competitiveness and national prosperity.

8.4.4 Creative Economy

Creative economy is probably the most widespread usage. Corporations and governments across nations increasingly favor creative economy, as inferred from sources consulted (World Economic Forum 2013). Regarding the word choice of *economy* instead of *era* to describe contemporary life on this planet, a movement may be afoot to use the creativity descriptor to politicize and commodify the economy, given that *creativity* is paired with *economy* in the public discourse. Creativity—tied to labor markets and creative industries (e.g., arts)—conjures a picture of creativity's role (and burden?) of ensuring world economies' vigor, wealth, and value (Boily et al. 2014; Ibbitson 2014; Johnson 2010).

Beyond diversity, another major creativity trend is urbanization. Creative productivity apparently increases when residents live among other creative city dwellers in places where creativity and innovation flourish; in fact, bustling cities are three times as creative as towns (Johnson 2010). Diversity and urbanization work hand-in-glove considering that greater cultural diversity occurs with access to multicultural capital.

Canada has long broadcast that the creative economy is a "dominant force in today's world economy" (Boily et al. 2014, p. 1). Its historic breakthrough in international testing in 2017 (BBC 2017) was preceded by the priority placed on economic success. Creativity was widely identified as the means to this end: "Addressing creativity in Canada will require a shift in culture," and "the creativity challenge requires appropriate incubation and tolerant and flexible environments" (p. 12). Asserted in this Canadian report is that "creative minds" must be "incubate[d]" so they "can thrive," with the demand for new jobs.

Canada's "greatest resource" is "its people" is a refrain in many sources (e.g., Boily et al. 2014). A strategy called for was the rewriting of innovation policies and "high-impact federal initiatives that could work to unite business leaders, academics and artists in building a more competitive and creative Canada" (Boily et al., p. 1). Concerned with economic prosperity, policymakers apparently "lookbeyond traditional economic metrics to include the importance of the development of people's creative potential" (Boily et al., p. 2). Acknowledged is the intangible type of creativity whereby citizens collaborate on new ideas leading to the design of creative products, albeit to ensure national economic prosperity.

Consider the creative dynamics involved in Canada's world standing. In a state of flux, just 3 years after much self-blaming as a tolerant–globally uncompetitive nation, in 2017 its global education status dramatically changed. Canada "climbed into the top tier of international rankings" on the Programme for International Student Assessment tests, "one of a handful of countries to appear in the top 10 for math, science, and reading" (BBC 2017). Racial tolerance remains a quintessential aspect of Canada's national identity, having long been its strong suit: "No country brings in as many immigrants…. In Canada, [each of the] national parties claims to be more pro-immigrant than the other[s]" (Ibbitson 2014).

Sexual tolerance has also made its mark in a nation where multiculturalism is the ultimate claim of creative achievement: "Our tolerance goes beyond race. Not only was Canada among the first countries to legalize gay marriage, Ontario [has] elected Canada's first lesbian minister" (Ibbitson 2014). Canadian sources reveal some honesty about the historic struggle with cultural diversity around Canada's tragic human rights abuses of its Indigenous community and other ethnic groups (Saul 2008).

Thus, hardship is entailed in becoming culturally tolerant and accepting. In current times, Canada accepts droves of migrants and refugees appearing at its borders despite backlash from Canadian anti-immigrationists whose intolerance is being largely attributed to U.S. President Trump's depictions of "outsiders as a frightening threat" (Ball 2016). Beyond Canada's overall diversity mindset, the positive economic impact of immigrants on economic growth helps explain the receptivity to outsiders (Ibbitson 2014).

Turning a problem into a solution, Canada is constantly re-creating itself. Creative products arising out of its culturally diverse identity include less tangible creativity through "restorative" (rather than "punitive") justice. This was "inspired by First Nations practices … used in Canadian justice systems now for over forty years" (Johnston and Jenkins 2017, pp. 1–2). For example, "innovative expression in memorials [honors] a growing Indigenous assertion of identity, spirituality, activism, and loss" (pp. 1–2). Besides these memorials, tangible creative production extends to the "new sustainable communities" that "address critical housing inadequacies … based on legacy Intuit knowledge of changing climate and respect for the unique traditions of community" (pp. 1–2). The making and remaking of cultural creative identity in Canada vividly illustrates dynamic creativity on a historic and modern day scale (Glăveanu and Tanggaard 2014).

In the creativity era, a question worth posing is, have we truly shifted from the knowledge-based era to embrace more fully creativity? Within many globally competitive cultures (e.g., China and the United States), teachers and learners reportedly suffer from testing circumstances and stifling pedagogies. High-stakes accountability cultures neglect opportunities to exercise the imagination and creative capacity (Mullen 2017a, b). Imitation and literal comprehension, competencies valued in the nineteenth-century, cannot advance global education (World Economic Forum 2013). As Zhao (2014) attests, even the best schools are not usually working with the global competencies of creativity and entrepreneurship. Global-ready graduates should be able to creatively generate meaning, problem-solve, actively reflect, produce collaboratively, and work collectively.

8.5 Select Creativity Theories in Psychology

Here I address influential academic theories that inform dynamic perspectives on creativity. The literature and Internet searches revealed a frequency of citations to Kaufman and Beghetto's (2009) 4-C creativity model and Csikszentmihalyi's (1996, 1999) systems creativity model. Moreover, peer scholars describe these Western theories, solidifying their value and influence. The select models have even guided study of creative pedagogies in international educational settings (e.g., Mullen 2017a, b, 2018).

8.5.1 Four C Model

The 4-C model (Beghetto and Kaufman 2007; Kaufman and Beghetto 2009) has four forms/levels/types of creativity: "Mini-c" is novel and personally meaningful experiences, "Little-c" is everyday problem-solving in work and life, "Pro-C" is a category belonging to creative professionals (not famous), and "Big-C" is creativity of great magnitude reserved for famous works. Creative are personal meaning-making, problem-solving, professional value, and cultural innovation.

8.5.1.1 Mini-c

Mini-c feeds professional creativity and other types that would not otherwise come into being. As Eisner (2004) describes, meaning-making is itself an aesthetic process, neglected because it is elusive and challenging. Creative beings do not just *have* experiences—we make meaning of them. Communicating our discoveries, we enliven Mini-c's capacities by attributing meaning to our experiences of events and dynamics (Eisner 1991). We creatively render these these using images, schemas, and more. Artists have long "convey[ed] their visions in new technologies such as cinema [and] virtual realities," writes Gardner (2011, p. 65), endorsing creativity in the form of digital self-expression.

8.5.1.2 Little-c

Humans constantly encounter problems to be solved or resolved. Many simply react to problems rather than anticipating them, which arguably takes a greater creative capacity. We creatively use physical or digital objects and tools without much thought about our own artistry. In everyday problem-solving, creativity has endless possibilities—even the word *problem* is multifaceted. When we puzzle over something, we are trying to solve a problem. And when we make inferences and decisions and arrive at a solution or judgment, we might very well be creatively problem-solving. A creative person might ask, What does *problem* mean in this context? What is the nature of this problem that I am *anticipating*? (Schwab 2004)

8.5.1.3 Pro-C

Pro-C professional creativity recognizes highly accomplished creativity. Kaufman and Beghetto (2009) added it to their 2007 model, reintroducing it in 2009 as the Four Cs of Creativity. Such distinguished contributions move a discipline in a new direction or even completely change it. Pro-C contributions vary widely, from replication or improvement of pre-existing products to "reiniation," where "[creators try] to move the field to a new (as-yet-unreached) starting point and then progress from there" (p. 6).

Likely, leading creative professionals who study unsystematic, difficult problems beat others to them, not sticking with problems already evident in the field or domain. Schwab's (2004) takes is that complex problems demand "anticipatory consideration." The "eye" of pro-C individuals, he states, is illuminated "by possible fresh solutions to problems, new modes of attack, and new recognitions of degrees of freedom for change [to occur]"; they don't miss the "novel features of new problems" (pp. 114–115). Attraction to novelty and originality as meaning makers and problem solvers can lead to recognized creative breakthroughs. Creative risk-takers, Pro-C creators use, disrupt, and remake structures of knowledge, what Csikszentmihalyi (1996) refers to as the rules and procedures (symbolic knowledge) of a field or domain.

8.5.1.4 Big-c

Big-C's famous works of human creative achievement transform societies, even the world. Dewey (1934) believes that when artwork becomes Big-C by "attain[ing] classic status, it somehow becomes isolated from the human conditions under which it was brought into being and from the human consequences it engenders in actual life-experience" (p. 3). Everyday conditions and influences (e.g., activities) that imaginatively inform aspects of life should count as part of the cultural treasury. Such story lines are intrinsic to the aesthetics of art-making and the art of making things.

Creativity researchers building on the 4-C creativity model acknowledge that while "extraordinary accomplishments" (in science, art, technology, etc.) are eminent, Big-C's breakthroughs come from "myriads of Little-c creativity accomplishments" (Stoeger 2003, p. 3). "Numerous creative learning decisions" are involved as we set goals, deal with obstacles, and become more efficient with learning (p. 3).

8.5.2 Csikszentmihalyi's Systems Theory

Csikszentmihalyi (1996) illustrates his creativity framework using science, specifically astrology, to depict conditions and influences for creative discovery as well as breakthrough. Pertinent across disciplines, his theory demystifies falsehoods associated with creators and their lifeworld. The take on creativity conveys "interaction among domain, field, and person" (p. 29) as the source of creativity, not just an individual.

This position contradicts the assumption that creativity occurs "inside people's heads," as "some sort of mental activity" belonging to "special people" (Csikszentmihalyi 1996, p. 23). Instead, creativity is "a systematic rather than an individual performance" (p. 23), meaning that while someone may stake a claim in a creative act, there is no way to judge it without reference to standards and a social process of evaluation belonging to a domain (academic or professional livelihood).

A creative idea does not change a domain or field in social isolation; to manifest, others must understand it, "it must pass muster with the experts," and "it must be included in the cultural domain to which it belongs" (Csikszentmihalyi 1996, p. 27). Creativity, "observed only in the interrelations of a system" (p. 27), is a systems model situating the creator within a dynamic ethos of field and domain.

8.5.2.1 Systems Model of Creativity

Csikszentmihalyi's (1996) systems model of creativity encompasses three levels:

1. *Domain* (macro) "consists of a set of symbolic rules and procedures" that are "nested in … culture, or the symbolic knowledge shared by a particular society, or by humanity."
2. *Field* (next level of macro) includes "gatekeepers to the domain [whose] job is to decide whether a new idea or product should be included in the domain."
3. *Person* (micro) "has a new idea or sees a new pattern" that "use[s] the symbols of a given domain" (e.g., engineering), and "this novelty is selected … for inclusion." (pp. 27–28)

(For graphical depictions of Csikszentmihalyi's systems model, see Kahl and Hansen 2015.)

8.5.2.2 Systems Model Illustrations

From interviews with 91 exceptional contributors of knowledge to their domain, Csikszentmihalyi (1996) validates his suppositions. The vignette of an astronomer enlivens his creativity interaction model; her Pro-C discovery was that a galaxy's stars do not always rotate in the same direction. While she had shown herself to be creative, domain experts would have to decide whether to corroborate her accomplishment. Validation did result. Her work was funded and discovery published, and her finding was admitted into astronomy's canon. At the macro level, a complicated, long-term interaction would have transpired, allowing the creator's work to become known and possibly have impact.

Of course, within a knowledge domain, external factors can significantly affect an outcome. Hurdles range from an organization's cultural dynamics, a nation's politics, a domain's prohibitive structures, and an individual's circumstances. For example, a domain may not appreciate a creator's discovery or see it as such. Yet, despite barriers, a known creation may still result.

8.5.2.3 Select Theories' Generative Possibilities

Kaufman and Beghetto (2009) recognize the value of Csikszentmihalyi's (1996) systems creativity model. They confirm their predecessor's idea of creativity as an interaction among person, domain, and field, concurring that creativity's synergies extend well beyond a person's idea or work. Regardless, they assert the importance of "person" as creativity's primary source.

For Csikszentmihalyi (1996), because the creator is de-emphasized, shaping forces (i.e., field and domain) that impact one's creative capacities come to the fore—hypothetically, all of the synergies that influence success are exposed. Hence, the creative person is but one of multiple energetic forces at play within a complex web. However, the literature suggests that the creative person is at the center of creative processes, with minimal attention on context. For Kaufman and Beghetto, like Csikszentmihalyi, creator and environment interactively influence creative processes and outcomes. Differing it seems is the perspective as to which force predominantly influences the creative sphere—creator (Kaufman and Beghetto) or milieu (Csikszentmihalyi), with the ever-present influence of context flagged within these creativity paradigms.

While these models are not polar opposites, as Fig. 8.1 may suggest, their emphasis differs regarding human creativity and influences from the milieu. Thus, evident in Kaufman and Beghetto's (2009) explanation, external forces are still highly influential within this worldview. However, due credit is given to the seeds of generativity (i.e., Mini-c and Little-c) for formulating ideas, making gains, and experiencing breakthroughs. In my own theory-building, the two psychology frames intersect not in perfect harmony but more as complementary perspectives on creativity, which I have extended with the notion of an overlap. A new type of creativity ("Hidden-c") is discussed later.

However, societies have a bias toward "eminent creativity" (Kaufman and Beghetto 2009, p. 1), favoring cultural icons. This lopsided view may help to explain why "the quality of creative products in schools" do not attract much attention and lack "clear reference standards" and why creativity goes without a common definition in education policy and curricula (Collard and Looney 2014, pp. 3, 351).

Worth noting, efforts to raise awareness of creativity that are *not* about Big-C famous works but rather everyday life also has a history (see Dewey 1934). Of continuing deep interest, then, is the near invisible, barely detectable Mini-c and Little-c creative processes (Beghetto 2006).

8.6 Systems Theory and Life Systems

An ecological take on creativity is that all sectors of society (e.g., schools) are life systems subject to change and growth. Adaptation to changing demographics and global trends is paramount if these are to thrive, innovate, and lead (Wheatley 2017). Creative thinking, critical thinking, and problem solving are capacities for success

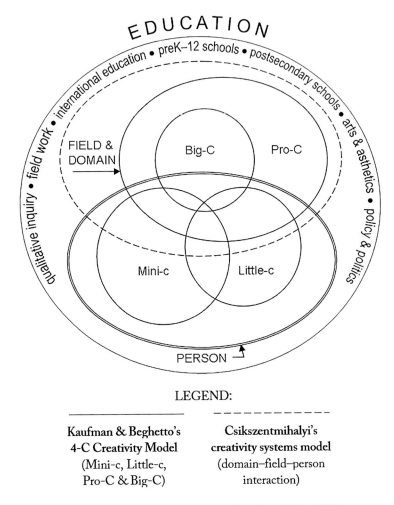

Fig. 8.1 A synthesis of select models of creativity for education. (Mullen 2017a)

in innovative, globalized economies (Heyl 2014). Rigid dispositions, customary patterns, and the status quo do not serve innovation and adaptation (Bandura 1997), yet the struggle to survive is not without politics. "Survival of the fittest" is how Li and Gerstl-Pepin (2014) describe the rhetoric of economic innovation and revitalization dispossessed of creative vision.

In the creative economy, transforming nations and their subsystems (e.g., institutions) seek to provoke a level of instability, not stabilize equilibrium. Such creative behavior disrupts the existing state of affairs, allowing for new and complex learning (Wheatley 1992). Being innovative and creative as a growing, adapting system necessitates "self-organizing interaction" (Stacey 1992) and a "transformative interactive" among peers (Ferdig and Ludema 2005). This kind of work and relationship crosses organizational, disciplinary, and other borders. Team members creatively cross boundaries as they interact and combine elements from different contexts to generate the new and unfamiliar (Akkerman and Bakker 2011; Mullen 2017a).

In changing work environments, creativity is a condition of innovation and a crucial component of organizational excellence. In such life systems, transformation is not readily subjected to one person's vision (Stacey 1992). Any powerful entity is not the sole proprietor of creative vision. Perhaps this is why Akkerman and Bakker (2011) identify innovation in teamwork and creativity of organizational collaborators as influencers of expert performance and organizational excellence. Importantly, in disequilibrium, the collective (e.g., activist communities) and influential sectors of society (e.g., tech-savvy youth) enact vision that may conjure exciting (or dangerous) possibilities for creativity.

Alive with possibility, living systems interact with their environment through the flow of ideas, energies, and data. Living systems—cells, organisms, groups, organizations, and societies—survive by forming, adapting, sustaining, and, importantly, even reinventing themselves in relation to systems (Wheatley 1992). Like other living things, the system (e.g., organization) has a personality, values, and structures, in addition to interactive patterns and internal practices (Brown and Moffett 1999). People's micro movements (re)create systems; as such, every exchange and action might help with conceiving or executing creative processes.

Beyond dialogue and action, renewal of a system depends on an attitude of possibility. Wheatley (1992) agrees that a spirit of possibility supports change (Ferdig and Ludema 2005). Human-centric conceptualizations can generate momentum for inquiry and change, no matter how uncertain. Life itself is dynamic, unlike an organizational chart's static representation of life systems (Wheatley and Kellner-Rogers 1996). To Wheatley (1992), life forces are fluctuations; like those in the universe, these are the "primary source of creativity" creating disturbances and imbalances (p. 20): "Every organization is an identity in motion, moving through the world, trying to make a difference" (Wheatley and Kellner-Rogers, p. 58). Viewing the world as a living organism (rather than a machine) is a lesson taken from Wheatley's (2017) new life science model—systems as organisms are unstable, unpredictable, uncertain, and yet identifiable. Dynamic creativity feeds off such dynamics.

Systems flourish when regenerated and reinvented (Brown and Moffett 1999). Within such institutions, structures, practices, programs, and policies are attuned culturally and globally. With systems aging, vitality, flexibility, and fluidity diminish, as does "capacity" for "meet[ing] challenges from unexpected directions" (Gardner 1963, p. 3). Holding onto worn-out ways of thinking and behaving may be preferred. But, as Heyl (2014) explains, "a world of distributed learning" confronts "the short shelf life of knowledge" (p. 254).

In a dynamically creative world, power hierarchies give way to new patterns of interaction, collaboration, interdisciplinary, and cross-cultural work. A driving question is how best to revitalize aging, outdated organizations to meet 21st century demands of increasing diversity in school populations. Mature civilizations and their sectors and organizations retool in fundamental ways, such as through diverse strategic alliances. Growth is thriving, functions are team supported, and vibrancy is perceptible.

8.6.1 Culture Frame

Creativity within high-stakes testing cultures is a challenge to foster within stymied life systems (Zhao 2014). Creative expression and innovative in such schooling contexts, spanning the West and the East, is a struggle to cultivate. A pedagogic problem is "teachers' desire to avoid discouraging learners' self-expression" by giving "little guidance" to learners "on how they might improve or deepen their work." Consequently, "Neither teachers nor learners are encouraged to develop their own sense of what counts as high-quality creative work" (Collard and Looney 2014, p. 351).

Within China's testing milieu, teachers are expected to help students achieve high scores on tests and unquestioning respect of authority (Lee and Pang 2011). Low scores on entrance exams limit future possibilities for Chinese citizens, with severe consequences being poor quality of life and even suicide (Zhao 2014). China's competitive mindset dominates, undermining such collectivist strengths as its strong sense of social belonging (Staats 2011).

Paradoxically, while China's labor markets control education systems and hinder creativity (Staats 2011), China is recognized as accrediting the collective with being creative (Sternberg 2006). The collectivist tradition should make it amenable to collaborative expressions of creativity and cooperative groupings, but another constraint is that classes are typically large and teacher centered (Starr 2010).

In mainstream China, it is difficult to teach a twenty first-century curriculum that advances global competencies. Classroom pedagogies must align with rote-based testing goals even though the World Economic Forum (2013) identifies creativity and entrepreneurship as proficiencies needed for global literacy. However, generative possibilities exist within this test-centric environment where Chinese students—presumed to lack creativity (Li and Gerstl-Pepin 2014)—have opportunities to experience interventions of creativity. In one such case, 34 Chinese education undergraduates produced dynamic cultural frames of creativity in response to Kaufman and Beghetto's (2009) 4-C creativity model (Mullen 2017a). Cooperative work groups and a collectivist orientation supported the creative learning (see next section).

Chinese students' reduced creativity likely reflects not their human capacity but their culture, environment, or teacher pedagogy. In Niu and Sternberg's (2001) study, evaluators rated the creativity of Chinese and American college students, finding the American artwork more creative and aesthetic. Negative influences in China are the learning environment's task constraints and teacher absence of directives to be creative. Similarly, Niu et al. (2007) attributed performance-based differences between college students in the United States and Hong Kong to cultural influences. (Americans proved stronger in creative thinking on creative writing and problem-solving tasks involving insight.) Being challenged by such studies is the stereotype that Asians are not creative based on perceived genetics, characteristics, talents, abilities, or motivations.

Prevailing, though, is the unfortunate stereotype that Chinese learners are uncreative, even robotized. China's government believes its citizens lack creativity and are incapable of flexible and divergent thinking, critical thinking, and higher order thinking. The global news and even published research perpetuate this deficit Asian stereotype, which could interfere with creative behavior and expression. In China, students take their directions from teachers whose signals are from authorities, all carriers of the regime. Given its millions of followers, Confucianism has likely reinforced allegiance to the nation's government. Chinese students have had to become very good at tested subjects, sacrificing development in open-ended problem-solving. However, despite the generalization that this population is creativity-poor and math-smart, creative expression and innovation do exist in not only China's entrepreneurial sector but also its educational sector (Woetzel and Towson 2013).

8.6.2 Introducing Hidden-c

Interacting with select creativity models from educational psychology requires invoking my adapter and shaper role. In this creative capacity, I identify a fifth C—Hidden-c—as aligning well with conceptions of dynamic creativity (Corazza 2016) and as a complement to Kaufman and Beghetto's (2009) 4-C creativity model. Using theory-informed application to ground Hidden-c, I approach it as a generative possibility for which theoretical perspectives and Chinese learning contexts serve as touchstones.

Hidden-c refers to creative self-beliefs and behaviors that trigger the personal power of creativity and capacity for engaging in dynamic creativity. Moreover, making a dynamic creative achievement by shifting and changing over time and overcoming challenges encountered quite possibly mobilizes the capacity for influencing and being influenced by environments. Putting personal creativity center stage as a creator or instructor is strategic (i.e., Hidden-c), for it emphasizes the capability of human beings to engage actively in the exploratory experience of originality and effectiveness, perhaps even altering conditions and situations that affect generative work.

To further contextualize Hidden-c in the literature upon which I am drawing, when creative potential is realized, it manifests as creative *achievement* (Corazza 2016) in one of the 4Cs, typically Little-c's sphere of problem-solving or above. (However, a case could also be made for achieving within Mini-c's meaning-making domain.) Conversely, when the potential for creativity is not fulfilled (for internal or external reasons), then one remains in a state of what Corazza describes as creative *inconclusiveness*, that is, the Hidden-c condition. In this view, educating for creativity becomes an effort aimed at promoting higher and higher levels of potential for originality and effectiveness, as well as the conditions that transform Hidden-c into some form of creative achievement (Ronald Beghetto and Giovanni Emanuele Corazza, personal communication, February 18, 2018).

Importantly, for decades, educators have asserted that teacher beliefs (such as all students are naturally creative) are more powerful than teacher knowledge. Xu (2012) confirms that "teachers are highly influenced by their beliefs, which in turn are closely linked to their values, to their views of the world, and to their understanding of their place within it" (p. 1397). Based on Xu's review of the literature, we know that teacher belief affects how educators define problems, make decisions, and even act. Because creative self-beliefs form at a young age, these tend to stay the same, she contends. However, they *can* change when individuals are exposed to enriching opportunities for expressing creative behaviors, a conception that deserves to be fully developed and extensively tested.

Quite possibly, before human beings can creatively and dynamically generate meaning, problem-seek, and problem-solve—let alone contribute to professions and even to the world—they must believe in their potential for creativity. Self-belief, also creative self-belief, is rooted in the long-established concept of *creative self-efficacy*, defined most directly as the "perceived confidence to creatively perform a particular task" (Beghetto and Karwowski 2017, p. 3). Creative self-belief can be explained as that which is "triggered when a person encounters a performance situation, … result[ing] in a self-judgment about one's confidence to creatively perform an impending task at a particular level (e.g., 'I am confident that I can creatively solve three of these five problems')" (Beghetto and Karwowski, p. 7). These creativity researchers also classify creative self-efficacy as one main type of creative self-belief. (For a description of creative self-beliefs relative to definitions, dimensions, and measurement ideas, see Table 1.1 in Beghetto and Karwowski 2017.)

Beyond theorizing, consider an empirical validation of the hypothesis that self-belief is fundamental to creative processes and probably the very capacity to be creative. Beghetto's (2006) US-based survey study of 1322 middle and secondary students' judgements of their creative abilities advances the fundamental premise that "Although creative ability is necessary for creative expression, it is not sufficient. Creative expression, like other forms of behavior, seems to be influenced by self-judgments of one's ability to generate novel and useful outcomes" (p. 447). A possible interpretation of *self-judgment* as Beghetto refers to it, or Hidden-c from my perspective, is that it is both a catalyst for all creative endeavor—and thus a form/level/type of creativity unto itself—and a shaping force that underlines the 4Cs. At all levels of creativity and across types, creators who persist with the doubts, uncertainties, and unknowns typical of long-term, complicated creative processes may learn something valuable from the failed attempt(s) or potentially discover an original outcome. A Pro-C or even Big-C creative achievement signals success, but educative insight comes from first-hand knowledge of the dynamics behind it.

Given this framework and study finding of creative self-belief, perhaps mysteriously, then, the Chinese preservice sophomores I taught did prove to be creative (Mullen 2017a, 2018). Despite feeling long suppressed (and overly regulated by test-centric curricula) to the point of believing they were uncreative, they rose to the occasion. And, despite not having worked previously as peer collaborators in their classrooms, all were on task and productive. Within cooperative groups in a Chinese university's ministry-set general curriculum exclusive of the liberal arts, students read and interpreted the basic 4C classification (Kaufman and Beghetto 2009). In teams and alone, they produced writing and graphics signifying Mini-c and the other three categories of creativity, in addition to unifying images of their homeland for which they felt proud (e.g., Confucius, to them a beloved teacher–philosopher).

These undergraduates also creatively and collaboratively performed their achievements on our classroom's stage, complete with a microphone and their self-made 4C props, and later for another live audience. In direct response to Niu and Sternberg's (2001) and Niu et al.'s (2007) findings, task constraints within the Chinese learning environment were removed in favor of a creative work space and directives to be creative. These were explicitly articulated in the course title Creativity and Accountability in Education and the syllabus, in addition to instructions accompanying all exercises, as well as in the English–Mandarin communication, both spoken and written.

In this Chinese course the generation of creative products suggested personal and professional growth by way of dynamic Mini-c and Little-c collective immersion. These were individual (e.g., personal essays of creativity) and joint productions of original products (e.g., 3D paper posters representing each of the 4Cs) that had engaged students' (inter)subjectivities and imaginations. As noted earlier, Corazza (2016) has identified these processes as intrinsically dynamic. Negotiating conceptions and representations, cooperative groups moved from the intrapersonal (Mini-c and Little-c) to the professional/cultural (Pro-C), to the societal/global (Big-C), articulating possibilities for Pro-C and Big-C creativity.

Paradoxically, with the pervasive message that Chinese people are uncreative, half of the students' essays on personal creativity expressed the belief of *not* being creative (Mullen 2017a, 2018). Some of these Chinese participants could not recall ever having had a creative experience, or if they had, an adult or other external force had disrupted it. Brainstorming beyond their personal essays, teams generated drawings, captions, and integrative images of the 4Cs (e.g., butterfly, compass, birthplaces). Poster designs—3D folded renderings of books, clothing, filmstrips, and more—were fresh, novel creations connoting practical value. Self-reported was 4C curiosity, task engagement, and peer enjoyment, all outcomes associated with creativity (Kaufman and Beghetto 2009). Students strongly preferred the group projects, without acknowledging the self-reflective groundwork in creativity originating with their individual essays. Evidencing high creativity, the dynamic teams had no avenue available for imitating or replicating the 4C model, such as by consulting the Internet or student samples.

This course's rapid pace and brevity further suggested some level of self-confidence or perhaps shared confidence. Like the marginalized learners (e.g., girls, English language learners) in Beghetto's (2006) study, being at a disadvantage can challenge one's beliefs about the capacity for creativity. Because feedback from peers and teachers about one's ability influences creative self-efficacy, when positive or encouraging this can boost the most vulnerable student and his or her learning. Influential authority figures and peers factor into the creative learning process and experience, as do perceptions. Contextual dynamics (e.g., teacher acceptance) can bring about feelings of belonging (Beghetto 2006), which in the Chinese classroom was evidenced as a feeling of communal bonding and friendship arising out of a safe space for taking creative risks and expressing oneself.

Csikszentmihalyi's (1996) model focuses on "domain" and "field," serving as reminders that influential forces, visible and invisible alike, constantly exert influence. Within classrooms, the teacher is a gatekeeping force. On the scale of a field or profession, gatekeeping by expert peers who evaluate the quality of products (e.g., manuscripts) is a deciding factor in what counts as a creative contribution to a discipline or profession. Such real-life dynamics can affect anyone's creative self-efficacy, motivation, doubt, and even desire to persist.

Situations in which creativity is blocked do not necessarily negate being creative and in fact can strengthen one's resolve and thus capacity to be creative (Beghetto 2006).

Some creators do persist with creative challenges, even changing their circumstances while courageously modeling what is possible for others. While creative people whose socialization or circumstances may inhibit the development of positive creative self-beliefs, contradictorily they may find they can engage in creative tasks and performances where these are energized and modeled or imposed and scaffolded (Mullen 2017a, 2018).

From this perspective, creative self-belief and learning is both a paradox and possibility in restrictive learning environments. This outcome emerged from a pedagogical intervention enabling study of a Chinese preservice teacher classroom where Hidden-c surfaced as a creative force in students' learning performances. Learners were immersed in a novel situation—their classroom was organized into a work studio with roundtables inside a theater and their curriculum was steeped in a collectivist orientation, organized around project-based learning within cooperative groups (Mullen 2018). However, it was not known at the time if the experiential conditions and new activities intended to foster creativity would in fact stimulate creative thinking and yield creative products, as well as overall success.

8.7 Takeaways, Implications, and Possibilities

Future directions for theory, research, and practice emerge from this layered treatment of several ideas of creativity. The main concept considered was dynamic creativity, with creative self-belief (extended to Hidden-c) touched upon, and with discussion of public discourse about creativity. Also included were Canadian and Chinese examples of creative and cultural learning.

8.7.1 Dynamic Creativity in Hindsight

Dynamic creativity—the central construct herein—was introduced as a new concept of creativity and it was illustrated with examples. This key sense-making device allowed for the exploration of select influential theory, public discourse, and generative possibility. A speculation was that dynamic creativity involves generative possibility on many different levels, from adaptive and flexible learning to the changing self-beliefs of individuals and nations.

Hopefully, something new has been conveyed about complex, dynamic interplays of creativity among individuals, systems, and cultures. Certain understandings underlying this writing are that creativity can be operationalized in experiential terms through "creative activity and creative products" and that creativity "will always depend upon the judgment process" and "who the judges are" (Corazza 2016, p. 259). Vital to this picture are attitudes of possibility in expressing and manifesting creativity, as the various life systems' examples and cases Suggest.

8.7.2 Hidden-c's Creative Potential

Also presented was the emergent idea of Hidden-c, with grounding in the creativity theories of Kaufman and Beghetto (2009), Csikszentmihalyi (1996), and Corazza (2016). While perhaps an extension of the 4Cs theory, the generative possibility of Hidden-c was more a demonstration of dynamic creativity along the lines of Corazza's thinking. The life systems interpretation of Csikszentmihalyi's (1996) creativity framework also served to advance dynamic possibilities for thinking about different kinds of systems in which creative learning is essential for adaptation and growth. Notably, the creative synthesis of Kaufman and Beghetto and Csikszentmihalyi's models may provide creative openings for readers to rethink, rework, re-create, or even apply the idea.

What does hidden-c suggest? Based on viewpoints ventured, Hidden-c may be in service of creative thought and action for which the belief in oneself as a creative being is a generative force. Dewey (1934) teaches that the human condition through which creativity manifests must not be lost—everyday creativity born out of circumstance and conflict should be part of any cultural story. For Dewey (1934) and Eisner (2004), creativity is the soul of the human condition. Schools, if transformed, enable creative teaching and learning in the development of creative societies for which Kaufman and Beghetto, Csikszentmihalyi, and Corazza's theories can be utilized.

8.7.3 Creative Self-Belief Emergence

While not focused on teacher and learner beliefs, this writing has implications for study of this area. As noted, a finding of breakthrough studies is that Chinese students' reduced creativity likely reflects their culture, environment, or context rather than any natural ability to be creative (e.g., Niu and Sternberg 2001; Niu et al. 2007). Significant interferences with the creative process from youth can socialize preservice teachers and other adults to think they have a creativity deficiency. Consider the scale of this problem for students intending to become teachers who will in turn influence the young. Not only is this self-belief a serious hindrance for the preservice teacher but also for societies struggling to adapt and excel in the creativity economy.

Theory building about dynamic creativity could enrich the self-belief construct with study of how nations understand their capacity to be creative and reflective. Entire nations as living systems possess dynamic creativity, including generative regimes. Considered was creative self-belief relative to Canada's tolerance of migrants and refugees. While Canada persists with new challenges of multiculturalism and embrace in a changing world of human migration patterns, it seeks notoriety on competitive international testing. These endeavors may be culturally contested goals and dynamics, in effect subjecting school-aged immigrants to a mindset of belonging contingent on attaining top scores in the tested areas.

Imagine such ideas becoming powerful in the hands of the worldwide community of creativity scholars capable of addressing creative self-belief on the scale of nations and their influence on personal, professional, and eminent creativity. In effect, new insights into creativity could emerge on an entirely new level that, specific to Hidden-c, affect people's belief in their capacity to creatively contribute and accomplish as part of something larger than themselves.

8.7.4 Public Discourse About Creativity

Follow-up could also inform the issue of creativity within the nonacademic public realm. Not taken up to the extent one might expect in the creativity literature, this quasi-visible, prevailing force likely profoundly influences creative work, but how? The discourse around creativity's role in ensuring socioeconomic prosperity, breakthrough innovations and inventions, and competitive international rankings probably has many linkages to what influential gatekeepers (e.g., funders and sponsors) deem professional ("Pro-C") and especially eminent ("Big-C") creative contributions. How do such external forces affect creators' work?

Creative economy is a prevalent way of seeing and quite possibly structuring and rewarding creativity. Yet the importance of this reality does not seem to be a topic in the literature. Additional scrutiny also concerns powerful and influential entities' goals, values, interests, affiliations, and impact on societal and educational systems, including academies around the world. I would be remiss not to mention that affirmations of creativity exist in some world leaders' discourse around such topics as active acceptance of cultural difference being valued over mere tolerance. Another idea is to compare discourse about creativity within the public realm and academic community. Such analysis could uncover areas of similarity and dissimilarity, quite possibly critical or provocative in nature, and even offer a roadmap for the professoriate.

8.7.5 Canadian and Chinese Creativity Cases

Another takeaway is that creativity is *not* limited to a particular application. A universal application, creativity, like good teaching, is integral to all learners. Seed ideas for creative learning, growth, and transformation were contained in the Canadian and Chinese cases, each with different ways of relating to the world's high-stakes testing ethos and opportunities for creative innovation. In fact, the richness of these illustrations—Canada a story of a nation's vibrant cultural identity undergoing creative change and China a story of collective strengths evidenced in grassroots creativity—is about the larger narrative of dynamic creativity. Dynamic creativity makes possibility palpable and breathes life into education.

8.8 A Final Word

Readers may choose to adapt any of these ideas to help inform their own theories, studies, and pedagogies. My hope is that this introduction to dynamic creativity, with application to influential theory, public discourse, and generative possibility, offers something of interest. Hidden-c's creative potential may be worth developing and mining in new contexts to advance dynamic creativity.

References

Akkerman, S. F., & Bakker, A. (2011). Boundary crossing and boundary objects. *Review of Educational Research, 81*(2), 132–169.
Ball, M. (2016, September 2). Donald Trump and the politics of fear. *The Atlantic*. Retrieved from https://www.theatlantic.com/politics/archive/2016/09/donald-trump-and-the-politics-of-fear/498116
Bandura, A. (1997). *Self-efficacy: The exercise of control*. New York: Freeman.
BBC. (2017, August 3). How Canada became an education superpower. *Education News*. Retrieved from http://www.educationviews.org/canada-education-superpower
Beghetto, R. A. (2006). Creative self-efficacy: Correlates in middle and secondary students. *Creativity Research Journal, 18*(4), 447–457.

Beghetto, R. A., & Kaufman, J. C. (2007). Toward a broader conception of creativity: A case for mini-c creativity. *Psychology of Aesthetics, Creativity, and the Arts, 1*, 73–79.

Beghetto, R. A. (2016). Creative openings in the social interactions of teaching. *Creativity Theories–Research–Applications, 3*(2), 261–273. https://doi.org/10.1515/ctra-2016-0017.

Beghetto, R. A., & Karwowski, M. (2017). Toward untangling creative self-beliefs. In J. C. Kaufman (Ed.), *Creative self: Effect of beliefs, self-efficacy, mindset, and identity* (pp. 3–22). London: Elsevier.

Boily, P., Chapdelaine, N., Hartley, M., Kent, L., Suurkask, K., & Wong, J. C. (2014). *Creativity unleashed: Taking innovation out of the laboratory and into the labour force.* Retrieved from http://www.actioncanada.ca/wp-content/uploads/2014/04/AC-TF3-Creativity-Report-EN-web.pdf

Brown, J. L., & Moffett, C. A. (1999). *The hero's journey: How educators can transform schools and improve learning.* Alexandria: ASCD.

Collard, P., & Looney, J. (2014). Nurturing creativity in education. *European Journal of Education, 49*(3), 348–364. https://doi.org/10.1111/ejed.12090.

Conference Board of Canada. (2008, August). *Valuing culture: Measuring and understanding Canada's creative economy.* Ottawa: Author. Retrieved from http://www.conferenceboard.ca/e-library/abstract.aspx?did=2671

Corazza, G. E. (2016). Potential originality and effectiveness: The dynamic definition of creativity. *Creativity Research Journal, 28*(3), 258–267.

Craft, A., Cremin, T., Burnard, P., Dragovic, T., & Chappell, K. (2012a). Possibility thinking: Culminative studies of an evidence-based concept driving creativity? *International Journal of Primary, Elementary and Early Years Education, 41*(5), 538–556. https://doi.org/10.1080/03004279.2012.656671.

Craft, A., McConnon, L., & Matthews, A. (2012b). Creativity and child-initiated play: Fostering possibility thinking in four-year-olds. *Thinking Skills and Creativity, 7*(1), 48–61.

Cropley, D., & Cropley, A. (2010). Functional creativity: "Products" and the generation of effective novelty. In J. C. Kaufman & R. J. Sternberg (Eds.), *The Cambridge handbook of creativity* (pp. 301–317). New York: Cambridge University Press.

Csikszentmihalyi, M. (1988). Society, culture, and person: A systems view of creativity. In R. J. Sternberg (Ed.), *The nature of creativity* (pp. 325–339). New York: Cambridge University Press.

Csikszentmihalyi, M. (1996). *Creativity: The psychology of discovery and invention.* London: HarperPerennial.

Csikszentmihalyi, M. (1999). Implications of a systems perspective for the study of creativity. In R. Sternberg (Ed.), *Handbook of creativity* (pp. 313–335). Cambridge: Cambridge University Press.

Culture. (2017). *Merriam-Webster.* Retrieved from https://www.merriam-webster.com/dictionary/culture

Dewey, J. (1934). *Art as experience.* New York: Perigee Books.

Dynamic. (2017). *Wiktionary.* Retrieved from https://en.wiktionary.org/wiki/dynamic

Eisner, E. W. (1991). *The enlightened eye: Qualitative inquiry and the enhancement of educational practice.* New York: Macmillan.

Eisner, E. W. (2004). What does it mean to say that a school is doing well? In D. J. Flinders & S. J. Thornton (Eds.), *The curriculum studies reader* (2nd ed., pp. 297–305). New York: Routledge.

Ferdig, M. A., & Ludema, J. D. (2005). Transformative interactions: Qualities of conversation that heighten the vitality of self-organizing change. *Research in Organizational Change and Development, 15*, 171–207.

Gardner, J. W. (1963). *Self-renewal: The individual and the innovative society.* New York: Harper & Row.

Gardner, H. (2011). *Truth, beauty, and goodness reframed: Educating for the virtues in the age of truthiness and Twitter.* New York: Basic Books.

Glăveanu, V. P., & Tanggaard, L. (2014). Creativity, identity, and representation: Towards a sociocultural theory of creative identity. *New Ideas in Psychology, 34*, 12–21.

Hennessey, B. A. (2013). Foreword. In A.-G. Tan (Ed.), *Creativity, talent, and excellence* (pp. vii–ix). New York: Springer.

Heyl, J. D. (2014). Globalization and the U.S. university: Reactions, trends, and a teachable moment. In S. Harris & J. Mixon (Eds.), *Building cultural community through global educational leadership* (pp. 254–266). Ypsilanti: NCPEA.

Hunt, L. (2014). *Writing history in the global era*. New York: W.W. Norton.

Hunter, G. S. (2013). *Out think: How innovative leaders drive exceptional outcomes*. Mississauga: Wiley.

Ibbitson, J. (2014, July 2). Why is Canada the most tolerant country in the world? Luck. *Globe and Mail*. Retrieved from https://www.theglobeandmail.com/news/politics/why-is-canada-the-most-tolerant-country-in-the-world-luck/article19427921

Jacobs, B. A. (2006). *Race manners for the 21st Century: Navigating the minefield between Black and White Americans in an age of fear*. New York: Arcade Publishing.

Johnson, S. (2010). *Where good ideas come from: The natural history of innovation*. New York: Penguin Group.

Johnston, D., & Jenkins, T. (2017). *Ingenious: How Canadian innovators made the world smarter, smaller, kinder, safer, healthier, wealthier, and happier*. New York: Penguin Random House.

Kahl, C. H., & Hansen, H. (2015). Simulating creativity from a systems perspective. *CRESY Journal of Artificial Societies and Social Simulation, 18*(1), 1–22. https://doi.org/10.18564/jasss.2640.

Kaufman, J. C., & Beghetto, R. A. (2009). Beyond big and little: The four C model of creativity. *Review of General Psychology, 13*(1), 1–12.

Kaufman, J. C., & Sternberg, R. J. (Eds.). (2010). *The Cambridge handbook of creativity*. New York: Cambridge University Press.

Keller-Mathers, S., & Murdock, M. (1999). Research support for a conceptual organization of creativity. In A. Fishkin, B. Cramond, & P. Olszewski-Kubelius (Eds.), *Investigating creativity in youth* (pp. 49–71). Cresskill: Hampton Press.

Lee, J. C. K., & Pang, N. S. K. (2011). Educational leadership in China: Contexts and issues. *Frontiers of Education in China, 6*(3), 331–241.

Li, Q., & Gerstl-Pepin, C. (Eds.). (2014). *Survival of the fittest: The shifting contours of higher education in China and the United States*. Heidelberg: Springer.

Mullen, C. A. (2017a). *Creativity and education in China: Paradox and possibilities for an era of accountability*. New York: Routledge.

Mullen, C. A. (2017b). Creativity in Chinese schools: Perspectival frames of paradox and possibility. *International Journal of Chinese Education, 6*(1), 27–56.

Mullen, C. A. (2018). Creative learning: Paradox or possibility in China's restrictive preservice teacher classrooms? *Action in Teacher Education, 40*, 186–202.

Mumford, M. D. (2003). Where have we been, where are we going? Taking stock in creativity research. *Creativity Research Journal, 15*, 107–120.

Neber, H., & Neuhaus, B. J. (2013). Creativity and problem-based learning (PBL): A neglected relation. In A.-G. Tan (Ed.), *Creativity, talent, and excellence* (pp. 43–56). New York: Springer.

Niu, W., & Sternberg, R. J. (2001). Cultural influences on artistic creativity and its evaluation. *International Journal of Psychology, 36*(4), 225–241. https://doi.org/10.1080/00207590143000036.

Niu, W., Zhang, J. X., & Yang, Y. (2007). Deductive reasoning and creativity: A cross-cultural study. *Psychological Reports, 100*(2), 509–519 https://doi.org/10.2466/pr0.100.2.509-519.

Robinson, K. (2015). *Creative schools: The grassroots revolution that's transforming education*. New York: Viking.

Saul, J. R. (2008). *A fair country: Telling truths about Canada*. Toronto: Viking Canada.

Sawyer, K. (2012). Extending sociocultural theory to group creativity. *Vocations and Learning, 5*, 59–75.

Schwab, J. (2004). The practical: A language for curriculum. In D. J. Flinders & S. J. Thornton (Eds.), *The curriculum studies reader* (2nd ed., pp. 103–117). New York: Routledge.

Staats, L. K. (2011). The cultivation of creativity in the Chinese culture—past, present, and future. *Journal of Strategic Leadership, 3*(1), 45–53.

Stacey, R. D. (1992). *Managing the unknowable: Strategic boundaries between order and chaos in organizations.* San Francisco: Jossey-Bass.

Starr, J. B. (2010). *Understanding China: A guide to China's economy, history, and political culture* (3rd ed.). New York: Farrar, Straus and Giroux.

Stasis. (2017). *Merriam-Webster.* Retrieved from https://www.merriam-webster.com/dictionary/stasis

Sternberg, R. J. (2006). Introduction. In J. C. Kaufman & R. J. Sternberg (Eds.), *The international handbook of creativity* (pp. 1–9). Cambridge: Cambridge University Press.

Stoeger, H. (2003). Learning as a creative process. In A.-G. Tan (Ed.), *Creativity, talent, and excellence* (pp. 1–11). New York: Springer.

Tan, A.-G. (2013). Psychology of cultivating creativity in teaching and learning. In A.-G. Tan (Ed.), *Creativity, talent, and excellence* (pp. 27–42). New York: Springer.

Wheatley, M. J. (1992). *Leadership and the new science: Learning about organization from an orderly universe.* Oakland: Berrett-Koehler.

Wheatley, M. J. (2017). *Who do we choose to be? Facing reality, claiming leadership, restoring sanity.* Oakland: Berrett-Koehler.

Wheatley, M. J., & Kellner-Rogers, M. (1996). *A simpler way.* Oakland: Berrett-Koehler.

Wierzbicki, A. P., & Nakamori, Y. (2006). *Creative space: Models of creative processes for the knowledge civilization age.* New York: Springer.

Woetzel, J., & Towson, J. (2013). *The 1 hour China book.* Cayman Islands: Towson Group LLC.

World Economic Forum. (2013). The global competitiveness report: 2013–2014. Geneva: Author. Retrieved from http://www3.weforum.org/docs/WEF_GlobalCompetitivenessReport_2013-14.pdf

Xu, L. (2012). The role of teachers' beliefs in the language teaching–learning process. *Theory and Practice in Language Studies, 2*(7), 1397–1402. https://doi.org/10.4304/tpls.2.7.1397-1402.

Zhao, Y. (2014). *Who's afraid of the big bad dragon?* Thousand Oaks: Jossey-Bass.

Zimmermann, K. A. (2015). *What is culture? Definition of culture.* Retrieved from https://www.livescience.com/21478-what-is-culture-definition-of-culture.html

Chapter 9
Content-Driven Pedagogy: On Passion, Absorption and Immersion as Dynamic Drivers of Creativity

Lene Tanggaard

Abstract The passion for learning and teaching, the pleasure of being lost in a compelling story, the awe and excitement of participating in great drama or producing original art, the engrossing study of pond life and engaging with the wonders of nature, the time to be consoled over a lost friendship– all these things that make classrooms wondrous and stay with children for the rest of their lives have been superseded in many places by the push for higher test scores, the obsession with numerical achievement data, and the narrow concentration on bulldozing through the basics at the price of everything else. (Hargreaves and Fullan, *Professional kapital – en forandring af undervisningen på alle skoler* [Professional capital – a change of teaching in all schools]. Frederikshavn: Dafolo Forlag, 2016, p. 35).

9.1 Introduction

Is there anything better than passion, absorption and the enchantment of immersion in subjects as described in the above quotation from the book *Professional Capital*? If anything, many of us will eventually remember exactly such moments. Some might also remember the feeling of being measured on standardised tests time and again. The quotation pinpoints the existence of a neoliberal movement that is at risk of reducing school to those outputs that can be delivered on measurable scales. Here, absorption and passion for a case or a subject are held to play a very minimal role in the learning process.

The intent of the present chapter is to highlight the role of engagement in the subject matter (reading a lovely essay, learning about the photosynthesis or the genres of art) and a content-driven pedagogy for the development of teachers' and students' creativity in school. My point is that this requires that absorption and passion for a subject are held as key drivers to this ambition. As stated by Simonton

---

L. Tanggaard (✉)
Department of Communication & Psychology, Aalborg University, Aalborg, Denmark
e-mail: lenet@hum.aau.dk

© Springer Nature Switzerland AG 2019
R. A. Beghetto, G. E. Corazza (eds.), *Dynamic Perspectives on Creativity*, Creativity Theory and Action in Education 4,
https://doi.org/10.1007/978-3-319-99163-4_9

(2017), most eminent creators benefit more from having broad interests and a passion for something that eventually lead them in the direction of producing something new, valuable and effective, e.g. something judged as creative. The role of formal education for the development of creativity is more questionable when studying the history of great inventors: "*Big C creativity presents a curvilinear, inverted function of the level of formal education achieved*" (2017, p. 16). For example, Galileo's involvement in the visual arts paved the way for his telescopic discoveries and seemed more important than anything else for his achievements, the great filmmaker Steven Spielberg dropped out of college, and Facebook's Mark Zuckerberg is also a college drop-out. Simonton himself did well in school, but "*I too frequently felt that studying, homework, and assignments was interfering with what I really would rather do*" (2017, p. 12). However, can anything be done to pave the way for students to experience deep involvement and meaningful learning in school? Is this possible and, if so, what is the task for teachers interested in cultivating creativity in today's school- and educational environment?

One argument put forth in this paper is that creativity must be understood as a dynamic, substantial component of subject matter and learning among students. Many debates on creativity critique the conservative focus in schools on traditional subjects and cultural reproduction (Robinson 2011). Doubts seem to be voiced in this connection as to whether it still makes sense to preserve and maintain existing knowledge and pass it on in school to generations to come. In this chapter, I argue that is does make sense, if teachers also focus their work on making way for student's own perspectives on the matter at hand.

The traditional school subjects such as maths or history and arts can be drivers in the creative process. Put simply, there is a need for striking a better balance between content and strategies in the discussion of creativity in school and in teaching. Creativity in specific domains requires in-depth information about that domain. This is why children's creative potential often reveals glimmers of impressive achievement, but why they cannot consistently reach the levels of adult "creatives". There is a persistent social meme that children are born creative geniuses (which is ridiculous given the content knowledge necessary for eminent levels of creative achievement). Conversely, one can spend a lifetime acquiring higher and higher expertise on a subject, and never take a step out of the common knowledge domain. This is when strategies/mind-set/abilities for creative thought (including implementation) become useful and perhaps necessary. The history of art, science, and technology is full of examples of great innovations coming from persons that were not the highest experts in their field: their marginal position was actually crucial to their success (Simonton 2017). This is an interesting tension. Too much formal education can be a drawback for creativity to unfold. On the other hand, it is dangerous to see creativity as only a meta-competence with no direct link to content-matter. The point in this chapter is that the latter drives more than we think in relation to creativity.

Below, I will propose several reasons why I believe this is so. First, by analysing the pure and narrow ideal of learning that seems to dominate current educational discourse, and then by means of examples that show, in contrast to the ideal of pure learning, that content drives more than we think. This is an argument aligned with Corazza's (2016) dynamic conception of creativity where creativity is understood as a dynamic rather than a static phenomenon. The dynamic conception of creativity, and the impure idea of learning presented in this chapter, draws on pragmatist philosophy from James, Pierce and Dewey. Pragmatism underlines that validity of a given action or product depends on a judgement of its effects in concrete situations. This may involve a degree of subjectivity and time-dependency. The basic premise behind this dynamic conception of creativity is that we will not know what will be the creativity of tomorrow. It is to be judged in the situation at hand, in the future. In regards to education, one line following from this is that we don't need to focus on content and existing knowledge. It will soon become obsolete. However, in this chapter, I take another direction. Because of the need for a dynamic conception of creativity and the development of the creative potential of pupils in school and students in the educational system, we need content understood as the driver of student engagement and creativity.

9.2 Pure Learning and Creativity

In the educational system, we are witness to an intensified focus on meta-competencies. Creativity is one of these celebrated competences of the future (Corazza 2016). In Denmark, where this chapter was written, prominent figures from our national pedagogical university has stated that learning in school is now less about gaining insight into something or getting a grasp of some topic (Rasmussen et al. 2007). Now is has to do with lifelong learning and the acquisition of meta-competences such as the ability to learn. There seems to be a sort of consensus, not only in Denmark, that the educational system should prepare students for an insecure future by means of equipping them with a set of meta-competences (collaborative skills, problem-solving skills, learning skills etc.), but the question is whether this really makes us more creative?

9.3 What Do We Need to Become Creative?

Researchers struggle to find an inclusive definition of creativity, but most researchers agree that creativity is about the new and the valuable fitting the specific context in question (Corazza 2016), even if creativity researchers disagree a bit on the exact formula (Simonton 2017). Beghetto and Kaufmann (2014) defines creativity as a process striving for movement and dynamic progress; but whether this means that already-existing knowledge ceases to be a driver for the development of the new – that is a good question. One thesis advanced in this chapter is that there is no such thing as pure development or movement, but that it is always materialized and occurs because of something other than itself. Creativity is what I have previously described as a socio-material process, meaning that creativity enters the world because of an dynamic interaction over time (leading to something new, valuable and surprising) between the people, materials and tools involved (Tanggaard 2013), and in pedagogical contexts because of teaching in which the subject is mediated by intelligent teachers who create opportunities for the pupils to be creative either in the class-room (Tanggaard and Hjorth 2017) or when students go home to experiment with what they might have encountered or learned in school or elsewhere (Tanggaard 2014; Simonton 2017).

Following on from these ideas, in a series of three anthologies, Danish colleagues and I have formulated what we call an impure pedagogy (Rømer et al. 2011, 2017; Tanggaard et al. 2014). In these books, we assert that learning processes are impure because they are formed and given content by something that constitutes the learning process itself. Just as in the quotation above from Hargreaves and Fullan (2016), where it is precisely absorption in and enchantment with the subjects that is seen as a driving force.

Thus, there is something driving the thing we want. The subjects and the teaching mean something for the development of creativity, because they give access to what has been. The social conceptions (c.f. Taylor's (2004) concept of 'Modern Social Imaginaries') that bind a country, a society and a community together are not just something we can think of as a constant that does not need to be taken care of. They arise and are learnt through exposure to and immersion in these communities' narratives, art and literature.

These conceptions enable community and practice, and they are about the ways in which we conceive social existence, the ways we live together with others, the expectations we have, and the deeper normative ideas and images that guide our life with each other (Taylor 2004, p. 23). These social conceptions are important repertories for creativity in a given context and teaching can make us acquainted with these. Displacing content with forms and meta-learning in school might make us less familiar with these repertories and accordingly, we may have access to less creative potential.

The displacement of content in pedagogical reality with meta-learning can be seen as the worst enemy of creativity, even if it is often framed differently. It is obvious from the introductory quotation from the Canadian authors that a global struggle is going on over the school, in which skills, wisdom and the joy of immersion in material are supplanted by a numerical obsession with test results and scores, or an understanding of learning as a continuous lifelong process of skills development, often associated with the creative. The coupling of the tight focus on functional skills testing with the idea of meta-learning is, however, partly contradictory, because it emphasizes the measurement of functional skills in the school just when these skills are expected to lose ground in the future as the emphasis shifts to the so-called meta-competencies. This is paradoxical in itself, and no wonder the individual practitioner in the school and in the educational system sometimes becomes confused and perhaps also disengaged.

My point in this chapter is precisely that our attention has moved away from content as a driver in pedagogical work with creativity and focused instead on measurements, or meta-learning. I believe that we are missing the target by focusing on processes and competences as drivers in themselves.

Below, I will dwell briefly on Hargreaves and Fullan's book on professional capital in order to specify why from a creativity point of view, too, we need something other than what a purely functional paradigm makes possible. Namely, a content-driven pedagogy which is also the gate-way to a dynamic conception of creativity in which immersion in something gives rise to the new and the valuable in specific contexts.

9.4 Towards a Content-Driven Creative Pedagogy

In the quotation that introduces this chapter, Hargreaves and Fullan criticize the current preoccupation with numerical performance data in schools. The focus of Hargreaves and Fullan's book is on the creativity, complexity and passion needed to drive good teaching, but they do not shrink from criticizing teachers themselves, or their trade unions, for failing to offer alternative solutions and options for the testing regime and enthusiasm for figures that predominate in school systems of all kinds around the world (Hargreaves and Fullan 2016, p. 36).

Hargreaves and Fullan argue that a possible alternative lies in the concept of professional capital, which they see as '*the product of human capital, and social capital, and decisional capital*' (ibid., p. 29). Human capital is developed early in childhood and through school and the education system, while social capital concerns the strength of the interactions, exchanges, circulations and knowledge sharing that teachers are involved in, and decisional capital, as the word implies, is about the judgement and determination sometimes needed to make difficult decisions in complicated situations. This is not a matter of blindly trusting or just applying research-based knowledge, but precisely of building up teachers' and pedagogues' professional capital, which can be challenged again and again in a dynamic interaction between, for example, theory and practice, or education and profession.

In the above-mentioned book and in his earlier publications, Hargreaves is in my view one of the foremost 'impure' thinkers in the pedagogical landscape, because he insists on a linkage between the pedagogical tradition and the demand for renewal and critique of that tradition grounded in anything other than a pure, technocratic view of the optimization of school activity and the individual pupil's learning processes. There is therefore every reason to listen to his balanced and at the same time pointed views.

As I see it, there is much to suggest that we have forgotten the content and the pedagogical significance of the content, and that this is leading us into a foggy, technocratic labyrinth. In research, there is a tendency, rather than researching what there is, to insist on an instrumentalist research logic about what will work (based on purely probabilistic considerations), and the debate about learning seems to have lost the sense of there being a *something* (a societal issue, a teacher, a content and a case) that drives learning processes. As Brinkmann and the present author put it in our first joint article on pedagogy, 'In Defence of an Impure Pedagogy' in 2008, we are always learning about something, and we learn best when we have forgotten that we are learning.

Below, I will show on the basis of empirical examples how content is a driving force in learning processes and therefore neither can nor should be allotted a minimal role, even when it comes to developing so-called meta-competencies such as creativity. First, a case from real life.

9.4.1 Have We Lost Focus on the Content? A Case from Real Life

> On 7 September 2015, I gave a lecture and workshop for over 250 health service clinical advisors at Aarhus University Hospital. The title of my lecture was 'Have we lost focus on the case?', and it had been prompted by an inspiring dialogue with the planning group behind the conference. When I told the group during initial planning that I work with an understanding of learning in which content, case and professionalism are seen as a driver for creative learning processes, it was as if a great weight had literally been lifted from them. I quoted the Danish theologian K.E. Løgstrup as follows: 'While we are grappling with the task, the character that determines its solution is being developed. The formation of character is a result of the pleasure to be found in the happy result, and already during the struggle against difficulties. But it is a fatal error to turn one's back to the task and one's face to one's character so as to take pleasure in it. That quickly becomes destructive, and in more than one way. The character trait freezes and becomes a caricature of itself, and self-satisfaction grows (Løgstrup 1972, p. 20). The reaction when I read the quotation to the planning group was remarkable. They told me that they had for a long time been under the influence of a quite different type of thinking that focused attention on relationship work, coaching and facilitation, and that saw the role of the teacher and advisor as a matter of finding the right methods to awaken what was already in the students. They increasingly felt themselves required to focus on students' personality and appreciate the students' personal learning style and strategies. They felt this was to the detriment of a focus on the content of teaching and their own professional knowledge. I took detailed notes during the meeting, including direct transcription of quotations from the planning group such as: 'There has been a "personalization" of pedagogy', 'None of us can stand for anything or have an opinion on behalf of a subject or professional pride any more', 'We have become squeamish about contact, but we don't think we are helping students by letting them be alone with themselves', 'It is OK, isn't it, to stand by some professional ideals and insights, and at the same time let them be criticized, knowing full well that the world is contingent and changing, and that our professional insights have to be challengeable?

This conversation was the prelude to a day seminar at which we discussed how, when and in what ways learning processes can or should be made to be about the case, rather than being frozen in a relationships-oriented caricature where we, as Løgstrup (1972) put it, begin to circle around each other in a strange, singular and self-absorbed manner. Many will no doubt argue that the advisors mentioned above are mistaken, and that nobody has asked them to shift focus away from content and their own role as initiative-takers, and onto learning processes. Of course, the fact that I read out the quotation during the meeting also has an effect, as it necessarily colours the subsequent comments, but they had invited me for a particular reason. Impure pedagogy as we have formulated it in our books had inspired them and touched something that they themselves experienced but that they did not feel they had the legitimacy to oppose seriously, or perhaps the language to criticize.

My point for the present is precisely that the concepts and language we use to describe good teaching and counselling is of great importance, and not least that this language has become 'purer' and thus lost its connection to subject didactics. Perhaps this happens because we, out of misconceived deference, have allowed the pure learning concept to dominate?

The advisors discussed above feel that the professional – professional pride and authority – is currently being excluded from the pedagogical conversation. There are several reasons for this. One is the current enthusiasm for the functional meta-learning paradigm. For example, have a look at this quotation from James Nottingham's trendsetting book *Challenging Learning*. In his book, Nottingham writes: 'When I behave like a personal trainer – someone who encourages the students, gives individual feedback and above all challenges them as much as possible – that is when the students develop most. It is also when students learn how to learn, and in the process gain better self-esteem, become more independent and get better results' (Nottingham 2014, p. 19).

The characteristic feature of the book is a logic derived from the psychology of cognition focusing on *'thinking strategies, self-perception, metacognitive knowledge and cognitive tactics and strategies'* (Nottingham 2014, p. 24).

There is on the face of it nothing either epoch-making or wrong about the conclusions drawn in the above extracts. Feedback has for decades been one of the most tried-and-tested methods in learning research, and being encouraged and challenged may be assumed to be conducive to any learning process, but what is remarkable is that students' cognitive strategies and approaches should be the primary focus. It could equally have said that the most important tool for any teacher is to be firmly grounded in a subject area, but in fact that is not mentioned at all. Or that it is about awakening the joy of wonder through the teacher him- or herself standing for something. Rather, one gets the feeling that teaching, for the teacher, is primarily about having knowledge of the crucial learning-promoting factors that can be identified by research in the field. No wonder, perhaps that teachers such as those in the above example from the hospital sector may feel that they need to be able to act as a sort of psychological coach to the students, in order to cope with the demands on their abilities. Let us examine another case from real life.

9.4.2 Mastering the Material

> One year after the above-mentioned day seminar, I was at a conference in the USA. I attended a presentation by the American researcher Patti Lather, whose work has had an enormous influence on the movement that is today best described as post-humanist, feminist-inspired, qualitative research. During her presentation, Patti Lather suddenly said

that she lets her students read texts they don't understand. If they are to find their way around a theorist's world, they should not start by identifying their own learning style and strategies. They are simply asked to read, and, if they don't understand, they have to read again. There is no way around the material, and this is a form of learning process that is not initially oriented towards understanding. At all events, the material comes before understanding, desire, meaning and metacognitive awareness. Some will perhaps argue that this is an obsolete, old-fashioned way of approaching material, but Patti's students, who were also present on the day in question, said that they saw it as the only way of getting deeply into the material, and that they also saw Patti as their guarantee that it would ultimately make sense to go through this learning process. Here, then, the subject specialist inspires confidence that it is worthwhile getting to grips with the material. When Nottingham writes, referencing Hattie, that 'performance is strengthened as a function of feedback' and that 'performance is improved to the extent that students and teachers together agree appropriate, specific and challenging goals', this seems to be a long way from Patti's example, where students are not learning via feedback as such, but rather, in fact, on the basis of a trust-based instruction to read specific material.

The above is an example of immersion in an initially apparently uninteresting and incomprehensible text driving a learning process forward. The dynamic drivers are trust in the material and in the teacher. A literary example is to be found in Elena Ferrante's book about two friends, Elena and Lila, in 1950s and 1960s Naples. Elena, the main character, describes how she learns to do well at school without getting much help at home. After a visit to her teacher at a party at her house, at which Elena is impressed by all the political and literary discussions going on, apparently quite naturally, in the house, she decides to start by quite simply imitating the words the others use and learning them by rote. She wears out the books at school with reading them. Her strategy is soon a great success. She becomes a legitimate participant in conversations and discussions.

It is fashionable to assert that the form of learning that Elena engages in leads only to parroting the facts and an impersonal, external and superficial relationship to what has been learnt, but in Elena's case it is, in fact, her only way in to a world that is foreign to her. To enter into something, to want it and thereby slowly achieve understanding – not the other way round. Superficial learning can quite simply lead to deep learning, and there need not be any contradiction between the two. It is self-evident that rote learning, where one maintains an external relationship with what is learnt, which means nothing to the learner personally, will not necessarily lead to what has been learnt being used creatively or for the purpose of understanding. On the other hand, there is nothing to suggest that one can become creative by not knowing anything (see also Tanggaard 2016).

While there is good reason to warn against superficial learning and aimless parroting of particular material, and against the trend for education policy to move in that direction with an eye fixed firmly on the performance data, there is equally good reason to warn against the 'decontentification' of the education system that we are witnessing, where dubious forecasts are used as the basis for radical reforms, where pure functional learning models predominate, and where content is thrown out with the bathwater, partly on the strength of the creativity discourse when that discourse becomes too pure. However, if there is nobody (a teacher, an advisor, or some particular material, a text, a source) to point at the landscape and show where the main traffic arteries and the hiding-places and the shortcuts are, it becomes difficult to find one's way, and a lot of energy may be spent unnecessarily going down roads that turn out to be blind alleys. As the apprentices I followed as part of my Ph.D. project told me, they were happy to take responsibility for their own learning, but it can be hard to tell what is worth learning if nobody helps by pointing it out, as they put it. Hence, they preferred a concept of mutual responsibility for learning, and this indicates the need for a wall to throw the ball against at times when you have to learn something that you are not yet confident with (Tanggaard 2006). That one must then consider, as Hattie and Yates also say, in fact, in their book on visible learning, how teachers manage their expertise, whether they are at all suited to teaching, whether their knowledge gets in the way of their pedagogical practice (who has not had the experience of being taught be someone who knows a lot but cannot really explain it?) – this must self-evidently be taken into account (Hattie and Yates 2014).

So, we learn to learn by learning something, and we perhaps also learn best when we do not notice that we are learning and thus do not focus on our own meta-competencies (Tanggaard and Brinkmann 2008). There is nothing wrong with reflecting on one's own learning strategies or developing one's meta-competencies, but these empty or pure processes are not in themselves drivers of either learning or creativity.

9.5 Why Are Creativity Seen as a Meta-competence?

If passion for something drives most people to create (Simonton 2017), when why is creativity simultaneously seen as a pure meta-competence? Is it because there are elements in the history of psychological creativity research that can lead to creativity being conceived as a pure, individual process that, so to speak, merely requires one to open up to inspiration, while the more laborious work with materials is pushed into the background?

A great faith in ideas is what laid the foundation for creativity research. In early creativity research, creativity was perceived in terms of divine inspiration (Sternberg and Lubart 1995), and in ancient Greece the Muses were the metaphorical image of the source of true creation and creativity. With the Renaissance, creativity came to be seen in earnest as something biologically determined and hereditary (Montuori and Purser 1995). Whether one saw creativity as a matter of inspiration or as a biologically determined phenomenon, one studied creativity as an individual attribute.

This habit of locating creativity in individuals, with a focus on connections between intelligence and creativity, personality, mind-set, neurological correlates etc., continues today. Here, idea generation and divergent thinking are typically used as measures of creativity or creative potential, and this is also what is typically taught in schools when increased creativity is the goal (Tanggaard 2016).

In this perspective, attention is very rarely paid to what people actually do in the workplace, in their lives as such, or what everyday life in the classroom looks like.

The focus on testing a potential aptitude for divergent thinking continues to contribute to the classic distinction between inspiration and perspiration or hard work, with the hard work or the many hours on the practice track often being undervalued in the actual understanding of what creativity is.

The main issue is that inspiration and new ideas are not the whole story of creativity. The Swedish creativity researcher Lindström emphasized in 2009 (Lindström 2009, p. 8ff) that creativity is never created from nothing. A person who succeeds in being creative will often select and combine elements that are part of his or her existing repertoire; creativity is therefore rooted in reality, in a form of reorganization of what one can do or what one knows. Even though a person can have the experience of a 'sudden flash of creativity', it is still based directly, or perhaps more indirectly, on a continuation of what the person already knows, or on breaking with or deviating from styles that already exist.

There is therefore a growing acknowledgement in creativity research of a need for new and more nuanced evaluations of creativity; different ways of measuring and evaluating creativity are therefore being used. Of course, there are still the classic creativity tests involving, as mentioned, measurement of individuals' aptitude for divergent thinking; but there is also evaluation of creative products, where people are asked to report on their own experience of creativity, in the form of diary entries, interviews or questionnaires. The way staff experience their managers' support for creativity can be evaluated. Creative environments are observed and ethnographic studies carried out on them; historically based studies of creative achievements are conducted, in the form of case studies, for example (Mumford et al. 2012).

My point in this chapter has been that the conception of creativity in the school also needs revision. It is time to do away with simple 'quick fix' ideas about creative processes as merely a question of techniques for mastering idea generation. There is a need for what I call a content-based pedagogy, in which the dynamic relationships between subject teaching and students' development of creativity takes centre stage.

One must know a lot in different ways in the creative process in order to succeed. Knowledge can sometimes be the pre-requisite for having ideas, and at other times knowledge gets in the way, but in the long run very few people succeed in developing new products, new services or new organizations and companies without a large helping of knowledge. It is this point that can show us that creativity is not reducible to a meta-competency or to something that comes of its own accord. Creativity is the result of hard work, in the school and elsewhere, and subject teaching has an important role as the place where students can build up a repertoire so that, later on, they can play with ideas from different domains and combine them into new, worthwhile products and initiatives.

There are studies that demonstrate again and again that people acknowledged as creative in different domains have often accumulated 10 years' experience before they can contribute creatively to a field (Gardner 1982). This means, then, that while on the one hand we are born creative, and the creative is an essential part of being human, on the other it must be said that a high level of creativity demands expertise, that it takes time, and that it requires a lot of work. Nevertheless, we rather surprisingly continue to believe that great discoveries such as Darwin's theory of evolution or Edison's discovery of electric light are based on ideas. How did they get the big idea, do we ask? We should instead be asking how long it took them to learn the subject, and how many years they spent describing and selling their inventions.

This exaggerated focus on ideas is the result of our tendency to look for insights when we seek creativity, instead of looking for hard-won expertise and the arduous long haul. Ordinary people, psychologists researching creativity and creative people themselves are all concerned with identifying the moment when creativity happens, the stage known as 'illumination' in Wallas's famous typology (Wallas 1926). It is therefore no surprise that creativity is often illustrated with liberal use of glowing lightbulbs, but as long as we see creativity as what happens 'in the moment', we ignore what happens before and after. We don't talk about the long periods of tedious training, day-to-day work and experiments that can lead to our having a good idea. A more dynamic conception of creativity will include these dimensions in future work on developing and evaluating the efforts being made in our schools to develop creativity.

9.6 Conclusion

Taking a case from Denmark as a starting-point and with reference to international studies, this chapter has shown that we are witnessing the emergence of a learning discourse in which content and subject are not seen as essential to the learning process. The most important thing for a teacher and a student is to know their learning and teaching strategies and the develop meta-competencies. In the chapter, I have shown that we can take another route that is far more fertile. Here, cases, content, subjects, immersion and passion play a major part in learning processes. Here, teachers and advisors regain an authority as the ones who show the way in the landscape. Here, meta-competencies such as creativity are acquired through something other than the meta-competencies in themselves. Here, one may lose oneself in some material precisely in order to gain insight into oneself. Here, it is perhaps when we forget that we are learning that we learn most. Here, there is no contradiction between knowledge and experience or between immersion and creativity. Here, ingrained contradictions are broken up so as to create new possibilities for pedagogical researchers and practitioners. In the chapter I have placed Hargreaves and Fullan, especially, into what we call an impure paradigm, thereby showing that the sources that are sometimes thought of as research-based sources for a pure, functionalist paradigm of learning cannot automatically create a foundation for that paradigm. In Hargreaves and Fullan there is no rejection of cases, content or the professional judgement of reflective teachers. In a word, we need to ask both 'what shall we read?' and 'what shall we learn?' Sometimes, we also simply need to leave all these questions and engage with cases, activities and content. There is something to be learnt from that, too. And that is the point being made above.

So what can teachers do? Beghetto writes in one of his latest pieces (Beghetto 2017) that teachers can both teach about creativity, for creativity and through creativity. I agree. A major point to be taken from this chapter is that content matters. This is both the case then teachers teach about, for and through creativity. A few bullets with advice based on the present chapter at the end might help teachers interested in cultivating student's creativity.

- Don't be afraid to show an interest in something. It will be highly stimulating for students to see that passion is possible
- Teach students through experimenting with subject matter and with the teaching. They will learn that experiments are possible and creativity needs it.
- Even if content might become absolute in the future, knowing something makes is easier to know what one do not know. Teach students something and tell them to keep experimenting with what they know and don't know yet.
- Develop trust with students and they will trust you, also in criticizing and debating the content matter put forth in the teaching situation.
- Don't be afraid of boring teaching. It might help students' mind wandering generate good ideas.
- Teach students something and teach them how to recognize and develop their learning strategies. Find a suitable balance between content and strategies.

Work with students' potential. In a dynamic conception of creativity, we will not know the requirements of tomorrow. Keep an eye open towards the unexpected, also among students and work with it when it happens in the teaching situation.

References

Beghetto, R. (2017). Creativity in teaching. In J. C. Kaufman, J. Baer, & V. P. Glăveanu (Eds.), *Cambridge handbook of creativity across different domains*. New York: Cambridge University Press.

Corazza, E. G. (2016). Potential originality and effectiveness: The dynamic definition of creativity. *Creativity Research Journal, 28*(3), 258–267.

Gardner, H. (1982). *Art, mind, and brain: A cognitive approach to creativity*. New York: Basic Books.

Hargreaves, A., & Fullan, M. (2016). *Professional kapital – en forandring af undervisningen på alle skoler* [Professional capital – a change of teaching in all schools]. Frederikshavn: Dafolo Forlag.

Hattie, H., & Yates, G. (2014). *Synlig læring og læringens anatomi* [Visible learning and the atonomy of learning]. Frederikshavn: Dafolo.

Lindström, L. (2009). Produkt- og procesvurdering i kreativ virksomhed [Product- and process assessment in creative work]. In L. Tanggard & S. Brinkmann (Eds.), *Kreativitetsfremmende læringsmiljøer i skolen* [Promoting creativity and learning in school] (pp. 151–170). Frederikshavn: Dafolo Forlag.

Løgstrup, K. E. (1972). Opdragelse og etik [Education and ethics]. *København: Pædagogik nr., 1*, 9–27.

Montuori, A., & Purser, R. (1995). Deconstructing the lone genius myth: Toward a contextual view of creativity. *Journal of Humanistic Psychology, 35*(3), 69–112.

Mumford, M. D., Hester, K. S., & Robledo, I. C. (2012). Creativity in organizations: Importance and approaches. In M. D. Mumford (Ed.), *Handbook of organizational creativity* (pp. 3–16). San Diego: Elsevier.

Nottingham, J. (2014). *Udfordrende læring* [Challenging learning]. Frederikshavn: Dafolo Forlag.

Rasmussen, J., Holm, C., & Kruse, S. (2007). *Viden om uddannelse. Uddannelsesforskning, pædagogik og pædagogisk praksis* [Knowledge about education: Educational research and educational practice]. København: Hans Reitzels forlag.

Robinson, S. K. (2011). *Out of our minds – Learning to be creative.* London: Capstone.

Rømer, T. A., Tanggaard, L., & Brinkmann, S. (2011). *Uren pædagogik til debat* [Debating impure pedagogy]. Aarhus: Klim.

Rømer, T. A., Tanggaard, L., & Brinkmann, S. (2017). *Uren pædagogik [Impure Pedagogies].* Aarhus: Klim.

Simonton, D. K. (2017). Big C versus little c. Defintions, implications and inherent creative contradictions. In R. Beghetto & B. Sriraman (Eds.), *Creative contradictions in education* (pp. 1–19). Cham: Springer.

Sternberg, R. J., & Lubart, T. I. (1995). *Defying the crowd: Cultivating creativity in a culture of conformity.* New York: Free Press.

Tanggaard, L. (2006). *Læring og identitet* [Learning and Identity]. Copenhagen: Hans Reitzels Forlag.

Tanggaard, L. (2013). The socio- materiality of creativity. *Culture and Psychology, 19*(1), 20–32.

Tanggaard, L. (2014). *Fooling around: Creative learning pathways.* Charlotte: Information Age Publishing, incorporated (Advances in Cultural Psychology: Constructing Human Development).

Tanggaard, L. (2016). *FAQ – kreativitet* [FAQ – creativity]. Copenhagen: Hans Reitzels Forlag.

Tanggaard, L., & Brinkmann, S. (2008). Til forsvar for den urene pædagogik [In defense of an impure pedagogy]. *Nordisk Pædagogik, 28*(4), 303–314.

Tanggaard, L., & Hjorth, R. (2017). Promoting abduction – a teaching experiment on creative learning processes in a high school classroom context. In R. A. Beghetto & B. Sriraman (Eds.), *Creative contradictions in education: Cross disciplinary paradoxes and perspectives.* 1 udg (Vol. 1, pp. 221–247). Schweizerland: Springer.

Tanggaard, L., Rømer, T., & Brinkmann, S. (2014, red). *Uren pædagogik II* [Impure pedagogy II]. Aarhus: Klim.

Taylor, C. (2004). *Modern social imaginaries.* Durham/London: Duke University Press.

Wallas, G. (1926). *The art of thought.* New York: Harcourt, Brace.

Part II
Dynamic Conceptions & Future Directions

Chapter 10
Creativity as a Dynamic, Personal, Parsimonious Process

Mark A. Runco

Abstract This entire volume is intended to challenge static conceptions of creative action and thought. The present chapter introduces a particular dynamic definition of creativity. It also explores applications of that definition, primarily for education. The definition detailed herein is only one of several, as is evidenced by the other chapters in this same volume, and it may be that there is overlap. There may also be disagreement, the exploration of which will no doubt lead to further refinements and advance in our understanding of creativity. For obvious reasons the present chapter begins with a brief summary of previous definitions of creativity. The new dynamic definition will make the most sense after this summary (also see Corazza, GE. Creativity Research Journal, 28:258–267 (2016)).

10.1 Introduction

This entire volume is intended to challenge static conceptions of creative action and thought. The present chapter introduces a particular dynamic definition of creativity. It also explores applications of that definition, primarily for education. The definition detailed herein is only one of several, as is evidenced by the other chapters in this same volume, and it may be that there is overlap. There may also be disagreement, the exploration of which will no doubt lead to further refinements and advance in our understanding of creativity. For obvious reasons the present chapter begins with a brief summary of previous definitions of creativity. The new dynamic definition will make the most sense after this summary (also see Corazza 2016).

This chapter also explores the idea that there is a mechanism that explains how creativity comes about. This involves the *construction of original interpretations of experience*. That idea is detailed below, as is Piaget's idea that "to understand is to invent," for it too emphasizes a dynamic process. This chapter also brings in an interplay of top-down and bottom-up cognitive processes and describes how that interplay

M. A. Runco (✉)
American Institute for Behavioral Research and Technology, Vista, CA, USA

© Springer Nature Switzerland AG 2019
R. A. Beghetto, G. E. Corazza (eds.), *Dynamic Perspectives on Creativity*,
Creativity Theory and Action in Education 4,
https://doi.org/10.1007/978-3-319-99163-4_10

is dynamic. It defines creativity such that discretion is involved, and that too implies a dynamic as the individual decides when to be creative and when not to be creative.

10.1.1 The Standard Definition of Creativity

The "standard definition" of creativity has been used for decades (see review by Runco and Jaeger 2012). It is most easily interpreted as static rather than dynamic. It posits that creative things must be both original and effective. The ratio of originality to effectiveness may vary in different domains or even at different phases of a creative process, but regardless, all creativity is both original and effective. The static nature of this standard definition is tied to the fact that it is usually applied to *things*. More often than not the label given to creative things is *product*, which is one of the six major perspectives on creativity. The other perspectives refer to creative personality, creative places, creative processes (Rhodes 1961), creative persuasion (Simonton 1995), and creative potential (Runco 2008). Recognizing these 6 Ps is helpful because it brings up the possibility that creativity can be understood as a process rather than a product, and processes are by definition dynamic.

Before turning from the standard definition to dynamic creative processes, it behooves us to acknowledge that originality and effectiveness are not the only criteria of creative things and creative processes. The standard definition works fairly well but is far from perfect. Indeed, a slew of alternative definitions have been published in the last 2–3 years (Acar et al. 2017; Corazza 2016; Kharkhurin 2014; Martin and Wilson 2017; Simonton 2012; Weisberg 2015), and most include criteria in addition to originality and effectiveness. One criterion that stands out is *authenticity*. This may be the most useful addition to a definition of creativity because it helps to insure that such a definition applies across cultures (Tan 2016) and it fits nicely with what the humanists said about creative expression and self-actualization. Put simply, self-actualized individuals are psychological healthy, authentic (true to themselves, to others, and to the topic or experience at hand), and creative.

The addition of authenticity to a definition of creativity might be especially helpful because it is inherently dynamic. This is implied by much of the humanistic research, which tends to view life as a journey, a process, a developmental process. Life is a matter of growth and change, and these are of course processes, and thus to be true and authentic, changes must be acknowledged and perhaps even directed. But all we really need to do is consider the label, *self-actualization,* for any actualization is a process. For the humanists, the self-actualization process depends on authenticity and creativity (Maslow 1968; Rogers 1954).

10.2 Creativity as Dynamic Construction

The addition of authenticity to a definition of creativity is useful, but it would be even more useful to go beyond self-actualization and to bring in the cognitive contributions to creativity. It would also be useful to be able to describe what underlying mechanisms actually explain how creative things come about. This could easily be the most important question in all of the creativity research, and any mechanism will need to be dynamic. What is it about humans that allows creativity? How are we creative? What do we inherit that provides us with the capacity to create?

These questions led to a theory that relies on a dynamic definition of creativity and which focuses on a mechanism that actually offers at least a partial explanation of the creative process. The theory has been outlined before, but earlier descriptions were primarily intended to show that creativity depends on individuals rather than social processes. Indeed, this theory was proposed in reaction to the social and attributional theories that became the norm 20 and 30 years ago (e.g., Csikzentmihalyi 1990; Kasof 1995) and are still alive and well (Glaveanu 2010). These social theories are useful because they describe how culture and Zeitgeist influence judgments of creativity, but they go too far and often conclude that without social recognition, there is no creativity. Elsewhere I have argued that there *is* creativity, even it the end result or product is not social recognized, and in fact even if there is no manifest product! That is a hint of the dynamic nature of personal creativity: it relegates static products and outcomes. The theory of personal creativity is a process theory with very broad implications (Runco 1995, 1996, 1997, 1999, 2003; Runco and Pina 2013).

Given that this theory started in reaction to static product and social views of creativity, it may make sense to introduce it by outlining what is misleading or even wrong with those alternative views. Just above I alluded to one thing what is wrong with static views: they are unrealistic. Life is a process, and creating is a process. Also important is that products do not tell us about the process that was used to create the product. Thus they do not help us to understand the causal mechanism underlying creation. They aren't really explanations at all. A scientific explanation must include causality, otherwise it does not really explain anything. Admittedly, the creative process may lead to a creative product, and that is one reason the creative process should be nurtured, but judgments of products often vary (Runco 1989; Runco et al. 2010, 2016; Runco and Smith 1992), an in fact some things are deemed creative at one point in time only to be deemed uncreative later! There are all kinds of reasons to recognize that creativity is a process.

Not all social views of creativity are product views, so something more should be said about the problems of social views, above and beyond problems of product views. The main problem with social views is that they over-emphasize judgments, attributions, and social reactions. Indeed, many of them go as far as to say that, without social recognition, there is no creativity (Csikzentmihalyi 1990; Glaveanu 2010; Kasof 1995). The fact of matter is that social recognition is distinct from creativity. It is extricable from it–and should be extricated because that is how the creative process works. Attributions follow the creation and are not required for the actual creation. Simplifying, a creative process occurs, and sometimes it results in an outcome that is judged as creative. There are at least two steps–creation and social recognition–and the first step can happen without the second. Just as important, the second step does not help in any way to explain the first. Including social recognition in a definition of creativity is therefore quite misleading. It conflates creation with social recognition. This is especially disconcerting given the scientific need for parsimony (Runco 2010).

So the creative process does not depend on social attributions and is therefore personal. In addition, the personal processes offer a parsimonious view of creativity and describe a mechanism that may explain how creativity comes about. What is required for personal creativity? Three things, the first being the *construction of original interpretations of experience* mentioned briefly earlier. This is how original ideas, insights, and ideas come about. The term *interpretations* is used because so much is known about how the human mind uses both top-down (conceptual) and bottom-up (data-driven) processes such that the individual constructs a meaningful understanding. And it is a construction; it is not just a snapshot of what is experienced. That would be all bottom-up, but instead the individual brings something to the construction of interpretations. It is in precisely this fashion that creativity is dynamic. There is a kind of interplay between the individual and his or her experience. Interpretations are always original, at least for the individual him- or herself, and we do not construct meaning in a random fashion–or it would not be meaningful! The fact that it is meaningful indicates that it is effective, though again, it might be only for the individual him- or herself.

One highly attractive feature of the theory of personal creativity is that interpretations, and thus the creation of meaningful interpretations, rely on a mechanism that is possessed by each of us. Children have the capacity for interpretation, older adults have it, individuals in all domains (e.g., art, mathematics, music, athletics, dance, design) have it. Dynamic creativity is a part of what it means to be human. It results from the deployment of cognitive capacities we all possess.

Personal creativity also involves *intentions*. A person is creative if his or hermeaningful and original interpretations result from effort; they are not serendipitous. Creative breakthroughs do sometimes occur by chance or accident, but including serendipity would probably lead to a mechanism that does not apply broadly. The process does also require *discretion*. In this context discretion refers to knowing when to invest in creativity, or when to construct original interpretations, and when instead to rely on memory, habit, tradition, or assumption. Life requires this kind of discretion because, although the creation of original ideas is frequently useful, it is always necessary, and in fact is sometimes inefficient or wasteful. Sometimes it is best to save one's resources for creative opportunities and to *satisfice*, which means to invest minimal effort. Assumptions, habits, and routines are sometimes very useful; they allow us to process information quickly when effortful processing would be a waste.

Then there is the fact that we are social animals (Aronson 1980). We need to get along, at least some of the time, and maybe most of the time! This in turn requires conformity or at least compliance to conventions. You might look at it this way: what kind of students and employees and citizens do we want? I suggest the ideal is to support people who retain the capacity for originality and creativity, but at the same time can get along with others. They know when to invest in new ideas and when to conform. That depends on discretion.

Discretion may sound a bit like the judgments that were criticized above, as part of the social recognition that is too often glued to creativity when it should be extricated. Actually, discretion is dynamic, at least in the sense that it is a process. The creative person exercises discretion in that he or she recognizes that one context lends itself to creativity, while a different context, encountered another time, does not, and indeed each context in which the person finds him- or herself is judged as right for creativity or not. That is a dynamic process, as the person moves from context and setting to context and setting.

One important implication of this view of creativity as interpretive follows from Piaget's (1976) theory of cognition and invention. He used the label *assimilation* to describe how an individual processes information and, in order to grasp it, actually alters it to understand it. He gave examples such as a child calling a dog a cat because both share four legs and live around people. This child's cognitive structures are apparently limited, probably because of experience (e.g., the family owns a cat but not a dog), and the child is not sure what to call the dog, but since it has four legs and two ears and is around the house, well, close enough, it's a cat. The information about the dog is forced into the schema for a cat. In doing so the child ignores the woof and many other features of the concept of "dog," and does so in order to process the information. Assimilation is enormously useful because it allows new information to be processed, even if not fully understood, and does so by altering what is processed. It is quite dynamic, and the Piagetian way to describe the initial stages of the construction of new knowledge, new schema, new understandings. Of relevance is the title of Piaget's (1976) monograph on this topic, namely "to understand is to invent." To my reading he may have used the word "create" instead of "invent." As was proposed earlier in this chapter, people create by constructing–or "inventing," or "creating"– meaning.

One reason I bring in the Piagetian view is because he also argued that true development requires assimilation and the invention of new understandings. For Piaget, if the person does not go through the adaptive process (which begins with assimilation), there is no real development. The person can memorize something, but that is not the same as understanding. Thus Piaget ties the invention of knowledge to development, and if I am correct that the same process helps us to understand creativity, it follows that creativity is required for development. I am using the word "development" here instead of "learning" because Piaget and others felt there were differences between and among growth, development, and learning; but in essence the idea here is that creativity is required for intellectual growth. The important point is that education must focus on personal creativity or students will not really learn (Runco 2003). They may memorize, but that won't serve them well when they leave school and are faced with the natural environment and ill-defined problems. Creativity is what is needed in the natural environment.

10.3 Implications and Clarifications

Several points need to be examined further. First is the idea that social recognition can be extricated from actual creativity. This does not mean that socially recognized creativity requires a different process from that described as personal creativity.

There is creativity that is only personal, but there is also socially recognized creativity. The difference? The former may not lead to a product and may not be observed and judged by any audience whatsoever. It may be creative and meaningful, but only for the individual. Of great significance is that socially recognized creativity also starts with the same process, the construction of an original interpretation, but it may lead to something that is shared and socially recognized. So *personal creativity and socially recognized creativity both start with and depend on the same constructive process*. The difference is that the latter goes further such that something is shared and attributed with creativity by an audience. That "something further" is not required for creativity, however, and it is not a part of the explanatory mechanism (i.e., the construction). Indeed, we should see creativity as one thing and attributions and recognition as other (social) things.

That being said, audiences can be creative when they attribute meaning to a product or person. This follows from the fact that they experience the result of the personal creative process (e.g., they may hear a new song that one individual composed) and they construct their own personal interpretations of it. That process may very well be the same as that used by the songwriter! It may be a construction of meaning, in this case the meaning of the song. Hence creators may construct new meaning, and audiences may experience that creation and construct their own creative interpretations of it. They may not do this; they could just listen to others in the audience and conform or agree. But they may actively construct their own interpretations, in which case they are also being creative, just as the songwriter or original creator was creative.

Indeed, all kinds of interesting questions arise, once the creativity of the audience is recognized. Consider, for example, that something may be creative that is meaningful in one (personal) way to the creator but is meaningful in another (creative) way to the audience–but their interpretations may differ! This difference has been debated for some time. Literary critics, for example, have debated "the text" for years, the idea being that all a critic needs to judge is the written product–the text–and he or she can formulate his or her own meaningful judgment. But others believe that, to judge a creation, be it textual or otherwise, judges should take into account the creator's view and situation. The theory outlined herein implies that judges should be free to create their own meanings and may ignore the creator, but here I merely wish to acknowledge the debate as an example of how both creators and audience may be creative and yet disagree with one another.

10.4 Conclusions

Admittedly this chapter describes only one view of how creativity involves a process and is dynamic. Then again, note the different ways that creativity is dynamic, given the personal and constructive view outlined here. Creative ideas and insights result from an interplay of bottom-up and top-down processes, for example, which is a dynamic interplay. In addition, discretion is required or the person would be blindly original but not necessarily creative, and such discretion means that the individual is actively deciding about when to be creative and when not to be creative–another dynamic aspect of the creative process. I leave it to the other contributors to this volume to explore other aspects of a dynamic creativity. I myself will be satisfied if we recognize that products tell us little about the underlying process, and thus lack explanatory power; and that to understand the *how* people create, we must look to processes.

References

Acar, S., Burnett, C., & Cabra, J. F. (2017). Ingredients of creativity: Originality and more. *Creativity Research Journal, 29*, 133–144.

Aronson, E. (1980). *The social animal*. New York: Worth.

Corazza, G. E. (2016). Potential originality and effectiveness: The dynamic definition of creativity. *Creativity Research Journal, 28*, 258–267.

Csikzentmihalyi, M. (1990). The domain of creativity. In M. A. Runco & R. S. Albert (Eds.), *Theories of creativity* (pp. 190–212). Newbury Park: Sage.

Glaveanu, V. P. (2010). Creativity as cultural participation. *Journal for the Theory of Social Behaviour, 41*(1), 48–67.

Kasof, J. (1995). Explaining creativity: The attributional perspective. *Creativity Research Journal, 8*, 311–366.

Kharkhurin, A. (2014). Creativity.4in1: Four-criterion construct of creativity. *Creativity Research Journal, 26*, 338–352.

Martin, L., & Wilson, N. (2017). Defining creativity with discovery. *Creativity Research Journal, 29*, 417–425.

Maslow, A. (1968). Creativity in self actualizing people. In *Toward a psychology of being* (pp. 135–145). New York: Van Nostrand Reinhold.

Piaget, J. (1976). *To understand is to invent*. New York: Penguin.

Rogers, C. R. (1954). Towards a theory of creativity. *ETC: A Review of General Semantics, 11*, 249–260.

Rhodes, M. (1961). An analysis of creativity. *Phi Delta Kappan, 42*, 305–310.

Runco, M. A. (1989). The creativity of children's art. *Child Study Journal, 19*, 177–189.

Runco, M. A., & Jaeger, G. (2012). The standard definition of creativity. *Creativity Research Journal, 24*, 92–96.

Runco, M. A. (1995). Insight for creativity, expression for impact. *Creativity Research Journal, 8*, 377–390.

Runco, M. A. (1996). Personal creativity: Definition and developmental issues. *New Directions for Child Development, 72*(Summer), 3–30.

Runco, M. A. (1997). Personal creativity: Lessons from literary criticism. In L. Dorfman & C. Martindale (Eds.), *Emotion, creativity and art* (Vol. 1, pp. 305–317). Perm: Perm State Institute of Arts and Culture.

Runco, M. A. (1999). Creativity need not be social. In A. Montuori & R. Purser (Eds.), *Social creativity* (Vol. 1, pp. 237–264). Cresskill: Hampton.

Runco, M. A. (2003). Education for creative potential. *Scandinavian Journal of Education, 47*, 317–324.

Runco, M. A. (2008). Creativity and education. *New Horizons in Education, 56*(1), 107–115.

Runco, M. A. (2010). Education based on a parsimonious theory of creativity. In R. A. Beghetto & J. C. Kaufman (Eds.), *Nurturing creativity in the classroom* (pp. 235–251). New York: Cambridge University Press.

Runco, M. A., & Pina, J. (2013). Imagination and personal creativity. In M. Taylor (Ed.), *Oxford handbook of the development of imagination* (pp. 379–386). New York: Oxford University Press.

Runco, M. A., & Smith, W. R. (1992). Interpersonal and intrapersonal evaluations of creative ideas. *Personality and Individual Differences, 13*, 295–302.

Runco, M. A., Kaufman, J. C., Halliday, L. R., & Cole, J. C. (2010). Change in reputation as index of genius and eminence. *Historical Methods, 43*, 91–96.

Runco, M. A., Acar, S., Kaufman, J. C., & Halliday, L. R. (2016). Changes in reputation and associations with fame and biographical data. *Journal of Genius and Eminence, 1*, 52–60.

Simonton, D. K. (1995). Exceptional personal influence: An integrative paradigm. *Creativity Research Journal, 8*, 371.

Simonton, D. K. (2012). Taking the U.S. Patent office criteria seriously: A quantitative three-criterion creativity definition and its implications. *Creativity Research Journal, 24*, 97–106.

Tan, C. (2016). Creativity and confucius. *Journal of Genius and Eminence, 1*, 84–89.

Weisberg, R. (2015). On the usefulness of "value" in the definition of creativity. *Creativity Research Journal, 27*, 111–124.

Chapter 11
Polyphonic Orchestration: The Dialogical Nature of Creativity

Ingunn Johanne Ness and Vlad Glăveanu

Abstract In this chapter, we aim to propose and develop a dialogical account of creativity. While creativity is often understood as a feature of a person or products, we offer a different account. We believe creativity is not a static "object" (personal trait or product feature) but rather the dynamic and evolving quality of the relationships we develop with others within a shared cultural environment (Glăveanu VP, The creative self: effect of beliefs, self-efficacy, mindset, and identity. Academic Press, Waltham, 2017). The chapter builds on an extensive ethnographic fieldwork of innovative idea development in organisational settings. Our focus is thus on the concrete case of creativity in multidisciplinary groups in order to illustrate and develop further the concept of Polyphonic Orchestration (see Ness IJ, Eur J Innov Manag 20:557–577, 2017). The empirical research we build on showed that when leaders are open to co-construction and dialogue in the groups, the chance of succeeding in building a creative culture improves considerably. This is in contrast to the way leadership is often viewed as a set of managing strategies, almost coming in from the "outside", to manage the creative processes. The concept of Polyphonic Orchestration portrays creativity at once, as an individual and social, personal and cultural process. This notion is central, we propose, to a dialogical account of creating as it brings forward the pre-condition of dialogue and points to the necessity of guiding the social exchanges that are at the heart of creativity.

I. J. Ness (✉)
University of Bergen, Bergen, Norway
e-mail: Ingunn.Ness@uib.no

V. Glăveanu
Webster University, Bellevue, Switzerland

11.1 Introduction

The aim of this chapter is to propose and develop a dynamic, contextual, and perhaps most importantly dialogical account of creativity. This account stands in sharp contrast to the "standard" definition of creativity in terms of the originality and effectiveness of creative products (Runco and Jaeger 2012). While many creativity researchers would largely agree that creativity is a process rather than a feature of persons or products, the field itself is still oriented towards the psychometric measurement of individual abilities or product characteristics. Studying creativity as a process is methodologically difficult given the fact that processes involve action, movement, and change. The statistical apparatus we want to use in relation to creativity is not well equipped to deal with change. In particular, it is oriented towards numerical values based upon static properties. We can therefore ask, what is the alternative?

In this chapter, we will build on dialogism as a concept to (re)capture the dynamic quality of creativity, understood not as an ability but as a process of being in the world and relating to it. According to this epistemological standpoint, creativity is not a "thing" but rather the evolving quality of our relationships with others, with objects, institutions and everything that makes up our cultural environment (Glăveanu 2014). Based on dialogism (Bakhtin 1986; Marková 2003), we postulate that such relationships are best described as dialogues. The notion of dialogue is interesting on many accounts, but most of all because it suggests a bidirectional exchange. In a dialogue, there is not only a speaker and a listener, or addressor and addressee, but an exchange between these two positions. More than this, speakers are, simultaneously, listeners (Mead 1934) and both positions build on and contribute to a shared context of cultural signs and meanings.

Creativity as dialogue (see also Glăveanu 2017) is a first step towards the dynamic, relational, and contextual account we envision. Instead of a phenomenon grounded in person or product, we have one that necessarily involves two or more positions. Even when creators work in complete solitude, they are still in dialogue with themselves, with the ideas of others and with a wide array of material and institutional conditions that make their activity possible in the first place. Dialogues are not only relational and temporal; they are also open towards the future. Bakhtin (1986) pioneered the view that "true" dialogues are on-going because they incorporate positions and views that are always in tension with each other. He contrasted this with the monologue in which one voice overpowers all others and effectively excludes the differences and tension that are the engine of creativity (see Glăveanu and Beghetto 2017). Monologism is, in this paradigm, is the very antithesis of creativity as it would hinder free expressions and explorations of other perspectives in a conversation.

Bakhtin (1986, p. 132) argued that the monological word is often attached to power and thus to leaders (see also Dysthe 1997 and Ness 2017). For, Bakhtin there is a contradiction between dialogue and monologue, meaning the internally persuasive word and the authority's word.

> …the internally persuasive word is half-our and half-someone else's. Its creativity and productiveness consist precisely in the fact that such a word awakens new and independent words that it organizes masses of our words from within, and does not remain in an isolated and static condition. (Bakhtin 1981, pp. 345–346).

If dialogue is a necessary condition of creativity, it is not always a sufficient one. To illustrate this point we can think about the concrete example of group creativity. There are many cognitive and social factors that interfere in and shape the relationships between people and their voices or perspectives (Paulus and Nijstad 2003). Unfortunately, diversity of points of view is a double-edged sword and the polyphony or multi-voicedness that characterises teamwork often leads to frustration or even dead-ends and non-consensus. This is due to the fact that the divergent nature of dialogues and polyphony in general requires a balancing factor represented by guidance and even convergence. In other words, the multiple voices or perspectives placed in relation to with each other in the creative process need some form of orchestration if they are to turn potential into achievement.

In this chapter, we will focus on the concrete case of creativity in multidisciplinary groups in order to illustrate and develop further the concept of polyphonic orchestration (see also Ness 2017). This notion is central, we propose, to a dialogical account of creativity as it brings forward the pre-condition of dialogue and points to the necessity of guiding dialogues. We also continue the aural or musical analogies built on by Bakhtin who used polyphony – and heteroglossia – as key concepts in his work. To orchestrate means both to listen and act, to guide and be guided, to create harmonies by building on dissonance in an on-going cycle. This is traditionally the role of leaders within a group. But this is also what each one of us enacts in our daily life whenever we produce new and meaningful ideas, objects or projects. The orchestration of creativity is, at once, an individual and social, personal and cultural process. As follows, we will illustrate it within an organisational context and then reflect on its general principles. But before, let's revisit briefly the "voices" about creativity we are responding to here.

11.2 Creativity: From Individual Product to Social Process

The historical trajectory of creativity as a topic of research experienced a few "moments" of rupture and transformation. One of the most notable took place around the time of the Renaissance (at least in Western history), when men – sadly not necessarily women – replaced God as the only possible creator (see Weiner 2000). This Copernican move empowered creativity and innovation, even if in the case of the few rather than the many. A more recent shift, largely associated with mid-twentieth century psychology, saw a "democratisation" of creative potential and a growing belief that each and every person is creative in one way or another (Glăveanu 2010). For as liberating as this modern conception is, however, it still places the focus on isolated individuals and their achievements, particularly in stereotypically creative domains such as art, science or design. Measuring creativity by considering products, the cornerstone of the first scientific studies in this area, has gradually been replaced by a concern for process (see Lubart 2001). It is only in recent years, however, that this concern for process has been used to challenge the traditionally static definition of creativity itself (see, for instance, Corazza 2016).

What this contemporary movement stresses is the fact that creative products and processes are dynamic and inter-related. Dialogism makes a powerful contribution to this new trend by effectively moving the debate away from products and processes altogether. Within a dialogical framework it does not make sense to separate the two but integrate them within a broader conception of positions, perspectives, dialogues, polyphony and, last but not least, the orchestration of creativity. Let us consider these concepts in turn.

For a long time the focus in creativity research has been on the creativity of the person and his or her intra-psychological attributes, mainly intelligence and personality (e.g., Barron and Harrington 1981). Paradoxically, by considering these psychological "elements" separately and in a static manner, these kind of investigations tend to lose sight not only of the concept of creativity, but of the person as well. People create as individual dynamic systems embedded within larger social, and equally dynamic systems. If we are to understand the contribution of personality, intelligence, motivation, or any other psychological function, to creativity, we need to respect the integrative, holistic nature of the agents doing the creating and the world that supports and responds to their actions. In other words, we need to understand the person not as an isolated, self-contained entity, but in a multiple and dynamic relationship with others, within society. The notion of position is essential in this regard. Individuals and positions are not identical: a person can occupy – and does occupy – multiple positions at the same time and, most importantly, move between them (Gillespie and Martin 2014). Positions can be defined in physical terms (e.g., where people stand in space), in social terms (e.g., depending on the social roles people adopt), and symbolic terms (e.g., depending on the meaning they give to the world from their standpoint). By exchanging positions – physical, social and symbolic – we become flexible in our relation to ourselves and the world and are able to act in a creative and dialogical manner.

What happens when we re-position ourselves? Effectively, we change our perspective. Perspectives can be defined, in a pragmatist way, as action orientations (Gillespie 2006) since they guide our thinking and our behaviour. Every position is associated with one or multiple perspectives. For example, two people who sit at different ends of the table have quite different perceptual perspectives of the table, the room, and each other. Students and teachers – two specific social and symbolic roles – develop and act based on different perspectives about the situation they find themselves in. The fact that the people in the first example and the teacher and students in the second one do talk to each other – engage in dialogue – and they have the potential, physically or imaginatively, to exchange positions, is crucial for bridging the gap between them, building common ground, and acting creatively (see Glăveanu 2015a).

These dialogical relationships are the bedrock of creativity. It is because we can communicate and exchange perspectives, through re-positioning, that we can reach new understandings and develop new forms of action and interaction. Dialogues are grounded in perspective taking. We need to be able to take the perspective of those we are exchanging with for communication to continue and be successful. Equally, creative people build on their capacity to understand, both cognitively and emotionally, the perspective of other people or what it means to occupy different positions in the world. In Bakhtin's terms, they develop a polyphonic way of seeing the world, one filled by the voices of other people. In fact, there is a deep parallel between the notions of perspective and that of voice. Both are social, interactive, and enabled by culture. In this chapter, we will use them interchangeably, even though they come from different theoretical traditions (pragmatism and dialogism) and have their specificity.

The last theoretical step is represented by orchestration. Positions, perspectives or voices do not exist in isolation from each other. On the contrary, they are defined precisely by their relational value; for instance, the separate roles of teacher and student would be unimaginable without the other. This relationship, however, changes over time. If it didn't, we would not have the possibility to re-position or take the perspective of others. Each one of these positions introduces us to a new sphere of experience that enriches our imagination (Zittoun and Gillespie 2015) and diversifies the resources of our creative action. But re-positioning and perspective taking are not taking place at random. They are coming out of a certain life course, they respond to the needs of the current situation, and they anticipate a certain future. In other words, they are orchestrated, in the here and now, by the web of actions and interactions the creative agent participates in.

Polyphonic orchestration is thus placed at the core of the creating, and is directing the processes taking place in what Ness called the "Room of Opportunity" (Ness and Søreide 2014). In this metaphorical room, multiple voices or perspectives co-exist and become articulated with each other. They are effectively orchestrated by the participants in the interaction or, in the case of solitary work, by the different positions internalised by the creative person. In what follows we will present the research that documented this process, led by the first author, and discuss her findings regarding collaborative creativity, multidisciplinarity, summed up in what she called Polyphonic Orchestration. After this, we will return to the dialogical approach to creativity and derive some general principles that underpin polyphonic orchestration and their theoretical and practical consequences. If we accept that creativity is dialogical then this has deep implications for how we understand, study and cultivate it. Dynamic, relational and contextual accounts of creating cannot operate within the same psychometric logic that dominated the field since its inception. A new science of creativity is to be (re)invented and, with it, a new methodological apparatus.

11.3 The Polyphonic Orchestration of Creativity in Multidisciplinary Groups

With the research questions "What characterizes creative knowledge processes in multidisciplinary groups working with developing innovative ideas, and how are these processes facilitated?" as a point of departure, the interest was in understanding more about how members of multidisciplinary groups develop new knowledge and ideas dialogically, and also how such processes are facilitated by leaders.

Consequently, she sought access to groups doing authentic innovation work in the hope that access to groups working with developing innovative ideas, would ensure rich and interesting data. Thus, the selection of research groups was a careful selection of possible organisations, using a combination of convenience and a purposive sample (Patton 2002).

Access to this particular field – groups working with innovation – turned out to be a challenge, however. Innovation is highly business sensitive due to strong competition in the market and thus organisations hesitate to let outsiders enter such groups in order to avoid the risk of leaked information. One of the groups was based at the heart of the Innovation Department in the International Oil and Gas Company, Statoil, another group worked with strategy in Statoil, and the last group was based in a Norwegian Research Institute. Thus, the research field was highly confidential. Still, after meetings and e-mail correspondence where the intentions of the project were presented with a project plan, trust was gained from the management in the organisations and access to three different groups. Then various confidentiality agreements were signed. We are not allowed to report the *content* of what was discussed and developed, as this was all confidential. In particular, this was important in the Statoil groups. Fortunately, the focus for the research was more on *how* these group members worked, collaborated, interacted and thus on creative dialogical *processes*.

All three groups had as mandate to develop innovative ideas. See Table 11.1 below, describing the groups.

Table 11.1 Groups that participated in research (in Ness 2016, pp. 39–40)

Group name	Formal group task/aim	Group composition
Strategy group	Strategy development	Core group: 3 male members from different parts of the organization with different experiences and competences, including legal and on/offshore logistics and engineering
Oil and gas company	Their aim was to develop a business case with cost-efficient solutions and with a competitive instinct	
		Group meetings were supplemented with 3–10 members with specific knowledge
Innovation group	Idea/innovation development	Core group: 5 males and 1 female researchers with different expertise and competences, including engineering, business, geophysics, cyber technology
Oil and gas company	Their aim was to develop radical ideas based on needs and challenges across the organization	
		In some meetings the group was supplemented with 3-7 members with specific knowledge
Research group	Their aim was to develop innovative research projects and write applications for external funding	3 males and 1 female researchers with different expertise and competences
Research institute		

After the three groups were identified, courses were undertaken in order to get an entrance card. This made it possible to come and go as one pleased and to follow the groups over a long period.

In order to understand what characterized creative knowledge processes leading to innovative ideas and how they were facilitated, the researcher investigated the social interactions, communication, and relational processes specific for the three workgroups. The focus was on *how* the group members negotiated and collaborated when they developed innovative ideas. As the development of new ideas, in a dialogical perspective, takes place *between* the group members rather than *within* each individual group member, it was applied concepts and ideas drawn from sociocultural theories, primarily the idea that knowledge emerges and develops through a process of co-construction and dialogue. This co-construction is assumed to take place in the context of an active and dynamic relationship between the social and the individual. Knowledge is viewed as socially co-constructed through interaction with the social, cultural or physical environment, and in the context of a process distributed in both time and space.

While acknowledging that there are also important individual differences between people that play a great part in group creativity, the focus in this project has been on the dialogical relations established between participants. This focus doesn't deny but actually brings to the fore individual differences (in perspective or knowledge, for instance), while considering them in a very different light: individual-level diversity comes out of multiple and dynamic social relations and forms of belonging. In this sense, dialogical relations both thrive on individual differences and result in individual differentiation, but the process through which this occurs is thoroughly social.

The project was qualitative in nature and exploratory in scope. An ethnographic research design was chosen as it was necessary to experience the social life of the groups studied over longer periods of time in situ.

In accordance with ethnographic designs (Denzin and Lincoln 2000; Fangen 2010; Gerson and Horowitz 2003; Krumsvik 2014), the following wide range of methods of data collection were also used as part of the fieldwork: formal observations of workshops and meetings; formal field notes of group meetings; formal semi-structured interviews with the leaders of the three groups; formal semi-structured interviews with core group members who also were experienced leaders of innovation and development processes in their organisations; and informal field conversations with group leaders and group members. The fieldwork lasted for a period of 18 months and this allowed the researcher to collect an extensive amount of data. All dialogue and group work was then recorded and transcribed.

The analyses were inductive. First, the empirical observations were analyzed. This resulted in an understanding of the collaborative processes that reflects what was seen and experienced in the groups. This understanding helped to narrow the focus and ask new questions. The questions were then explored in the analysis of focus group interviews and contributed to further understanding of the phenomenon, helped once more to narrow the focus and to ask questions that are more specific. These questions were finally explored in the analysis of individual leader

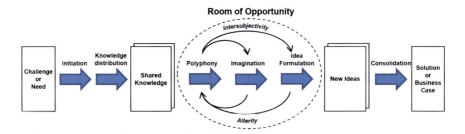

Fig. 11.1 Model, "The Room of Opportunity". (Ness and Søreide 2014, p. 557)

interviews. What came out of this sequential exploration was a deeper understanding of dialogical creativity, based on a triangulation of findings from both observations and interviews. In these analyses, the researcher interpreted the data and created meaning and categories that were not explicit in the text itself.

One of the main findings from this project was that group members developed their ideas by going through six phases (see also Ness and Søreide 2014) (Fig. 11.1).

The process started with some kind of challenge or need. Then the processes went through initiation and knowledge distribution when different group members were put together and shared knowledge on the task at hand. The process ended with a solution or business case after a consolidation of a concrete idea, in the two last phases, when the group members formulated and then consolidated their concrete ideas. When looking closer at the identified phases, it was concluded that group members learned from each other and built a knowledge platform during the first phases of the process, and this enabled the development of innovative ideas in the last phases. Group members came from different disciplines and thus had different fields of expertise. It was thus crucial that they could learn from each other in order to develop a shared knowledge. This helped them develop later on new ways of thinking and understanding, for instance, systems about which they already had some knowledge.

An example from the analyses is when Hannah, a member of the Innovation group, expressed her view on learning and the importance of bringing together people with different competences:

> Participation and enthusiasm is important – and building on each other's ideas and perspectives. When there are several people in the group with different competences, you get this dynamics which is so important. You are challenged by others. You learn to think in a new fashion when you hear how others talk about matters you thought you knew. (Ness and Søreide 2014, p. 553)

However, even though the diversity of perspectives among group members clearly could the engine for creativity, this diversity was also difficult to handle. Sometimes group members used very domain specific terminology and consequently they had problems understanding each other. Each group member brought with him or her their own set of knowledge, ideas and experiences and they struggled with communicating in a way that was constructive (i.e., trying to place this knowledge in the context of other people's expertise). Often the discussions centred on what a term actually meant or what definition would be the "right" one to use. This is often the case in cross boundary work. (For more see Edwards 2011; Ness and Riese 2015) Still, despite these challenges, the groups managed to progress with their innovation work.

We discovered that creativity and idea development peaked in the three middle phases since it was in this part of the process the group member started to negotiate and challenge new ideas. This was done in a circular movement in which group members went back and forth between the different identified phases in the discussions. In these discussions, they explored different ideas and scenarios and in this way could stretch the limits for what was possible at the time.

Consequently, these phases could be seen as a separate "room" within the process, characterized by many voices that stated, confronted, and built on different views and perspectives. It was a polyphonic phase that, once more, stimulated both individual and collective imagination. Consequently, this was called the "Room of Opportunity" (Ness and Søreide 2014).

Developing innovative ideas was, to a large extent, was about bringing together different perspectives and letting group members dialogue with each other and co-construct ideas. An example is when Arne in the Statoil Innovation group emphasized the importance of different perspectives. He said:

> I think that multidisciplinary settings stimulate creativity. It's important to bring together individuals who work towards the same problem, but they see things from different perspectives. They will have different views on the problem, right? (Ness and Søreide 2014, p. 552)

He explained that he thought it was important to have diverse and multidisciplinary working groups when working with innovation, an impression shared by other participants.

However, innovative ideas were not reached automatically. The process of building a common knowledge platform for enabling innovative ideas required that the group members, from different disciplines, had the ability to recognize and acknowledge others' competence and resources in addition to their own special expertise. Thus, these findings revealed that it was not enough to bring together group members from different disciplines; they needed additional relational competence in order for the collaboration to succeed and for creativity and learning to occur (Ness and Riese 2015).

An example that showed how the leader of the Innovation group, emphasized the value of the relational climate and collaboration in the group, was when he talked about group dynamics and how important it was to have trust between group members. He said:

> We have different competences gathered in one place so to say, and there is a huge potential in tossing things back and forth between the different people. This synergy is really good, that we can say what is on our mind – and if someone disagrees, that is ok too. There must be trust in the group so that everybody participates. And also respect and understanding for each other's special competence is important, I think. (Ness and Riese 2015, p. 36)

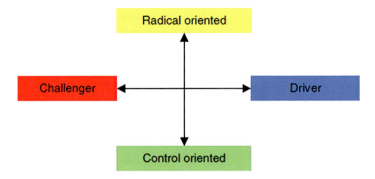

Fig. 11.2 Four roles in the relational dynamics in the groups

Furthermore, other findings in this research indicated the fact that effective leaders showed awareness of how imagination could be stimulated. Across all the three groups, the leaders sought a creative climate by forming groups that were characterized by both a diversity and polyphony in disciplinary perspectives, but also in the way group members related to each other. When looking closer at group dynamics, it was identified four complementary roles. These roles also could be organised along two axes in describing the interactions between members. The roles are: driver vs. challenger, and control oriented vs. radical oriented. The driver in the group would look for progression and moving forward with the discussions, while the challenger would often provide an opposite "force" and seeking further exploration or disagreeing so that progression stopped and the group spent more time discussing a matter. In this way there would be a push and pull dynamics between these two roles. Similar, the radical oriented role would push limits and go for wild and radical ideas out of the box and in which the sky is the limit with no reflections on limiting factors, while the control oriented role would have an opposite function and focus on costs and regulations which would limit and "weigh down" the more radical thinking. In this way, there was a dynamic between the four roles that influenced how creative the discussions were. These roles were dynamic and dialogically related, and they could be observed in the way members changed certain positions (perspectives or voices) during the discussions. Further, these roles seemed to have complementary functions in the relational space established within the group, and the leaders seemed to actively stimulate each one of them in order to create a dynamic that enabled creativity (Fig. 11.2).

The interaction between these four identified roles added a different "energy" to each group and moment within the process, and often provided tensions the groups could explore in a creative manner (Ness 2017).

We further observed that leaders seemed to orchestrate these roles in order to enable creativity in the groups and that this orchestration was about opening up for new ideas to occur by using a dialogical and open approach that was not too controlling. This way of orchestrating required the leaders to activate all the voices in the group and they achieved a creative climate by stimulating the different perspectives and roles involved. An example is when the leader of the Research Institute group, Craig, said:

> When creating innovation, one needs to create certain group processes and a movement towards new ideas. This requires a mix of different persons, and they all need to have the courage to open up and contribute actively with their personality and intellectual powers. There must be an impulse, which ignites motion – it does not just happen. It must be triggered and followed. You can call it roles. The roles can ignite that motion towards innovative ideas. (Ness 2017, p. 571)

In summary, these findings highlight the ways in which group members in multidisciplinary teams developed ideas and co-constructed knowledge in a collaborative and dialogical manner. The findings also show that the different perspectives and dynamics in the groups, including between the four different roles, were encouraged by the leaders and resulted in tensions that stimulated the imagination. However, this tension needed a safe environment in the groups in order to be constructive (Ness and Riese 2015). An emotional and supportive climate in the groups seemed thus to influence the group members' ability to use their imagination as a collective. Positive relationships supported imagination and creativity. The leaders orchestrated the creative knowledge processes by using a dialogical and open approach and this relational leader practice can be defined as Polyphonic Orchestration (Ness 2017).

11.4 Dialogical Creativity

The study discussed before offers a rich illustration of the processes of polyphonic orchestration within multidisciplinary groups. This research context is both exceptional – in the sense of a particular organisation, bringing experts to work together – and extremely mundane – we oftentimes find ourselves in situations that require collaboration and the sharing of expertise. While it might be argued that dialogical creativity characterises teamwork in particular, we want to use the set of findings above to reflect on a much wider range of contexts. Indeed, if we move away from individualistic conceptions of creativity we soon come to realise that creative processes always bring together a plurality of positions, roles and perspectives; these blur any sharp distinction between "individual" and "group" creativity and make both intrinsically collaborative (see also Barron 1999). What we call here "polyphonic orchestration" or the dynamic organisation of different voices or perspectives within creative action is both a personal and social phenomenon. In essence, it testifies to the dialogical nature of the mind doing the creating and its interconnection with the minds of others.

In this discussion we want to highlight some distinctive features of polyphonic orchestration or what, in other words, defines dialogical creativity.

1. *The dynamic tension between similarity and difference.* For Bakhtin (1986), dialogues never end in "sameness" or identical views. On the contrary, dialogical

forms of relating to each other are meant to further our understanding, to produce new meanings while maintaining differences. Paradoxically though, we need to build common ground in order to conserve difference and help the emergence of novelty. This is part of the lesson of studying multidisciplinary groups. The "room of opportunity" (Ness and Søreide 2014) in which creativity and imagination flourish is set up when enough sharing takes place that people can take each other's perspective *while* maintaining their own points of view. The act of perspective taking, essential for creativity (Glăveanu 2015a, b), is interesting to examine in this regard. First of all, we never "take" the perspective of others but, rather, construct perspectives in dialogue or interaction with them (see also Glăveanu and de Saint Laurent in press). We thus understand – at a cognitive, affective or action level – the standpoint of other people without fully letting go of our own. This is not an image of the solipsistic mind, generating mental representations in isolation, neither is it a romanticised account in which the positions of self and other constantly merge through identification and empathy. We learn from Bakhtin, 1984, p. 110 that: "Truth is not born nor is it to be found inside the head of an individual person, it is born *between people* collectively searching for truth, in the process of their dialogical interaction". It is, in fact, the dialogue that relates the perspective of self and that of others that defines perspective taking and makes it so fertile for creativity. This dialogue produces new meanings by cultivating reflexivity or the possibility to see oneself and one's view as an other would (Mead 1934; de Saint-Laurent and Glăveanu 2016). Dialogical creativity is thus grounded in the productive tension between similarity and difference, closeness and distance, the perspective of self and those of others.

2. *The cooperation and movement between different roles.* The notion of role is interesting for dialogism as, in some ways, it corresponds to that of position. We can think of roles as positions that are defined in social terms. Indeed, a role can only be conceived in relation to other roles within a social arena. While many theories refer to roles as institutionally defined positions (e.g., Gillespie and Martin 2014), for instance, buyer and seller, doctor and patient, teacher and student, there is much more to this notion than established social categories. The research discussed in this chapter uses this notion in wider sense when identifying the interplay between challenger, driver, radical oriented and control oriented roles within multidisciplinary groups. In effect, these are positions within the group that make accessible a certain range of perspectives rather than others. For instance, challengers would probably foster critical perspectives while control oriented people would favour predictability. The interesting thing is that these roles or positions are not fixed. Indeed, one and the same person might play multiple roles in a group or change roles depending on context and moment within the life course. Importantly, these positions and their associated perspective become internalised and represent, in Bakhtin's terms, voices that contribute to the orchestration of creativity within as well as between people. What matters the most from a dialogical standpoint is not so much the number of roles, positions or voices but the movement between them. Being able to re-position one-

self, adopt new roles and thus understand those who "speak" from their position, is crucial for both collaboration and creativity. It allows enough flexibility to be able to notice new meanings and possibilities for action. It also contributes to the balance mentioned above between sameness and difference, attachment to a certain role and openness to others, including radically different ones. In many ways, the process of "divergent thinking", often mentioned in relation to creativity (Baer 2014), is being reconceptualised by dialogism as the capacity to exchange positions and perspectives in relation to a topic or situation.

3. *Polyphonic orchestration is not a given but a collaborative achievement.* Another important lesson derived from the study presented here is that successful group work has specific antecedents. Among them, openness, curiosity and respect for each other's perspectives stand out as particularly important (see Ness and Riese 2015). These allow group members to develop mutual trust, which is essential for the development of creativity and, more generally, the development of a healthy and well-functioning self (Winnicott 1971). An atmosphere of trust enables the exploration, experimentation and playfulness specific for creative action, both individual and collective. In fact, the three conditions identified by Ness in her study are important pillars for dialogical creativity. Openness implies the recognition of the fact that other positions exist and their perspectives can and should be explored. Curiosity underpins the motivation to start this exploration process, to get to know more about others and their views (and, through reflexivity understand better oneself and one's own views in this process). Finally, respect is crucial for going beyond the simple recognition of other voices or perspectives. It effectively legitimises them and considers them implicitly valuable for the task at hand. Processes of polyphonic orchestration build on each one of these conditions which, for as basic as they might sound, are often difficult to achieve in practice. There are multiple barriers – personal, interpersonal and cultural – preventing us from recognising other's points of view and engaging with their perspective (see Glăveanu and Beghetto 2017). And these barriers become apparent not only in situations of group work but also when we are creating in solitude. What makes certain perspectives not come to mind? What makes us easily dismiss others? The dialogical approach to creativity expands the role of openness, curiosity and respect from external to internal interactions and dialogues. In the end, what is being orchestrated within creativity is a polyphony of voices and points of view. If you are not able to identify these voices as valuable, there is little chance of learning from them or creating with their help.

4. *Effective leadership and facilitation is essential for the polyphonic orchestration of creativity.* Leadership is a topic that receives more and more attention in relation to creativity (Carmeli et al. 2013). And yet, very often, it is treated as a separate phenomenon or set of processes that comes in, from the "outside", to shape or guide creative processes. Based on the findings of the study discussed here we can see how leadership is much more ubiquitous than this. According to Dysthe (1997, p. 85), a leader who acknowledges a dialogical perspective, an understanding of the importance of the internally persuasive word and the asymmetry

in the relation between a leader and a co-worker, will have greater chance of succeeding in building a creative culture. The groups under investigation had formal leaders but the successful leaders among them were those who knew how to adapt their leadership style to the dynamic of the group and the different stages of the creative process (Ness 2017). In other words, effective leadership involved the capacity to take multiple positions or adopt different roles in order to contribute to the overall orchestration of the process. The notion of orchestration itself is revealing in this regard. Orchestras need conductors but the conducts are not standing apart from the music. They are active listeners and capable of adapting and guiding the process from the inside. The same applies to dialogic creativity: its dialogues and tensions need facilitation and guidance. We would argue in fact that successful creators are those who understand their own processes and have internalised good leadership models to help manage them. Of course, what constituted good or effective leadership and facilitation is highly contextual and will depend on the team, the task, and stage in the process. When working alone, leadership is not absent but reflected in the way in which different perspectives are managed by the person. In both cases, the task of leadership is to cultivate the diversification of perspectives and their meaningful integration (Glăveanu and Gillespie 2015). Like a masterful director, leaders who aim for creative or innovative outputs need to cultivate the openness, curiosity and respect mentioned above. They should be mindful of the different roles and positions present in the group or situation and allow them to develop and interact with each other. Last but not least, leadership is not the opposite of polyphony for as long as they are not aiming to close the debate and make everyone reach the same conclusion. Itself, the task of leading or facilitating is a polyphonic one, drawing its strength from multiplicity rather than sameness and uniformity.

The four characteristics of dialogical creativity presented above nuance our understanding of polyphonic orchestration and can be used to guide its practical application. Taken together, these features challenge many of our usual assumptions about creativity and, more broadly, about our existence as agentic, social beings. Creativity is not grounded only in difference and novelty. It does not simply emerge when multiple voices or perspectives are available. And it is not separate from leadership and facilitation. The notion of polyphonic orchestration paints a different picture of this process, bringing together its multiple and oftentimes antagonistic facets. Creativity is, at once, individual and social, shared and different, common and unique, constrained and free.

What would be the implications of a dialogical theory of creativity for education? Acknowledging and utilizing different perspectives in course activities are important if universities aim to educate autonomous thinkers, endowed with an awareness of different ways of conceiving a topic and abilities of thinking creatively. According to Biesta (2013), education works in three overlapping domains: qualification, socialization, and subjectification. Through education we become qualified to do certain things, we become socialized into a culture of certain ways of thinking and acting, and we (can) become autonomous subjects of moral judgement, responsibility and action. Depending on context, different domains may be more or less in the foreground. However, in light of the developments and massification of higher education over the last decades (Guri-Rosenblit et al. 2007; Hornsby and Osman 2014), it seems particularly important that university programs aim to facilitate course activities that provides growth in all three domains. In order to do this, a dialogical practice is crucial because if we look to Higher Education, we find that the number of students enrolling in this sector has increased drastically. In the case of Norway, for instance, the number of students enrolled at Universities has gone from 6.983 students in 1997 to 82.193 in 2017 (NSD 2018). As a result, student groups have become more diverse, encompassing young people with different cultural and socio-economic backgrounds (Biggs and Tang 2011). These changes have contributed to transforming universities from elite institutions to institutions concerned with mass education, and put more strain on the way the institutions teach because "more diverse groups of students need better pedagogical facilitation" (Michelsen and Aamodt 2007, p. 14, translated from Norwegian). However, this diversity is not simply a challenge that needs to be overcome, but also an opportunity to promote dialogues between a wide range of perspectives (Ness and Egelandsdal forthcoming). Polyphonic Orchestration is a tool to help teachers in how to utilize such diversity by creating situations where the students can engage with each other and the material, and thus support the students' development into a field of study. Our dialogical account of creativity bridges the individual and the social and points to the necessity of scaffolding the social exchanges that are at the heart of creativity.

11.5 Concluding Thoughts

In this chapter, we have developed a dialogical account of creativity that contrasts the "standard" definition of creativity in terms of the originality and effectiveness of creative products (Runco and Jaeger 2012). This view goes beyond static understandings of creativity that define it in terms of personal traits or characteristics of products and focuses our attention on the dialogical nature of creating with and for others, within a socio-material and cultural context. The dialogical view of creativity is not meant to replace existing approaches to creativity, even when they are mainly individual-based (e.g., cognitive or motivational theories), but give this kind of work a social and cultural basis (see Glăveanu 2015b). This is because, in fact, dialogism does not deny the individual; on the contrary, it gives it gives the person a priviledged place as the source of difference and differentiation in the social field. But the dialogical ontology is markedly different than that of traditional, positivist science (Marková 2003) in that it considers individual uniqueness as ultimately social in its origin, expression, and consequences. Adopting such an epistemology does not deny previous work in the psychology of creativity but can enrich existing conclusions and lead to new insights, as we hope to have demonstrated here.

The chapter has built on an extensive ethnographic fieldwork of innovative idea development in organisational settings in order to highlight the process characteristics of polyphonic orchestration, its outcomes, facilitators and obstacles. A particular focus was placed on the role of leaders and facilitators within the group and the way they fostered dialogical relations between members and cultivated a sense of openness and possibility specific for creative work. Some distinctive features of polyphonic orchestration and what defines dialogical creativity have been discussed.

First, *the dynamic tension between similarity and difference* shows how dialogical forms of relating to each other are meant to further our understanding, to produce new meanings while maintaining differences. Further, *the cooperation and movement between different roles* is also central, and in dialogism the notion of role is interesting in how it corresponds to that of position and how we change perspectives in a continuous movement. We also highlighted that *Polyphonic Orchestration is not a given but a collaborative achievement.* Successful group work has some conditions and some of these are openness, curiosity and respect for each other's perspectives (see Ness and Riese 2015). These allow group members to develop mutual trust, which is essential for the development of creativity. Finally, we also drew attention to how *effective leadership and facilitation is essential for the polyphonic orchestration of creativity.* Leadership it is often seen as a set of processes that comes in, from the "outside", to shape creative processes. The reality is, however, that leadership for creativity is more ubiquitous than this. When leaders open up for a co-construction and dialogue in their work groups, they will improve the chance of building a culture of innovation and creativity.

The concept of Polyphonic Orchestration portrays creativity as a dynamic process meant to articulate, at once, self and other, sameness and difference, the real and the imagined, with transformative consequences for creators, culture, and society.

References

Baer, J. (2014). *Creativity and divergent thinking: A task-specific approach.* New York: Psychology Press.
Bakhtin, M. M. (1981). *The dialogic imagination: Four essays.* Austin: University Texas Press.
Bakhtin, M. M. (1986). *Speech genres and other late essays.* Trans. by Vern W. McGee. Austin: University of Texas Press.
Barron, F. (1999). All creation is a collaboration. In A. Montuori & R. Purser (Eds.), *Social creativity* (Vol. I, pp. 49–59). Cresskill: Hampton Press.
Biesta, G. (2013). *The beautiful risk of education.* London, UK: Paradigm publishers.
Barron, F., & Harrington, D. (1981). Creativity, intelligence, and personality. *Annual Review of Psychology, 32,* 439–476.
Carmeli, A., Gelbard, R., & Reiter-Palmon, R. (2013). Leadership, creative problem-solving capacity, and creative performance: The importance of knowledge sharing. *Human Resource Management, 52*(1), 95–121.

Corazza, G. E. (2016). Potential originality and effectiveness: The dynamic definition of creativity. *Creativity Research Journal, 28*(3), 258–267.
de Saint-Laurent, C., & Glăveanu, V. P. (2016). Reflexivity. In V. P. Glăveanu, L. Tanggaard, & C. Wegener (Eds.), *Creativity: A new vocabulary* (pp. 121–128). London: Palgrave.
Denzin, N. K., & Lincoln, Y. S. (2000). Introduction: The discipline and practice of qualitative research. In N. K. Denzin & Y. S. Lincoln (Eds.), *Handbook of qualitative research (2 ed., pp. 1–29). California*. Thousand Oaks: Sage Publications.
Dysthe, O. (1997). Leiing i eit dialogperspektiv. In O. L. Fuglestad & S. Lillejord (Eds.), *Pedagogisk ledelse – et relasjonelt perspektiv* (pp. 72–93). Bergen: Fagbokforlaget.
Edwards, A. (2011). Building common knowledge at the boundaries between professional practices: Relational agency and relational expertise in systems of distributed expertise. *International Journal of Educational Research, 50*(2011), 33–39.
Fangen, K. (2010). *Deltakende observasjon* (2nd ed.). Bergen: Fagbokforlaget.
Gerson, K., & Horowitz, R. (2003). Observation and interviewing: Options and choices in qualitative research. In T. May (Ed.), *Qualitative research in action* (pp. 199–224). London: Sage Publications.
Gillespie, A. (2006). *Becoming other: From social interaction to self-reflection*. Greenwich: Information Age Publishing.
Gillespie, A., & Martin, J. (2014). Position exchange theory: A socio-material basis for discursive and psychological positioning. *New Ideas in Psychology, 32*, 73–79.
Glăveanu, V. P. (2010). Paradigms in the study of creativity: Introducing the perspective of cultural psychology. *New Ideas in Psychology, 28*(1), 79–93.
Glăveanu, V. P. (2014). *Distributed creativity: Thinking outside the box of the creative individual*. Cham: Springer.
Glăveanu, V. P. (2015a). Creativity as a sociocultural act. *Journal of Creative Behavior, 49*(3), 165–180.
Glăveanu, V. P. (2015b). The status of the social in creativity studies and the pitfalls of dichotomic thinking. *Creativity: Theories–Research–Applications, 2*(1), 102–119.
Glăveanu, V. P. (2017). The creative self in dialogue. In M. Karwowski & J. C. Kaufman (Eds.), *The creative self: Effect of beliefs, self-efficacy, mindset, and identity* (pp. 119–137). Waltham: Academic.
Glăveanu, V. P., & Beghetto, R. A. (2017). The difference that makes a 'creative' difference in education. In R. A. Beghetto & B. Sriraman (Eds.), *Creative contradictions in education* (pp. 37–54). Cham: Springer.
Glăveanu, V. P., & de Saint Laurent, C. (in press). Taking the perspective of others: A conceptual model and its application to the refugee crisis. Special issue in *Peace and Conflict: Journal of Peace Psychology*.
Glăveanu, V. P., & Gillespie, A. (2015). Creativity out of difference: Theorising the semiotic, social and temporal origin of creative acts. In V. P. Glăveanu, A. Gillespie, & J. Valsiner (Eds.), *Rethinking creativity: Contributions from social and cultural psychology* (pp. 1–15). Hove: Routledge.
Guri-Rosenblit, S., Šebková, H., & Teichler, U. (2007). Massification and diversity of higher education systems: Interplay of complex dimensions. *Higher Education Policy, 20*(4), 373–389. https://doi.org/10.1057/palgrave.hep.8300158.
Hornsby, D. J., & Osman, R. (2014). Massification in higher education: Large classes and student learning. *Higher Education, 67*(6), 711–719. https://doi.org/10.1007/s10734-014-9733-1.
Krumsvik, R. J. (2014). *Forskingsdesign og kvalitativ metode; ei innføring*. Bergen: Fagbokforlaget.
Lubart, T. I. (2001). Models of the creative process: Past, present and future. *Creativity Research Journal, 13*(3–4), 295–308.
Marková, I. (2003). *Dialogicality and social representations. The dynamics of mind*. Cambridge, MA: Cambridge University Press.
Mead, G. H. (1934). *Mind, self, and society from the standpoint of a social behaviorist*. Chicago: University of Chicago Press.

Michelsen, S., & Aamodt, P. O. (2007). *Evaluering av Kvalitetsreformen - Sluttrapport*. Oslo: Norges forskningsråd.

Ness, I. J. (2016). *The room of opportunity: Understanding how knowledge and ideas are constructed in multidisciplinary groups working with developing innovative ideas*. Doctoral thesis. University of Bergen, Norway.

Ness, I. J. (2017). Polyphonic orchestration: Understanding how leaders facilitate creative knowledge processes in multidisciplinary groups working with innovation. *European Journal of Innovation Management, 20*(4), 557–577.

Ness, I. J., & Egelandsdal, K. (forthcoming). STEPRE – model: Knowledge development in student groups in higher education. *Designs for Learning*.

Ness, I. J., & Riese, H. (2015). Openness, curiosity and respect: Underlying conditions for developing innovative knowledge and ideas between disciplines. *Learning, Culture and Social Interaction, 6*, 29–39.

Ness, I. J., & Søreide, E. G. (2014). The room of opportunity: Understanding phases of creative knowledge processes in innovation. *Journal of Workplace Learning, 26*(8), 545–560.

Patton, M. Q. (2002). *Qualitative research & evaluation methods* (3rd ed.). Thousand Oaks: Sage.

Paulus, P., & Nijstad, B. (2003). Group creativity: An introduction. In P. Paulus & B. Nijstad (Eds.), *Group creativity: Innovation through collaboration* (pp. 3–11). New York: Oxford University Press.

Runco, M. A., & Jaeger, G. J. (2012). The standard definition of creativity. *Creativity Research Journal, 24*(1), 92–96.

Weiner, R. P. (2000). *Creativity and beyond: Cultures, values, and change*. Albany: State University of New York Press.

Winnicott, D. W. (1971). *Playing and reality*. London: Routledge.

Zittoun, T., & Gillespie, A. (2015). *Imagination in human and cultural development*. London: Routledge.

Chapter 12
The Dynamic Definition of Creativity: Implications for Creativity Assessment

Lindsey Carruthers and Rory MacLean

Abstract Within this chapter, we consider the dynamic definition of creativity within a practical context, with roots in psychological measurement. A discussion of some of the existing measures of creativity is provided, with an attempt to assimilate them to the dynamic definition of creativity, as proposed by Corazza (Creat Res J 28:258–267, 2016). In most cases, some adaptations to the measures are required in order to acknowledge new criteria, such as creative inconclusiveness, and some ideas are presented here for future researchers to consider. Ultimately, it is argued that the dynamic definition of creativity is timely, necessary, and an important step in developing the field of creativity research.

12.1 Introduction

Everyone has an idea of what creativity is, yet when attempting to define it, it is one of those notoriously difficult psychological concepts that words can never seem to accurately represent. If defining creativity is difficult, reaching a consensus of its definition is near impossible. However, a consensus amongst creativity researchers (at least) is required now more than ever if we hope to credit the field with consistent and reliable empirical investigations that build on the findings of those before us. Creativity has been measured in many different ways: through convergent thinking tasks (e.g., Mednick 1962), the creation of a product (e.g., collages; Amabile 1982; Baer 1996; poems: Kasof 1997; and stories; Wolfradt and Pretz 2001), and also with larger batteries that include divergent thinking tests (e.g., Guilford 1967; Torrance from 1966). These measures were all designed with various versions of a definition of creativity in mind. This chapter will consider these existing creativity tests, and will discuss their compatibility with the new dynamic definition of creativity, with adaptations suggested where possible. We take our definitions from Corazza (2016),

---

L. Carruthers (✉) · R. MacLean
School of Applied Sciences, Edinburgh Napier University, Edinburgh, Scotland, UK
e-mail: L.Carruthers@napier.ac.uk; R.MacLean@napier.ac.uk

as there he details the intricacies of both the previous standard definition of creativity, and the newly proposed dynamic definition of creativity. The standard definition used is: "creativity requires originality and effectiveness" (Corazza 2016, p. 259). The dynamic definition of creativity is: "creativity requires potential originality and effectiveness" (Corazza 2016, p. 262).

Specifically, the measures we consider here are divergent thinking, the Consensual Assessment Technique, self-report, historiometry, and the Remote Associates Test. We provide a brief explanation of each measure, before analysing its compatibility with the dynamic definition of creativity, and include possibilities for altering the method to investigate various aspects within the dynamic definition, such as creative inconclusiveness, or the creative process.

It is near impossible to determine how creativity is currently measured in education establishments, if it is at all. The dynamic definition of creativity looks to the future, and it is hoped that some of the measures described here could be utilised in schools, colleges, and universities to develop powerful, maybe even longitudinal data, that will aid our understanding of the creative process.

12.2 Divergent Thinking

The invention of tasks measuring divergent thinking (a creative act in itself) aided a rise in creativity research as requested by Guilford in his Presidential speech at the American Psychological Association in 1950, and most of the subsequent research publications measuring creativity empirically have used a form of a divergent thinking task. As tests of divergent thinking are so commonly used, and are quick and convenient to administer, this seems an appropriate starting point for discussing creativity in relation to the new dynamic definition.

Divergent thinking involves the production of numerous answers for one given question or problem, an example being 'list unusual uses for a tin can' (Torrance et al. 1992). Divergent thinking tests are thought to facilitate the measurement of creativity, as the participant has an opportunity to provide multiple original and effective ideas or answers, thus conforming to the definition of creativity itself. Specifically, fluency, flexibility, and originality scores are the most commonly recorded scores from a divergent thinking task. Fluency is the number of ideas the participant produced, flexibility is the number of different types of response, and originality is a measure of how unique or novel the idea is. (Occasionally elaboration, the amount of detail included, is also measured in tasks requiring drawn responses.)

Divergent thinking seems to have become synonymous with creativity, which does not reflect the complex nature of creativity, but does give merit to the importance of divergent thinking tasks in the measurement of creativity. Specifically, tasks of this type are considered to be predictors of creative potential (Kuhn and Holling 2009; Runco 2004; Torrance et al. 1992), in line with the standard definition of creativity. These types of tests would therefore be ideal for use by educators, to begin the tracking of the creative potential of new generations.

It is important that explicit instructions emphasising the importance of originality in the production of the ideas are given to the participant before they begin any divergent thinking tasks. For example, an instruction such as 'think of ideas that other people might not think of' (Torrance et al. 1992) helps to raise creativity scores as it encourages participants to avoid listing menial, 'normal' ideas that would not contribute to their flexibility or originality scores. It is therefore assumed that with that instruction, participants who complete a divergent thinking task are actively trying to think creatively, thus are in pursuit of a creative goal (as defined by Corazza (2016, p. 262): "A creativity goal is the intention to generate items, pertaining to a focus area, showing originality and effectiveness").

A key element of the dynamic definition of creativity is that outcomes should have the potential to be original and effective, but responses that are not deemed to be adequately original or effective at that point should still be considered as important aspects of the creative process. Corazza (2016) refers to this as creative inconclusiveness, and provided a full definition: "Creative inconclusiveness corresponds to insufficient attribution of originality and/or effectiveness to the represented outcomes of a creative process by any estimator at a specific time" (p. 263).

The most common way of assessing divergent thinking test performance – fluency – does not involve making any judgements about the originality or effectiveness of the responses; all that is measured is the number of responses. As the participants are instructed to think creatively, in this way, fluency could be seen as assessing creative inconclusiveness. Responses may be unoriginal or ineffective, but would still count towards the fluency score and represent attempts to be creative and the pursuit of a creative goal.

Although not as commonly reported, the assessment of flexibility in divergent thinking task performance is valuable and could contribute to an understanding of the creative process, defined by Corazza (2016, p. 263) as "a process enacted by an agent in the pursuit of its creativity goals". For example, if the responses are considered in the order they are presented by the participant, it may be possible to identify the development of ideas across the course of the task. With the addition of a participant dialogue, where they verbally describe their ideas as they come to them, the creative process experienced in that task could be qualitatively analysed for the strategies used and associations made. This could be a valuable method of studying the thought process in pursuit of a creativity goal.

Arguably, originality should be the most valued measurement taken from a divergent thinking task. Traditionally, originality is determined by the statistical (in)frequency of responses, and in large batteries, this can be based on the previous performance of large normative samples (e.g., Torrance Tests of Creative Thinking, from 1966), or frequency may be relative to others within the current sample. This way of assessing originality is convenient and objective, but could allow for original but not particularly effective responses to be counted. It could be said that statistical infrequency does not fully address the construct of originality, which presumably also incorporates elements of subjective judgement, such as surprise (as perhaps experienced by the scorer). An alternative approach to assessing the originality of divergent thinking tests therefore would be to have the responses rated for originality (by an estimator or the creative agent themselves). Given that the dynamic definition places emphasis on the subjective judgement of estimators, this method of scoring would appear to fit the dynamic definition well.

12.3 Consensual Assessment Technique

Recognition of the potential for originality and effectiveness can come from two sources. The first from the individual themselves (self-report as later discussed). The second, is from the perspective of others. The Consensual Assessment Technique recruits judges (usually experts in the relevant field, although not exclusively) to use their own subjective definitions and opinions of what is creative, to assign a mark out of five or ten to each product/solution generated by the participants (Amabile 1982). This can be used for almost any type of product made, such as divergent thinking solutions, collages and artwork, poetry, and written/verbalized ideas. Reliability ratings between judges and across tests using Cronbach's alpha coefficient have been found to be high, with scores typically ranging from .7 to .9 (Kaufman et al. 2008a). This scoring method is thought to be ecologically valid as it is similar to the method by which creative products are judged in real life, by critics.

The Consensual Assessment Technique is considered by some to be the gold standard of creativity assessment (e.g., Kaufman et al. 2008b), and we suggest here that with some minor adaptations, it could still be a powerful assessment tool alongside the new dynamic definition of creativity. In fact, through the Consensual Assessment Technique, it may be possible to study multiple aspects of dynamic creativity, including the creative potential of an agent, the product of a creative process, the representation of a creative product, and the estimator.

Firstly, we briefly consider the assessment of the creative potential of an agent or participant, for which Corazza (2016) gave the following definition: "The quality and quantity of resources invested by an agent in the pursuit of creativity goals" (p. 263). One very simple way of measuring the creative potential of an agent within laboratory studies, would be to provide participants with a variety of materials and the instruction to create a collage, or an item of art of some kind. This could be assessed using the Consensual Assessment Technique by showing estimators the resources (time, environment) and materials that were available to the agents, alongside the final products of the creative process. The estimators could then use this information to provide their score on how creatively the items have (or have not) been used.

The key characteristic of the Consensual Assessment Technique is the judges, or estimators. Corazza (2016) provided the following definition of an estimator: "An agent observing the representations of the outcomes of a creative process and conceiving the ensuing potential effects in terms of originality and effectiveness"

(p. 263). In this context, we consider the assessment tool in relation to the judgement of the represented product of the creative process (as opposed to the agent or process itself). The "definition of product of a creative process [is]: "An outcome of the process with a potential for originality and effectiveness"" (Corazza 2016, p. 263). These definitions could be incorporated into the Consensual Assessment Technique, with an adaptation to the instructions to the estimators. In evaluating products such as artwork or inventions, estimators could firstly provide their subjective creativity rating as usual. Then, the estimators could be asked to score the products again, this time with their own views on the potential originality and effectiveness, meaning the estimators could be asked to provide three scores rather than just one. The creativity score should be rated first and separately to the secondary scores, so that it is not affected by them. This could be a valuable first step in aligning the Consensual Assessment Technique to the dynamic definition of creativity, as analysis comparing the three scores could be conducted, revealing any differences between scores according to the instruction type (i.e., subjectively rate for creativity, vs. rate potential originality/effectiveness). If there were no differences, then the adaptation suggested would not be necessary, and the assessment method would be suitable for the dynamic definition without change.

Following the provision of ratings, the expert estimators could contribute a qualitative statement on why, or why not, a product has been scored as potentially original and effective. Although these suggestions convolute the Consensual Assessment Technique, which until now is more streamlined, it would add a level of richness to the data that can be used in numerous ways.

Firstly, the mean creativity scores from the estimators could be used to represent the perceived creativity of the product. Secondly, the two additional scores proposed here could represent the perceived creative potential of the product. Thirdly, the qualitative data could be highly valuable, as it could highlight potential uses, or applications of the product beyond what was originally conceived. Experts within a field could view the products differently, and this could result in a wide scope for creative potential. This could be expanded even further by using experts from across different fields. For example, engineers, artists, and designers would all consider an item differently, and where a product may be ineffective and unoriginal in one field, it could be exemplary in another. Indeed, if there was disagreement amongst the estimators with a consensus not being possible, this would be interesting from a dynamic creativity perspective.

The Rite of Spring, a ballet by Stravinsky, for example, is particularly well known for dividing opinion. At the first public performance in 1913, some audience members disliked it so much that there was nearly a riot and critics were split in their reviews. Yet, it is now regarded as one of the most influential orchestral works of the last century. Famous painting Le Déjeuner sur l'Herbe (1863) by Édouard Manet was scandalous and notorious in its day, with the Salon in Paris refusing to exhibit the piece. Now, Manet's style is considered ground-breaking, and made way for the impressionist movement in the following years.

Perhaps strong disagreement by estimators could be a sign of creative potential, or disruptive innovation, especially in public works, as controversy leads to attention, which could lead to the work having a real impact. Some of the most groundbreaking, paradigm-shifting creative products are those most likely to divide opinion. Thus, research in to consensus of creativity can teach us a lot, but perhaps research in to non-consensus would yield more dynamic and realistic findings.

Another important aspect to consider here is that the Consensual Assessment Technique could aid in the study of originality and effectiveness over time, which could lead to a more 'literal' measurement of creative potential. It is well known that the works of many famous creators were valued years later, as was the case for Stravinsky and Manet, or even posthumously, meaning their work was potentially effective, and it reached that potential, but at a later time.

This proposed adapted method would result in thorough, rich data that go beyond the standard way of assessing creativity, to consider a product dynamically. The short, medium, and long term effectiveness of the products could also be measured if the procedure was repeated over time. Whereas the earlier version of the Consensual Assessment Technique (Amabile 1982) provides a 'snapshot' measurement of creativity, the adaptations here provide a dynamic, rounded assessment of the creative product. However, it is not deniable that this whole assessment would be time and resource expensive. It is certainly the case that further research would be required to support the statistical validity and reliability of this assessment method, and researchers may wish to adapt these ideas on a small scale initially. Importantly, the qualitative aspect here should prevent the creative agent, process, and product from being replaced by numbers and statistics, thus protecting the essence of creativity, which arguably cannot be calculated numerically.

Having discussed the judgement of others on a creative piece, it is appropriate to examine self-judgement, in the form of self-report measures of creativity.

12.4 Self-Report

A crucial element of the dynamic definition of creativity is that the creative process and its outcomes are subjectively assessed for creative potential, and the first person to estimate such potential is always the creative agent themselves. It would therefore make sense to consider self-report measures of creativity as possible methods of assessing the dynamic definition. Such measures have been suggested as having a higher degree of face validity than other methods of assessing creativity (Hocevar and Bachelor 1989), and the best predictor of future creative behavior is previous creative behavior (Colangelo et al. 1992). Self-report measures are usually quick and inexpensive to administer, and can ask individuals to report on creative activities, achievements, behaviors, and thoughts, and so may well represent a convenient, flexible, and comprehensive approach to assessing creativity.

This section will consider some of the most popular and useful self-report methods currently in use, and how well they encompass the dynamic definition of creativity. (Please see Silvia et al. 2012; and Kaufman et al. 2008a, b for helpful reviews).

The Creative Achievement Questionnaire (Carson et al. 2005), is a popular measure, used in a number of studies (e.g., Agnoli et al. 2016; Mar et al. 2006; White and Shah 2011). Unsurprisingly given its name, the Creative Achievement Questionnaire focuses on creative achievements, and considers significant creative accomplishments in 10 different domains: visual arts, music, dance, architectural design, creative writing, humor, inventions, scientific discovery, theatre and film, and culinary arts. Participants indicate achievements in each creative domain (e.g., for music, options include "I play one or more musical instruments proficiently", "I have composed an original piece of music", and "My compositions have been critiqued in a national publication"), and can receive a score for each domain as well as a total score combining the domains. This scale therefore only focuses on observable achievements and does not take into account inconclusive outcomes or the creative behaviors behind such achievements – the final creative achievement is all. As such, the Creative Achievement Questionnaire is undoubtedly useful for investigating creative success, but perhaps does not encompass the full range of creative activity under the dynamic definition.

Some other similar measures focus on creative activities and accomplishments, but also allow for the more everyday creative behaviors. The Creative Behavior Inventory was developed by Hocevar (1979, 1980), and later adapted by Dollinger (2003), Dollinger et al. (2007). In both versions, participants are presented with a list of activities and accomplishments considered to be creative and are asked to indicate the frequency of those behaviors in adolescence and adult life. In the dynamic definition, creative achievement requires both originality and effectiveness, and although some items in the Creative Behavior Inventory refer to creative outcomes judged to be effective (e.g., "Had artwork or craft work publicly exhibited"), originality rarely features explicitly (e.g., "Prepared an original floral arrangement"). However, rather than this being a shortcoming, it may offer an opportunity to adopt a broader understanding of creativity. The Creative Behavior Inventory merely asks participants to report the frequency of creative behaviors – whether these lead to particularly effective or original outcomes is not the main issue. It could consequently be argued that this focus on engagement in creative behaviors allows for a broader and more dynamic understanding of creativity to be assessed. Several items make no reference to originality or effectiveness; for example, the item "Made your own holiday decorations" does not state that these decorations should be original and effective, nor does it ask participants to make judgements about the creativity of these decorations. In responding to this item, participants could include decorations that are unoriginal (same as previous years, copied from the internet) and/or ineffective (poorly made, unattractive, do not resemble what they were meant to), as well as highly original and effective decorations, and so items such as this can encompass both creative inconclusiveness and creative achievement – key elements of the dynamic definition of creativity.

Batey's (2007) Biographical Inventory of Creative Behaviors (BICB) is an alternative measure of creative behavior, which, like the Creative Behavior Inventory, offers the opportunity to assess the dynamic definition of creativity to some extent. In the BICB participants are asked to indicate in which of 34 creative activities they have been involved over the past 12 months. While most of the activities involve an identifiable creative achievement or outcome (e.g., "Written a novel", "Formed a sculpture using any suitable materials"), in only a few items is the originality or effectiveness of the achievement actually specified (e.g., "Had an article published", "Invented and made a product that can be used"); in other cases, the outcome has the potential to be original and effective, thus allowing for a more dynamic interpretation of creativity to be assessed.

More recently, Benedek, Jauk and colleagues (Diedrich et al. 2017; Jauk et al. 2013, 2014) developed the Inventory of Creative Activities and Achievements (ICAA), which combines elements of the CBI and CAQ in that both creative activities and creative achievements are assessed. Respondents are asked to indicate the frequency of creative activities and behaviours across a range of different domains, over a period of 10 years, as well as rate the level of achievement in the domains. The timescale covered in the ICAA is longer than that in the BICB, and shorter than in the CBI, and thus seems to be a happy compromise. The ICAA appears to provide a comprehensive and versatile assessment of real-life creativity across a range of different creative domains, and at different levels of creative achievement, and findings suggest that it will be a useful addition to the assessment of creative activities and achievements.

Some other self-report measures of creativity take a different approach, and, rather than focusing on frequency of observable behaviors or accomplishments, ask participants to self-rate their own creativity. For instance, Kaufman et al. (2009a) developed the Creativity Domain Questionnaire, in which participants rate their own creativity over 56 domains, covering seven different areas of creative behavior: artistic/visual, artistic/verbal, performance, math/science, problem solving, interpersonal, and entrepreneur; a shortened modified version – the Revised Creativity Domains Questionnaire – was developed (Kaufman et al. 2009b), with 21 domains over four areas: math/science, drama, interaction, and arts. What is crucial here is that in both measures participants use their own definition of creativity, thus allowing for subjectivity in assessment, and the possibility that some participants' responses may reflect potential for originality and effectiveness, and creative inconclusiveness, and not just creative achievement. However, without having a clear understanding of which definition an individual is using, it is difficult to determine if the dynamic definition is being assessed. The Kaufman Domains of Creativity Scale (Kaufman 2012) also requires participants to self-rate creativity, but items make reference to specific examples of outcomes and accomplishments within domains, rather than focusing on the overall domains. In this way, some items directly refer to originality and/or effectiveness (e.g., "Composing an original song", "Choosing the best solution to a problem"), whereas others offer a more dynamic interpretation (e.g., "Making up rhymes", "Enjoying an art museum"). What is more, when participants have not actually done one of the listed acts, the Kaufman Domains of Creativity Scale instructs them to estimate their creative potential in these activities. Thus, a dynamic approach could apply here.

The final type of self-report measure considered here goes further, and focuses on the thought processes behind creative outcomes, and individuals' creative self-beliefs. Beghetto and Karwowski (2017) helpfully make a distinction between creative self-efficacy, which reflects perceived confidence in relation to an impending creative task; creative metacognition, which represents beliefs about knowledge about one's own creative strengths and weaknesses, as well as knowledge about the creative contexts; and creative self-concept, which refers to a more generalized judgment about one's own creative ability. Taken together, it is argued that these three concepts contribute to creative identity, and Beghetto and Karwowski (2017) urge creativity researchers to be clear and specific about which concepts and definitions they are using.

Previous measures of creative self-efficacy have included short, simple questionnaires, such as Beghetto's (2006) three items: "I am good at coming up with new ideas", "I have a lot of good ideas", and "I have a good imagination", and Jaussi et al. (2007) proposed an additional four-item self-efficacy questionnaire: "In general, creativity is an important part of my self image", "My creativity is an important part of who I am", "Overall, my creativity has little to do with who I am" (reversed scoring), and "My ability to be creative is an important reflection of who I am". However, Beghetto and Karwowski (2017) now recommend that measures of creative self-efficacy should be future-oriented, and should focus on confidence in performance, rather than competence, and so the previous questionnaires arguably do not fit this stricter definition.

The concept of creative self-efficacy is important as those with high self-efficacy are more likely to gear their behavior towards fulfilling a specific goal as they believe they can achieve this, whereas those with low self-efficacy are likely to envisage failing to achieve, and will therefore place obstacles in their way (Bandura 1993). It has been stipulated that strong self-efficacy in this context is essential for creative production, motivation, and the ability to behave creatively (Bandura 1997; Tierney and Farmer 2002).

When assessing creative metacognition, Beghetto and Karwowski (2017) recommend that researchers should take into account the accuracy of one's own confidence in performing a task and whether that matches with actual performance. In addition, a true measure of creative metacognition should also assess an individual's ability to regulate their creative behaviour and beliefs in relation to the context (e.g., try a new strategy, persist with current approach).

At a broader level, researchers can also assess creative self-concept, which reflects more stable general beliefs about creative abilities in different domains (Beghetto and Karwowski 2017). This can include assessments related to competence and/or enjoyment (e.g., "I am good at writing poetry" vs. "I enjoy writing poetry"), and should focus on more holistic assessment of past performance.

The Runco Ideational Behavior Scale (Runco et al. 2001) is a 23-item questionnaire which assesses the thought processes associated with creative behaviour, and consequently taps into creative self-efficacy, creative metacognition and creative self-concept. Items reflect an individual's thinking and ideas related to creativity (e.g., "I would rate myself highly in being able to come up with ideas"; "I am good at combining ideas in ways that others have not tried"; "I like to play around with ideas for the fun of it"). The focus here, and in other similar measures, is on ideational behaviour and self-belief, and not necessarily on the creative outcome, and so could be seen as allowing for creative inconclusiveness as well as creative achievement, and is therefore a promising method of assessing the dynamic definition of creativity.

Taken together, self-rated measures of creativity offer researchers the opportunity to examine the creative agent's own perception of their creativity, and in some instances go beyond creative accomplishment, with items that allow the incorporation of creative inconclusiveness. It would appear then, that these measures can already assess numerous aspects of the dynamic definition of creativity.

12.5 Historiometry

The historiometric approach to assessing creativity focuses on eminent individuals who are universally recognized as being creative as subjects (Simonton 1997b), and involves quantitative analysis with large numbers of eminent creators, with the aim of identifying general rules or laws. On first inspection, with such an emphasis on creative success and quantifiable creative achievements, historiometry may not appear to fit well with the dynamic definition of creativity; however, some elements of this approach do in fact lend themselves to a more dynamic definition.

A key part of the dynamic definition is that outcomes may have the potential to be original and effective, but judgement of these outcomes is not static or absolute – it can vary over time. Simonton (1998a) adopted the historiometric approach to examine precisely this. Looking across 496 operas by 55 different composers spanning 332 years, he saw that the contemporary aesthetic judgement of an opera is related to how an opera was initially received, but this relationship changes over time in a cyclical fashion. A similar cyclical pattern was found in relation to the melodic originality of classical music themes (Simonton 1984, 1998b). Thus, this research would appear to support the dynamic definition, and suggests that estimating creativity at one point in time may provide a limited view of the phenomenon.

Other historiometric studies look at creative productivity over time, and examine the number of creative products generated within a specific time period (e.g., Simonton 1997a). The historical data sources for this type of investigation, such as encyclopedias, will only include outcomes which, over the passage of time, have been judged to be of importance by critics within the field of interest and are thought to be worthy of inclusion. This recognizes the subjective, context-dependent and time-related element to the judgement of creativity; indeed, there are numerous examples of individuals whose creative work was not fully appreciated by contemporary audiences, but who were later recognized for their eminent creativity (e.g., Vincent van Gogh, Paul Gauguin, Franz Kafka). By adopting a historical approach, historiometry allows the investigation of creators and creative products whose creative potential was only later realized.

However, the historiometric approach still focuses predominantly on creative achievements. Creative inconclusiveness could perhaps be investigated (e.g., by looking over drafts of novels, or sketches), but this would rely on historical records being complete, reliable, and accurate, which may be difficult to achieve. Nonetheless, this approach to creativity assessment offers a historical and dynamic perspective, which would appear to be unique. This approach may be a good starting place for students of creativity, to encourage consideration of the processes behind creative works, the idea that we rarely see evidence of inconclusiveness, yet it absolutely must exist.

12.5.1 Remote Associates Test

The last measure to be considered here is the Remote Associates Test, which warrants discussion as it is a popular measure, likely due to its neat design and convenient nature. The associative theory of creativity posits that successful creative thinking may be the result of forming new and useful associations between disparate concepts (e.g., Mednick 1962; Schmajuk et al. 2009). The thought that creativity consists of an associative process is an "old and sturdy" (Barron and Harrington 1981, p.12) theory in psychology, with the most well-known contribution being from Mednick (1962). An association is a link between two ideas, elements, or stimuli, which can be strong or weak, although Mednick (1962) argued that the weaker or more remote the association is, the more creative it is. Within the associative theory, word association tasks are frequently used. The original Remote Associates Test was produced by Mednick (1962; more recently updated and made readily available by Bowden and Jung-Beeman 2003) for the purpose of measuring creative thought through association. Each trial comprises three words, and the participant is required to produce a fourth word that relates to each word separately. An example trial is: cottage, Swiss, cake; the solution being cheese (cottage cheese, Swiss cheese, and cheese cake).

It could be argued that the Remote Associates Test is useful for assessing how individuals think about words, and how they can be flexible in thinking beyond the immediate meaning of words. This relates to the old concepts of fixation breaking, and venturing outside perceived limitations (in this case, of language) detailed in problem solving theories (e.g., Luchins 1942; Ohlsson 1992). By some, this is thought to be key to the production of creative ideas, as breaking perceived barriers can lead to novel associations being made (Ansburg and Hill 2003; Mednick 1962). One's ability to commonly break fixations and mind-sets, as measured by the Remote Associates Test may therefore be indicative of their potential to be original, in line with the dynamic definition of creativity. However, getting from a word association task to determining creative potential does not appear to be straight forward.

It is the contention of the authors that the Remote Associates Test is an inappropriate measure of creativity, as it does not allow participants to be original, a requirement of the standard definition of creativity, and that it in fact measures other facets of cognition instead, such as vocabulary and verbal intelligence. The studies run by

Mednick and colleagues claiming to have found constructive and predictive validity for the Remote Associates Test did not control for participant intelligence, and featured participants who were arguably both highly intelligent and creative; architects, scientists, and engineers (see Mendelsohn 1976 for a review). The Remote Associates Test is still frequently used in creativity research today, however it may not be manageable for participants with limited vocabulary or knowledge of the verbal cues used. The reliance on convergent thinking and intelligence, rather than creative thinking, may be too high within the Remote Associates Test, making it unsuitable for purpose. In support of this, it was found that the Remote Associates Test has higher correlation values with IQ, specifically aspects of verbal IQ, working memory, cognitive speed and accuracy, and school achievement, than it does with any creativity scores (as measured by tests of divergent thinking, Lee et al. 2014; Taft and Rossiter 1966). Whereas it has been demonstrated that tests of divergent thinking, for example, have predictive validity with other measures of creativity (e.g. Runco 2004), the Remote Associates Test has rarely been even moderately related to divergent thinking (Lee et al. 2014). This implies that the Remote Associates Test may involve processes outwith those in creative thinking.

Furthermore, beyond the study of creativity, the Remote Associates Test has been used in studies investigating bipolar and manic-depressive disorders (Fodor 1999), the effect of feedback on performance (McFarlin and Blascovich 1984), search strategies (Smith et al. 2013), social intelligence (Keating 1978), and even erotomania in celebrity worship (McCutcheon et al. 2003). This highlights that the Remote Associates Test is a flexible measure, which thereby demonstrates its lack of construct validity.

In consideration of the dynamic definition of creativity described previously, it is posited here that the Remote Associates Test does not allow for potential originality, as there is only one correct answer that the participants are expected to produce. While the correct solution may be effective, if a participant came up with an original, novel solution that linked all three words in an abstract way, it would be scored as incorrect, thus the test may actually be anti-creativity. The existence of a preexisting solution removes the possibility of demonstrating originality, novelty, and uniqueness, but also inherently eliminates the opportunity for establishing potential. As the test stands, the solution is the final step, and there is no opportunity for ideas to develop, or for creative elaboration in any way, like there is with divergent thinking tasks, or in the construction of creative products. It is also very difficult to comprehend what an adaptation of the Remote Associates Test would look like in order to sufficiently address both the standard and the dynamic definitions of creativity.

The associative theory however, could still be a useful model in investigation of the creative process, and there could be scope for utilising and testing this. For example, the process behind verbal creativity could be measured by asking participants to produce word association maps, perhaps in relation to an idea they have themselves, or cued in a laboratory setting. Participants could be presented with two random words, and using word association they could draw out links that might eventually connect the two words. Similarly, this method may be used effectively in the case of a divergent thinking task, such as the Unusual Uses Test. With the target object at the top of the page, participants could be asked to list their ideas as normal, but could use arrows to indicate where one idea has been linked to, or has come from, another. This would illustrate the development of ideas (thus their potential, probably to a limited degree), and the associations that have been made along the process of being creative, if indeed this was the method used by the participant in being creative. If an individual did not use an associative process, fewer of their ideas would be linked, and this would be clearer. It could be hypothesized that the more connections made, the more remote the ideas become. Alternatively, if originality is poor, this could lead to the measurement of creative inconclusiveness in the creative process. A dynamic scoring system would need to be implemented, probably one that combined the methods of Torrance (1990), and the adapted Consensual Assessment Technique, as proposed above.

Where there is possibility for the associative theory of creativity to be useful in the measurement of dynamic creativity, it is concluded here that the Remote Associates Test is an unsuitable measure of creativity, be it standard or dynamic.

12.6 Implications and Conclusions

Having presented a discursive analysis of existing creativity measures and their compatibility (or not) with the dynamic definition of creativity, we will now briefly consider two important implications, ecological validity and considering creative products as 'unfinished'.

Firstly, ecological validity is arguably a prominent problem in all studies that use laboratory based experiments to test human behavior and cognitive processes. Creativity within non-specialist samples may not naturally occur in a laboratory setting, and creativity tests may inadvertently inhibit creativity and creative potential, as opposed to facilitating it. For example, in consideration of a typical verbal divergent thinking task, a participant is limited to producing solutions that fit the requirements of the task (i.e., based on the target product in an unusual uses task) – and their output is taken as a measure of their creativity. But a musician, or a chef, or an artist, might not be creative in this verbal manner. The Consensual Assessment Technique looks to score creative products in an ecologically valid way, but the self-report measures discussed here, such as the Creative Behavior Inventory and Kaufman Domains of Creativity Scale, may be more suitable to combat this issue, and should perhaps be used in conjunction with other laboratory based measures.

For the dynamic definition of creativity to work in research, it may be that we need to consider all products made in testing sessions as 'unfinished'. Thinking of an item as finished leaves no room for development, which may limit the item's potential for originality and effectiveness. If the item is considered unfinished, this leaves options open for further developments and adaptations of item, which could form the basis of a highly original and effective solution. We may also need to consciously separate the creator's intended purpose of the product, from the potential purpose of the product. This may be required in order to fully contemplate an item's potential for originality, but this could only really be carried out by outsiders, those independent from the project. Doing so would open possibilities for the utility of the solutions. However, it can be argued that in order for a product to be effective at all, it should fit the brief of the task set. Outwith research, in 'real' creative situations, this may lead to a disparity between the creator and the critic, but the creator in any case would likely have different ideas of the purpose and the potential of their work compared to an outsider. This may be more of a philosophical issue that researchers may want to consider in future work.

Although Corazza (2016) proposes the dynamic definition of creativity is backward compatible with existing measures of creativity, it is important to remember that previous measures were not designed with this definition in mind. Thus, past methods may not fully address aspects such as creative inconclusiveness, and may not be suitable for measuring future potential. Of the measures and adaptations considered here, there are a number of promising options, but in order to fully encompass the dynamic definition of creativity, new original and effective assessment methods are required.

These methods may be of particular interest to educators. We believe that of particular importance to education, is an emphasis on creative inconclusiveness. Students (of all ages) should be encouraged to engage in their creative process with an emphasis on the value of this experience, but without the pressure of perfecting their masterpiece. If educators are made aware of the dynamic definition of creativity, and inconclusiveness in particular, this could rejuvenate the assessment of creative products. Rather than basing grades on a 'finished' creative product, new assessment methods could be designed that incorporate documentation and reflection on the experience of being creative.

Fundamentally, if creativity researchers wish to fully understand creativity, we should all adopt a consistent definition of the complex construct. In 1950, Guilford inspired the advancement of creativity research that was noticeably missing within psychological literature. The dynamic definition of creativity as fully described by Corazza (2016) is an impressive, modern, and thorough re-evaluation of the field of creativity generally, and specifically introduces new and important concepts such as creative inconclusiveness, which have not been valued previously. The dynamic definition is flexible, comprehensive, and offers new directions for investigation that should provide the momentum required for the next era of creativity research.

References

Agnoli, S., Corazza, G. E., & Runco, M. A. (2016). Estimating creativity with a multiple-measurement approach within scientific and artistic domains. *Creativity Research Journal, 28*(2), 171–176. https://doi.org/10.1080/10400419.2016.1162475.

Amabile, T. M. (1982). Social psychology of creativity: A consensual assessment technique. *Journal of Personality and Social Psychology, 43*(5), 997–1013. https://doi.org/10.1037/0022-3514.43.5.997.

Ansburg, P. I., & Hill, K. (2003). Creative and analytic thinkers differ in their use of attentional resources. *Personality and Individual Differences, 34*, 1141–1152. https://doi.org/10.1016/S0191-8869(02)00104-6.

Baer, J. (1996). Does artistic creativity decline during elementary school? *Psychological Reports, 78*, 927–930. https://doi.org/10.2466/pr0.1996.78.3.927.

Bandura, A. (1993). Perceived self-efficacy in cognitive development and functioning. *Educational Psychologist, 28*(2), 117–148. https://doi.org/10.1207/s15326985ep2802_3.

Bandura, A. (1997). *Self-efficacy: The exercise of control*. New York: W.H. Freeman.

Barron, F., & Harrington, D. M. (1981). Creativity, intelligence, and personality. *Annual Review of Psychology, 32*, 439–476. https://doi.org/10.1146/annurev.ps.32.020181.002255.

Batey, M. (2007). *A psychometric investigation of everyday creativity*. Unpublished doctoral dissertation. University College, London.

Beghetto, R. A. (2006). Creative self-efficacy: Correlates in middle and secondary students. *Creativity Research Journal, 18*(4), 447–457. https://doi.org/10.1207/s15326934crj1804_4.

Beghetto, R. A., & Karwowski, M. (2017). Towards untangling creative self-beliefs. In M. Karwowski & J. C. Kaufman (Eds.), *The creative self: Effect of beliefs, self-efficacy, mindset, and identity* (pp. 3–22). San Diego: Elsevier Academic Press.

Bowden, E. M., & Jung-Beeman, M. (2003). Normative data for 144 compound remote associate problems. *Behavior Research Methods, Instruments, & Computers, 35*(4), 634–639. https://doi.org/10.3758/BF03195543.

Carson, S. H., Peterson, J. B., & Higgins, D. M. (2005). Reliability, validity and factor structure of the creative achievement questionnaire. *Creativity Research Journal, 17*(1), 37–50. https://doi.org/10.1207/s15326934crj1701_4.

Colangelo, N., Kerr, B., Hallowell, K., Huesman, R., & Gaeth, J. (1992). The Iowa Inventiveness Inventory: Toward a measure of mechanical inventiveness. *Creativity Research Journal, 5*, 157–163. https://doi.org/10.1080/10400419209534429.

Corazza, G. E. (2016). Potential originality and effectiveness: The dynamic definition of creativity. *Creativity Research Journal, 28*(3), 258–267. https://doi.org/10.1080/10400419.2016.1195627.

Diedrich, J., Jauk, E., Silvia, P. J., Gredlein, J. M., Neubauer, A. C., & Benedek, M. (2017). Assessment of real-life creativity: The inventory of creative activities and achievements (ICAA). *Psychology of Aesthetics, Creativity, and the Arts*. Advance online publication. https://doi.org/10.1037/aca0000137.

Dollinger, S. J. (2003). Need for uniqueness, need for cognition, and creativity. *Journal of Creative Behavior, 37*(2), 99–116. https://doi.org/10.1002/j.2162-6057.2003.tb00828.x.

Dollinger, S. J., Burke, P. A., & Gump, N. A. (2007). Creativity and values. *Creativity Research Journal, 19*(2–3), 91–103. https://doi.org/10.1080/10400410701395028.

Fodor, E. M. (1999). Subclinical inclination toward manic-depression and creative performance on the Remote Associates Test. *Personality and Individual Differences, 27*(6), 1273–1283. https://doi.org/10.1016/S0191-8869(99)00076-8.

Guilford, J. P. (1967). *The nature of human intelligence*. New York: McGraw-Hill.

Hocevar, D. (1979, April).*The development of the Creative Behavior Inventory (CBI)*. Paper presented at the annual meeting of the Rocky Mountain Psychological Association (ERIC Document Reproduction Service No. ED 170 350).

Hocevar, D. (1980). Intelligence, divergent thinking, and creativity. *Intelligence, 4*, 25–40. https://doi.org/10.1016/0160-2896(80)90004-5.

Hocevar, D., & Bachelor, P. (1989). A taxonomy and critique of measurements used in the study of creativity. In J. A. Glover, R. R. Ronning, & C. R. Reynolds (Eds.), *Handbook of creativity* (pp. 53–75). New York: Plenum.

Jauk, E., Benedek, M., Dunst, B., & Neubauer, A. C. (2013). The relationship between intelligence and creativity: New support for the threshold hypothesis by means of empirical breakpoint detection. *Intelligence, 41*, 212–221. https://doi.org/10.1016/j.intell.2013.03.003.

Jauk, E., Benedek, M., & Neubauer, A. C. (2014). The road to creative achievement: A latent variable model of ability and personality predictors. *European Journal of Personality*. https://doi.org/10.1002/per.194.

Jaussi, K. S., Randel, A. E., & Dionne, S. D. (2007). I am, I think I can, and I do: The role of personal identity, self-efficacy, and cross-application of experiences in creativity at work. *Creativity Research Journal, 19*(2–3), 247–258. https://doi.org/10.1080/10400410701397339.

Kasof, J. (1997). Creativity and breadth of attention. *Creativity Research Journal, 10*(4), 303–315. https://doi.org/10.1207/s15326934crj1004_2.

Kaufman, J. C. (2012). Counting the muses: Development of the Kaufman Domains of Creativity Scale (K-DOCS). *Psychology of Aesthetics, Creativity, and the Arts, 6*(4), 298–308. https://doi.org/10.1037/a0029751.

Kaufman, J. C., Plucker, J. A., & Baer, J. (2008a). *Essentials of creativity assessment*. Hoboken: Wiley.

Kaufman, J. C., Baer, J., Cole, J. C., & Sexton, J. D. (2008b). A comparison of expert and non-expert raters using the consensual assessment technique. *Creativity Research Journal, 20*(2), 171–178. https://doi.org/10.1080/10400410802059929.

Kaufman, J. C., Cole, J. C., & Baer, J. (2009a). The construct of creativity: A structural model for self-reported creativity ratings. *Journal of Creative Behavior, 43*(2), 119–134.

Kaufman, J. C., Waterstreet, M. A., Ailabouni, H. S., Whitcomb, H. J., Roe, A. K., & Riggs, M. (2009b). Personality and self-perceptions of creativity across domains. *Imagination, Cognition and Personality, 29*(3), 193–209. https://doi.org/10.2190/IC.29.3.c.

Keating, D. P. (1978). A search for social intelligence. *Journal of Educational Psychology, 70*(2), 218. https://doi.org/10.1037/0022-0663.70.2.218.

Kuhn, J.-T., & Holling, H. (2009). Exploring the nature of divergent thinking: A multilevel analysis. *Thinking Skills and Creativity, 4*, 116–123. https://doi.org/10.1016/j.tsc.2009.06.004.

Lee, C. S., Huggins, A. C., & Therriault, D. J. (2014). A measure of creativity or intelligence? Examining internal and external structure validity evidence of the Remote Associates Test. *Psychology of Aesthetics, Creativity, and the Arts, 8*(4), 446–460. https://doi.org/10.1037/a0036773.

Luchins, A. S. (1942). Mechanization in problem solving: The effect of Einstellung. *Psychological Monographs, 54*(6), i–95. https://doi.org/10.1037/h0093502.

Mar, R. A., DeYoung, C. G., Higgins, D. M., & Peterson, J. B. (2006). Self-liking and self-competence separate self-evaluation from self-deception: Associations with personality, ability, and achievement. *Journal of Personality, 74*(4), 1047–1078. https://doi.org/10.1111/j.1467-6494.2006.00402.x.

McCutcheon, L. E., Ashe, D. D., Houran, J., & Maltby, J. (2003). A cognitive profile of individuals who tend to worship celebrities. *The Journal of Psychology, 137*(4), 309–322. https://doi.org/10.1080/00223980309600616.

McFarlin, D. B., & Blascovich, J. (1984). On the Remote Associates Test (RAT) as an alternative to illusory performance feedback: A methodological note. *Basic and Applied Social Psychology, 5*(3), 223–229. https://doi.org/10.1207/s15324834basp0503_5.

Mednick, S. A. (1962). The associative basis of the creative process. *Psychological Review, 69*(3), 220–232. https://doi.org/10.1037/h0048850.

Mendelsohn, G. A. (1976). Associative and attentional processes in creative performance. *Journal of Personality, 44*, 341–369. https://doi.org/10.1111/j.1467-6494.1976.tb00127.x.

Ohlsson, S. (1992). Information-processing explanations of insight and related phenomena. *Advances in the Psychology of Thinking, 1*, 1–44.

Runco, M. A. (2004). Creativity. *Annual Review of Psychology, 55*, 657–687. https://doi.org/10.1146/annurev.psych.55.090902.141502.

Runco, M. A., Plucker, J. A., & Lim, W. (2001). Development and psychometric integrity of a measure of ideational behavior. *Creativity Research Journal, 13*(3–4), 393–400. https://doi.org/10.1207/S15326934CRJ1334_16.

Schmajuk, N., Aziz, D. R., & Bates, M. J. B. (2009). Attentional-associative interactions in creativity. *Creativity Research Journal, 21*(1), 92–103. https://doi.org/10.1080/10400410802633574.

Silvia, P. J., Wigert, B., Reiter-Palmon, R., & Kaufman, J. C. (2012). Assessing creativity with self-report scales: A review and empirical evaluation. *Psychology of Aesthetics, Creativity, and the Arts, 6*(1), 19–34. https://doi.org/10.1037/a0024071.

Simonton, D. K. (1984). *Genius, creativity, and leadership: Historiometric inquiries.* Cambridge, MA: Harvard University Press.

Simonton, D. K. (1997a). Creative productivity: A predictive and explanatory model of career trajectories and landmarks. *Psychological Review, 104*(1), 66–89. https://doi.org/10.1037/0033-295X.104.1.66.

Simonton, D. K. (1997b). Historiometric studies of creative genius. In M. A. Runco (Ed.), *The creativity research handbook* (Vol. 1, pp. 3–28). Creskill: Hampton Press.

Simonton, D. K. (1998a). Fickle fashion versus immortal fame: Transhistorical assessments of creative products in the opera house. *Journal of Personality and Social Psychology, 75*(1), 198–210. https://doi.org/10.1037/0022-3514.75.1.198.

Simonton, D. K. (1998b). Masterpieces in music and literature: Historiometric inquiries. *Creativity Research Journal, 11*(2), 103–110. https://doi.org/10.1207/s15326934crj1102_2.

Smith, K. A., Huber, D. E., & Vul, E. (2013). Multiply-constrained semantic search in the Remote Associates Test. *Cognition, 128*(1), 64–75. https://doi.org/10.1016/j.cognition.2013.03.001.

Taft, R., & Rossiter, J. R. (1966). The Remote Associates Test: Divergent or convergent thinking? *Psychological Reports, 19*, 1313–1314. https://doi.org/10.2466/pr0.1966.19.3f.1313.

Tierney, P., & Farmer, S. M. (2002). Creative self-efficacy: Its potential, antecedents and relationship to creative performance. *Academy of Management Journal, 45*(6), 1137–1148. https://doi.org/10.2307/3069429.

Torrance, E. P. (1966). *The torrance tests of creative thinking: Norms-technical manual research edition. verbal tests, forms A and B, figural tests, forms A and B.* Princeton: Personnel Press.

Torrance, E. P. (1990). *Torrance tests of creative thinking: Manual for scoring and interpreting results.* Bensenville: Scholastic Testing Service, Inc..

Torrance, E. P., Ball, O. E., & Safter, H. T. (1992). *Torrance tests of creative thinking: Streamlined scoring guide, figural A and B.* Bensenville: Scholastic Testing Service, Inc..

White, H. A., & Shah, P. (2011). Creative style and achievement in adults with attention-deficit/hyperactivity disorder. *Personality and Individual Differences, 50*(5), 673–677. https://doi.org/10.1016/j.paid.2010.12.015.

Wolfradt, U., & Pretz, J. E. (2001). Individual differences in creativity: Personality, story writing, and hobbies. *European Journal of Personality, 15*, 297–310. https://doi.org/10.1002/per.409.

Chapter 13
Interdisciplinary Exploration and Domain-Specific Expertise Are Mutually Enriching

Don Ambrose

Abstract Interdisciplinary and domain-specific investigative trajectories represent very different approaches to the study of creative intelligence. They proceed in opposing directions and seem to generate contradictions. Interdisciplinary work seems to make domain-specific inquiry look excessively insular while domain-specific work seems to undermine the credibility of investigations that cross disciplinary borders. In actuality, these two very different approaches can enrich each other if their adherents develop healthy forms of mutual respect.

13.1 Introduction

In order to extend our knowledge of creativity and other dimensions of creative intelligence such as giftedness and talent development we need to employ both domain-specific inquiry and interdisciplinary exploration. Both of these investigative tracks have been established in creative intelligence fields but they seem to be moving along without doing much to inform each other. If we can find ways to share more ideas between these tracks we might accelerate progress.

Scholarship on domain-specific expertise has become vibrant in creativity studies (e.g., Baer 1998, 1999, 2010, 2012a, b, 2013, 2015, 2016a, b; Baer and Kaufman 2015; Beghetto et al. 2015; Kaufman et al. 2017; Silvia et al. 2009; Simonton 2009). It also influences gifted education (e.g., Olszewski-Kubilius et al. 2017; Subotnik et al. 2011). The core idea behind much of this work is that creativity and giftedness go beyond general cognitive processing and are more dependent on the development of knowledge, skills, and dispositions within specific domains. For example, a person can be a creative writer but not a creative composer if she developed considerable expertise and talent in the domain of writing but has little interest or talent in music.

D. Ambrose (✉)
College of Education and Human Services, Rider University, Lawrence Township, NJ, USA
e-mail: ambrose@rider.edu

There also has been some interdisciplinary inquiry aimed at clarification and extension of our knowledge of creative intelligence (e.g., Ambrose 1996, 1998, 2003, 2005a, b, 2006, 2009, 2014a, b, 2016, 2017a, b; Ambrose et al. 2003, 2012, 2014; Ambrose and Cross 2009; Ambrose and Sternberg 2012, 2016a, b; Gardner 1988, 2006; Gruber and Bödeker 2005; Kalbfleisch and Ambrose 2008; Lindauer 1998; McLaren 2003; Root-Bernstein 2014; Root-Bernstein 2001, 2003; Sawyer 1998; Shiu 2014; Sriraman and Dahl 2009; Thiessen 1998; VanTassel-Baska and Stambaugh 2006). Key ideas in this work have to do with the notion that our conceptions of creativity, giftedness, and talent development can be enriched by borrowing theories and research findings from diverse disciplines, many of which are not normally associated with high ability. Notably, the *Journal of Creative Behavior* and the *Creativity Research Journal* explicitly recognize the importance of interdisciplinary work in the field of creativity studies.

My work is primarily on the interdisciplinary inquiry track. When research on domain-specific expertise began to accelerate I first wondered if it would run counter to interdisciplinary investigation and undermine it in some way because the two tracks pursue very different, seemingly contradictory purposes. But I now think those concerns were somewhat premature.

A metaphor can be helpful here. Assume that a group of scholars show up in "Creative Intelligence City," an imaginary metropolis encompassing all of the phenomena pertaining to creativity, giftedness, and talent development. Those who are inclined to carry out domain-specific inquiry will lodge themselves within a big, prominent office building in the city and explore the inner workings of that particular "domain." The building is analogous to an academic discipline or professional field. Assuming that the field is well established and rich with accumulating professional knowledge, that domain is a lofty, sturdy skyscraper. The steel frame in the superstructure and the pilings drilled down into the bedrock provide the theoretical and philosophical frameworks of the field. The floors are where the work of the field takes place. The valuable, practical work of the field is done in the lower floors where the professional practitioners labor and interact with "customers" who come in from the streets. Researchers navigate around in these floors as well but their offices are located in higher floors where more abstract knowledge production takes place. The top floors are where the eminent leaders and gatekeepers of the field make many of the decisions about the operations that take place in the building. The external walls are the epistemological borders that separate the field from other fields in the external environment. These walls are insular or somewhat porous depending on the size of the windows and whether or not they open fully. The basement of the building is where resources and old ideas are stored. While the building looks well established and solid it can change over the course of time. New findings and emerging theories can initiate the building of additional floors or wings, and parts of the structure can be dismantled, but most skyscrapers stay quite stable over the course of time. The evolution of the field mostly takes place through the addition of knowledge and the discarding of no longer valid constructs within the structure.

There certainly is more than enough work to do within a skyscraper so those who are inclined to do domain-specific work like to confine their thinking within the walls of the building. When they take a break every now and then to gaze through the windows they capture occasional glimpses of other domain buildings but they quickly get right back to producing and using domain-specific knowledge. Moreover, the infusion of rapidly evolving information technology enables them to generate far more professional knowledge than ever before so the knowledge is accumulating at a very rapid pace making it exceedingly difficult for any single professional or researcher to master everything in the building. This disinclines them from going beyond their walls to explore other buildings, even though they have technology that can facilitate networking among multiple office towers.

In contrast, interdisciplinary explorers tend to be based in a domain building but they like to explore throughout Creative Intelligence City. First, they explore electronically to see what's out there. Then they walk, Uber, or take the bus or subway throughout the city stopping at multiple skyscrapers and wandering into them, riding up the elevators, visiting with some of the theorists, researchers, and practitioners in offices on the various floors, and then moving on to other buildings. They gather theories and research findings from these diverse buildings and attempt to figure out how foreign ideas might be relevant to the work done in their home building and how to synthesize those constructs when possible.

One of these buildings has a big sign over the front door saying "creativity studies." Another neighboring building is labeled "gifted education." Yet another building houses "special education." A cluster of close together but separate buildings on a single block are labeled "cognitive psychology," "neuropsychology," "positive psychology," "psychobiology," and "school psychology," among others. Looking beyond the district encompassing the creativity-giftedness-psychology towers we come across other city blocks with other domain skyscrapers that don't seem directly related to creative intelligence but actually have some intriguing connections with the topic. These include "economics," "sociology," "political science," "anthropology," "law," "biotechnology," "behavioral genetics," "neuroscience," "biochemistry," and even "theoretical physics," among many others.

So, here we have a conundrum. Can we understand everything we need to know about creative intelligence by staying within a single building? Conversely, won't we become overwhelmed with far too many borrowed constructs to make sense of creative intelligence if we wander throughout the city stepping into many diverse buildings?

The limitations of staying within the same domain-specific building without engaging in exploration of other buildings in the city become obvious when we consider some insights that interdisciplinary explorers have brought back to the creativity studies and gifted education skyscrapers. Just a few examples can illustrate what can be gained from that. A special issue of the *Roeper Review* (Kalbfleisch and Ambrose 2008) solicited insights from cognitive neuroscientists and applied them to giftedness and creativity. One of these insights was the discovery that the brain-mind systems of mathematically gifted children are significantly different from their peers (O'Boyle 2008). These differences show up in heightened interhemispheric exchanges of information within the neocortex generating an unusual degree of neural connectivity as well as exceptional strengths in mental imagery. The professionals in both the creativity studies and gifted education office towers can benefit from that borrowed insight.

Another example of an insight borrowed from other skyscrapers in Creative Intelligence City comes from the results of work done by an interdisciplinary team years ago. A group of prominent scholars from four academic disciplines (economics, political science, English studies, analytic philosophy) came together to investigate the structure and dynamics of their disciplines (Bender and Schorske 1997). They eventually determined that two of the fields (economics and analytic philosophy) were unified, insular, and firmly policed. The other two (political science and English studies) were fragmented, porous, and contested. In the first of these patterns, the field is unified around a dominant theory. It is insular because it resists the intrusion of theories and research findings from foreign disciplines. It is firmly policed because the gatekeepers of the field won't publish articles or books that diverge from the orthodoxy. In contrast, a field following the second pattern is fragmented and contested because it is made up of warring theoretical and/or philosophical camps. No single theory comes to dominate and if one does gain some prominence it doesn't rule the majority of minds for very long. The field is porous because it cannot or will not stop invasions of theories and research findings from foreign disciplines.

After coming across these insights about the structure and dynamics of foreign fields I applied them to creativity studies (Ambrose 2006) and engaged with colleagues to inject them into gifted education (Ambrose et al. 2010), determining that both of these fields fit the fragmented, porous, contested pattern at the time of the analyses. It's highly unlikely that these insights would have been applied to creativity studies and gifted education if the interdisciplinary exploration had not turned up these patterns that were hidden away in other skyscrapers in Creative Intelligence City.

13.2 How Interdisciplinary Exploration and Domain-Specificity Can Help Each Other

It seems counterintuitive that these two very different investigative trajectories can support each other but it's quite likely that they can. Domain-specific experts can help interdisciplinary explorers be more cautious as they wander through unfamiliar parts of Creative Intelligence City. Meanwhile, interdisciplinary explorers can bring back foreign ideas and patterns that shed new light on the concepts within a domain-specific skyscraper.

13.2.1 Domain Specific Experts Making Interdisciplinary Explorers More Accurate in Their Work

First, the work on domain-specific expertise in creative intelligence fields can help interdisciplinary explorers be more careful about the work they do. For example, in the first few years of my interdisciplinary excursions I was excitedly tramping through the terrain of multiple disciplines coming across conceptual gemstones that appeared to be relevant to clarification and extension of theory and research on creativity and giftedness. But then I started interacting with an economist. We communicated frequently and collaborated on the development of some in-depth articles over the course of more than 18 months until he had to withdraw from the project because he was trepidatious about the flack he might get from colleagues in his field. The articles were turning out to be critical of the dominant theoretical framework in economics and that firmly policed field is notorious for coming down hard on dissenters.[1]

My extensive communication with this economist enriched my understanding of the nuances of multiple economic concepts, which I previously thought I understood fully but then realized I didn't. Since then I've been more cautious about importing constructs from foreign disciplines. I still do it but I vet them more carefully by triangulating multiple sources and securing opinions from experts when they are available. In essence, my collaboration with the economist revealed how deep and rich domain-specific expertise really is. Of course, I should have known this from observing researchers and theorists in my own domain skyscraper but that form of awareness seems to be hidden away from academics who tend to forget, to some extent, the depth and complexity of expertise in their domains and how long it takes to develop it. Suffice it to say that interdisciplinary scholars always should strive to escape the dogmatism of excessive certainty so they can appreciate the extensive knowledge bases within each domain-specific skyscraper they visit and the complex nuances that the theories and research findings can have. This enables them to value the worthiness of their domain-specific colleagues.

13.2.2 *Interdisciplinary Explorers Enriching the Work of Domain-Specific Experts by Providing Domain-Transcending Patterns and Conceptual Gemstones*

High levels of intelligence do not inoculate the minds of individuals and groups from infection by dogmatism (Elder and Paul 2012; Sternberg 2002). This applies to both interdisciplinary and domain-specific scholars. In the prior section I mentioned a form of dogmatism that can infect the minds of interdisciplinary investigators if they are not careful. Domain-specific experts can fall prey to a different form of dogmatism. It is possible for a domain-specific skyscraper to become a dogmatic field and the nature of the dogmatism depends on the structure and dynamics of the field as mentioned earlier–unified, insular, firmly policed or fragmented, porous, contested.

A unified, insular, firmly policed domain skyscraper has thick walls and small, tightly closed windows, forcing the scholars and practitioners within to align with a dominant theory. So a few gatekeepers in the top floor control much of what goes on

---
[1] I'm withholding the name of my colleague and the title of the articles to protect him.

in the floors below. Meanwhile, very few ideas from other skyscrapers can sneak through the small, closed windows so interdisciplinary work is difficult, if it's considered at all. Consequently, the dogmatism that can infect the minds of the professionals in this skyscraper is a form of excessive certainty or unwarranted confidence in the dominant theoretical construct and the findings it generates. Thomas Piketty (2014) is one of a growing number of prominent, rebellious economists who have pushed open some windows in their insular domain. He employed the term *scientific illusion* to signify how economics has avoided dealing with important contextual influences from the sociocultural and political environments. He recommended that his field engage in more interdisciplinary work to escape from this form of insular dogmatism.

The dogmatism Piketty was lamenting derives from the rational actor model of the individual economic decision maker, which is the dominant theoretical framework in mainstream economics. According to this framework, a person participating in the economy is exceptionally rational, operating on the basis of complete information sets, for entirely selfish reasons (Beckert 2002; Stiglitz 2010). The model works nicely as an efficient guide for the empirical work and model building in economics but it doesn't map onto reality very well. Seldom is any individual human entirely rational and the vast majority are at least somewhat altruistic. In addition, very seldom does anyone have access to perfect information sets about complex phenomena, even as they pertain to typical economic decisions. Because of this flawed model rooted in the dogmatism of a unified, insular, firmly policed domain skyscraper the economy has suffered. The biggest twenty first-century disaster based on this form of dogmatism was the 2008 economic collapse, as described by dissenting economists (e.g., Kotz 2015; Madrick 2014; Piketty 2014; Stiglitz 2010; Temin and Vines 2013).

Interdisciplinary explorers can help the excessively sequestered professionals in a unified, insular, firmly policed domain skyscraper by importing fresh ideas that can encourage them to think differently about narrowly confined constructs. For example, Morson and Schapiro (2017) recognized that economics tends to be excessively sanitized of altruism and ethics because it focuses too narrowly on rational self-interest. Consequently, they recommended some interdisciplinary synthesizing based on injecting the study of literature into economics because literature tends to evoke altruistic feelings and ethical awareness due to the visceral experiences readers gain from the plight of literary characters. This recommendation represents an opportunity for a highly creative modification of the work carried out in an enormously influential domain-specific office tower.

A fragmented, porous, contested domain skyscraper generates somewhat different forms of dogmatism. Because it is theoretically and philosophically contested it produces warring camps within it. So there are prominent gatekeepers in various competing offices on the top floor lobbing criticisms at one another and pushing researchers and practitioners to head in competing directions. And because their epistemological windows are open they allow ideas to drift in from other domain buildings causing additional turbulence and occasional chaos. Consequently, the field ends up looking somewhat schizophrenic and plagued by some degree of angst.

13.3 Examples of Transdisciplinary Patterns and Conceptual Gemstones That Can Generate Creativity in Domains

Interdisciplinary exploration can take us into scores of domain-specific towers where thousands of theories and research findings can be borrowed for importation into one's home domain. Here are just a few of these constructs, some of which already have been imported into creativity studies and gifted education, and others that can be imported to promote new forms of creative thinking in these fields.

13.3.1 Patterns from Complexity Science

Interdisciplinary wanderers can help the anxious professionals within a fragmented, porous, contested domain skyscraper by bringing them constructs and insights that can help establish some sense of order or common ground, thus reducing the conflict within the building and generating some excitement about a productive new inquiry path. For example, an easy to grasp pattern from the interdisciplinary field of complexity science can establish some common conceptual ground in a fragmented field by providing a pattern of similarity that applies to many, perhaps most phenomena of interest within that field. The *edge of chaos hypothesis* developed by complexity theorists Langton and Packard (see Kauffman 1995; Langton 1990; Packard 1988; Waldrop 1992), provides the basis for the *chaos-order continuum*, which portrays complex adaptive systems as oscillating along a continuum from excessive order to excessive chaos with productive complexity arising in the middle (Ambrose et al. 2014). Most complex adaptive systems studied within most academic disciplines and professional fields tend to align well with the continuum. Complex adaptive systems include the human brain-mind, groups of human minds (e.g., K-16 classrooms, teams in entrepreneurial organizations), animal populations in ecosystems, economies within and among nations, traffic patterns in major cities, chemical reactions, and many more.

When a complex adaptive system moves too far toward the order end of the continuum it becomes rigid, locked into a particular structural or behavioral pattern. When it moves too far toward the chaos end of the continuum it becomes frenetic and unstable. At either of these ends of the continuum the behavior is not complex because there is no systematic, complex pattern in the structure or dynamics of the system. But when the system finds the *edge of chaos* in the middle of the continuum where chaos and order are in exquisite dynamic tension, its structure and/or behavior becomes intricately complex. For example, a schizophrenic human mind is fragmented and chaotic as it pushes too far toward the chaos end of the continuum. In contrast, a dogmatic human mind engages in rigid, narrow, superficial, thought because it is firmly locked into an unyielding idea framework. But when a creative human mind is deeply engaged in a challenging, complex problem it can find the edge of chaos in the middle of the continuum and generate enormously complex, highly productive theoretical, philosophical, or practical work. It does this because it benefits from the dynamic tension between the chaos-generating ambiguity of the complex problem and its order-generating constraints.

Arguably, interdisciplinary travelers moving throughout Creative Intelligence City can deliver the chaos-order continuum construct into a wide range of high-rises, including the following (explained in detail in Ambrose 2014b).

- *Economics.* The centralized planning of the Soviet Union in the twentieth century was excessively ordered; consequently, it didn't develop sufficient complexity to produce the goods and services needed by a large population. In contrast, the excessive deregulation of the global economy due to neoclassical economic theory, and its ideological cousin neoliberalism, generated economic chaos that produced the 2008 economic collapse. A vibrant economy requires dynamic tension between the chaos of free-market dynamics and the order of prudent regulation. Creative, entrepreneurial economic action can be guided by more awareness of the dynamic tension between chaos and order.
- *Political science.* Totalitarian governments establish exceedingly firm control over the policymaking apparatus, legal institutions, and the media in a nation, thus producing counterproductive, excessive order that severely limits the freedom of the population. In contrast, when a nation falls into anarchy it lacks the political authority to establish and maintain the rule of law so the political system falls into excessive chaos. But when a nation finds the exquisite balance between individual freedom and communal solidarity it develops a healthy democratic governance system, which allows for optimal levels of creative self-actualization among its citizens along with social justice through the effective provision of public goods.
- *The structure and dynamics of academic disciplines.* The aforementioned analyses of academic disciplines and professional fields, which portrayed them as unified, insular, and firmly policed or fragmented, porous, and contested, fit neatly onto the chaos-order continuum. When a field is extremely unified, insular, and firmly policed it can fall prey to excessive order because the dominant theory firmly locks the minds of theorists, researchers, and practitioners into a single conceptual framework. When a field is extremely fragmented, porous, and contested its lack of adherence to an agreed-upon conceptual framework can make it excessively chaotic. From the viewpoint of the chaos-order continuum, academic disciplines and professional fields could establish bases for stronger theory development, research, and practical work if they avoid either extreme. This likely would require more nuanced judgment on the part of all involved. Nuanced judgment is a form of critical thinking that enables participants to avoid conceptual polarization by searching for shades of gray between opposing, either-or positions (Elder and Paul 2012; Resnick 1987). Such judgment could encourage a field to hold an influential theory lightly, using it as a lamp that enables searching through darkened corners of the conceptual terrain while avoiding the temptation to securely lodge that lamp in a particular location in the landscape, pointing it in a single direction. This could make more

room for creative inquiry by preventing a field from locking itself too firmly into a single theoretical perspective. Theoretical entrenchment seems to be an ongoing problem throughout the history of science as evidenced by the periodic emergence of starkly contrasting scientific paradigms (Kuhn 1962).

- *The dynamics of teaching and learning.* Veteran teachers tend to resonate with the chaos-order model because they recognize processes from curriculum and instruction that fit along the continuum. Here are just a few examples:

  - Classroom management: the authoritarian teacher vigorously presses toward excessive order. Laissez-faire teachers allow excessive chaos. Student-centered teachers employing problem-based learning enable their students to manage themselves through complex, intrinsic motivation.
  - Assessment: Excessive reliance on standardized testing pushes school systems to the excessive order end of the continuum due to overemphases on the pseudo-quantitative precision of easily measured, superficial learning. The impulsive assessment used by teachers who do not engage in sufficient planning generates instructional chaos. Authentic assessment generates productive complexity arising from intriguing, deep immersion in real-world problems and the focus on complex thought processes.
  - The science and art of teaching: Teachers adhering too rigidly to proven methodologies (the science of teaching) can lock themselves into excessive order. Those who rely too heavily on their intuitive impressions of how things are going (the art of teaching) can fall prey to excessive chaos. But blending the science and art of teaching can lead to highly complex constructivist learning processes.

13.3.2 Benefiting from Diverse Minds Within and Between Domains

Another borrowed insight comes from a leading scholar who has done some of his own interdisciplinary exploration through several skyscrapers in Creative Intelligence City. Scott Page (2007, 2010, 2017) synthesized research from economics and the interdisciplinary field of complexity science to portray the value of cognitive diversity in the performance of work groups throughout a variety of governmental and corporate organizations. Cognitively diverse work teams encompass diverse backgrounds, theories and philosophical perspectives, problem-solving heuristics, and belief systems. Such teams consistently outperform cognitively homogenous teams even when the latter teams are superior in measured intelligence.

These findings have some interesting implications when it comes to the work done within and among the various domain-specific office towers in Creative Intelligence City. First, it becomes important to ensure that the professionals and researchers within a domain-specific tower come from varying professional and cultural backgrounds. But such diversity is difficult to achieve in a unified-insular-firmly policed domain that is dominated by a particular theoretical perspective. The professionals and academics in that domain are very likely to think along very similar lines about difficult, complex problems. Even if they are extremely strong in measured intelligence and domain-specific expertise their collective homogeneity probably will drag down their group performance.

Consequently, the somewhat greater diversity encompassed by the collective minds of professionals and academics in fragmented-porous-contested domain-specific towers could be an advantage when dealing with complex problems. Nevertheless, the wars over theoretical constructs and methodological tools that commonly take place in a fragmented domain likely suppress problem-solving performance within that domain. In view of this, it would be wise if researchers in the creativity studies and gifted education office towers were to devote more attention to the dynamics of cognitive diversity when they carry out their research.

13.4 An Interdisciplinary Economic Framework for Analyzing Inequality and Fairness

Venkatasubramanian (2017) produced a mathematical framework for analyzing the extent to which fairness is considered in income distributions throughout a society. The framework; which is derived from an interdisciplinary synthesis of constructs from economics, political science, information theory, game theory, systems engineering, and statistical mechanics; addresses the lack of attention mainstream economics pays to economic fairness. Venkatasubramanian went on to use the framework to analyze some of the world's economies. In one example the framework shows that Scandinavian nations have close to ideal fairness while the United States is extremely unfair. This innovative, interdisciplinary framework analyzing an important dimension of economics can be applied readily to work on dark creativity in the field of creativity studies (see Cropley et al. 2010; Gutworth et al. 2016; Majid al-Rifaie et al. 2016). For example, influential players in national and global economic systems can be revealed as engaging in dark creativity when they pull economic and political levers to keep those systems pushing toward even more severe inequalities. The previously mentioned 2008 economic collapse, largely caused by highly creative, unethical manipulation of the world's financial system, is a specific example of this form of dark creativity.

13.4.1 Cutting Holes in Veneer Theory

Another topic mostly investigated beyond the walls of the creativity studies and gifted education office towers is the extent to which altruism is rooted in our biology and evolutionary processes or, conversely, tends to be applied as a thin layer over our baser, brutish natures. Sociobiology and its neighboring fields tend to magnify the biological and evolutionary bases for human nature, including some aspects of moral-ethical behavior (see Dawkins 2006; Wilson 1975, 1978). A few insights from sociobiology have made their way through the partially open windows of the creativity studies office tower (e.g., McLaren 2003). But most of the work in this field remains in other buildings in Creative Intelligence City.

For example, primatologist Frans De Waal (2006) argued that our conceptions of morality have been distorted by scholarship from the past in evolutionary biology and philosophy. Some of the past research in evolutionary biology portrayed human nature as extremely selfish (Trivers 1971; Wilson 1978). When we go back centuries to the work of the eminent philosopher Thomas Hobbes (1651/1985), deep in the cobwebbed recesses of the philosophy building, we are confronted with his portrayal of human nature as innately asocial or antisocial and brutish. De Waal argued that *veneer theory* arises from these distortions of human nature essentially portraying humans as much less worthy and ethical than they typically are. Veneer theory suggests that morality is a thin veneer that covers the core of human nature, which is immoral, or at best amoral. Supposedly, in normal circumstances the veneer prevents us from abusing and exploiting one another; however, when crises such as resource shortages or tragedies scratch the veneer, our harmful core dispositions escape and enable us to engage in evil behavior.

De Waal pointed out that evil does tend to emerge in these conditions but that veneer theory overemphasizes it while hiding the altruism that also comes forth in desperate circumstances. To counter veneer theory, De Waal (2006) provided a more optimistic portrayal of human nature, which is based on decades of observing the behavior of primates. His findings show that altruism actually is common among primates, emerging from their visceral emotional responses to the suffering of others. He also argued that the emergence of altruism is evolutionarily adaptive because it promotes group cohesion and groups in which the members look out for one another survive much better than do loosely affiliated groups and selfish, atomistic individuals. Finally, he specified that this form of altruism goes much deeper than reciprocal altruism in which the generous person is expecting some kind of payback from the beneficiary. Of course, reciprocal altruism does exist but it doesn't dominate human behavior because it is not nearly as powerful as genuine altruism.

De Waal's magnification of genuine altruism and criticism of veneer theory could inject some helpful ideas into the creativity studies and gifted education towers in Creative Intelligence City. First, it could encourage more attention to generosity and kindness in creative work while illustrating how misguided, or at least limited, selfish conceptions of human nature can be when it comes to creativity. This could be an important dimension of continued work on dark creativity. Second, it could become a focal point for work on group creativity because De Waal's work in primatology shows that the group cohesion resulting from genuine altruism is evolutionarily adaptive. All kinds of groups from entrepreneurial startups, to corporations, to NGOs, to educational institutions could benefit from more attention to genuine altruistic behavior.

13.4.2 A Continuum of Global Relations

If we want to encourage big-picture thinking in creativity studies and gifted education we should borrow from disciplines that explore large-scale contextual influences on human thought and action. Political theorist Michael Walzer (2001) provided a helpful framework for this kind of thinking about creative intelligence. He created a continuum illustrating a variety of political arrangements that can take shape in international society. Seven possible international arrangements fit along the continuum from a highly centralized global system to an extremely decentralized, somewhat anarchic system. The following is a brief portrayal of these positions on the continuum:

1. A global state. A tightly centralized world government exerts considerable control over the thoughts and actions of global citizens, all of whom possess similar obligations and rights.
2. Imperial hegemony. A single dominant nation controls a global empire and establishes some differentiation between itself and all other nations. This is a small step away from the tightly controlled centralization in position 1. Here, there is sufficient centralized control to prevent conflict while still allowing for some cultural independence; however, the outlier states don't enjoy secure freedom because their fate rests in the hands of the dominant state, which could exert considerable control over them at any time. Also, citizens in the dominant state have more rights than those in other nations.
3. Federation of nation states. This system is analogous to a United States of the world. An influential central political entity has significant power, which is ceded to it by member nations that are somewhat independent. There is a guaranteed separation of powers and rights are protected by an effective judicial system. However, there is the potential for drift toward oligarchy because some member nations likely will enjoy more power than others.
4. Independent nations strongly influenced by non-state agents. According to Walzer, this system provides the most potential for the creation of peace, individual rights, justice, and cultural diversity. It provides insulation against the emergence of tyranny because it includes a strong United Nations peacekeeping force and international regulation of capital, labor, and environmental standards.
5. Borderless, international civic associations pressuring nation states to cooperate. These volunteer associations would be stronger than our current international organizations but they would have difficulty preventing abuses produced by powerful multinational corporations that find it easy to dodge accountability in a highly decentralized world.
6. Largely independent states blended with weak global organizations. In this arrangement no single state possesses sovereignty over the others. Nations engage in some limited cooperation through weak international organizations such as the World Bank, the World Court, and the United Nations. There is some pressure to prevent international conflict but wars and atrocities still emerge

periodically and socioeconomic inequality is rampant. According to Walzer, this point on the continuum closely approximated the global situation at the time he generated the framework. Arguably, the globalized socioeconomic system in the year 2018 still fits this position on the continuum.
7. Completely independent sovereign nations. There is no global authority and no stable organizations of states. Temporary agreements and treaties may emerge between some nations but these are unstable because they are not enforceable by third parties.

According to Walzer (2001) the worst forms of international relations would emerge at the extremes of the continuum because they are conducive to insecurity, inequality, and human rights abuses.

If theorists and researchers studying creativity and giftedness employed Walzer's continuum as an analytic framework they could clarify some of the contextual influences on creative intelligence. For example, position 7, completely independent sovereign nations, would require visionary, creative leadership similar to Sternberg's (2003, 2005, 2009) WICS model (wisdom, intelligence, and creativity synthesized) in order to prevent severe international conflicts and human rights abuses. WICS leadership also would be important in the highly centralized global state at position 1 on the continuum because a world government exerting control over global citizens would have to be guided by ethics to maintain the optimal balance of rights and obligations in the citizenry. Walzer's continuum also magnifies the importance of paying more attention to the dynamics of the dark side of creativity.

13.5 Encouraging Domain-Specific and Interdisciplinary Professionals to Collaborate

As mentioned at the outset, the inclinations and interests of domain-specific and interdisciplinary professionals can diverge considerably; however, their work can and should be complementary. But professionals can be locked dogmatically into established mindsets (see Ambrose and Sternberg 2012; Ambrose et al. 2012). In order to diminish the chances that counterproductive dogmatism will prevent potential, rich syntheses of domain-specific and interdisciplinary work we can make the potential of collaboration more visible. One way to do this is to employ the jurisprudential synthesis creative and critical thinking strategy (see, Arends and Kilcher 2010; Joyce and Weil 1992). This strategy, which isn't well known, enables groups and individuals to identify opposing, polarized positions on a complex, controversial issue and then build a compromise position between the two. First, participants explore the controversial issue and then establish the opposing positions, putting one of them in column A of a 3 column table and the other in column C. Then they find arguments and evidence for each of these two opposing positions putting them under the title of each position in the two outside columns. The step requiring the most creative and critical thinking involves the establishment of a compromise

Table 13.1 A jurisprudential table synthesizing the work of domain-specific and interdisciplinary professionals in Creative Intelligence City

Position A: Domain-specific work is best	Position C: Domain-specific and Interdisciplinary professionals work together	Position B: Interdisciplinary exploration is best
Working inside our domain-specific office towers provides the most important insights about creative intelligence by far. Wandering outside in the streets is a waste of time and generates confusion.	Both domain-specific knowledge generators and interdisciplinary explorers do important work. Moreover, their work is complementary because each provides insights about complex phenomena that are inaccessible to the other.	Traveling throughout creative intelligence city establishes clarity about creative intelligence by revealing patterns that appear from one city block to another. Hiding inside a single domain-specific tower can make you myopic.
(Participants load arguments and evidence supporting position A into this column)	(Participants load arguments and evidence supporting their synthesizing, compromise position in this column)	(Participants load arguments and evidence supporting position B into this column)

position that goes in the middle column. After naming the compromise position, participants find arguments and evidence for it and complete the middle column. The compromise can lean somewhat toward position A or B but cannot grossly violate either one.

The beginning of a proposed jurisprudential synthesis for domain-specific and interdisciplinary work shows up in Table 13.1. Domain-specific expertise is position A, interdisciplinary exploration is position B, and synthesizing domain-specific and interdisciplinary work is position C. Hopefully, those who favor one or the other opposing position will come to appreciate the points in the compromise position C, which shows how collaboration with those in the other "camp" can enrich the work of all. I would have benefited from this when I was somewhat narrow-minded about my favoritism of interdisciplinary work over domain-specific discovery.

13.6 Concluding Thoughts

There certainly are daunting barriers that make interdisciplinary work difficult within a domain. Imported constructs can seem strange because they can emerge from very different epistemological and even ontological frameworks. The knowledge base within a domain can be very complex and adding foreign constructs will add to this complexity. Moreover, the foreign origins of these constructs make it likely that they will generate communication difficulties because they won't fit into the dominant terminology of the field. Some have seen these communication difficulties as analogous to the conditions that give rise to pidginization of language during communication between representatives of different cultures (Baer 2012b; Galison 2001). Given these barriers, it's much easier to ignore constructs from foreign domains and focus on building more solid and expansive domain-specific knowledge bases using the constructs generated within a domain.

But these barriers shouldn't dissuade adventurous investigators from attempting to enrich their fields with foreign constructs that can shed new light on puzzling domain-specific phenomena. The primary argument here is that creative intelligence fields such as creativity studies and gifted education should engage in more interdisciplinary exploration; however, these fields are fragmented, porous, and contested (Ambrose 2006; Ambrose et al. 2010). Porous fields already have constructs from various disciplines wafting in through their open windows so they need interdisciplinary borrowing less than the unified, insular, firmly policed domain-specific towers. Nevertheless, even fragmented, porous, contested fields can benefit from more systematic interdisciplinary borrowing, especially in the context of twenty first-century globalization, which encourages the strengthening of cognitive diversity (Page 2007, 2010, 2017) and international, interdisciplinary scientific networking (Nielsen 2011; Suresh 2013). Importing more theories and research findings from diverse disciplines can ensure that more cognitive diversity emerges in teams of professionals in a domain-specific field, and in the individual minds of theorists, researchers, and practitioners.

Of course, these recommendations should be guided by the previous warnings about the forms of dogmatism that can arise in freewheeling, somewhat careless interdisciplinary exploration and excessively closed domain-specific work. If those who wander through the streets of Creative Intelligence City borrowing constructs from various office towers and those who labor within domain-specific towers truly appreciate the value in these different very different kinds of work they will be able to invigorate research and theory development in creative intelligence fields.

References

Ambrose, D. (1996). Unifying theories of creativity: Metaphorical thought and the unification process. *New Ideas in Psychology, 14*, 257–267.

Ambrose, D. (1998). A model for clarification and expansion of conceptual foundations. *Gifted Child Quarterly, 42*, 77–86.

Ambrose, D. (2003). Barriers to aspiration development and self-fulfillment: Interdisciplinary insights for talent discovery. *Gifted Child Quarterly, 47*, 282–294.

Ambrose, D. (2005a). Aspiration growth, talent development, and self-fulfillment in a context of democratic erosion. *Roeper Review, 28*, 11–19.

Ambrose, D. (2005b). Interdisciplinary expansion of conceptual foundations: Insights from beyond our field. *Roeper Review, 27*, 137–143.

Ambrose, D. (2006). Large-scale contextual influences on creativity: Evolving academic disciplines and global value systems. *Creativity Research Journal, 18*, 75–85. https://doi.org/10.1207/s15326934crj1801_9.

Ambrose, D. (2009). *Expanding visions of creative intelligence: An interdisciplinary exploration.* Cresskill: Hampton Press.

Ambrose, D. (2014a). Invigorating innovation and combating dogmatism through creative, metaphorical business leadership. In F. K. Reisman (Ed.), *Creativity in business* (pp. 52–66). London: KIE Conference Book Series.

Ambrose, D. (2014b). The ubiquity of the chaos-order continuum: Insights from diverse academic disciplines. In D. Ambrose, B. Sriraman, & K. M. Pierce (Eds.), *A critique of creativity and complexity: Deconstructing clichés* (pp. 67–86). Rotterdam: Sense.

Ambrose, D. (2016). Borrowing insights from other disciplines to strengthen the conceptual foundations for gifted education. *International Journal for Talent Development and Creativity, 3*(2), 33–57.

Ambrose, D. (2017a). Interdisciplinary exploration supports Sternberg's expansion of giftedness. *Roeper Review, 39*, 178–182.

Ambrose, D. (2017b). Interdisciplinary invigoration of creativity studies. *Journal of Creative Behavior, 51*, 348–351. https://doi.org/10.1002/jocb.205.

Ambrose, D., & Cross, T. L. (Eds.). (2009). *Morality, ethics, and gifted minds*. New York: Springer Science.

Ambrose, D., & Sternberg, R. J. (Eds.). (2012). *How dogmatic beliefs harm creativity and higher-level thinking*. New York: Routledge.

Ambrose, D., & Sternberg, R. J. (Eds.). (2016a). *Creative intelligence in the 21st century: Grappling with enormous problems and huge opportunities*. Rotterdam: Sense.

Ambrose, D., & Sternberg, R. J. (Eds.). (2016b). *Giftedness and talent in the 21st century: Adapting to the turbulence of globalization*. Rotterdam: Sense.

Ambrose, D., Cohen, L. M., & Tannenbaum, A. J. (Eds.). (2003). *Creative intelligence: Toward theoretic integration*. Cresskill: Hampton Press.

Ambrose, D., VanTassel-Baska, J., Coleman, L. J., & Cross, T. L. (2010). Unified, insular, firmly policed or fractured, porous, contested, gifted education? *Journal for the Education of the Gifted, 33*, 453–478.

Ambrose, D., Sternberg, R. J., & Sriraman, B. (Eds.). (2012). *Confronting dogmatism in gifted education*. New York: Routledge.

Ambrose, D., Sriraman, B., & Pierce, K. M. (Eds.). (2014). *A critique of creativity and complexity: Deconstructing clichés*. Rotterdam: Sense.

Arends, D., & Kilcher, A. (2010). *Teaching for student learning: Becoming an accomplished teacher*. New York: Routledge.

Baer, J. (1998). The case for domain specificity of creativity. *Creativity Research Journal, 11*, 173–177.

Baer, J. (1999). Domains of creativity. In M. A. Runco & S. R. Pritzker (Eds.), *Encyclopedia of creativity* (pp. 591–596). New York: Academic.

Baer, J. (2010). Is creativity domain specific? In J. C. Kaufman & R. J. Sternberg (Eds.), *The Cambridge handbook of creativity* (pp. 321–341). New York: Cambridge University Press.

Baer, J. (2012a). Domain specificity and the limits of creativity theory. *The Journal of Creative Behavior, 46*, 16–29.

Baer, J. (2012b). Unintentional dogmatism when thinking big: How grand theories and interdisciplinary thinking can sometimes limit our vision. In D. Ambrose & R. J. Sternberg (Eds.), *How dogmatic beliefs harm creativity and a higher-level thinking* (pp. 157–170). New York: Routledge.

Baer, J. (2013). Teaching for creativity: Domains and divergent thinking, intrinsic motivation, and evaluation. In M. B. Gregerson, H. T. Snyder, & J. C. Kaufman (Eds.), *Teaching creatively and teaching creativity* (pp. 175–181). New York: Springer.

Baer, J. (2015). The importance of domain-specific expertise in creativity. *Roeper Review, 37*, 165–178.

Baer, J. (2016a). Creativity and the common core need each other. In D. Ambrose & R. J. Sternberg (Eds.), *Creative intelligence in the 21st century: Grappling with enormous problems and huge opportunities* (pp. 175–190). Rotterdam: Sense.

Baer, J. (2016b). *Domain specificity of creativity*. San Diego: Academic.

Baer, J., & Kaufman, J. C. (2015). Bridging generality and specificity: The amusement park theoretical (APT) model of creativity. *Roeper Review, 27*, 158–163.

Beckert, J. (2002). *Beyond the market: The social foundations of economic efficiency*. Princeton: Princeton University Press.
Beghetto, R. A., Kaufman, J. C., & Baer, J. (2015). *Teaching for creativity in the Common Core classroom*. New York: Teachers College Press.
Bender, T., & Schorske, C. E. (Eds.). (1997). *American academic culture in transformation: Fifty years, four disciplines*. Princeton: Princeton University Press.
Cropley, D. H., Cropley, A. J., Kaufman, J. C., & Runco, M. A. (Eds.). (2010). *The dark side of creativity*. New York: Cambridge University Press.
Dawkins, R. (2006). *The selfish gene* (3rd ed.). New York: Oxford University Press.
De Waal, F. B. M. (2006). *Primates and philosophers: How morality evolved*. Princeton: Princeton University Press.
Elder, L., & Paul, R. (2012). Dogmatism, creativity, and critical thought: The reality of human minds and the possibility of critical societies. In D. Ambrose & R. J. Sternberg (Eds.), *How dogmatic beliefs harm creativity and higher-level thinking* (pp. 37–49). New York: Routledge.
Galison, P. (2001). Material culture, theoretical culture, and delocalization. In J. W. Scott & D. Keates (Eds.), *Schools of thought: Twenty-five years of interpretive social science* (pp. 179–193). Princeton: Princeton University Press.
Gardner, H. (1988). Creativity: An interdisciplinary perspective. *Creativity Research Journal, 1*, 8–26.
Gardner, H. (2006). *Five minds for the future*. Boston: Harvard Business School Press.
Gruber, H. E., & Bödeker, K. (Eds.). (2005). *Creativity, psychology and the history of science*. New York: Springer.
Gutworth, M. B., Cushenbery, L., & Hunter, S. T. (2016). Creativity for deliberate harm: Malevolent creativity and social information processing theory. *Journal of Creative Behavior*. https://doi.org/10.1002/jocb.155.
Hobbes, T. (1985). *Leviathan*. New York: Penguin (Original work published 1651).
Joyce, B., & Weil, M. (1992). *Models of teaching* (4th ed.). Needham Heights: Allyn & Bacon.
Kalbfleisch, L., & Ambrose, D. (2008). The cognitive neuroscience of giftedness [special issue]. *Roeper Review, 30*(3 & 4).
Kauffman, S. (1995). *At home in the universe: The search for the laws of self-organization and complexity*. New York: Oxford University Press.
Kaufman, J. C., Glăveanu, V. P., & Baer, J. (Eds.). (2017). *The Cambridge handbook of creativity across domains*. New York: Cambridge University Press.
Kotz, D. M. (2015). *The rise and fall of neoliberal capitalism*. Cambridge, MA: Harvard University Press.
Kuhn, T. (1962). *The structure of scientific revolutions*. Chicago: University of Chicago Press.
Langton, C. G. (1990). Communication at the edge of chaos: Phase transitions and emergent computation. *Physica D, 42*, 12–37.
Lindauer, M. S. (1998). Interdisciplinarity, the psychology of art and creativity: An introduction. *Creativity Research Journal, 11*, 1–10.
Madrick, J. (2014). *How mainstream economists have damaged America and the world*. New York: Alfred A. Knopf.
Majid al-Rifaie, M., Cropley, A., Cropley, D., & Bishop, M. (2016). On evil and computational creativity. *Connection Science, 28*(2), 171–193. https://doi.org/10.1080/09540091.2016.1151862.
McLaren, R. B. (2003). Tackling the intractable: An interdisciplinary exploration of the moral proclivity. *Creativity Research Journal, 15*, 15–24.
Morson, G. S., & Schapiro, M. (2017). *Cents and sensibility: What economics can learn from the humanities*. Princeton: Princeton University Press.
Nielsen, M. (2011). *Reinventing discovery: The new era of networked science*. Princeton: Princeton University Press.
O'Boyle, M. W. (2008). Mathematically gifted children: Developmental brain characteristics than their prognosis for well-being. *Roeper Review, 30*, 181–186.

Olszewski-Kubilius, P., Subotnik, R. F., & Worrell, F. C. (2017). The role of domains in the conceptualization of talent. *Roeper Review, 39*, 59–69.

Packard, N. H. (1988). Adaptation toward the edge of chaos. In J. A. S. Kelso, A. J. Mandell, & M. F. Shlesinger (Eds.), *Dynamic patterns in complex systems* (pp. 293–301). Singapore: World Scientific.

Page, S. E. (2007). *The difference: How the power of diversity creates better groups, firms, schools, and societies*. Princeton: Princeton University Press.

Page, S. E. (2010). *Diversity and complexity*. Princeton: Princeton University Press.

Page, S. E. (2017). *The diversity bonus: How great teams pay off in the knowledge economy*. Princeton: Princeton University Press.

Piketty, T. (2014). *Capital in the twenty-first century*. Cambridge, MA: Harvard University Press.

Resnick, L. B. (1987). *Education and learning to think*. Washington, DC: National Academy Press.

Root-Bernstein, R. (2001). Music, creativity, and scientific thinking. *Leonardo, 34*(1), 63–68. https://doi.org/10.1162/002409401300052532.

Root-Bernstein, R. (2003). The art of innovation: Polymaths and universality of the creative process. In L. V. Shavignina (Ed.), *The international handbook on innovation* (pp. 267–278). Oxford: Elsevier Science.

Root-Bernstein, M. (2014). *Inventing imaginary worlds: From childhood play to adult creativity across the arts and sciences*. Lanham: Rowman & Littlefield.

Sawyer, R. K. (1998). The interdisciplinary study of creativity in performance. *Creativity Research Journal, 11*, 11–19. https://doi.org/10.1207/s15326934crj1101_2.

Shiu, E. (Ed.). (2014). *Creativity research: An inter-disciplinary and multi-disciplinary research handbook*. New York: Routledge.

Silvia, P. J., Kaufman, J. C., & Pretz, J. E. (2009). Is creativity domain-specific? Latent class models of creative accomplishments and creative self-descriptions. *Psychology of Aesthetics, Creativity, and the Arts, 3*(3), 139–148.

Simonton, D. K. (2009). Varieties of (scientific) creativity: A hierarchical model of domain-specific disposition, development, and achievement. *Perspectives on Psychological Science, 4*(5), 441–452.

Sriraman, B., & Dahl, B. (2009). On bringing interdisciplinary ideas to gifted education. In L. V. Shavignina (Ed.), *International handbook on giftedness* (pp. 1235–1256). New York: Springer Science.

Sternberg, R. J. (2002). Effecting organizational change: A "mineralogical theory" of organizational modifiability. *Consulting Psychology Journal: Practice and Research, 54*, 147–156. https://doi.org/10.1037/1061-4087.54.3.147.

Sternberg, R. J. (2003). WICS as a model of giftedness. *High Ability Studies, 14*, 109–137. https://doi.org/10.1080/13598130320000163807.

Sternberg, R. J. (2005). WICS: A model of giftedness in leadership. *Roeper Review, 28*, 37–44.

Sternberg, R. J. (2009). Reflections on ethical leadership. In D. Ambrose & T. L. Cross (Eds.), *Morality, ethics, and gifted minds* (pp. 19–28). New York: Springer Science.

Stiglitz, J. E. (2010). *Free fall: America, free markets, and the sinking of the world economy*. New York: W. W. Norton.

Subotnik, R. F., Olszewski-Kubilius, P., & Worrell, F. C. (2011). Rethinking giftedness and gifted education: A proposed direction forward based on psychological science. *Psychological Science in the Public Interest, 12*(1), 3–54.

Suresh, S. (2013, October). To tap the world's vast and growing potential for new ideas, we need new rules. *Scientific American, 309*(4), 60.

Temin, P., & Vines, D. (2013). *The leaderless economy: Why the world economic system fell apart and how to fix it*. Princeton: Princeton University Press.

Thiessen, B. L. (1998). Shedding the stagnant slough syndrome: Interdisciplinary integration. *Creativity Research Journal, 11*, 47–53.

Trivers, R. (1971). The evolution of reciprocal altruism. *Quarterly Review of Biology, 46*, 35–57.

VanTassel-Baska, J., & Stambaugh, T. (2006). *Comprehensive curriculum for gifted learners* (3rd ed.). Boston: Allyn & Bacon.

Venkatasubramanian, V. (2017). *How much inequality is there? Mathematical principles of a moral, optimal, and stable capitalist society*. New York: Columbia University Press.

Waldrop, M. M. (1992). *Complexity: The emerging science at the edge of order and chaos*. New York: Touchstone.

Walzer, M. (2001). International society: What is the best that we can do? In J. W. Scott & D. Keates (Eds.), *Schools of thought: Twenty-five years of interpretive social science* (pp. 388–401). Princeton: Princeton University Press.

Wilson, E. O. (1975). *Sociobiology: The new synthesis*. Cambridge, MA: Harvard University Press.

Wilson, E. O. (1978). *On human nature*. Cambridge, MA: Harvard University Press.

Chapter 14
Thought Dynamics: Which Role for Mind Wandering in Creativity?

Manila Vannucci and Sergio Agnoli

Abstract For a long time, mainstream psychological research on cognitive processes has been focused on the investigation of externally-oriented cognition, namely deliberate processes generated in response to cues provided by the experimenter and associated with specific experimental paradigms. During the last two decades, there has been a surge of interest in both psychology and neuroscience toward the investigation of internally-oriented cognition, and, among the different kinds, a growing interest has been devoted to mind wandering (MW), which represents a shift in the contents of thought away from an ongoing task and/or from events in the external environment, toward internal mental contents. By definition, MW is characterized by a flow of thought, and it occurs without a fixed course or a drive to reach a specific goal. Creative thinking also involves dynamic shifts between different information and mental states. Does mind wandering contribute to creativity? Here we briefly review mixed findings on the association between MW and creativity and we outline a new multidimensional dynamic approach, in which the associations between different kinds of MW (i.e. spontaneous and deliberate) and different forms of creativity are considered. Practical implications of this approach are discussed.

M. Vannucci (✉)
Department of NEUROFARBA-Section of Psychology, University of Florence, Florence, Italy
e-mail: manila.vannucci@psico.unifi.it

S. Agnoli (✉)
Marconi Institute for Creativity (MIC), Villa Griffone, Sasso Marconi, Italy
e-mail: sergio.agnoli@unibo.it

14.1 Introduction

For a long time mainstream research has been focused on the investigation of externally-oriented and deliberate cognitive processes, associated with specific cognitive tasks (*task-centric view of mental processes*, Christoff et al. 2016, p. 1). This task-centric view of mental processes contrasts with our everyday life experience. In many situations of daily life, as for example while reading a book, attending a lecture, or driving, we may notice, to our dismay, that our attention drifts away from the primary task and the external environment and our mind starts wandering elsewhere towards internal thoughts, such as memories, current concerns, prospective thoughts, whose content is unrelated to the ongoing task. Usually, it takes some time (ranging from seconds to minutes) to bring our attention back to the primary task and the external environment. We refer to this *"shift in the focus of attention away from the here and now towards one's private thoughts and feelings"* (Smallwood et al. 2007, p. 818) as mind wandering, hereafter MW.

By definition, MW is characterized by a flow of thought, and it occurs without a fixed course or a drive to reach a specific goal. As we briefly review in the following, the functional and neural processes engaged in MW are becoming reasonably well established. However, as argued by Smallwood (2013), any comprehensive account of MW is expected to address and explain both the dynamics of the initial occurrence of MW as well as its maintenance-continuity over time (i.e., the process-occurrence framework; Smallwood 2013).

Recently, a series of studies have started addressing the key question of the neurocognitive mechanism by which MW arises: *Why* does the mind start wandering? And *how* does this mental state arise? To this regard, an important contribution has been provided by research studies on individual differences in MW, which introduced a crucial distinction between different types of MW, namely spontaneous and deliberate MW. The difference between the two is in the mental dynamics underlying the onset of the experience of MW: how attention shifts from external to internal information, how the change in mental state occurs, whether it occurs spontaneously or, somehow, under the individual's mental control.

The shift form external to internal information, as well as the involvement of implicit thinking processes and explicit control processes (e.g., Beaty et al. 2016) are key questions also in the study of creative thinking. Creative thinking involves indeed dynamic shifts between different information and mental states. Does mind wandering dynamics contribute to creativity? This is the question we will address in this chapter. As we will outline in the next paragraphs, identifying the processes that stimulate the initial occurrence of MW (its onset) and distinguishing between different kinds of MW, on the basis of the different dynamics of thought, can improve our understanding of how MW might contribute to different processes underpinning creative thinking.

14.2 Functional and Neural Mechanisms of MW

The phenomenon of MW has been first studied by a handful of researchers almost 50 years ago (e.g., studies on daydreaming in the 1960–1970s, Antrobus et al. 1966; Klinger 1971; Singer 1966), but only during the past two decades, it has received a widespread scientific attention, with a dramatic surge of interest in psychology and neuroscience. Our understanding of MW greatly benefited from the use of the "strategy of triangulation" (Smallwood and Schooler 2015), whereby self-reports, behavioural measures and physiological measures are combined together in the same study to make inferences about covert mental experiences.

Converging evidence suggests that MW is a ubiquitous and pervasive mental activity, common across different cultures and groups (see for a review, Smallwood and Schooler 2015). Experience sampling studies have indeed shown that people spend between 25% and 50% of their daytime engaged in MW (e.g., Killingsworth and Gilbert 2010), and the frequency of MW might even increase during well-practiced tasks (e.g., driving, reading) (Mason et al. 2007).

Neurocognitive research has clearly shown that MW is far more than a failure to constrain attention to perception, but it is instead a remarkable mental activity, which entails complex higher-order functional and neural mechanisms. An important functional mechanism involved in MW is the disengagement of attention from perception (known as *perceptual decoupling*): when the mind wanders, the attention is internally directed and the processing of sensory input is strongly decreased. This reduction has been observed in a range of physiological responses, such as pupil dilation, eye blink, and recording of event-related potentials (ERPs) (see for a review, Smallwood and Schooler 2015). Perceptual decoupling contributes to maintaining MW state insulating the internal train of thought from the distracting influence of external information, but it can, eventually, lead to a poor performance in tasks (e.g., increase in the number of errors).

Self-reports of the content of MW episodes suggest that, during MW, individuals tend to engage in *mental time travel*, mainly wandering into the personal past (involuntary recollections of autobiographical memories) and future (planning and simulation of future events). The contents of MW episodes are also mostly *self-related* and centred heavily on subjects' current concerns and goals, consistent with the notion that its thematic content is mostly driven, directly or indirectly, by the individual's goal or current life concerns, especially when taking an appropriate action toward the goal is not possible (Klinger 1971, 2013).

Neuroimaging studies (e.g., Christoff et al. 2009) provides support for these claims, showing that periods of MW involve high activations in the major hubs of the "default mode network" (DMN) as well as in executive prefrontal areas. This observed parallel recruitment of executive and default network regions – two brain systems that are often found to act in opposition – is consistent with the prevalence of a self-referential processing and with the relevance of current concerns and unresolved issues in the first-person reports, and may reflect an ongoing (if unconscious) effort to address them.

14.3 Why and How Our Mind Starts Wandering: Spontaneous and Deliberate MW

As argued by Smallwood (2013), any comprehensive account of MW is expected to address and explain the process of the initial occurrence of MW (i.e., the mental shifts between state of external and internal focus) as well as its maintenance-continuity over time (i.e., the processes that ensure the continuity of an internal train of thought once initiated, the process-occurrence framework; Smallwood 2013). *Why* does the mind start wandering at that specific moment? And *how* does this mental state arise?

The question of "*why*" is concerned with the identification of the processes and events that directly influence and control the occurrence of MW. One of the reasons for the inability to determine the onset of MW is the difficulty in causally linking MW to a preceding event that triggers the onset of MW (i.e., imperative stimulus; Smallwood 2013). In the MW literature MW episodes have been mainly described as self-generated (e.g., Smallwood 2013) and stimulus-independent (Antrobus 1968), terms that emphasize their independence from external stimuli and ongoing actions. However, during the last few years, increasing evidence has been reported suggesting for a role of external stimuli in MW (McVay and Kane 2013; Plimpton et al. 2015; Song and Wang 2012; Vannucci et al. 2017).

For example, in the experience sampling study by Song and Wang (2012), in most MW samples (88%) participants could report the trigger for the MW and nearly a half was reported to be associated with internal (49%) and half with external (51%) cues. Using an experimental paradigm, Plimpton et al. (2015) and Vannucci et al. (2017) could show that the majority of reported MW experienced during a monotonous vigilance task had an identifiable external trigger, and, in most cases, the trigger was one of the task-irrelevant verbal cues presented on the screen during the task.

How does the mind start wandering? How does the attentional shift from external to internal information occur? How does the change in mental state occur? To this regard, an increasing number of studies has demonstrated the importance of distinguishing between spontaneous (without intention) and deliberate (with intention) MW (see for a review, Seli et al. 2016c). The difference between these two kinds of MW stems from the mental dynamics underlying the onset of the experience of MW: whether the attentional shift (external-internal) occurs spontaneously or, somehow, under the individual's mental control. Specifically, in cases of deliberate MW, attention is *intentionally shifted* from the focal task to internal thoughts, whereas in cases of spontaneous MW, task-unrelated thoughts *capture one's attention*, triggering an uncontrolled shift from the task at hand to other trains of thought.

An important contribution understanding the two kinds of MW has been provided by research on individual differences in MW. Although MW is a ubiquitous and pervasive mental activity, a number of studies reported high inter-individual variability in the frequency of MW (for a review, see Smallwood and Schooler 2015), and the stability of these differences over time and across different contexts (i.e., in the laboratory and in everyday life, Ottaviani and Couyoumdjian 2013), suggests that MW is a relatively stable characteristic of the individuals.

Recently, Carriere et al. (2013) developed and validated two self-report scales assessing individual differences in trait levels of spontaneous and deliberate MW, the Mind Wandering-Spontaneous (MW-S) and the Mind Wandering-Deliberate (MW-D) scales, respectively. A series of studies has shown that, although the MW-S and the MW-D scales were positively correlated (*rs* ranging from .30s to .50s in Carriere et al. 2013), they are differentially associated with a number of psychological traits. In their seminal paper, Carriere et al. (2013) found that individual differences in spontaneous, but not deliberate, MW were uniquely and positively associated with self-reported fidgeting and self-reported propensity to act mindlessly. Moreover, the MW-S scale was moderately associated with attentional distraction (as measured by the Attentional Control-Distraction scale) and difficulties with attentional shifting (as measured by the Attentional Control-Shifting scale), whereas only small correlations with the same measures were found for the MW-D scale. Subsequent studies provided further evidence that the tendency to spontaneous MW may reflect difficulties in controlled processing: spontaneous but not deliberate MW was associated with attention-deficit/hyperactivity disorder (ADHD) symptomatology (Seli et al. 2015b) and with higher reports of obsessive-compulsive disorder (OCD) symptoms (Seli et al. 2016a). In a recent study Seli et al. (2015a) have shown that spontaneous and deliberate MW had opposing unique associations with some aspects of mindfulness: specifically, rates of deliberate mind wandering uniquely and positively predicted the tendency to be non-reactive to personal inner experiences, whereas spontaneous mind wandering negatively predicted the same dimension. Conflating the two kinds of MW as well as the different dimensions of mindfulness would likely produce underspecified, confounded, or even misleading conclusions.

A very recent study by Vannucci and Chiorri (2018) has shown that the two kinds of MW are also differentially associated to two distinct motivational dispositions related to self-consciousness: spontaneous MW was associated to self-rumination, whereas deliberate MW was associated to self-reflection. Previous studies on the two subtypes of self-consciousness have consistently shown that self-reflection is an openness-related self-focus, mainly motivated by intellectual curiosity and need for cognition, whereas self-rumination is a neuroticism-related self-focus (Trapnell and Campbell 1999). However, the results of this study showed that spontaneous and deliberate MW were uniquely predicted by self-rumination and self-reflection, respectively, and not by more general traits such as neuroticism and need for cognition.

Recently it has been also shown that two types of mind-wandering are related to their corresponding state-levels when assessed in the laboratory and that during easy task, deliberate MW is more frequently reported than is spontaneous MW (Seli et al. 2016b). Even more interesting, the two kind of MW have been also found to be distinguishable in terms of their neural associates (Golchert et al. 2017).

In their seminal study, Golchert et al. (2017) used multi-modal magnetic resonance imaging (MRI) analysis, to examine the cortical organisation that underlies inter-individual differences in spontaneous or deliberate MW. The authors found that participants who reported higher rates of deliberate mind-wandering tended to show a pattern of heightened integration between the default mode network (DMN) and regions of the fronto-parietal network (FPN). This pattern was observed primarily in prefrontal regions, including the medial prefrontal cortex and the anterior cingulate cortex, as well as in regions of the rostral and dorsolateral prefrontal cortex. By contrast, participants who reported higher rates of spontaneous mind-wandering showed cortical thinning in regions of the right parietal cortex, which encompassed adjacent regions of both the DMN and the FPN. As the authors conclude "these results support the hypothesis that more effective communication between regions of the DMN and the FPN is associated with MW that is more aligned with an individual's intentions" (p. 233).

Globally, these findings consistently demonstrate that spontaneous and deliberate MW are different cognitive experiences and that different cognitive mechanisms might play a role in prompting the arising of these two types of MW experiences.

14.4 The Dynamics of Creative Thinking: Which Role for MW?

The complex dynamics defining MW find a conceptual parallel in the dynamic shifts between different mental states during the creative thinking process. The thinker's mind indeed goes through a series of distinct mental states during her/his attempt to generate potential original and effective ideas (Corazza 2016). A number of models to describe the different mental states and constituents defining the creative thinking process have been proposed, such as the four-stages model by Wallas (1926), the articulation of the mental abilities by Guilford (1950), the eight dynamic stages with the elimination of all non-conscious elements from the model by Mumford et al. (1991), the Geneplore model (Finke et al. 1992), or the DIMAI model (Corazza and Agnoli 2015), just to citing a few. Even if creative thinking is usually ascribed in the common sense to a unspecific generative attitude, where the thinker is consumed in front of the challenging goal of generating a new idea, reality and empirical evidence depicted creative thinking as a complex dynamical phenomenon where idea generation is only a phase of the process, which furthermore involves inter-relations between lower-order cognitive, emotional, and attitudinal components. However, as stated elsewhere (Corazza and Agnoli 2015, 2018), should we simplify the creative thinking process to the maximum possible level, we would describe at least three necessary macro-states: gathering and structuring of information elements, ideation, and verification of the effects. Each of the three states is defined by higher-order functional mechanisms and by lower-order cognitive and motivational components.

The role of attentive mechanisms in particular have been highly explored in relation to the first two macro-states defining the process (Carson et al. 2003; Mendelsohn 1976; Necka 1999). Attentive processing seems emerging as central in the shift between the two states, representing a sort of gate either for the recruitment of external information or for the exploration of internal thoughts. A wide breadth of attention, which allows a large range of stimuli into the thinking process through the mechanism of *irrelevance processing* (Agnoli et al. 2015), seems to produce benefit for the creative performance, in that it has been hypothesized to allow a much larger pool of associations during the creative activity (Simonton 1988). An externally-directed attention able to detect a wide range of stimuli seems to be essential in defining the first macro-state of the creative thinking process, i.e., gathering and structuring of information elements. An active debate exists instead on the role of attention during the ideation mental state. A shift towards an internally directed attention is currently the most accreditated hypothesis in the scientific literature. Empirical evidence comes in particular from the neuroscientific research, which showed stable effects by brain activities associated to an internally directed attention focus during creative ideation. Event-related alpha synchronization, specifically, has been repeatedly demonstrated over the frontal and posterior cortical sites during ideation, in particular during ideation associated to divergent thinking (Fink and Benedek 2014; Neubauer and Fink 2009). Is has been suggested that this increase in alpha activity may reflect active top-down inhibition of task-irrelevant brain regions, such as the inhibition of long term semantic memory or the inhibition of vision-related regions, in order to inhibit the processing of irrelevant stimuli (Jensen et al. 2002). This brain activity in different cortical regions seems therefore to subsume a dynamic activity under the control of an attentive focus which acts as a strong controller of the process itself (Mastria et al. 2018). However, as shown in a recent study by Benedek et al. (2014), the increase of alpha activity over the parietal regions might be associated to the strength of task-focused attention rather than reflecting only the direction of the attention (internal vs. external). The enhancement of alpha activity over the right parietal region might be interpreted as a measure of the depth of the ongoing mental imagination process, representing therefore a valid proxy of the cognitive processes specific for creative ideation (Benedek et al. 2014), even if recent evidence has been provided also on the role of the enhancement of beta activity over this brain region for creative imagination and creative cognition (Agnoli et al. 2018b).

How interfering information or thoughts can influence the process is therefore a highly debated issue in the creativity literature. According to some authors the handling of apparently irrelevant information is a core constituting function in the creative thinking process (Agnoli et al. 2015; Carson et al. 2003; Corazza and Agnoli 2015; Simonton 1988). Mind wandering seems to represent a particularly informative mental activity in this sense, since it concerns the shift in the focus of attention from a defined task or activity towards thoughts and feeling not related to the ongoing activity. Moreover, the recent distinction between spontaneous and deliberate MW might represent a new interpretative key to understand the role of the control over the introduction of information during different phases of the creative thinking process. However, controversial anecdotal evidence exists on the role of mind wandering for creativity. Virginia Wolf just before the writing of "To the lighthouse" wrote "*My summer's wanderings with the pen have ... shown me one or two new dodges for catching my flies. I have sat here like an improviser with his hands ram-*

bling over the piano" (Wolf 1980, p. 37). Getting lost in our own thoughts might therefore represent a fruitful mental activity to promote the generation of original ideas. Contrary to the experience described by Virginia Wolf, Schopenhauer reported that he was unable to filter out incidental sound and that this inability was shared by many other eminent creators: "*Distinguishing minds have always shown extreme dislike to disturbance in any form, as something that breaks in on and distracts their thoughts*" (Schopenauer 1900, p. 163). According to this latter experience, a creative mind should be focalized, and un-focused thoughts are detrimental to the creative ideation.

14.5 A First Proposal to Explore the Relationships Between Spontaneous and Deliberate MW and Creative Thinking

The relationship between MW and creativity is not however a new topic in creativity research. The role of this mental activity has been indeed explored in a series of studies. However, echoing the contrasting anecdotes emerging from the experience of great creators of the past, the results of the research on the relationship between MW and creative cognition appear to be inconsistent (Baird et al. 2012; Hao et al. 2015). On the one hand, some studies have shown that taking a break involving an undemanding task characterized by a high level of unrelated thoughts might improve creative performance as measured by classic divergent thinking tasks (Baird et al. 2012; Gilhooly et al. 2012). These results have been explained by means of MW's increase in unconscious associative processing, which produces a spreading activation conducive to higher creative performance (Baird et al. 2012). On the other hand, evidence has reported that MW during creative idea generation might be detrimental to creative thinking, as measured by a classic divergent thinking task (Hao et al. 2015). Given that creative idea generation has been shown to involve a top-down executive process characterized by many control processes (inhibition of interfering stimuli, inhibition of dominant but not novel responses, judging and refining of initial ideas, etc.), these results seem to confirm that MW can be considered a control-resource consuming process.

Even if apparently contrasting, these results might not be incompatible. As we previously said, the creative thinking is not an unitary phenomenon, but it is instead characterized by a complex process involving both implicit associative processes and explicit control processes (Beaty et al. 2016), and MW might inversely influence these different processes. Moreover, as we reviewed above, MW is not a unitary and homogeneous class of experiences. The distinction between spontaneous and deliberate MW is fundamental, especially in the light of the important role of focused and de-focused attention during different phases of the creative thinking process. We indeed hypothesize that the dynamics characterizing the two forms of MW could potentially give new insight for the comprehension of the dynamic organization of the creative process.

Based on this hypothesis, in a recent seminal paper, we investigated for the first time the distinct contributions of spontaneous and deliberate MW to creative achievement and creative ideation (Agnoli et al. 2018a). In the study, we took into account the complexity of both constructs. As for MW, we assessed separately spontaneous and deliberate MW. As for creativity, we did not measured only creative ideation, but we also assessed a general form of creativity, which could give us indications on the effect of MW on real-word creativity. We indeed used both a creative-thinking performance index (i.e., response originality on a divergent thinking task) and a general index of creative success (i.e., creative achievement as measured by the Creative Achievement Questionnaire; Carson et al. 2005).

A total of 77 undergraduate students enrolled at the University of Firenze (Italy) took part in the study. Each participant completed the Mind Wandering: Deliberate and Mind Wandering: Spontaneous scales, that measure everyday deliberate and spontaneous MW, respectively (Carriere et al. 2013; Italian validation in Chiorri and Vannucci in press) and The Five Facets Mindfulness Questionnaire (FFMQ; Baer et al. 2006; Italian adaptation by Fossati et al. 2013), a self-report questionnaire composed of five subscales assessing different facets of a general tendency to be mindful in daily life: observing (i.e., attending to sensations, perceptions, thoughts and feelings), describing (i.e., labeling feelings, sensations and experience with words), acting with awareness, not judging inner experience, and being nonreactive to inner experience. Two measures of creativity were also administered, that is Creative Achievement Questionnaire (CAQ; Carson et al. 2005), a widely used measure of creative accomplishments, and The Titles Task (Guilford 1968), a measure of participants' divergent thinking ability.

The results of our study showed the unique and interactive role of MW and mindfulness dimensions in predicting creative performance and creative achievement. MW dimensions interacted indeed with mindfulness dimensions in predicting the two indexes of creativity. Here, for the purposes of the present chapter, we will however discuss only the main direct results of spontaneous and deliberate MW on creative thinking. When originality and creative-achievement variances were predicted in a single model, taking into account the within nature design used in our study, spontaneous and deliberate MW were significant direct predictors of originality. Specifically, deliberate MW emerged as a main positive predictor, whereas spontaneous MW was negatively associated with originality.

The control over the MW state can be considered a central element in the creative production insofar as it may increase response originality by introducing thought not apparently related to the creative focus into the thinking process. Spontaneous MW was, on the contrary, detrimental to originality, suggesting once again that control of the thinking process is a central requirement for creative thinking. The importance of deliberate metacognitive controls over the creative process has been already highlighted by past research. Feldhusen (1995) suggested that metacognition (i.e., control over goal setting, planning, use of cognitive processes, etc.) is one of the main prerequisites for creative thinking. As previously mentioned, the ability to control the switch of attention from the actual focal task could be considered a main mechanism to manage the introduction of irrelevant information into the divergent thinking process (i.e., irrelevant processing; Agnoli et al. 2015), which is a main attentional mechanism yielding higher originality. On the contrary, the lack of control over the introduction of information during the ideative phase of the process can be detrimental to the creative performance. This result seems to be particularly in line with the neuroscientific studies on creative ideation, where an increase of alpha activity in the posterior region has been explained as accounting for a shielding mechanism of sustained internally-directed attention that prevents external stimuli from interfering with internal processes (Benedek et al. 2014, 2016). More generally, the opposite pattern, which was obtained with the two kinds of MW, might, at least in part, contribute to explaining the mixed findings reported in the literature on the association between MW and creativity (Baird et al. 2012; Hao et al. 2015).

Interestingly, the two MW dimensions are associated in our study to the responses originality in a divergent thinking task, a measure of individual creative potential (Runco and Acar 2012). We can therefore assume that the beneficial (in the case of deliberate MW) and detrimental (in the case of spontaneous MW) effects of MW can be expressed in the whole phenomenological representation of creative potential, from personal expressions to the most outstanding achievements of creative thinking. Creativity is not indeed limited to those individuals who achieve success as a results of their creative acts, but a broad consensus exists in literature on the fact that creative potential is widely distributed (Beghetto and Kaufman 2007; Runco and Richards 1998; Sternberg et al. 2004). We believe in particular that the deliberate use of MW can find expression also in everyday creative acts, i.e., in the phenomenon defined by Beghetto and Kaufman (2007) as "mini-c" creativity. According to this vision, any information coming from the environment is not received passively, but it is interpreted and transformed by the individual through a personal lens on the basis of past experiences and personal histories, so that it assumes a new personal meaning (Beghetto and Kaufman 2007). In every personal creative act, the individual chooses to act differently, to interpret and transform reality according to her/his personal vision, to ignore convention, so that she/he can, using discretion (Runco 1996), chose deliberately to let the mind wander in order to include new and unexpected environmental information into the thinking process. Distraction becomes therefore a tool in the hand of the creative person that helps to maintain, using Stein's (1953) words, "permeable boundaries that separate the self from the environment".

14.6 Concluding Remarks and Future Developments

The control over internally-directed mental processes seems essential to understand the role of MW on creative thinking. The dynamics defining and distinguishing spontaneous and deliberate MW emerged indeed in our study to be discriminant in predicting creative performance. However, this multidimensional approach to MW should join a dynamic approach to the creative thinking process. Although speculative at present, we indeed believe that the distinction between spontaneous and deliberate MW might be even more informative if the different phases of the creative thinking process are taken into account. We can indeed suggest that the two dimensions of MW might play a different role during the distinct phases of creative process. On the basis of our previous findings and of the results of research showing the role played by internally- and externally-oriented attention, we could expect that spontaneous and deliberate MW can reveal new aspects of the dynamics defining the three macro phases of the creative thinking process, gathering and structuring of information elements, ideation, and verification of the effects. While most of the research has explored the ideation phase, it would be particularly important to show the effect of the two distinct mental processes during the other phases of the process, and dynamically explore how their involvement can define or predict the final creative performance.

Moreover, in considering the different roles of intentional and spontaneous MW in creativity, it should be noted that intentionality (and spontaneity) is not restricted to the onset (initial occurrence) of a MW episode. As pointed out by Seli et al. (2016c) "*intentional mind-wandering can also manifest as an allowance of the continuation of a previously unintentionally progressing episode. […] Similarly, unintentional mind-wandering can manifest as an intended episode of mind-wandering that has gone beyond an intended stopping point*" (p. 9). The control over the distribution of attentional resources might dynamically change over time. Elucidating these processes can improve our theoretical understanding of the interactions between MW and creativity and it will be a very important avenue for future research.

Future studies on the association between MW and creativity will benefit from the adoption of a neuro-phenomenological approach, that combines first-person measures/experience sampling of MW and creativity processes with measures of neural activity. Clarifying how the different types of MW and subprocesses of creative thinking interact in our brain could improve our understanding of the functional roles of MW in creativity. In particular, exploring the association between MW and the alpha brain activity emerging as central during the ideational phase of the creative thinking process (Benedek et al. 2014, 2016) could potentially explain whether the internally directed processes characterizing this creative phase are associated to the mental mechanism of wandering in "*one's private thoughts and feelings*"(Smallwood et al. 2007, p. 818).

Beyond having important theoretical implications, these fine-grained neurocognitive look at MW and creativity will have also important implications for applied research in educational and professional (i.e., workplace) contexts. For a long time, research on MW has focused almost exclusively on detrimental effects of MW in educational/learning and professional contexts (e.g. Risko et al. 2012; Smallwood et al. 2011). Mind wandering during lectures has been investigated with laboratory studies, presenting thought probes during video-recorded lectures (e.g., Risko et al. 2012; Szpunar et al. 2013) and with classroom studies, presenting thought probes during lectures, and other class-related activities (e.g., discussions, problem-solving activities, students presentation).

Globally, these studies have shown that frequent MW during lectures is associated with decreased lecture quiz scores ($r = .32$, Risko et al. 2012) and impaired later retention of information from the lecture (e.g., Lindquist and McLean 2011;

see Schacter and Szpunar 2015 for a review). Although the frequency of MW has been found to be reduced during more engaging "active learning situations" (e.g., problem-based small-group discussions), it occurs also during these activities 15–25% of the time (e.g., Geerlings 1994). On the basis of these findings, applied research aimed at developing methods (e.g., mindfulness meditation) and educational practices (i.e., taking notes, interpolated memory tests) to reduce MW during lessons (see for a discussion, Kane et al. 2017).

However, recent studies have shown that not all types of MW have the same effects on learning performance. For example, in a very recent study Kane et al. (2017) have found that off-task thoughts which are not focused on the here-and-now of the ongoing lecture but related to the lecture topics (e.g., thoughts related to the course themes) positively predicted learning ($r = .26$, with scores on the post-test). The only study (Wammes et al. 2016) in which intentional and spontaneous MW were assessed separately reported that rates of intentional MW negatively correlated with quiz scores at the end of the lecture ($r = -.21$) whereas rates of spontaneous MW correlated with final exam score ($r = -.20$), suggesting that the two types of MW might have different effects on learning performance.

Moreover, all these studies focused on the effects of MW *during* a lecture on learning performance of the lecture contents, and they did not investigate whether trainings of MW might have more general beneficial effects on academic achievement and scholastic success in educationally relevant contexts.

To this regard, our findings on the association between MW and creativity highlight the importance for future research to examine the possibility of developing methods to increase MW under certain conditions and to study the effects of this increase on the creative performance and academic achievement.

For example, future studies should investigate whether MW trainings, in which students learn making room for intentional MW during monotonous and repetitive tasks, might increase both the level of meta-awareness and control over MW and their creative performance. Moreover, given the positive association between creative thinking abilities and academic achievement (Beghetto 2016; Gajda et al. 2017), training intentional MW might also indirectly affect scholastic success, through the mediation of enhanced creative ideation.

This approach however can only be assumed adopting a dynamic framework to the study of creativity and MW, which does not consider the two phenomena as static mono-dimensional constructs, but as complex thinking processes which mutually and dynamically define each other.

References

Agnoli, S., Franchin, L., Rubaltelli, E., & Corazza, G. E. (2015). An eye-tracking analysis of irrelevance processing as moderator of openness and creative performance. *Creativity Research Journal, 27*, 125–132. https://doi.org/10.1080/10400419.2015.1030304.

Agnoli, S., Vannucci, M., Pelagatti, C., & Corazza, G. E. (2018a). Exploring the link between mind wandering, mindfulness, and creativity: A multidimensional approach. *Creativity Research Journal*. Advance online publication. https://doi.org/10.1080/10400419.2018.1411423

Agnoli, S., Zanon, M., Mastria, S., Avenanti, A., & Corazza, G. E. (2018b). Enhancing creative cognition with a rapid right-parietal neurofeedback procedure. *Neuropsychologia*. https://doi.org/10.1016/j.neuropsychologia.2018.02.015.

Antrobus, J. S. (1968). Information theory and stimulus-independent thought. *British Journal of Psychology, 59*(4), 423–430. https://doi.org/10.1111/j.2044-8295.1968.tb01157.x.

Antrobus, J. S., Singer, J. L., & Greenberg, S. (1966). Studies in stream of consciousness. *Perceptual and Motor Skills, 23*(2), 399–417. https://doi.org/10.2466/pms.1966.23.2.399.

Baer, R. A., Smith, G. T., Hopkins, J., Krietemeyer, J., & Toney, L. (2006). Using self-report assessment methods to explore facets of mindfulness. *Assessment, 13*, 27–45. https://doi.org/10.1177/1073191105283504.

Baird, B., Smallwood, J., Mrazek, M. D., Kam, J. W., Franklin, M. S., & Schooler, J. W. (2012). Inspired by distraction: Mind wandering facilitates creative incubation. *Psychological Science, 23*, 1117–1122. https://doi.org/10.1177/0956797612446024.

Beaty, R. E., Benedek, M., Silvia, P. J., & Schachter, D. L. (2016). Creative cognition and brain network dynamics. *Trends in Cognitive Sciences, 20*, 87–95. https://doi.org/10.1016/j.tics.2015.10.004.

Beghetto, R. A. (2016). Creative learning: A fresh look. *Journal of Cognitive Education and Psychology, 15*, 6–23. https://doi.org/10.1891/1945-8959.15.1.6.

Beghetto, R. A., & Kaufman, J. C. (2007). Toward a broader conception of creativity: A case for "mini-c" creativity. *Psychology of Aesthetics, Creativity, and the Arts, 1*(2), 73. https://doi.org/10.1037/1931-3896.1.2.73.

Benedek, M., Schickel, R. J., Jauk, E., Fink, A., & Neubauer, A. C. (2014). Alpha power increases in right parietal cortex reflects focused internal attention. *Neuropsychologia, 56*, 393–400. https://doi.org/10.1016/j.neuropsychologia.2014.02.010.

Benedek, M., Jauk, E., Beaty, R. E., Fink, A., Koschutnig, K., & Neubauer, A. C. (2016). Brain mechanisms associated with internally directed attention and self-generated thought. *Scientific Reports, 6*, 1–8. https://doi.org/10.1038/srep22959.

Carriere, J. S. A., Seli, P., & Smilek, D. (2013). Wandering in both mind and body: Individual differences in mind wandering and inattention predict fidgeting. *Canadian Journal of Experimental Psychology, 67*(1), 19–31. https://doi.org/10.1037/a0031438.

Carson, S., Peterson, J. B., & Higgins, D. (2003). Decreased latent inhibition is associated with increased creative achievement in high-functioning individuals. *Journal of Personality and Social Psychology, 85*, 499–506. https://doi.org/10.1037/0022-3514.85.3.499.

Carson, S. H., Peterson, J. B., & Higgins, D. M. (2005). Reliability, validity, and factor structure of the creative achievement questionnaire. *Creativity Research Journal, 17*, 37–50. https://doi.org/10.1207/s15326934crj1701_4.

Chiorri, C., & Vannucci, M. (in press). Replicability of the psychometric properties of trait-levels measures of spontaneous and deliberate mind wandering. *European Journal of Psychology Assessment*. Advance online publication. https://doi.org/10.1027/1015-5759/a000422.

Christoff, K., Gordon, A. M., Smallwood, J., Smith, R., & Schooler, J. W. (2009). Experience sampling during fMRI reveals default network and executive system contributions to mind wandering. *Proceedings of the National Academy of Sciences of the United States of America, 106*(21), 8719–8724. https://doi.org/10.1073/pnas.0900234106.

Christoff, K., Irving, Z. C., Fox, K. C. R., Spreng, R. N., & Andrews-Hanna, J. R. (2016). Mind-wandering as spontaneous thought: A dynamic framework. *Nature Reviews Neuroscience, 17*(11), 718–731. https://doi.org/10.1038/nrn.2016.113.

Corazza, G. E. (2016). Potential originality and effectiveness: The dynamic definition of creativity. *Creativity Research, 28*(3), 258–267. https://doi.org/10.1080/10400419.2016.1195627.

Corazza, G. E., & Agnoli, S. (2015). On the path towards the science of creative thinking. In G. E. Corazza & S. Agnoli (Eds.), *Multidisciplinary contributions to the science of creative thinking* (pp. 3–20). Singapore: Springer.

Corazza, G. E., & Agnoli, S. (2018). The creative process in science and engineering. In T. Lubart (Ed.), *The Creative process: Perspectives from multiple domains*. London: Palgrave Macmillan.

Feldhusen, J. F. (1995). Creativity: A knowledge base, metacognitive skills, and personality factors. *Journal of Creative Behaviour, 29*, 255–268.

Fink, A., & Benedek, M. (2014). EEG alpha power and creative ideation. *Neuroscience and Biobehavioral Reviews, 44*, 111–123. https://doi.org/10.1016/j.neubiorev.2012.12.002.

Finke, R. A., Ward, T. B., & Smith, S. M. (1992). *Creative cognition: Theory, research, and applications*. Cambridge, MA: MIT Press.

Fossati, A., Somma, A., Maffei, C., & Borroni, S. (2013). Il ruolo dei deficit di mindfulness nella disregolazione emotiva e comportamentale: uno studio italiano su soggetti non clinici [The role of Mindfulness deficiencies in emotional and behavioural dysregulation: An Italian study on non-clinical subjects]. *Psicoterapia Cognitiva e Comportamentale, 19*, 43–62.

Gajda, A., Karwowski, M., & Beghetto, R. A. (2017). Creativity and academic achievement: A meta-analysis. *Journal of Education & Psychology, 109*, 269–299. https://doi.org/10.1037/edu0000133.

Geerlings, T. (1994). Students' thoughts during problem-based small-group discussions. *Instructional Science, 22*(4), 269–278.

Gilhooly, K. J., Georgiou, G. J., Garrison, J., Reston, J. D., & Sirota, M. (2012). Don't wait to incubate: Immediate versus delayed incubation in divergent thinking. *Memory & Cognition, 40*(6), 966–975. https://doi.org/10.3758/s13421-012-0199-z.

Golchert, J., Smallwood, J., Jefferies, E., Seli, P., Huntenburg, J. M., Liem, F., & Margulies, D. S. (2017). Individual variation in intentionality in the mind-wandering state is reflected in the integration of the default-mode, fronto-parietal, and limbic networks. *NeuroImage, 146*, 226–235. https://doi.org/10.1016/j.neuroimage.2016.11.025.

Guilford, J. P. (1950). Creativity. *American Psychologist, 5*, 444–454.

Guilford, J. P. (1968). *Creativity, intelligence and their educational implications*. San Diego: EDITS/Knapp.

Hao, N., Wu, M., Runco, M. A., & Pina, J. (2015). More mind wandering, fewer original ideas: Be not distracted during creative idea generation. *Acta Psychologica, 16*, 110–116. https://doi.org/10.1016/j.actpsy.2015.09.001.

Jensen, O., Gelfand, J., Kounios, J., & Lisman, J. E. (2002). Oscillations in the alpha band (9-12 Hz) increase with memory load during retention in a short-term memory task. *Cerebral Cortex, 12*, 877–882. https://doi.org/10.1093/cercor/12.8.877.

Kane, M. J., Smeekens, B. A., von Bastian, C. C., Lurquin, J. H., Carruth, N. P., & Miyake, A. (2017). A combined experimental and individual-differences investigation into mind wandering during a video lecture. *Journal of Experimental Psychololgy General, 146*, 1649–1674. https://doi.org/10.1037/xge0000362.

Killingsworth, M. A., & Gilbert, D. T. (2010). A wandering mind is an unhappy mind. *Science, 330*, 932. https://doi.org/10.1126/science.1192439.

Klinger, E. (1971). *Structure and functions of fantasy*. New York: Wiley.

Klinger, E. (2013). Goal commitments and the content of thoughts and dreams: Basic principles. *Frontiers in Psychology, 4*, 415. https://doi.org/10.3389/fpsyg.2013.00415.

Lindquist, S. I., & McLean, J. P. (2011). Daydreaming and its correlates in an educational environment. *Learning and Individual Differences, 21*, 158–167. https://doi.org/10.1016/j.lindif.2010.12.006.

Mason, M. F., Norton, M. I., Van Horn, J. D., Wegner, D. M., Grafton, S. T., & Macrae, C. N. (2007). Wandering minds: The default network and stimulus-independent thought. *Science, 315*, 393–395. https://doi.org/10.1126/science.1131295.

Mastria, S., Agnoli, S., Zanon, M., Lubart, T., & Corazza, G. E. (2018). Creative brain, creative mind, creative person. In Z. Kapoula, J. Renoult, E. Volle, & M. Andreatta (Eds.), *Exploring transdisciplinarity in art and science*. Basel: Springer.

McVay, J. C., & Kane, M. J. (2013). Dispatching the wandering mind? Toward a la-boratory method for cuing "spontaneous" off-task thought. *Frontiers in Psychology, 4*, 570. https://doi.org/10.3389/fpsyg.2013.00570.

Mendelsohn, G. A. (1976). Associative and attentional processes in creative performance. *Journal of Personality, 44*, 341–369. https://doi.org/10.1111/j.1467-6494.1976.tb00127.x.

Mumford, M. D., Mobley, M. I., Uhlman, C. E., Reiter-Palmon, R., & Doares, L. M. (1991). Process analytic models of creative capacities. *Creativity Research Journal, 4*, 91–122. https://doi.org/10.1080/10400419109534380.

Necka, E. (1999). Creativity and attention. *Polish Psychological Bulletin, 30*, 85–97.

Neubauer, A. C., & Fink, A. (2009). Intelligence and neural efficiency. *Neuroscience and Biobehavioral Reviews, 33*, 1004–1023. https://doi.org/10.1016/j.neubiorev.2009.04.001.

Ottaviani, C., & Couyoumdjian, A. (2013). Pros and cons of a wandering mind: A prospective study. *Frontiers in Psychology, 4*, 524. https://doi.org/10.3389/fpsyg.2013.00524.

Plimpton, B., Patel, P., & Kvavilashvili, L. (2015). Role of triggers and dysphoria in mind-wandering about past, present and future: A laboratory study. *Consciousness and Cognition, 33*, 261–276. https://doi.org/10.1016/j.concog.2015.01.014.

Risko, E. F., Anderson, N., Sarwal, A., Engelhardt, M., & Kingstone, A. (2012). Everyday attention: Variation in mind wandering and memory in a lecture. *Applied Cognitive Psychology, 26*, 234–242. https://doi.org/10.1002/acp.1814.

Runco, M. A. (1996). Personal creativity: Definition and developmental issues. *New Directions for Child and Adolescent Development, 1996*(72), 3–30.

Runco, M. A., & Acar, S. (2012). Divergent thinking as an indicator of creative potential. *Creativity Research Journal, 24*(1), 66–75. https://doi.org/10.1080/10400419.2012.652929.

Runco, M. A., & Richards, R. (Eds.). (1998). *Eminent creativity, everyday creativity, and health*. Norwood: Ablex.

Schacter, D. L., & Szpunar, K. K. (2015). Enhancing attention and memory during video-recorded lectures. *Scholarship of Teaching and Learning in Psychology, 1*, 60–71. https://doi.org/10.1037/stl0000011.

Schopenauer, A. (1900). *Studies on pessimism*. New York: Boni & Liveright.

Seli, P., Carriere, J. S. A., & Smilek, D. (2015a). Not all mind wandering is created equal: Dissociating deliberate from spontaneous mind wandering. *Psychological Research, 79*, 750–758. https://doi.org/10.1007/s00426-014-0617-x.

Seli, P., Smallwood, J., Cheyne, J. A., & Smilek, D. (2015b). On the relation of mind wandering and ADHD symptomatology. *Psychonomic Bulletin & Review, 22*(3), 629–636. https://doi.org/10.3758/s13423-014-0793-0.

Seli, P., Risko, E. F., Purdon, C., & Smilek, D. (2016a). Intrusive thoughts: Linking spontaneous mind wandering and OCD symptomatology. *Psychological Research, 81*, 392–398. https://doi.org/10.1007/s00426-016-0756-3.

Seli, P., Risko, E. F., & Smilek, D. (2016b). Assessing the associations among trait and state levels of deliberate and spontaneous mind wandering. *Consciousness and Cognition, 41*, 50–56. https://doi.org/10.1016/j.concog.2016.02.002.

Seli, P., Risko, E. F., Smilek, D., & Schacter, D. L. (2016c). Mind-wandering with and without intention. *Trends in Cognitive Sciences, 20*, 605–617. https://doi.org/10.1016/j.tics.2016.05.010.

Simonton, D. K. (1988). *Scientific genius: A psychology of science*. New York: Cambridge University Press.

Singer, J. L. (1966). *Daydreaming. An introduction to the experimental study of inner experience*. New York: Random House.

Smallwood, J. (2013). Distinguishing how from why the mind wanders: A process-occurrence framework for self-generated mental activity. *Psychological Bulletin, 139*(3), 519–535. https://doi.org/10.1037/a0030010.

Smallwood, J., & Schooler, J. W. (2015). The science of mind wandering: Empirically navigating the stream of consciousness. *Annual Review of Psychology, 66*(1), 487–518. https://doi.org/10.1146/annurev-psych-010814-015331.

Smallwood, J., O'Connor, R. C., Sudbery, M. V., & Obonsawin, M. (2007). Mind-wandering and dysphoria. *Cognition & Emotion, 21*, 816–842. https://doi.org/10.1080/02699930600911531.

Smallwood, J., Mrazek, M. D., & Schooler, J. W. (2011). Medicine for the wandering mind: Mind wandering in medical practice. *Medical Education, 45*, 1072–1080. https://doi.org/10.1111/j.1365-2923.2011.04074.x.

Song, X., & Wang, X. (2012). Mind wandering in Chinese daily lives – An experience sampling study. *PLoS One, 7*(9), e44423. https://doi.org/10.1371/journal.pone.0044423.

Stein, M. I. (1953). Creativity and culture. *The Journal of Psychology, 36*(2), 311–322.

Sternberg, R. J., Grigorenko, E. L., & Singer, J. L. (Eds.). (2004). *Creativity: From potential to realization*. Washington, DC: American Psychological Association.

Szpunar, K. K., Khan, N. Y., & Schacter, D. L. (2013). Interpolated memory tests reduce mind wandering and improve learning of online lectures. *Proceedings of the National Academy of Sciences of the United States of America, 110*, 6313–6317. https://doi.org/10.1073/pnas.1221764110.

Trapnell, P. D., & Campbell, J. D. (1999). Private self-consciousness and the five-factor model of personality: Distinguishing rumination from reflection. *Journal of Personality and Social Psychology, 76*(2), 284–304. https://doi.org/10.1037/0022-3514.76.2.284.

Vannucci, M., & Chiorri, C. (2018). Individual differences in self-consciousness and mind wandering: Further evidence for a dissociation between spontaneous and deliberate mind wandering. *Personality and Individual Differences, 121*, 57–61. https://doi.org/10.1016/j.paid.2017.09.022.

Vannucci, M., Pelagatti, C., & Marchetti, I. (2017). Manipulating cues in mind wandering: Verbal cues affect the frequency and the temporal focus of mind wandering. *Consciousness and Cognition, 53*, 61–69. https://doi.org/10.1016/j.concog.2017.06.004.

Wallas, G. (1926). *The art of thought*. New York: Harcourt Brace.

Wammes, J. D., Seli, P., Cheyne, J. A., Boucher, P. O., & Smilek, D. (2016). Mind wandering during lectures II: Relation to academic performance. *Scholarship of Teaching and Learning in Psychology, 2*, 33–48. https://doi.org/10.1037/stl0000055.

Woolf, V. (1980). In A. O. Bell & A. McNeillie (Eds.), *The diary of Virginia Woolf* (Vol. 3). New York: Harcourt Brace & Company.

Chapter 15
From Dynamic Processes to a Dynamic Creative Process

Marion Botella and Todd Lubart

Abstract Since Wallas' (*The art of thought*. Harcourt, Brace and Company, New York, 1926) four-stage model, the sequential perspective on the creative process may be questioned. The creative process as a dynamic phenomenon is examined in this chapter. In order to understand how the creative process is dynamic, we start by examining the nature of dynamic processes in other fields such as education, cognitive science, health and social psychology. Based on the understanding of these dynamic processes, we develop hypotheses and observations on the dynamics of the creative process. This approach involves new methods to assess the complexity of the creative process.

15.1 Introduction

The creative process corresponds to "a succession of thoughts and actions that leads to original and adapted creations" (Lubart et al. 2015, p. 111). Two levels can be used to describe it (Botella et al. 2016): the *micro* level, which describes the mechanisms underlying the generation of ideas such as associative, divergent and convergent thinking (Guilford 1950; Martindale 1981, 1999; Mumford and Porter 1999; Runco 1991, 1999; Simonton 1980, 1990, 1999); and the *macro* level, which refers to the major stages of the process sequence (Amabile 1988; Busse and Mansfield 1980; Carson 1999; Doyle 1998; Goswami 1996; Lubart 2000–2001; Ochse 1990; Osborn 1953; Runco and Dow 1999; Treffinger 1995). However, authors do not agree on the name of stages, their number (from 3 to 9 stages) and their sequence. The most common model is also one of the first: the four-stage model of Wallas (1926) with preparation, incubation, illumination and verification. Cropley and Cropley (2012) note that the original version included seven stages: preparation,

M. Botella (✉) · T. Lubart
Institut de Psychologie, Laboratoire Adaptation Travail-Individu, Université Paris Descartes, Paris, France
e-mail: marion.botella@parisdescartes.fr

activation, generation, illumination, verification, communication and validation; and Sadler-Smith (2016) notes five stages, adding an intimation stage between incubation and illumination.

Even if there is still no consensus in the scientific literature, authors have explored factors involved in the creative process. These process dimensions include domain knowledge or expertise, personal motivation, personality characteristics, personal feelings, emotions and affects, product constraints, and environmental characteristics (Cropley et al. 2013; Runco and Dow 1999; Russ 1999; Shaw 1989, 1994).

15.1.1 What Is Dynamic?

Etymologically, the word "dynamic" comes from the Greek *dynamikós*. The adjective "dynamic" refers to a force, power or motion characterized by or producing change or progress; especially one that motivates, affects development or stability; thus, dynamic is opposed to *static*.

Is the creative process dynamic? From 1935, Patrick in her descriptive studies of artists, scientists and other engaged in creative work noted overlaps between Wallas' stages, especially between preparation and incubation (Patrick 1935, 1937, 1938). Vinacke (1952) believed that individuals can go back and move quickly from one stage to another, sometimes giving free rein to their thoughts and other times relying on their critical thinking. According to Vinacke, the ability to move from one stage to another of the creative process is essential, probably facilitating access to cognitive and affective processes. Armbruster (1989) even considered "there is a danger in using Wallas's model, because it implies that the process of creativity is linear" (p.178); the creative process is much more interactive and redundant. There is communication between the stages. Krashen (1984) found that the best writers do not follow a linear approach, but have many feedback loops returning to previous steps. In 1981, Ainsworth-Land (1981) was the first to title a paper "*The dynamics of the creative process*". To answer the question of whether the creative process is dynamic, we will first explore some dynamic processes in diverse fields such as education, cognitive sciences, health psychology and social psychology. The goal here is to explore the nature of dynamic processes and then bring this to bear on the creative process in order to define better and specify what is a dynamic creative process.

15.2 Dynamic Processes

Simonton (2001) described talent development as a dynamic process, based on the combination of multiple components such as physical, physiological, cognitive and dispositional traits. According to Simonton (2001), the domain-specific manifestation of talent will be due to the varieties of combinations of genetic components. Thus, individuals with very different profiles can have the same talent. Considering the non-additive (but multiplicative) emergent combination of the components, Simonton (2001) suggested that exceptional talent would be extremely rare and exhibit a skewed distribution. Based on empirical evidence from Waller et al. (1993), Simonton (2001) postulated that talent shows low heritability. In this approach, the dynamic process is a combination of multiple components.

15.2.1   Dynamic Learning

In a recent case study, learning a foreign language was described as a dynamic process and analyzed based on Complex Dynamic Systems (Sun et al. 2016). The authors explained that children's developmental learning is not linear but involves complex interactions with the environment. Based on previous work (Molenaar 2013; Molenaar and Campbell 2009; Van Geert and Steenbeek 2005) and the Complex Dynamic Systems perspective, Sun and collaborators (2016) argued that development is a real-time self-organizing process in which the system evolves from successive interaction of fluctuation and stability. Especially considering the learning of a foreign language, the authors described it as an open dynamic language characterized by a dependence on initial conditions, complete interconnectedness between various components, non-linearity, internal reorganization (learning capacity and adaptability for example), environmental interaction, internal and external resources (such as input from the teacher), attractor states, iteration, variation and emergent properties. In their case study, a 3-year-old boy during his first 5 months, named Jimmy, was observed. In the beginning, Jimmy used mainly body language to be understood. Then, over time, Jimmy started to be more flexible, using a verbal response and nonverbal behaviors. Sun and collaborators (2016) illustrated the flexibility and adaptation to the environment by the fact that Jimmy changed his developmental trajectory when a new teacher came. The verbal responses of Jimmy were also influenced by the teacher's repetitions. For Sun and collaborators (2016), a dynamic process is thus characterized by its regularity, complexity, and flexibility.

15.2.2   In Cognitive Science

Ward and Wickes (2009) considered that graded category structure is dynamic through the accessibility of exemplars and the rating of typicality. They examined this dynamic process manipulating the accessibility of exemplars. In this study, 228 students had to complete a 20-item pleasantness rating task with 5 fruits, 5 tools and 10 filler items. Then, participants had to complete a creative generation task in which they had either to imagine a fruit from another planet or to imagine a tool used by an intelligent species on another planet. Results indicated a primed accessibility effect: participants reported more fruits than tools when they had to imagine an alien fruit whereas they reported more tools than fruits when they had to imagine an alien tool. Indeed, Ward and Wickes (2009) showed the dynamics of category structure and its influence on creative generation. As it is possible to manipulate the accessibility of exemplars (primed effect), graded category structure is considered dynamic rather than static.

15.2.3 In Health Psychology

Yaniv (2012) described role reversal as a dynamic phenomenon. Role reversal is a method used in psychotherapeutic interaction to help two individuals to understand the point of view of the other, switching their role. Based on Kellermann (1994), Yaniv (2012) underlined the dynamics and interaction between the three stages of the role reversal process (empathic role taking, action reproduction and role feedback). For him, these three stages are interdependent. In the first, empathic role taking, individuals start to imitate the other from superficial imitation to a deeper and personal imitation. Then, in the action reproduction stage, individuals try to reproduce with their own subjectivity the other. Finally, in the last stage of role feedback, individuals exchange on how each other is seen. The work by Yaniv (2011) suggests that the dynamics of this process will be due to the involvement of empathy and creativity. Indeed, empathy activates self-other awareness and self-regulation of emotions and creativity inhibits partially focused attention. Both combined contribute to the dynamics of the role reversal process.

15.2.4 In Social Psychology

Leadership Foti et al. (2008) considered leadership perception as a dynamic phenomenon because of several factors such as "cognitive knowledge structures of followers, the context in which leader behaviors are embedded, and multiple pieces of information occurring simultaneously and over time" (p. 178). For these authors, the dynamics of leadership perception could be explained by connectionist and catastrophe theories. The connectionist approach is mainly used to model social stereotypes, leadership perceptions and skills. Each element of knowledge is not isolated but connected to many others. So, this theory explains that representations of leadership from memory are not static but constantly recreated based on the representations activated by all the interconnected elements and the context. Additionally, catastrophe theory explains the attractions and trajectories between the mental representations. According to this theory, the representation can fluctuate across time.

Dynamic Collaborative Process Multiparty collaboration operates when parties are able to see the problem from another point of view and to go through it to search for a solution (Gray 1989). The psychodynamics of collaborative processes was also studied (Prins 2006), considering the mutual influence of organizational structure on and by individual and collective processes. Prins (2006) analyzed the dynamic process "by taking into account subjective data, observations, as well as the context and history of the collaborative and its partners" (p. 351). Based on the scientific literacy, Prins (2006) considered that understanding the dynamics of such a process involves studying simultaneously the system and world views, objective and subjective experiences, accepting the ambiguity of the process studied. In her case study, Prins (2006) observed a group developing network organization in the domain of foster care during 1 year. She showed that each member had a specific point of view on the project and its outcome. Every interaction and meeting contributes to the subjectivity of participants and the collaboration, leading to evaluate each participant and also the dynamics of the group. The dynamic emerges from mutual influences between network's elements.

Bakker et al. (2013) studied the dynamics of creative project teams according to the time frame. In this experiment, the authors constructed teams of three students working together during 45 min to complete a creative project. Then the teams were randomly assigned to two experimental groups: either the team members will never work again together or they will work all together during the 1 year program. Students were informed about the assigned groups before the 45 min first task. Bakker and collaborators (2013) assessed the time orientation, task immersion, team conflict and cohesion, and processing of information at the end of the first task. The results showed that, compared to teams with longer time frame, teams with shorter time frame were more oriented toward the present, less immersed in the task, showed a tendency ($p < .10$) to prefer heuristic processing, and had less team conflict. So, Bakker and collaborators (2013) found different team dynamics during creative project work according to the time frame. In this paper, authors did not indicate if the order of the work process varies according to the time frame. However, Bakker and collaborators (2013) considered that the possibility to change the group collaboration by manipulating the time frame was a sign of a dynamic process.

15.2.5 In Others Fields

Entrepreneurship For Engel et al. (2017) entrepreneurial networking occurs in conditions of uncertainty because every action changes the network. So, the authors "encourage more research on the dynamic and reciprocal influence between individual cognition and actions, social networks, and entrepreneurial outcomes" (p. 36). Based on a large literature review, they proposed a dynamic process model of entrepreneurial networking under uncertainty including three parts (entrepreneurial uncertainty evaluation, effectual networking, and networking outcomes). Each part can be influenced by exogenous unexpected contingencies. They include also interactions between subcomponents (for example the perceived ambiguity of networking goals interacted with venture goals). Another interesting proposal was a cyclical model of goal convergence and means explanations from networking outcomes and entrepreneurial uncertainty evaluation. In this work, a dynamic process corresponds to cycles, interactions between parts (or subparts), several possible ways in the process and involvement of individual cognition, actions, networks and outcomes. Engel et al. (2017) illustrated their approach using the example from Ohanian (2014) with "Reddit", which is a startup that recently grew to over 175 million regular monthly users, when the founders of the start-up interacted with investors, who required them to develop a very different idea from their initial one.

Socio-Economic In the economic field, Fusari (2005) argued that the economy is dynamic through innovation, adaptation for profit, and uncertainty. Another dynamic process is the contingent valuation, which is a popular method to evaluate environmental goods in economics (Tisdell et al. 2008). For them, the dynamics in contingent valuation refers to the moment when individuals change their "willingness to pay" response according to the "environmental good (information provision), experiencing the good, and the lapse of time (memory decay) within a single valuation project in a continuous sequence" (p. 1444). In this study, Tisdell, and collaborators (2008) tested how much Australian people will to pay to save a mahogany glider without any information about it (Survey I: $24.99), and after information provision by a lecturer (Survey II: $35.67; $t = -1.52$, $p = 0.065$). They tested also an experienced good with participants visiting a park and seeing (or not) the mahogany glider. Results indicate a significant increase of "willingness to pay" when participants saw the glider but a no significant increase when they did not. This illustrates an interactive dynamic which influences attribution of value.

15.2.6 In Aesthetic and Creative Fields

Aesthetics Carbon (2010, 2011) examined the dynamics of aesthetic appreciation using the example of car exteriors; the results showed a dynamic aesthetic appreciation linked to curvature ratings of the cars between 1950 and 1999. In 2011, Carbon considered the dynamics of this phenomenon in terms of a highly flexible mechanism explaining why "we can adapt to an ever-changing world" (p. 711) and why "we can identify "streams", "movements" or "periods"." (p.711). He proposed a two-step model with a first stage of confrontation with many innovative exemplars and a second step based on adaptation of them. The dynamic aspect in this model is that the "end" of the aesthetic appreciation process is not really an end. For Carbon (2011), it is just a temporary state (taste) that leads to cycle to a new process: "this process is a dynamic one that never reaches full stability, as experience with new stimuli will always start and revive the process again" (p.715). To illustrate the change of curvature, Carbon (2010) used the example of the Volkswagen Beetle (1960; high curvature) which moved into the Golf I (1974; low curvature) and then Golf V (2003; high curvature again).

Dynamics of Emotions The dynamic relation between emotions and creativity was studied in a game playing situation (Yeh et al. 2016). In this empirical study, the emotions of 266 undergraduates were assessed before and during game play in term of valence (positive or negative), activation (high or low), and regulatory focus (prevention with an expanded attentional scope or promotion with a constricted attentional scope). Regression analyses showed that baseline emotions could not predict creativity; but emotions experienced during the game did. In particular, positive emotions associated with a high activation and a promotion focus facilitated creative thinking whereas negative emotions associated also with a high activation and a promotion focus decreased performance. In this study, the dynamic aspect refers to emotions during game playing, which are more predictable of creativity than emotions at the baseline.

Dynamic External Support Pearson and collaborators considered that creative mental imagery is a dynamic process (Pearson et al. 1999, 2013; Pearson and Logie 2000). In 2015, Pearson and Logie tested the involvement of mental imagery process in creative synthesis through internal and external representations with static or dynamic sketches. In the creative synthesis task, all participants had to follow the verbal instructions to combine letters, symbols and/or number into a new pattern during 6 trials (for example, combine rotated D and J into umbrella). Authors designed four conditions (16 participants per condition): imagery alone (internal representation), drawing-in-air (participants draw with the finger in the air), sketching (external static representation in which participants actually draw on a blank paper) and graphic package use (external dynamic representation using a computer software allowing participants to generate, to rotate, to size the symbols). Participants in the dynamic support condition identified correctly more patterns than in others conditions. Pearson and Logie (2015) explained this result by a reduction in working memory load and by a "greater superiority of external representations for supporting changes to the frame of reference in which synthesized patterns are interpreted" (p. 106). In this study, the dynamic aspect is the possibility to externalize the creation of mental image through software, and so, the possibility to manipulate directly the image during its creation.

15.3 Dynamic Creative Processes

Now that we have seen examples of dynamic processes relevant to research on creativity, we will present some models that focus on creativity. Then, we discuss the creative process in terms of a dynamic phenomenon.

15.3.1 Dynamic Definition of Creativity

Recently, Corazza (2016) proposed a variant to the standard definition of creativity which initially includes only originality and effectiveness. Based on the fact that the product of the creative process can be inconclusive at one time but considered creative later, Corazza (2016) added "potential" offering a dynamic definition of creative: "creativity requires potential originality and effectiveness" (p. 262). This addition makes an important point suggesting that a product is not necessarily finished but it can be a part of a more global creative process as well and can be reevaluated later by estimators. If we combined several definitions of elements of creativity, proposed by Corazza (2016), the creative process is "a process enacted by an agent (a single individual or a group of individuals) in the pursuit of its creative goals (the intention to generate items, pertaining to a specific portion of a knowledge domain at a defined time, showing originality and effectiveness)" (p. 263). So, according to this definition of creativity and especially in terms of the creative process, the dynamic aspect here comes from the inclusion of the temporal dimension.

15.3.2 Emotional Resonance Model

The emotional resonance model (Lubart and Getz 1997) proposes that the emotional aspects of past experiences contribute to access and create associations of concepts. There is an emotional substratum of psychic life – always present and more or less active – that colors our perceptions, our decisions, the memory we have of people we meet, situations lived and objects used in our activities. The emotional resonance model has three components: (1) endocepts, which represent idiosyncratic emotions experienced and attached to concepts or representations in memory; (2) an automatic resonance mechanism, which propagates the emotional profile of an endocept through memory and activates other endocepts; (3) a resonance detection threshold, which determines whether a resonance-activated endocept (as well as the concept or representation to which it is attached) enters working memory.

Each concept or representation in memory is associated with traces corresponding to the emotional experiences experienced by the individual. These traces, called "endocepts" (Arieti 1976; Averill and Nunley 1992), encode idiosyncratic emotions related to concepts, images representing objects, people or situations. These representations are individualized and multidimensional. For example, if the concept "elevator" is activated in memory, its mental representation may be associated with a mixture of boredom, anxiety, fear, or any other type of emotion related to the experiences in elevators.

An endocept is activated when the concept and/or image to which it is linked is also activated. The activation of an endocept propagates the emotional tone of the latter as a wave through memory, following routes which are distinct from those of cognitive associative networks. If the profile of another endocept is close to the propagated profile, the two endocepts will resonate; the resonance force of each endocept depends on the similarity of its multidimensional emotional profile with that of the transmitter endocept attached to the initial concept. The fact that the resonance between two endocepts is accessible to working memory depends on the sensitivity of the individual to his/her own emotions and the resonance force between two endocepts. For example, an individual who has a high detection threshold may have as much difficulty detecting a link with a strongly resonant endocept as someone who has a low threshold for an endocept that is weakly resonant. Once detected, resonance allows the establishment of an association between two emotionally close concepts, which may otherwise be cognitively distant. The emotional resonance model leads to the creation of an association between a source concept (activated during a task) and another concept that is linked to it in an endoceptual way. From this core, it is possible to develop forms of associations which may be quite idiosyncratic, and therefore original. The dynamic aspect is the creation of transitory resonance patterns, which arise naturally when a concept is activated during problem solving activities.

15.3.3 The Bumper Effect

Greeley (1977) described the dynamics of the bumper effect in the creative process. The Bumper Effect Dynamic (BED) corresponds to a subconscious fit to the internal order and/or conception of the creator. Greeley described this effect as follows: "when you are composing a poem and write a word which stops the movement of thought so you cannot proceed, you cross out that word or sentence, and continue with the thought movement in a different direction. It is as if a" bumper" were preventing you from going astray by guiding and keeping you on the correct path" (p. 261). Here, the author did not explain if the entire creative process is dynamic but he considered that a part, at least, is.

15.3.4 Cycles of Experimentation

Roels (2014) explored the creative process of eight music composers, taking particularly one as an example with pre and post- interviews after the performance. The author considered "experimentation to be a dynamic and transformation between mind and matter" (p. 229). Experimentation involves combining emotional and cognitive processes with actions. The dynamics of the creative process appears when a composer changes ideas ("what the composer thinks, imagines, and feels while composing also changes during the creative process", p. 230), visible through the traces of the actions. According to Roels (2014), to examine one isolated experimentation leads to "absurd observations" (p. 234) and researchers have to observe a cycle of experiments. For example, the first version of the case study described was to compose a *lamento*; the second version was still a *lamento* but with a slower tempo written through a paper sketch; the third version was a digital copy of the previous one; the fourth version add a viola da gamba; and the final version exchanged it with a cello solo. Roels (2014) explained that the modifications of the production were not very important for this composer maybe because the composer used this composition more as a technical exercise rather than a real composition explaining why the composer did not experiment a lot.

15.3.5 Dynamics of Divergent Thinking

Hass (2017) considered that participants do not complete linearly divergent thinking tasks of alternative uses. The "participants' cognition is dynamic" (p. 234) due to the semantic retrieval process itself. To support this idea, Hass (2017) investigated responses of 226 undergraduates on four thinking tasks of alternative uses. Results highlighted the semantic distance at the beginning of the iteration process to find an original and novel answer. The study suggests that divergent thinking is not linear and the creative process involves divergent thinking. This result was also confirmed by dynamic interactions between brain regions (Beaty et al. 2015), especially default and control networks (Beaty et al. 2016).

15.3.6 Dynamics of Narrative Writing

Some authors examined the dynamics of narrative writing by logging key strokes (von Koss Torkildsen et al. 2016). The dynamics of the process appears in transcription fluency, pausing and revisions. For example, studying 42 elementary children, von Koss Torkildsen and collaborators (von Koss Torkildsen et al. 2016) showed that a large majority of children made local revisions directly on the word as they were typing it. Moreover, the better stories were written by children who transcribed faster and made the most revisions. This study suggests that the dynamics of narrative writing can be linked to the creativity of productions.

15.3.7 Dynamic Creative Process

Lubart (2009) examined creative writing and the role of evaluation of ideas in the creative process of composing a story. University students wrote a story based on a title and the creativity of the productions were rated by experienced judges. During the student's creative process, students received prompts to evaluate their ideas as they were working. These evaluative moments occurred either early in the work process, late, or at an even pace. The results indicated that early evaluation of work in progress, by the student creators themselves, was linked to more creative stories compared to later evaluations, evenly-paced evaluations or random evaluation in a control condition. In a follow-up study, using naturally-occurring differences in evaluation during story generation, the same benefits for those who engage in early evaluation were observed. These findings suggest that the moment when a sub-process of creative thinking occurs can on average lead to more creative productions. In the case of university students completing a writing task, it is likely that early evaluation led them to recognize that their initial idea was weak or flawed and to make an effort to improve their basic storyline. Thus, the moment when certain sub-processes occur can provoke a dynamic that favors originality.

Since 2011, we have been studying the dynamics of the creative process in art (Botella et al. 2011, 2013), in scriptwriting (Bourgeois-Bougrine et al. 2014), in science-engineering (Peilloux and Botella 2016), design (Botella and Lubart 2015), and music (Glaveanu et al. 2013). Through interviews of experts in various creative fields (Glaveanu et al. 2013), we noted that interviewees had many difficulties to describe their creative process. They can explain the stages, the factors involved in it, but it seems very hard to relate how these stages interact, describe their co-occurrence or mutual influences and success factors linked to the process dynamics. In general, a dynamic creative process occurs when the stages are not sequential; creators "can return to "previous" stages of the process or engage several stages at the same time" (Botella et al. 2011).

We observed, as well, the dynamics of the creative process of art, design and science-engineering students when they had to create for their school projects (Botella and Lubart 2015). In this article, we observed that in all three domains, the creative process is dynamic, stages interact with each other (to define the problem and to search for documents), feedback is possible (from the reflection stage in which participants ask and interact with the work to the definition stage) and the time passed in each stage varies between domains (over time, design students marked the stage of divergent thinking 47% of the global time whereas science-engineering students reported it 29%). Following these studies, we suggested that the dynamics of the creative process can be assessed by repeated self-report of what participants do when creating, using a creative process report diary. In this diary, individuals describe their experience of the creative process by marking what stage(s) they are doing at a specific time (Botella et al. 2017).

15.4 Discussion

In this chapter, several dynamic processes within and outside the creative research field were presented. To begin, it is interesting to note that even if several studies referred to the term "dynamic", it is still not clearly explained. If we try to resume all the examples of dynamic processes, we find that several authors saw it as a component of the process itself (Fusari 2005; Hass 2017; von Koss Torkildsen et al.

2016). For Fusari (2005), economy is a dynamic process through innovation, adaptation for profit, and uncertainty; for Hass (2017), the dynamics of divergent thinking is due to the semantic retrieval itself; and for von Koss Torkildsen et al. (2016), the dynamics of the narrative writing appears in transcription fluency, pausing and revisions. A process can also be dynamic according to the accessibility and rating of its components (Ward and Wickes 2009). For others, a process is dynamic because of the combination of multiple components (Simonton 2001; Sun et al. 2016; Yaniv 2012).

Sun and collaborators (2016) proposed that a dynamic process occurs in real-time, and is self-organizing, evolving from successive complex interactions with the environment. This concept of a dynamic interaction between a person and his/her environment was sketched in early work by Kurt Lewin (1935). In the same vein, Prins (2006) defined a dynamic collaborative process by the mutual influence of organizational structure on and by individual and collective processes. This idea is echoed in Gruber's (1988, 1989) evolving systems approach to creativity, with ongoing interactions between a person's knowledge, purpose and affect "subsystems" which may amplify deviations and favor unique, original behavior. Furthermore, a dynamic process occurs within a temporal frame (Bakker et al. 2013; Corazza 2016) and depends on various information that is available simultaneously and unfolding over time (Foti et al. 2008). Nevertheless, Carbon (2010, 2011) suggested that the "end" is just a temporary state that can move to a new process due to new stimuli. So, a dynamic process is cyclic (Carbon 2010, 2011, 2012; Engel et al. 2017; Roels 2014).

According to all these authors, we can propose a definition of the term "dynamic" for the creative process: **the creative process is dynamic by its components itself, their organization, their combination, the successive interactions it maintains with the environment, the unfolding nature of a phenomenon over time and its cyclical nature**. So, a dynamic creative process is opposed to *static* and *linear* process (see Fig. 15.1). In Fig. 15.1, we contrast an essentially linear description of the creative process such as Wallas (1926) with a more dynamic description such as Botella et al. (2011). Here, we see clearly that linearity involves moving from one stage to another without any other possible way whereas a dynamic description involves many interactions between stages.

From this definition, we can consider that stages of the creative process occur in a dynamic way and interact with each other. The stages of the creative process correspond to micro-processes and their organization and combination correspond to a macro-process (Botella et al. 2016). The successive interactions with the environment and the time frame reinforce the importance of developing tools such as the Creative process Report Diary. Indeed, the CRD respects ecological validity – avoiding, as far as possible, placing the individual in "artificial" conditions (Brewer 2000) – and takes into account the time frame by repeated measures.

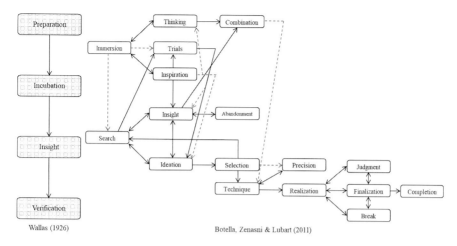

Fig. 15.1 Contrast between a linear approach (Wallas 1926) and a dynamic approach of the creative process (Botella et al. 2011)
Note. **In the dynamic model, the solid lines indicate the main transitions observed with art students between the stages; dotted lines indicate frequent transitions (Botella et al. 2011).**

15.5 Conclusion

From the presentation of some dynamic processes in diverse fields such as education, cognitive sciences, health psychology and social psychology and with a definition of what is a dynamic creative process, we can now formulate suggestions for educational practice:

- The creative process is not linear and Krashen (1984) found that the best writers do not follow a linear approach. Additionally, the better stories were written by participants who transcribed faster and made the most revisions (Lubart 2009; von Koss Torkildsen et al. 2016). According to these considerations, an educational practice could be to invite students to produce quickly something and to work again after to specify their idea by going back to previous stages. Combining emotional and cognitive processes, the teacher could provide cycles of experimentation to students (Roels 2014).
- For Carbon (2010, 2011), aesthetic appreciation is just a temporary state that leads to a new process. In this way, the teacher could invite the students to reinvest old products, to reevaluate them or to use them as a source of inspiration.
- The dynamic creative process is a combination of multiple components. Developing creativity could involve enhancing factors such as domain knowledge or expertise, personal motivation, personality characteristics, personal feelings, emotions and affects, product constraints, and environmental characteristics (Cropley et al. 2013; Runco and Dow 1999; Russ 1999; Shaw 1989, 1994), based on a multivariate approach (Lubart et al. 2015). Considering more especially the emotional resonance model (Lubart and Getz 1997), another suggestion for

educational practice would be the generation of emotions to facilitate the activation of endocepts and the association of ideas. In the same vein, Yeh and collaborators (2016) showed that positive emotions associated with a high activation and a promotion focus facilitated creative thinking. A part of the training could be dedicated to training emotions. Corazza (2016) has already proposed to develop an educational program on frustration from the inconclusiveness of the process.
- Because the dynamics of the creative process are too difficult to explain directly in interviews with the creator, researchers could use Creative process Report Diary (CRD) to improve knowledge on it. The CRD could also be used in class when pupils or students are creating to improve their metacognition about their own process. It is an easy tool to implement with adults (Botella and Lubart 2015; Botella et al. 2011) and even with pupils when it is presented visually with pictures (Didier et al. 2016). More globally, the use of tool could be a way to enhance the teaching of creativity. Pearson and Logie (2015) had shown that software externalizing the creation of mental images reduce working memory.
- Sun and collaborators (2016) described a process evolving from successive interaction of fluctuation and stability. In the same vein, Foti and collaborators (2008) described the perception of leadership by information occurring simultaneously and over time. The Bumper Effect Dynamic (Greeley 1977) prevents individuals from going astray by guiding and keeping them on the correct path. Based on these studies, we can imagine the teacher offering help when the process is too stable, by adding other constraints, by stopping an incorrect path, or changing the rhythm of the class for example.
- Based on Ward and Wickes (2009), the teacher could adjust the information given at the beginning of the teaching session to activate the accessibility of exemplars. The teacher could also propose exercises favoring the semantic distance between ideas (Hass 2017). More globally, based on the work of Tisdell and collaborators (2008), teachers could provide only a little information about the theme of the program, invite a lecturer or propose a living experience to encourage students to generate ideas and to be involved.
- Based on Yaniv's (2012) work on psychotherapeutic interactions, role reversal could be a method to help individuals to understand the creative process of others. As described by the author, first, the creator starts to imitate the other; second, the creator tries to reproduce the other with his or her own subjectivity; and finally, the creator exchanges the creative process. A better understanding of the creative process of others could give some ideas to improve one's own process.
- The creator is not alone during the creative process, especially in learning contexts. The teacher could invite students to enhance their social networks outside the class (Engel et al. 2017) or to collaborate during the class (Gray 1989). Moreover, the teacher could use constraints as Bakker and collaborators (2013) who proposed that team members will not work together again or that they will work all together during a 1 year program.

To conclude, the linear 4-stage model of the creative process (Wallas 1926) seems far from dynamic. However, the creative process appears to have an important dynamic structure. It is challenging to specify the components of the creative process, their organization, their combination, how they are influenced by the environment according to the time frame and also according to the creative domain studied. We suggest, however, that this dynamic approach is needed to capture the complex, idiosyncratic and seemingly unpredictable nature of the creative process and to develop potentially original and effective training.

References

Ainsworth-Land, G. (1981). The dynamics of creative process — Key to the enigmas of physics. *The Journal of Creative Behavior, 15*(4), 227–241. https://doi.org/10.1002/j.2162-6057.1981.tb00297.x.
Amabile, T. M. (1988). A model of creativity and innovation in organizations. *Research in Organizational Behavior, 10*, 123–167.
Arieti, S. (1976). *Creativity: The magic synthesis*. New York: Basic Books.
Armbruster, B. B. (1989). Metacognition in creativity. In J. A. Glover, R. R. Ronning, & C. R. Reynolds (Eds.), *Handbook of creativity* (pp. 177–182). New York: Plenum.
Averill, J. R., & Nunley, E. P. (1992). *Voyages of the heart: Living an emotionally creative life*. New York: Free Press.
Bakker, R. M., Boroş, S., Kenis, P., & Oerlemans, L. A. G. (2013). It's only temporary: Time frame and the dynamics of creative project teams. *British Journal of Management, 24*(3), 383–397 https://doi.org/10.1111/j.1467-8551.2012.00810.x.
Beaty, R. E., Benedek, M., Kaufman, S. B., & Silvia, P. J. (2015). Default and executive network coupling supports creative idea production. *Scientific Reports, 5*, 10964. https://doi.org/10.1038/srep10964.
Beaty, R. E., Benedek, M., Silvia, P. J., & Schacter, D. L. (2016). Creative cognition and brain network dynamics. *Trends in Cognitive Sciences, 20*(2), 87–95. https://doi.org/10.1016/j.tics.2015.10.004.
Botella, M., & Lubart, T. (2015). Creative processes: Art, design and science. In G. E. Corazza & S. Agnoli (Eds.), *Multidisciplinary contributions to the science of creative thinking* (pp. 53–65). Singapour: Springer.
Botella, M., Zenasni, F., & Lubart, T. (2011). A dynamic and ecological approach to the artistic creative process of arts Students: An empirical contribution. *Empirical Studies of the Arts, 29*, 17–38. https://doi.org/10.2190/EM.29.1.b.
Botella, M., Glaveanu, V., Zenasni, F., Storme, M., Myszkowski, N., Wolff, M., & Lubart, T. (2013). How artists create: Creative process and multivariate factors. *Learning and Individual Differences, 26*, 161–170.
Botella, M., Nelson, J., & Zenasni, F. (2016). Les macro et micro processus créatifs. In I. Capron-Puozzo (Ed.), *Créativité et apprentissage* (pp. 33–46). Louvain-la-Neuve: De Boeck.
Botella, M., Nelson, J., & Zenasni, F. (2017). It is time to observe the creative process : How to use a creative process report diary (CRD). *Journal of Creative Behavior*. https://doi.org/10.1002/jocb.172.
Bourgeois-Bougrine, S., Glaveanu, V., Botella, M., Guillou, K., De Biasi, P. M., & Lubart, T. (2014). The creativity maze: Exploring creativity in screenplay writing. *Psychology of Aesthetics, Creativity, and the Arts, 8*(4), 1–16.
Brewer, M. (2000). Research design and issues of validity. In H. Reis & C. Judd (Eds.), *Handbook of research methods in social and personality psychology* (pp. 3–16). Cambridge: Cambridge University Press.

Busse, T. V., & Mansfield, R. S. (1980). Theories of the creative process: A review and a perspective. *Journal of Creative Behavior, 14*(2), 103–132.

Carbon, C. C. (2010). The cycle of preference: Long-term dynamics of aesthetic appreciation. *Acta Psychologica, 134*(2), 233–244. https://doi.org/10.1016/j.actpsy.2010.02.004.

Carbon, C.-C. (2011). Cognitive mechanisms for explaining dynamics of aesthetic appreciation. *I-Perception, 2*, 708–719 https://doi.org/10.1068/i0463aap.

Carbon, C. C. (2012). Dynamics of aesthetic appreciation. *Human Vision and Electronic Imaging XVII, 8291*(A), 1–6. https://doi.org/10.1117/12.916468

Carson, D. K. (1999). Counseling. In M. A. Runco & S. R. Pritzker (Eds.), *Encyclopedia of creativity* (Vol. 1, pp. 395–402). New York: Academic.

Corazza, G. E. (2016). Potential originality and effectiveness: The dynamic definition of creativity. *Creativity Research Journal, 28*(3), 258–267. https://doi.org/10.1080/10400419.2016.1195627.

Cropley, D. H., & Cropley, A. J. (2012). A psychological taxonomy of organizational innovation: Resolving the paradoxes. *Creativity Research Journal, 24*(1), 29–40.

Cropley, D. H., Cropley, A. J., Chiera, B. A., & Kaufman, J. C. (2013). Diagnosing organizational innovation: Measuring the capacity for innovation. *Creativity Research Journal, 25*, 388–396.

Didier, J., Botella, M., Attanasio, R., & Lambert, M.-D. (2016). Construction of notebook to observe the creative process of young students during complex solving problems in educational context. *31st International Congress of Psychology*, July 24–29, Yokohama, Japan.

Doyle, C. L. (1998). The writer tells: The creative process in the writing of liberation fiction. *Creativity Research Journal, 11*(1), 29–37.

Engel, Y., Kaandorp, M., & Elfring, T. (2017). Toward a dynamic process model of entrepreneurial networking under uncertainty. *Journal of Business Venturing, 32*(1), 35–51 https://doi.org/10.1016/j.jbusvent.2016.10.001.

Foti, R. J., Knee, R. E., & Backert, R. S. G. (2008). Multi-level implications of framing leadership perceptions as a dynamic process. *Leadership Quarterly, 19*(2), 178–194. https://doi.org/10.1016/j.leaqua.2008.01.007.

Fusari, A. (2005). A model of the innovation-adaptation mechanism driving economic dynamics: A micro representation. *Journal of Evolutionary Economics, 15*(3), 297–333. https://doi.org/10.1007/s00191-005-0246-z.

Glaveanu, V., Lubart, T., Bonnardel, N., Botella, M., de Biaisi, P.-M., Desainte-Catherine, M., Georgsdottir, A., Guillou, K., Kurtag, G., Mouchiroud, C., Storme, M., Wojtczuk, A., & Zenasni, F. (2013). Creativity as action: Findings from five creative domains. *Frontiers in Psychology, 4*(April), 176. https://doi.org/10.3389/fpsyg.2013.00176.

Goswami, A. (1996). Creativity and the quantum: A unified theory of creativity. *Creativity Research Journal, 9*(1), 47–61.

Gray, B. (1989). *Collaborating: Finding common ground for multiparty problems*. San Francisco: Jossey Bass.

Greeley, L. (1977). The bumper effect dynamic in the creative process: The philosophical, psychological and neuropsychological link. *The Journal of Creative Behavior, 20*(4), 261–275.

Gruber, H. E. (1988). The evolving systems approach to creative work. *Creativity Research Journal, 1*, 27–51.

Gruber, H. E. (1989). The evolving systems approach to creative work. In D. Wallace & H. E. Gruber (Eds.), *Creative people at work: Twelve cognitive case studies* (pp. 3–24). New York: Oxford University Press.

Guilford, J. P. (1950). Creativity. *The American Psychologist, 5*, 444–454.

Hass, R. W. (2017). Tracking the dynamics of divergent thinking via semantic distance: Analytic methods and theoretical implications. *Memory and Cognition, 45*(2), 233–244. https://doi.org/10.3758/s13421-016-0659-y.

Kellermann, P. F. (1994). Role reversal in psychodrama. In P. Holmes, M. Karp, & M. Watson (Eds.), *Psychodrama since Moreno: Innovations in theory and practice* (pp. 263–279). London.: Routledge.

Krashen, S. (1984). *Writing: Research, theory, and applications*. Torrance: Laredo Publishing.

Lewin, K. (1935). *A dynamic theory of personality: Selected papers*. New York: McGraw-Hill.

Lubart, T. I., & Getz, I. (1997). Emotion, metaphor, and the creative process. *Creativity Research Journal, 10*(4), 285–301.

Lubart, T. I. (2000–2001). Models of the creative process: Past, present and future. *Creativity Research Journal, 13*(3–4), 295–308.

Lubart, T. (2009). In search of the writer's creative process. In S. B. Kaufman & J. C. Kaufman (Eds.), *The psychology of creative writing* (pp. 149–165). New York: Cambridge University Press.

Lubart, T. I., Mouchiroud, C., Tordjman, S., & Zenasni, F. (2015). *Psychologie de la créativité [psychology of creativity]* (2nd ed.). Paris: Armand Collin.

Martindale, C. (1981). *Cognition and consciousness*. Homewood: Dorsey.

Martindale, C. (1999). History and creativity. In M. A. Runco & S. R. Pritzker (Eds.), *Encyclopaedia of creativity* (Vol. 1, pp. 823–830). New York: Academic Press.

Molenaar, P. C. M. (2013). On the necessity to use person-specific data analysis approaches in psychology. *European Journal of Developmental Psychology, 10*, 29–39.

Molenaar, P. C. M., & Campbell, C. G. (2009). The new person-specific paradigm in psychology. *Current Directions in Psychological Science, 18*, 112–117. https://doi.org/10.1111/j.1467-8721.2009.01619.x.

Mumford, M. D., & Porter, P. P. (1999). Analogies. In M. A. Runco & S. R. Pritzker (Eds.), *Encyclopaedia of creativity* (Vol. 1, pp. 71–77). New York: Academic.

Ochse, R. E. (1990). *Before the gates of excellence: The determinants of creative genuis*. Cambridge: Cambridge University Press.

Ohanian, A. (2014). *From PlayStation to Y Combinator: The Reddit origin story, part 2*. Okhuysen: American Express Open Forum.

Osborn, A. F. (1953/1963). *Applied imagination* (3rd ed.). New York: Scribners.

Patrick, C. (1935). Creative thought in poets. *Archives of Psychology, 178*, 1–74.

Patrick, C. (1937). Creative thought in artists. *Journal of Psychology, 4*, 35–73.

Patrick, C. (1938). Scientific thought. *The Journal of Psychology, 5*, 55–83.

Pearson, D. G., & Logie, R. H. (2000). Working memory and mental synthesis. In S. O'Nuallan (Ed.), *Spatial cognition: Foundations and applications* (pp. 347–359). Amsterdam: John Benjamins Publishing.

Pearson, D. G., & Logie, R. H. (2015). A sketch is not enough: Dynamic external support increases creative insight on a guided synthesis task. *Thinking and Reasoning, 21*(1), 97–112. https://doi.org/10.1080/13546783.2014.897255.

Pearson, D. G., Logie, R. H., & Gilhooly, K. (1999). Verbal representations and spatial manipulation during mental synthesis. *European Journal of Cognitive Psychology, 11*(3), 295–314. https://doi.org/10.1080/713752317.

Pearson, D. G., Deeprose, C., Wallace-Hadrill, S., Burnett Heyes, S., & Holmes, E. A. (2013). Assessing mental imagery in clinical psychology: A review of imagery measures and a guiding framework. *Clinical Psychology Review, 33*(1), 1–23. https://doi.org/10.1016/j.cpr.2012.09.001.

Peilloux, A., & Botella, M. (2016). Ecological and dynamical study of the creative process and affects of scientific students working in groups. *Creativity Research Journal, 28*(2), 165–170. Retrieved from. https://doi.org/10.1080/10400419.2016.1162549.

Prins, S. (2006). The psychodynamic perspective in organizational research: Making sense of the dynamics of direction setting in emergent collaborative processes. *Journal of Occupational and Organizational Psychology, 79*(3), 335–355. https://doi.org/10.1348/096317906X105724.

Roels, H. (2014). Cycles of experimentation and the creative process of music composition. *Artistic Experimentation in Music: An Anthology*, 231–240.

Runco, M. A. (1991). *Divergent thinking*. Westport: Ablex Publishing.

Runco, M. A. (1999). Divergent thinking. In M. A. Runco & S. R. Pritsker (Eds.), *Encyclopaedia of creativity* (Vol. 1, pp. 577–582). New York: Academic.

Runco, M. A., & Dow, G. (1999). Problem Finding. In M. A. Runco & S. R. Pritzker (Eds.), *Encyclopaedia of creativity* (Vol. 2, pp. 433–435). New York: Academic.

Russ, S. W. (1999). Emotion/affect. In M. A. Runco & S. R. Pritzker (Eds.), *Encyclopaedia of creativity* (Vol. 1, pp. 659–668). New York: Academic.

Sadler-Smith, E. (2016). Wallas' four-stage model of the creative process: more than meets the eye ? *Creativity Research Journal, 27*(4), 342–352. https://doi.org/10.1080/10400419.2015.1087277

Shaw, M. P. (1989). The eureka process: A structure for the creative experience in science and engineering. *Creativity Research Journal, 2*(4), 286–298.

Shaw, M. P. (1994). Affective components of scientific creativity. In M. P. Shaw & M. A. Runco (Eds.), *Creativity and affect* (pp. 3–43). Westport: Ablex Publishing.

Simonton, D. K. (1980). Intuition and analysis: A predictive and explanatory model. *Genetic Psychology Monographs, 102*(1), 3–60.

Simonton, D. K. (1990). Creativity in the later years: Optimistic prospects for achievement. *The Gerontologist, 30*, 626–631.

Simonton, D. K. (1999). *Origins of genius: Darwinian perspectives on creativity*. London: Oxford University Press.

Simonton, D. K. (2001). Talent development as a multidimensional, multiplicative, and dynamic process. *Current Directions in Psychological Science, 10*(2), 39–43. https://doi.org/10.1111/1467-8721.00110.

Sun, H., Steinkrauss, R., van der Steen, S., Cox, R., & de Bot, K. (2016). Foreign language learning as a complex dynamic process: A microgenetic case study of a Chinese child's English learning trajectory. *Learning and Individual Differences, 49*, 287–296. https://doi.org/10.1016/j.lindif.2016.05.010.

Tisdell, C., Wilson, C., & Swarna Nantha, H. (2008). Contingent valuation as a dynamic process. *Journal of Socio-Economics, 37*(4), 1443–1458. https://doi.org/10.1016/j.socec.2007.04.005.

Treffinger, D. J. (1995). Creative problem solving: Overview and educational implications. *Educational Psychology Review, 7*(3), 301–312.

Van Geert, P., & Steenbeek, H. (2005). Explaining after by before: Basic aspects of a dynamic systems approach to the study of development. *Developmental Review, 25*, 408–442.

Vinacke, W. E. (1952). *The psychology of thinking*. New York: McGraw-Hill.

von Koss Torkildsen, J., Morken, F., Helland, W. A., & Helland, T. (2016). The dynamics of narrative writing in primary grade children: Writing process factors predict story quality. *Reading and Writing, 29*(3), 529–554. https://doi.org/10.1007/s11145-015-9618-4.

Wallas, G. (1926). *The art of thought*. New York: Harcourt, Brace.

Waller, N. G., Bouchard, T. J., Jr., Lykken, D. T., Tellegen, A., & Blacker, D. M. (1993). Creativity, heritability, familiarity: Which word does not belong? *Psychological Inquiry, 4*, 235–237.

Ward, T. B., & Wickes, K. N. S. (2009). Stable and dynamic properties of category structure guide imaginative thought. *Creativity Research Journal, 21*(1), 15–23. https://doi.org/10.1080/10400410802633376.

Yaniv, D. (2011). Revisiting Morenian psychodramatic encounter in light of contemporary neuroscience: Relationship between empathy and creativity. *Arts in Psychotherapy, 38*(1), 52–58. https://doi.org/10.1016/j.aip.2010.12.001.

Yaniv, D. (2012). Dynamics of creativity and empathy in role reversal: Contributions from neuroscience. *Review of General Psychology, 16*(1), 70–77. https://doi.org/10.1037/a0026580.

Yeh, Y. c., Lai, S. C., & Lin, C. W. (2016). The dynamic influence of emotions on game-based creativity: An integrated analysis of emotional valence, activation strength, and regulation focus. *Computers in Human Behavior, 55*, 817–825. https://doi.org/10.1016/j.chb.2015.10.037.

Chapter 16
Navigating the Ideology of Creativity in Education

Michael Hanchett Hanson

Abstract A growing number of scholars have come to see creativity, not as a trait or force or process, but as ideology – a set of seldom questioned values and assumptions about individuals and change that characterizes our time while unifying and reinforcing other ideological concepts, such as individualism and neophilia. What does this ideology look like in education? Can educators manage its impact, and even influence its meaning? In other words, inevitably working from *within* our ideology of creativity, what moves are available once we are aware of the stakes?

This chapter provides two examples of how the ideology of creativity can affect education. Then potential next steps in managing the ideology and influencing its development are proposed: adopting frameworks that promote participatory creativity, ensuring that analysis of complex systems is taught effectively and studying famous creative people with a broader social lens. This is a suggestive, not comprehensive, list. A form of creativity itself, this work will have to emerge from the complex interactions that constitute, maintain and drive both creativity research and education. More important than any specific recommendation, though, is awareness of the ideology – being attuned to the issues and discussing them.

16.1 Navigating the Ideology of Creativity in Education

A former graduate student contacts her professor (the author), a specialist in creative development to ask advice concerning her daughter. The teenager is a straight-A student and loves school. Her mother has been called to a special teacher conference, though, because the girl does not perform well during brainstorming sessions and, overall, her projects are not considered sufficiently creative. As a result of the conference, the mother and daughter are upset about the "poor performance" and wondering how to "help" the girl.

M. Hanchett Hanson (✉)
Teachers College, Columbia University, New York City, NY, USA
e-mail: mah59@tc.columbia.edu

Similarly, one of the respondents to E. Paul Torrance's longitudinal study on divergent thinking reported hating to receive the follow-up questionnaires as an adult. (The study has currently tracked for 50 years a portion of the elementary school students who took Torrance's divergent thinking tests from 1958–1964.) This woman had earned a PhD and two post-doctoral fellowships and worked as a scientific researcher. She had solved difficult problems in her field. As a child, though, she had found the divergent thinking tests frustrating and, in spite of her success, continued to feel insecure because she considered herself "very uncreative" (Torrance 2002, p. 2).

A successful entrepreneur comes to the author seeking advice. He made his fortune in an industry not related to education. He now wants to turn his attention to changing education through technology – making it creative! During the discussion, he explains that he has a diagnosed learning disability and never finished his own education. His goal is not to help schools simply accommodate students who might be challenged like him but to revolutionize education writ large. (There have been multiple versions of this kind of revenge on education discussion over the years.)

An article describing the DIY (do it yourself) educational movement, a project-based educational approach, quotes a psychologist as bemoaning the fact that current education does not teach children how to make things but instead how to be "scholars *in the narrowest sense of the word, meaning someone who spends their time reading and writing. Of course, most people are not scholars. We survive by doing things"* (Frauenfelder 2010, p. 44).

16.2 Creativity as Ideology

These stories reflect assumptions that everyone should be creative and, as expressed in much of the overall discourse on creativity, the more creativity the better. These assumptions have come with implicit, and often explicit, contempt for those who are not obviously creative, such as "scholars" or non-creative good students, virtuosos or historians – the people who maintain standards so that there is something for creative people to change. One is reminded of the Kurt Vonnegut (1990) quote: "Another flaw in human character is that everybody wants to build and nobody wants to do maintenance" (p. 238).

A striking aspect of these stories is how, without reflection, they make sense in the current rhetorical *zeitgeist*. The intelligent mother with her honors-student daughter did not react by laughing in the teacher's face. Why would an education system try to make the best students into failures? Somehow, not being sufficiently creative – measured in part by brainstorming participation! – seemed ominous and dangerous. (See further discussion of the danger of making students into failures in the quest for creativity in the classroom in Clapp 2017.)

First-glance validity may be the most striking aspect of the last vignette as well. The psychologist is quoted as juxtaposing scholarship to how most people learn, throwing in human survival for good measure. The descriptor of a scholar as "someone who spends their time reading and writing" seems reasonable until one is reminded of what daily life is actually like in the twenty-first century. Even 8 years ago, huge numbers of people, from executives to managers to clerical staffs, spent most of their days in front of screens *reading and writing*. Indeed, more than ever before in history, across the planet people were involved daily in the even more "scholarly" activity of searching for, evaluating and disseminating information. Of course, project-based learning is often a crucial aspect of good education, but juxtaposing it to scholarship does not make sense for education or for the world today.

There is a strong whiff of ideology in these examples. At least, they seem ideological in the everyday sense of powerful and unquestioned assumptions about how the world works which, at least at times, serves as smoke screen for questionable ends. Creativity has also become ideological in its punch. None of these stories would have such broad implications if creativity was an isolated construct, like say depth perception or technological aptitude. Instead, creativity is an umbrella term, linking many of today's powerful beliefs and social values, including individualism, motivation, fulfillment, risk taking, openness, play (spontaneity), market economics, social change, success, fame, and so on.

Not surprisingly, a growing number of scholars have come to see creativity as ideology. At the turn of the twenty first century, Weiner (2000) laid out the case for the historical development of the idea of creativity as ideology and asked what can come "beyond creativity." Well established creativity researchers, Runco and Albert (2010) have proposed that creativity can be seen as rational science or as ideology. Although psychology has usually embraced the rational science model, social displacements and resulting misery has led to the model of creativity as ideology. Others (e.g., Foucault, 1969/1998; Raunig et al. 2011; Rehn and De Cock 2009; Pope 2005) have analyzed the ideological functions of creativity from a number of critical positions. In what may be evidence of the growing power of the ideology of creativity, Pope (2005) has even argued for re-appropriation (with revisions) of the construct of creativity into critical theory rooted in Marxism.

16.2.1 What Kind of Ideology?

There is not room here to explore fully how the construct of creativity fits into the history of the equally complex concept of ideology and the current debates among ideology scholars.[1] Some consideration of how creativity can be ideological will be

---

[1] Freedan (2003) has argued that, based on convention, the term *ideology* proper should be limited to traditional ideologies: communism, socialism, liberalism, conservatism and fascism. The argument presented here obviously differs from that position, given the number of scholars who have talked about creativity as ideology. In addition, there does not seem to be another word that works as well in capturing the pervasive nature of unquestioned assumptions to so many aspects of life; the broad network of values, ideas and practices that fall under creativity; its use (in some contexts) as smokescreen for oppression as discussed by Weiner (2000), and its power within a particular period of time.

helpful in thinking about its functions in education, however. Is "creativity" a false class consciousness as Marx and Engels (1845/1998; Marx 1867/2010) used the term? In other words, does today's unquestioned enthusiasm for creativity lead to putting the onus for "recreating oneself" on the individual when a larger economic system puts her out of work in midlife? Pride in creativity and expectations of it would then deflect blame, preserving oppressive economic systems.

Or is the concept of creativity less encompassing: a powerful but more restricted idea that can function within and across ideologies? Everyone seems to think people should be creative but disagree about what that means. This is the conceptual umbrella function. Free enterprise advocates like to emphasize entrepreneurial individualism and risk taking. Social activists like to emphasize possibilities for changes in social values. People interested in spiritual development like the creativity discourse on fulfillment. Parents like the emphasis on child-like play as confirmation their children's value.

Alternatively, is the idea of creativity even more encompassing? Mannheim (1936/1954) described a paradoxical condition of ideology: any research works within ideologies so even the analysis of ideology is a product of ideology. In other words, this analysis of creativity as an ideology that carries unquestioned assumptions comes from within the influence of that very ideology which also promotes questioning assumptions. Indeed, I am not arguing that we can eliminate ideology, only that, by being more aware of its ideological functions, we can make the idea of creativity more relevant to our lives and to the challenges of eduction. In other words, this exercise turns creativity on itself.

Any of these positions is defensible and debatable. The point here is not to choose but to keep the possibilities in mind as we, first, quickly consider the historical development of our ideas of creativity and then specifically examine their functions in education.

16.2.2 History

But wait! Why would creativity be ideological? Is it not what distinguishes humanity? Part of our species like language and tool use? Yes and no. Using symbol systems, making and interpreting cultural products and developing new technologies – obviously, none of that is new. The idea of a near-magical *thing* within people and groups that is always good and promotes change *per se*, standing in opposition to conventions and traditions; a *force* that must be identified, nourished and channeled in order to fulfill lives, drive economics and save humanity; a *value* that does not just make room for different perspectives but also glorifies "rugged" (alienated) individualism; an *imperative* for everyone to look for value in the new – none of that is universal.

Most people do not realize how new and rapidly changing today's views of creativity are. *Creare* is a Latin verb, and scholars have traced key roots of the concept to European and American history (Mason 2003; Pope 2005; Weiner 2000). In spite of the Latin origin and the Romans' many innovations, however, they placed greater emphasis on tradition than novelty, and, in general – like the ancient Greeks – saw inspiration as coming from outside the individual, from the muses or gods. During the European Middle Ages, in most places it would be considered blasphemous to say that people created things. Only the Christian God created things. People made (*facere*) things. In the European Renaissance, the adjective *creative* started to be applied more liberally to people. Still, being creative was looked upon with suspicion until the later nineteenth century (Mason 2003; Weiner 2000). At that point, a number of related and reinforcing concepts and values emerged together in Europe and America, including increased interest in imagination, individualism, market economics, globalization, cultural analyses and… creativity.

After World War II as the United States with its focus on individualism and market economics became globally dominant, the idea of creativity grew alongside. At that time American psychology took on the study of creativity with more vigor than it had in the past. In 1950, J. Paul Guilford, outgoing president of the American Psychological Association, called for the psychological study of creativity, positing the idea of divergent thinking.

The mid-twentieth century was also, of course, the beginning of the Cold War. It is easy to forget the levels of American social anxiety that came with the realization that, in nuclear weapons, humanity had the power to destroy itself. Then the U.S.S.R. tested its first nuclear bomb in 1949. In this context Guilford's 1950 speech justified the study of creativity as a means to identify and properly *educate* superior American leadership in government and business.

Later, Carl Rogers and Abraham Maslow – humanistic psychologists – would explicitly justify the need for greater creativity as a Cold War strategy (Hanchett Hanson 2015, in press). Both men believed that there was one drive in life, to self-actualize, and self-actualization was strongly linked to creativity. For them, as well as other mid-twentieth century psychologists (e.g., Gruber 1989; May 1989), promoting creativity was also necessary for human survival in the nuclear age.

Education was central to the humanistic vision. Maslow (1971/1993) believed that with the right education, emphasizing creativity, a new kind of superior human being could be engineered. This "Heraclitian" human (p. 57) would produce continual change and be infinitely adaptable to it. He and Rogers (1954, 1961/1989, 1969) believed, as Guilford had argued, that promoting creativity in American education would give the United States the upper hand in global politics. One of the leading proponents of student-centered education, Rogers (1961/1989) argued that this kind of education could both to win the Cold War and the finally make America the world's leading intellectual force after so many years of dominance by European intellectuals. The logical problem with Rogers argument was that most of those European leaders had come from relatively rigid and demanding education systems, far from the student-centered approaches Rogers advocated.

Taken together, this discourse on creativity tended to present a classic double-bind: you cannot resist the power of creativity as an inevitable, natural condition of all humans, but to survive you must put all of your energy into giving it to more people. In spite of the apparent contradiction, note that the overall ideological drift: novelty was absolutely essential to solving problems. The problems were now huge and threatening humanity itself and so must be the novel solutions by implication.

Past experience, the lessons of history, traditional values and established conventions were devalued – and often explicitly vilified – as sources of needed solutions. Not surprisingly, education itself was in the cross-hairs. For Rogers and Maslow, received knowledge would keep the individual from experiencing the world as continually new in his or her own unique perspective. Less rhetorically extreme, the ideation theorists (divergent thinking and problem solving) were, nevertheless, working toward similar ends. Insisting that education promote creativity and defining it as divergent thinking inevitably meant moving from depth of knowledge to breadth of ideation with "idea" operationally defined as a brief phrase on a test. For the problem-solving researchers, the expectations of the world that came with experience and received knowledge would obstruct the ability to solve trick insight problems in experiments.[2]

In general, the emphasis on the individual constantly overcoming experience and learning – "thinking outside the box" – does not align with either the mission of education or case research on those who have done creative work (e.g., Gruber 1981; Hanchett Hanson 2005; Wallace and Gruber 1989). Weisberg (2006, 2011; Weisberg and Hanchett Hanson 2013) who has studied creativity through case studies as well as in experimental settings has concluded that creative people think specifically "inside their box" of experience and skills. What seems surprising to others ("outside the box") is the result of a long process of learning. This is in keeping with developmental points of view that define creative development as the construction of a distinctive point of view through experience, including education (Gruber and Wallace 1999). Furthermore, that experience is necessarily embedded in sociohistorical context (Gruber 1981, 2005; Hanchett Hanson 2015; John-Steiner 2015; Moran and John-Steiner 2003; Vygotsky 1930/2004). As will be described later, synthesizing the developmental and sociocultural perspectives, some creativity theorists have moved beyond the individualist assumptions. Nevertheless, the influence of the earlier lines of research have been pervasive and persistent, and divergent thinking tests are still used in research and education (see discussion, Hanchett Hanson 2015).

As both developmental and sociocultural frameworks would predict, however, there is also continuity between the old creativity views and the new ones. To draw lines between them too starkly would be a mistake. Many theorists working with humanistic clinical views, divergent thinking researchers and problem-solving theorists have readily acknowledged the complexity of life. The psychological construct of creativity, for all of its benefits and dangers, has not been built by naïve people or knee-jerk ideologues. If anything, inspired by their topic, creativity specialists have tended to be particularly socially aware, courageous and innovative (Hanchett Hanson 2015).

Many researchers across theoretical approaches have also acknowledged the crucial role of audiences, in addition to the individual thinker (e.g., Amabile et al. 1996; Beghetto 2016; Corazza 2016; Kaufman and Beghetto 2009; Plucker et al. 2004;

---

[2] See review of problem-solving and divergent thinking research in Weisberg (2006). For more in-depth discussion of all of these theories in relation to ideology, see Hanchett Hanson (2015).

Stein 1953). At least in the definition of creativity value must be recognized; some have considered the related social dynamics. Some have noted the changing meaning of the construct of creativity (e.g., Amabile et al. 1996; Sawyer 2012) and/or its ideological history and applications (e.g., Runco and Albert 2010; Sawyer 2012). Recently, more serious discussion of the possibilities of "dark sides" of creative work and the attendant ethical concerns have begun (e.g., Cropley et al. 2010; Moran 2010; Moran et al. 2014).

Indeed, the history of the psychological debates about creativity is itself a study in the tensions – affordances and limitations – between the individual perspectives of the theorists and their social and historical contexts. At the same time, however, the extreme individualist and neophilic values embedded in the history of the concept of creativity have been hard to shake. It has taken some time to move the more realistic and complex views of creativity from the introductions and discussions of research papers to the more powerful crux of the research and findings.

There are several take-aways from this very abbreviated history.

- The idea of creativity as a personal, psychological or social force is not necessary to build great buildings, write drama, produce art or institute new political systems. Many societies that did not attribute creativity to people or highly value creativity produced such works.
- A cornerstone of creativity theory has been extreme individualism. Society and its norms, including education, may then treated as irrelevant or worse – threats – rather than the resources from which people create and to which they contribute.
- Another cornerstone has been privileging the value of change itself, anything new over the learned or the traditional – *neophilia,* not as a description of just a type of person but as a social value. For some theorists, this has extended to experience itself with the goal of every moment feeling entirely new.
- Neither presumed privileging of the value of change nor imperatives for everyone to become agents of change have been common across history or societies. These are distinctly Modern values that arose in Europe and America and have grown dramatically since the late nineteenth century.
- Today's concepts of creativity have clear and more recent ideological roots in mid-twentieth century politics. The ideological functions of the concept of creativity have, thus, emerged over time and continue to evolve.
- Finally, education has long been central to the discussion as both scapegoat and – once *changed* – as promise for the future.

16.3 The Ideology in Education

The ideology presents creativity as answer to a wide range of problems from economic stagnation to individual fulfillment. Much of the research, curricula and assessment techniques have then aimed at giving everyone more of this good stuff. For educators, the results can easily seem like yet another activity and set of assessments in an already impossibly stretched day, not to mention yet another way for students to fail. What's more, teachers now have the daunting task of both teaching the rules and how to break them, often to a group of students with widely varying levels of understanding of those rules (math, grammar, spelling, scientific method, color theory and so on).

But what if educators took their cue from the broader controversies that have driven creativity research instead of the often reductive answers that some particular lines of research advocate? The history of the concept in psychology can be seen as a debate about the relationship of individual action to change. Do a few great individuals make history, or do socio-historical dynamics (*zeitgeist*) determine individual experience, ideas and actions? If such a dichotomy does not make sense, how do the dynamics between individual points of view and context work? Are the dynamics different in different times and places? Are they different in each case? Do they depend on the topic (domain)? How does one change affect later changes?

These are questions calling for education – questions that require in-depth knowledge of old and new ideas, as well as the circumstances of history; debates that call for critical thinking and logical argumentation, as well as synthesis of ideas, and concerns that, as the longstanding psychological deabtes have shown, are not easily resolved. These questions can help ground students' thinking across many topics including their own everyday experiences. In other words, presenting creativity as a series of questions, rather than an obvious and all-powerful answer, makes the concept both more realistic and more education friendly – and, frankly, more interesting.

What would this question-focused approach to creativity look like in education? There are almost endless examples, ranging from recognized controversies to very subtle assumptions. Consider two examples.

16.3.1 History Class

Let's start with an easy example. Every October in America there is a short cultural debate about the ethics of Christopher Columbus (e.g., Anderson 2015; Mach 2011; Shafer and Walsh 2017). Was he a bold and courageous explorer, a visionary who changed people's conception of the entire world? Or was he a ruthless and scheming slave trader who brought misery and death to the "New World"? A striking aspect of this controversy is that both sides usually assume that Columbus was exceptional – exceptionally bold or exceptionally cruel – and disproportionally responsible for the course of history. What if education changed the questions? How usual was he? What determined the impacts of his mistake: not finding a passage to Asia because he was wrong about how large the world was? (By the way, virtually all educated people of his day knew the world was round, Russell 1991.)

After all, Columbus could not have taken his voyage without the systems of beliefs, values, economics and technologies of the day, systems that involved millions of people, as well as his specific backers. Those systems were also key to determining what the world subsequently did with his accidental discovery. In other words, as sociocultural creativity theorists have argued (Clapp 2017; Csikszentmihalyi 1997, 1999; Hanchett Hanson 2015; Glăveanu 2014; Sawyer 2012), *the field* both made the discovery possible and determined its subsequent meaning and application – even though Columbus also had a hand in both. Better history textbooks today discuss the systemic social and economic pressures that have influenced change, and the technological advances that contributed as well.[3] They also usually give Columbus, the man, a lot of attention, reinforcing his "great man" status. Even then, with the systems and great-man evidence side-by-side, the questions of creativity, sketched above, are often more implicit than explicit. This is, of course, where the teacher can enter the scene with assignments highlighting the question of the relation of a given individual to the historical systems in which the person lives and works. For the students, this line of analysis is more important than the debate over the character of a particular man from the fifteenth century. After all, they will not discover the New World but will participate in today's versions of those systems, which facilitate and apply many discoveries and new opportunities for better or worse.

16.3.2 Art Class

As previously noted, history examples are easy targets. The "great man" (usually men and usually white) views of creativity and history are closely aligned. The individualism and neophilia of the ideology of creativity is not just in the textbooks, and not just in history class, though. These views are deeply embedded in the ways we think about students and education. Consider an example from art class. If creativity happens anywhere, it should be in art, right? I regularly evaluate and consult to educational programs, and have worked with a number of excellent art programs. An experienced teaching artist in a highly respected program came to me concerned about a specific set of lessons she was teaching about architecture and community. She was exceptionally reflective about her own teaching and came to me to discuss the creativity of her students. In an activity she designed, third graders learned how

---

[3] For example, the chapter on the meeting of the Native American, European and African worlds in Houghton Mifflin's *The Americans* (Danzer et al. 2012) describes the social, economic and political conditions of these three civilizations in the fifteenth century. Attention is also given to naval technologies that allowed Europeans to undertake colonial expansion. There is even a boxed text juxtaposing positive and negative historical views of Columbus. At the same time Columbus is definitely the central focus of the changes that occurred. This balancing of systemic and individualistic views is a step in the right direction but also confusing to read. The description of European society makes Columbus seem like a common type of man of his times, looking for upward mobility in one of the only ways possible at the time – trade – when naval technologies made such navigation possible, nation states were rising competitively and his backers, the monarchs of Spain, were particularly ambitious. Then the pages and quotes devoted to just Columbus, as well as the point/counterpoint about his legacy, seem to indicate that he was, for better or worse, both extraordinary and *the* cause of the change.

to make block prints and then designed a print of a house. All of the block prints would be put on long sheets of paper to form the blocks of a city, like the communities the children knew in Brooklyn. The teaching artist was concerned that all of the house designs looked so much alike. Indeed, the students openly copied each other's designs. Should they not be more creative, producing different kinds of designs? How could she get them to be more creative?

In the real world, though, architecture goes through styles in which people influence one another and borrow from one another. An educated eye can look at a building and, usually, identify when it was built by the style of fenestration, the materials used, the decorative details and so on. Like other domains of knowledge, architecture is a social discourse in which practitioners influence one another as they build on, and borrow from history. Yes, each Victorian house, Brooklyn brownstone, Parisian apartment building, or Cape Cod cottage has its own specific distinguishing elements, but overall their *styles* rely on elements that the buildings have in common, borrowed from one another, taught and learned in schools of architecture. Even in postmodern architecture, which tends to take similar attitudes toward decoration and unexpected elements but not necessarily replicate forms, there were leaders (most prominently Venturi and Brown 1972; Venturi 1977) and followers – all doing creative work.

The point: instead of imploring each student to be original in relation to the other students in the class, the learning opportunity concerning creativity is to make the students aware of the processes by which *their style* of housing develops within the group – its antecedents in their experiences, the ways borrowing affects the style, as well as distinctive elements within the details of the designs. How is this small-scale creative system working, and how are individuals contributing to it? Who introduced specific elements? What inspired the ideas for those elements and how did they become part of the classroom style? (That discussion would include, of course, any designs that differ from the dominant style emerging in the class.) Why were some elements of design copied and others not? This kind of education helps students understand how actual creative systems work, how multiple people take on different roles in the process and how and why variations in style emerge. Most importantly, it gives students an experience of how to participate in – and contribute to – a creative system, as well as a framework for understanding that experience.

Again, this example highlights how pervasive the themes of individualism and neophilia are. This teaching artist was not some wild-eyed ideologue. She was simply working within the current ideology of creativity which is so often presented as simultaneously self-evident and scientifically based.

16.4 Potential Next Steps

How can any educators navigate such pervasive and powerful assumptions? Furthermore, might rejecting extreme individualism and the dichotomy of tradition and creativity move us toward social inflexibility and hyper-conformity, competitive disadvantage in international economics, an Orwellian dystopia and lives of despair? So much of the rhetoric coming out of the Cold War and justifying creativity research for the last 60+ years have implied such dire consequences. Despite all of the work of psychology and sociology, neither history nor individual lives have proven predictable. Even in the United States where individualist views of creativity have been well integrated into business and self-help discourses, today there is little reason to believe that America is immune to autocracy and international competition or that Americans suffer less alienation and depression as a result. Indeed, it is possible that the expectations of creativity as panacea could make things worse by deflecting attention from meaningful policy debates and casting life's persistent hardships as failures to recreate oneself.

But what are the alternatives? As it turns out, there are already resources within creativity research and educational discourse that point toward the necessarily uncertain next steps in moving the ideology of creativity to a place that is more supportive of education. Again, I am not claiming that any of these moves will eliminate ideology but that they can move us toward concepts of creativity can be more relevant to actual lives and to education.

16.4.1 Participatory Creativity

First, within the study of creativity new frameworks are emerging that emphasize complexity and participation as context for individual agency (Clapp 2017; Glăveanu 2010, 2014; Hanchett Hanson 2015). *The individual is not lost or denied*. Indeed, individual perspectives are crucial to creative processes. But neither is the individual wildly ideating in a social and material vacuum. These emerging perspectives do not, themselves, claim to be new. They are syntheses of older theoretical and empirical work on creativity, extensions of discourse rather than revolutions. They draw from well-established developmental theories of creative development (themselves extending the works of Vygotsky and Piaget), sociocultural approaches to creative system dynamics and distributed cognition views of the social, material and temporal distribution of thought. (For further discussion see the chapter I wrote with Edward Clapp in this volume). In spite of this traditional grounding, the participatory perspectives mark a turn in the evolution of creativity theory. They point toward…

- *The affordances for change provided by history and tradition* – ideas do not spring magically from the mind but come from complex interactions with the social and material environment. In other words, thinking is socially, materially and temporally distributed within its sociohistorical context. Creative producers (an alternative term to "creator" or "creative genius") build upon, recombine and apply to new contexts the received knowledge and practices of their times.
- *The many roles in the creative process* – many people contribute to the work, its evaluation and application. Teachers, collectors, reviewers, connoisseurs, gallery owners, editors, consumers and so on become part of the creative process. This is a realistic reorientation of the concept of creativity. When people do real creative work in the world, they are thinking about their inspirations, the current state of their discipline, what they want their work to mean and who will determine that meaning.

- ***Interactions with the material world*** – symbol manipulation in the head is only meaningful within the context of *actions* in the social and material world. Creativity is work (Wallace and Gruber 1989). Painters become painters by painting, writers by writing, researchers by researching. Yes, knowledge and thought in the purely cognitive sense is important but only *takes form* through interactions with the material world. Even the most basic creative thought is supported by material actors, such as sketchbooks, notebooks, computers, brushes, paints, laboratories and so on.
- ***The longer-term biography of the idea*** – framing inquiries into creativity as contributions to the ongoing development of even larger ideas foregrounds the historical context and antecedents of any given contribution, as well as the social and material processes for integrating the contribution. This technique is meant to put individual contributions into context and highlight the agency of the many individuals needed to bring about change. For example, as described in the chapter on participatory creativity in this volume, a teacher can frame a module as Henry Ford's use of the assembly line to revolutionize manufacturing or frame it as the history of the assembly line (biography of the idea) to which Ford was a contributor who applied the idea in a powerful way.

16.4.2 Teaching Complexity

Second, in relation to participatory theories of creativity, students need to be able to think about the workings of complex social and material systems. Here, creativity offers a distinct opportunity. Whereas common examples of complex systems, such as circuitry, traffic patterns or weather systems, might be familiar but still abstract, most student are already directly – and often passionately – participating in creative social systems. They already take up multiple roles as consumers and recommenders of music and movies, makers of youtube videos, students of music, critics of fashion, and so on. In so doing they are contributing to the complex processes of creative production, evaluation and dissemination. What a good entry point to help them become comfortable conceptualizing and analyzing complex systems!

Here, again, the goal is not new. Within education, there is growing focus on how to teach thinking about complexity. Research (Kuhn et al. 2015) indicates that, although the principles of simple causality are more or less innate in human development, thinking about complex systems with multiple causes and multiple effects often needs to be taught. Analyzing complex systems is listed in the often-cited twenty first century skills educational framework s (p21.org). State guidelines usually include provisions for analyses of complexity, although the complexity standards are not always prominent or clearly defined. Having some standards does not, of course, guarantee that the standards are sufficient or that they will lead to effectively teaching complex systems analysis.

There are also caveats to keep in mind. Remember the DIY example cited at the beginning of this chapter where project-based learning and scholarship were juxtaposed. Project-based educational approaches can be very helpful in teaching complex systems. Without the "scholarly" work, though, these approaches can fall prey to *ad hoc* pragmatism. Students may learn what they need to for a given project but never get a larger view of (a) how what they are learning fits into broader domains of knowledge and (b) how and when to transfer the principles learned in one complex system to another.

16.4.3 *Studying Creative Lives*

So far, the emphasis has been on techniques that move the focus to the wide range of social and material actors, rather than the sole individual. The opposite approach – re-examining the famous individual – can be equally, if not more, powerful. A personal reflection here. One of the courses I teach is on case study method, using an expanded version of the evolving systems approach developed by Gruber and his associates (Gruber and Davis 1988; Gruber and Wallace 1999; Wallace and Gruber 1989). Students develop an extensive study of a famous individual's creative development. Each student chooses the person he or she will study and becomes immersed in that person's work and life story. From the beginning students are told that the method is designed to analyze creativity as a form of work in which individuals organize resources toward their emerging sense of purpose. That work is always specific to the sociohistorical context, and involves many people and material resources. It is *not* dependent on particular types of personalities or cognitive traits or universal processes. There is no trick to learn, but rather a developmental process to understand, a particular process that led to a unique point of view in a specific context. In spite of that presentation of the task, inevitably, about two-thirds of the way through the semester the students become agitated, and someone usually blurts out "I don't think creativity exists!" It is that hard for the students to give up the idea that creativity is either a magical trait to be identified or a formulaic process to be copied. After this short panic, everyone gets back to work and, in the end, most students say that the course is transformative. It changes how they think about creativity and development, as well as individual agency and social systems. It also gives a sense of empowerment – they see how many kinds of people can contribute with long-term work, if they know their questions and resources well and remain attuned to their own emerging sense of purpose.

There is no reason to wait until graduate school for these lessons. From at least middle school on, students are reading biographies of many of the same people that my graduate students are studying. True, such in-depth biographical analysis may not be explicitly written into curriculum standards, but it does not usually stand in opposition to them either. Many years of working in education have taught me that good educators are very creative.

16.5 Concluding Reflections: Dialogic Possibilities

The analysis of the ideology of creativity offered here is not a defense of all traditional education nor a retreat from the need to teach creativity. On the contrary, this is a call to address creativity more deeply in education. Nor is this a call for revolution. (The goal is not to overcome neophilia with something entirely new.)

16.5.1 Creativity Grounded in Education

The view of creativity advocated here is more complex than many concepts of creativity but arguably more realistic and, therefore, relevant to education. There are a few core premises. First, useful ideas do not come from getting outside of conceptual boxes, but reorganizing existing resources in processes of work and development over time. Education is, therefore, important. Second, received knowledge and socially recognized ideas and practices (traditions) are the alpha and omega of creativity – the resources that go into the work and the evaluation of the ultimate work. Third because of the dynamic nature of these social systems, meanings and practices inevitably change over time. Even the most orthodox traditions evolve, and many social practices are quite pliable. Therefore, the creative person does not have to lay siege to current ideas and practices but choose how to *participate* in change (help accelerate, slow, redirect etc.). To do so the student has to understand the current practices and meanings, causes and outcomes, well. Again, education comes to the fore. Finally, creativity occurs in distributed social and material systems over time. Individuals learn to take up many roles contributing to those systems. School itself is, thus, important. Whatever the learning formats and technologies, interactions are crucial – interactions among students, between students and teachers, between students and the world (technologies, artistic media and so on), as well as among teachers and administrators.

16.5.2 Ongoing Conversations

Within creativity research, the broader, participatory view advocated here has emerged from the foundations laid by previous approaches. Furthermore, dialogue between the older and newer views needs to continue. Most of the practices of the older, more reductive approaches can still have value even though the newer frameworks may shift how we see that value (Hanchett Hanson 2013). For example, based on the idea of divergent thinking, brainstorming was conceived as a way of magnifying ideational capacities through a group process. At first glance, it would seem that this widely used practice is in keeping with the principles of participatory creativity. After all, a group is producing the ideas, not an individual. Then decades of research that showed that brainstorming groups actually do not work that way. (In experiments, the same number of people working individually almost always come up with more, better ideas than the brainstorming groups, Nijstad et al. 2003). Those findings might seem to argue against participatory views.

Just making a group process out of a purely ideation-focused concept of creativity does not make it participatory, however. The development and organization of the distributed thought processes are not taken into account. How the individual contributes to the group and how the group contributes to the individual's point of view are crucial aspects of the participatory views. Asking a group of strangers to ideate on a random problem (the experimental condition) is not. In real-world practice, though, brainstorming can be used to facilitate participatory creativity. Indeed, it usually does. Repeated brainstorming sessions over time in an organization or classroom can help the group *develop* understanding of the knowledge and viewpoints of each member, build a sense of connection and commitment among the members, prime the group to tackle new topics and build a sense of excitement and motivation (Baer and Garrett 2010; Hanchett Hanson 2013; Starko 2014). All of these contribute to the recognition and organization of resources for creative purposes.

This is just one example of how dialogue between the older and newer views can work. The more interesting questions will be, no doubt, more difficult and less obvious. For example, how to think about, value and accommodate exceptional abilities? Participatory views move us away from unreasonable rhetoric of making everyone a creative genius, but what about the… actual genius? How to manage such students or coworkers or social outliers is still undertheorized in the participatory views. Pushing back on questions like this is the crucial importance of dialogues of old and new in moving forward.

The approach advocated here is not revolutionary within education either. Indeed, almost everything discussed above is advocated and/or covered in part by most of today's curriculum standards. Making sense of the application of those standards in the everyday interactions that constitute education will also be a conversation, and not necessarily an easy one. Here we add the many voices of educational systems to the creativity theory dialogues. Complicating the conversation will be the ideological remnants of older but powerful twin pillars of creativity as ideology: extreme individualism and neophilia. As shown in the art class example, these assumptions can be pervasive and subtle.

Indeed, the key point here is not the recommendations. Yes, adopting the framework of participatory creativity, ensuring that analysis of complex systems is taught effectively and asking students to study famous creative individuals with a critical lens – these would all seem to be logical steps. More important than any specific recommendation, however, is awareness of how the ideology of creativity functions in education. Becoming attuned to the issues and beginning to discuss them are the first, crucial steps. A form of creativity itself, this *work* will have to emerge from many contributions and complex interactions, just as described by the participatory theorists.

References

Amabile, T. M., Colins, M. A., Conti, R., Phillips, E., Picariello, M., Ruscio, J., & Whitney, D. (1996). *Creativity in context*. Boulder: Westview Press/Perseus Books Group.

Anderson, M. D. (2015, October 12). Rethinking history class on Columbus Day. *The Atlantic*. https://www.theatlantic.com/education/archive/2015/10/columbus-day-school-holiday/409984/. Accessed 25 Dec 2017.

Baer, J., & Garrett, T. (2010). Teaching for creativity in an era of content standards and accountability. In R. A. Beghetto & J. C. Kaufman (Eds.), *Nurturing creativity in the classroom* (pp. 6–23). Cambridge: Cambridge University Press.

Beghetto, R. A. (2016). Creativity and conformity: A paradoxical relationship. In J. A. Plucker (Ed.), *Creativity and innovation: Current understandings and debates*. Waco: Prufrock.

Clapp, E. P. (2017). *Participatory creativity: Introducing access and equity to the creative classroom*. New York: Routledge.

Corazza, G. E. (2016). Potential originality and effectiveness: The dynamic definition of creativity. *Creativity Research Journal, 28*(3), 258–267.

Cropley, D. H., Cropley, A. J., Kaufman, J. C., & Runco, M. A. (Eds.). (2010). *The dark side of creativity*. Cambridge: Cambridge University Press.

Csikszentmihalyi, M. (1997). *Creativity: Flow and the psychology of discovery and innovation*. New York: HarperPerennial (Original work published 1996).

Csikszentmihalyi, M. (1999). Implications of a systems perspective for the study of creativity. In R. J. Sternberg (Ed.), *Handbook of creativity* (pp. 313–315). Cambridge: Cambridge University Press.

Danzer, G. A., Klor de Alva, J. J., Krieger, L. S., Wilson, L. E., & Woloch, N. (2012). *The Americans*. New York: Houghton Mifflin Harcourt.

Foucault, M. (1998) What is an author? In J. D. Faubion (Ed.)., P. Rabinow (series Ed.), *Essential works of Foucault 1954–1984*, Volume 2: Aesthetics, method and epistemology (pp. 204–22). New York: The New Press (Original lecture in French 1969).

Frauenfelder, M. (2010, October). Technology: School for hackers: The do-it-yourself movement revives learning by doing. *Atlantic*, p. 44.

Freedan, M. (2003). *Ideology: A short introduction*. Oxford: Oxford University Press.

Glăveanu, V. P. (2010). Creativity as cultural participation. *Journal for the Theory of Social Behaviour, 41*, 48–67.

Glăveanu, V. P. (2014). *Thinking through creativity and culture: Toward an integrated model*. New Brunswick: Transaction Publishers.

Gruber, H. E. (1981). *Darwin on man: A psychological study of scientific creativity* (2nd ed.). Chicago: University of Chicago Press.

Gruber, H. E. (1989). Creativity and human survival. In D. B. Wallace & H. E. Gruber (Eds.), *Creative people at work* (pp. 278–287). Oxford: Oxford University Press.

Gruber, H. E. (2005). In H. E. Gruber & K. Bödeker (Eds.), *Creativity, psychology and the history of science*, Boston studies in the philosophy of science. Dordrecht: Springer.

Gruber, H. E., & Davis, S. N. (1988). Inching our way up Mount Olympus: The evolving systems approach to creative thinking. In R. J. Sternberg (Ed.), *The nature of creativity: Contemporary psychological perspectives* (pp. 243–270). Cambridge: Cambridge University Press.

Gruber, H. E., & Wallace, D. B. (1999). The case study method and evolving systems approach for understanding unique creative people at work. In R. J. Sternberg (Ed.), *Handbook of creativity* (pp. 93–115). Cambridge: Cambridge University Press.

Guilford, J. P. (1950). Creativity. *American Psychologist, 5*, 444–454.

Hanchett Hanson, M. (2005). Irony and conflict: Lessons from George Bernard Shaw's wartime journey. In D. B. Wallace (Ed.), *Education, arts and morality: Creative journeys*. New York: Kluwer Academic.

Hanchett Hanson, M. (2013). Creativity theory and educational practice: Why all the fuss? In J. B. Jones & L. J. Flint (Eds.), *The creative imperative: School librarians and teachers cultivating curiosity together* (pp. 19–37). Santa Barbara: ABC-CLIO.

Hanchett Hanson, M. (2015). *Worldmaking: Psychology and the ideology of creativity*. London: Palgrave Macmillan.

Hanchett Hanson, M. (in press). Tragedies of actualization. In V. P. Glăveanu(Ed.), *The creativity reader*. Oxford University Press, Oxford.

John-Steiner, V. (2015). Creative engagement across the lifespan. In V. P. Glăveanu, A. Gillespie, & J. Valsiner (Eds.), *Rethinking creativity: Contributions from social and cultural psychology* (pp. 31–44). New York: Routledge.

Kaufman, J. C., & Beghetto, R. A. (2009). Beyond big and little: The four C model of creativity. *Review of General Psychology, 13*, 1–12.

Kuhn, D., Ramsey, S., & Arvidsson, T. S. (2015). Developing multivariable thinkers. *Cognitive Development, 35*, 92–110.

Mach, A. (2011, October 10). Christopher Columbus: Five things you thought you knew about the explorer. *The Christian Science Monitor*. https://www.csmonitor.com/USA/2011/1010/Christopher-Columbus-Five-things-you-thought-you-knew-about-the-explorer/MYTH-Columbus-set-out-to-prove-the-earth-was-round. Accessed 20 Dec 2017.

Mannheim, K. (1954). *Ideology and utopia*. Wirth L, Shils E (trans). New York: Harcourt, Brace & Company (Original work published in German 1929. English translation first published 1936).

Marx, K. (2010). *Das kapital*. Pacific Publishing Studio. (Original published in 1867).

Marx K, Engels F (1998) The German ideology, including theses on Feuerebach (Great books in philosophy). Prometheus Books, Amherst (Original published in German, 1845).

Maslow, A. H. (1993). *The farther reaches of human nature*. New York: Penguin Books (Original work published 1971).

Mason, J. H. (2003). *The value of creativity: The origins and emergence of a modern belief*. Burlington: Ashgate Publishing.

May, R. (1989). The problem of evil: An open letter to Carl Rogers. In H. Kirschenbaum & V. L. Henderson (Eds.), *Carl Rogers: Dialogues* (pp. 239–251). Boston: Houghton Mifflin.

Moran, S. (2010). The roles of creativity in society. In J. C. Kaufman & R. J. Sternberg (Eds.), *The Cambridge handbook of creativity* (pp. 74–90). Cambridge: Cambridge University Press.

Moran, S., & John-Steiner, V. (2003). Vygotsky's contemporary contribution to the dialectic of development and creativity. In M. Marschark (Ed.), *Creativity and development* (pp. 61–90). Oxford: Oxford University Press.

Moran, S., Cropley, D., & Kaufman, J. C. (Eds.). (2014). *The ethics of creativity*. New York: Palgrave Macmillan.

Nijstad, B. A., Diehl, M., & Stroebe, W. (2003). Cognitive stimulation and interference in idea-generating groups. In P. B. Paulus & B. A. Nijstad (Eds.), *Group creativity: Innovation through collaboration* (pp. 137–159). Oxford: Oxford University Press.

Plucker, J., Beghetto, R. A., & Dow, G. (2004). Why isn't creativity more important to educational psychologists? Potentials, pitfalls, and future directions in creativity research. *Educational Psychologist, 39*, 83–96.

Pope, R. (2005). *Creativity: Theory, history, practice*. New York: Routledge.

Raunig, G., Ray, G., & Wuggenig U (eds) (2011) *Critique of creativity: Precarity, subjectivity and resistance in the 'creative industries.'* Mayflybooks, pp. 119–131. http://libros.metabiblioteca.org/handle/001/226. Accessed on 20 Dec 2017.

Rehn, A., & De Cock, C. (2009). Deconstructing creativity. In T. Rickards, M. A. Runco, & S. Moger (Eds.), *The Routledge companion to creativity* (pp. 222–231). New York: Routledge.

Rogers, C. R. (1954). Toward a theory of creativity. *Review of General Semantics, 11*(4), 249–260.

Rogers, C. R. (1969). In E. Charles (Ed.), *Freedom to learn*. Columbus: Merrill Publishing.

Rogers, C. R. (1989). *On becoming a person: A therapist's view of psychotherapy*. New York: Houghton Mifflin (Original work published 1961).

Runco, M. A., & Albert, R. S. (2010). Creativity research: A historical view. In J. C. Kaufman & R. J. Sternberg (Eds.), *The Cambridge handbook of creativity* (pp. 3–19). Cambridge: Cambridge University Press.

Russell, J. B. (1991). *Inventing the flat earth: Columbus and modern historians*. Santa Barbara: Praeger.

Sawyer, R. K. (2012). *Explaining creativity: The science of human innovation*. Oxford: Oxford University Press.

Shafer, L., & Walsh, B. (2017, October 5). *The Columbus Day problem*. Harvard Graduate School of Education. https://www.gse.harvard.edu/news/uk/17/10/columbus-day-problem. Accessed on 20 Dec 2017.

Starko, A. J. (2014). *Creativity in the classroom: Schools of curious delight* (5th ed.). New York: Routledge.

Stein, M. I. (1953). Creativity and culture. *The Journal of Psychology, 36*, 311–322.

Torrance, E. P. (2002). *The manifesto: A guide to developing a creative career*. Westport: Ablex Publishing.

Venturi, R. (1977). *Complexity and contradiction in architecture* (2nd ed.). New York: The Museum of Modern Art.

Venturi, R., & Brown, D. S. (1972). *Learning from Las Vegas*. Cambridge, MA: The MIT Press.

Vonnegut, K. (1990). *Hocus pocus*. New York: Berkeley Publishing Group.

Vygotsky, L. S. (2004). Imagination and creativity in childhood. *Journal of Russian and East European Psychology, 42*(1):7–97. (Original published 1930) http://lchc.ucsd.edu/mca/Mail/xmcamail.2008_03.dir/att-0189/Vygotsky__Imag___Creat_in_Childhood.pdf. Accessed on 20 Dec 2017.

Wallace, D. B., & Gruber, H. E. (Eds.). (1989). *Creative people at work*. Oxford: Oxford University Press.

Weiner, R. P. (2000). *Creativity and beyond: Cultures, values and change*. Albany: State University of New York.

Weisberg, R. W. (2006). *Creativity: Understanding innovation in problem solving, science, invention and the arts*. Hoboken: Wiley.

Weisberg, R. (2011). Frank Lloyd Wright's Fallingwater: A case study in inside-the-box creativity. *Creativity Research Journal, 23*, 296–311.

Weisberg, R. W., & Hanchett Hanson, M. (2013). Inside-the-box: An expertise-based approach to creativity in education. In J. B. Jones & L. J. Flint (Eds.), *The creative imperative: School librarians and teachers cultivating curiosity together* (pp. 71–84). Santa Barbara: ABC-CLIO.

Chapter 17
The Dynamic Universal Creativity Process

Giovanni Emanuele Corazza

Abstract In this chapter we introduce the Dynamic Universal Creativity Process (DUCP), defined as the active ensemble of all creativity episodes in the evolution of our cosmos. It is shown how this construct descends naturally through a shift in the leading perspective in creativity studies: from a focus on static creative achievements to the consideration of dynamic processes, which even transcend their agents. Four mechanisms for the dynamic extension in time and space of creativity episodes are presented: continued exploration, concatenation, estimation, and exaptation. The concepts of wide-sense and strict-sense creativity are introduced to allow the consideration of four layers of existence in the DUCP: material, biological, psycho-social, and artificial. The theoretical and practical implications of these definitions are discussed, also in view of contributing to the mending of the cultural fracture between science and the arts, under the flag of creativity studies. A description of the creativity mechanisms characterizing the material, biological, psycho-social, and artificial layers is provided, highlighting intra- and inter-layer concatenation potential and achievements. Among other concepts, complex systems, biological evolution, bipedalism, neoteny, individual and social mind-based behaviour, as well as artificial intelligence, all find an integrated place in the framework of creativity studies, under the DUCP umbrella. Implications on educational systems of the future are drafted in the final discussion.

17.1 Introduction

We live in a world of constant change, and there is a widespread feeling in society that the pace of this change is constantly increasing (Corazza et al. 2010; Feather 2013; Rosa 2003). Taking on an anthropocentric view, the human species should collectively be considered the prime actor in this accelerating evolution, which is

---

G. E. Corazza (✉)
DEI Department, Marconi Institute for Creativity, University of Bologna, Bologna, Italy
e-mail: giovanni.corazza@unibo.it

© Springer Nature Switzerland AG 2019
R. A. Beghetto, G. E. Corazza (eds.), *Dynamic Perspectives on Creativity*,
Creativity Theory and Action in Education 4,
https://doi.org/10.1007/978-3-319-99163-4_17

first and foremost cultural and economic, but it is also heavily affecting the environment, in both its geo-physical and biological dimensions. Considering the psychology of individuals and the sociology of their relationships, this enormous power for change can arguably be attributed to the creativity and anticipation powers of the human mind (Corazza 2017a), not at all in isolation but deeply intertwined with the fundamental human predispositions and abilities for communicating, learning, and for social life in general (Glăveanu 2011). Indeed, researchers in cultural evolution have recognized that creativity is necessary to explain the exponential growth of cumulative culture (Enquist et al. 2008). Even though creativity has always existed in our species, the current evolution in society calls for new interdisciplinary approaches and efforts to transform creativity studies into a self-standing scientific discipline, with important bearing upon human well-being, and with impact on developmental and educational matters (Corazza 2017b). This chapter should be considered a contribution in that direction, focusing more on ultimate than on proximal questions (Alessi 1992).

Our discussion begins by considering the definition for creativity. While the debate on the selection of requirements for creativity is still open (e.g., see Martin and Wilson 2017, and references therein), the so-called standard definition for creativity foresees that this phenomenon requires both originality and effectiveness (Runco and Jaeger 2012). In other words, for an entity to contribute to the growth of cumulative culture it must be original, i.e. novel, authentic and non-obvious, as well as effective in introducing new forms of (possibly domain-specific) value, such as utility or aesthetics. However, as discussed in (Corazza 2016), the possession of the attributes of originality and effectiveness actually define a creative *achievement*, i.e. the conditions for which the outcome of a creative process succeeds in being recognized as creative, at least by a group of people in a certain environment (Stein 1953). But creativity is a journey, and creative efforts are not always met with success: on the contrary, challenging the state-of-the-art, exploring new avenues, trying to solve ill-defined problems, engaging in new artistic compositions, or in general trying to contribute to the growth of cumulative culture invariably opens up the space for failed trials, frustration, and difficult interactions with an inside dialogue and an outside world which are quick to judge and reject. Recognizing that this blue side of the creativity medal is not only real but actually very important in the process, especially in the pursuit of developing creativity in educational settings (Beghetto 2010), a *dynamic definition for creativity* has been proposed (Corazza 2016): creativity requires a *potential* for originality and effectiveness. A single word carries the difference that makes the difference: *potential*. The higher the potential (which depends on task at hand, personal characteristics of all those involved in the creative act, goals, motivation, environmental characteristics, resources and blocks, etcetera), the higher the level of creative activity and the chance to arrive at one or more creative achievements, which are however never guaranteed *a priori*. In this framework, when out of the creative process a successful product emerges, the potential is realized and an instance of *creative achievement* occurs. On the contrary, when there is no outcome, or the outcome is rejected by internal or external assessment, it is possible to recognize an instance of creative *inconclusiveness*, from which very important lessons can be learned; and given that sufficient motivation and resources are still available, the process is not concluded but pushed forward in the pursuit of the original or modified objectives. Previous investment should not be wasted (Sternberg and Lubart 1991), and in fact it is well known that the history of artistic and scientific genius was paved by persistence (Albert 1983; Edison 1948; Eysenck 1995; Galton 1869; Simonton 1984).

It is important to underline how the introduction of potential *inside* the definition of creativity has the power to transform the framework from an analysis of static attributes (originality and effectiveness) to the description of a dynamic process characterized by the possible prospective to deliver items with the desired attributes. This, which is in line with dynamic approaches to cognition (Beer 2000), constitutes a very clear and distinct shift in emphasis from product to process, using the classic terminology of Rohdesian tradition (Rhodes 1961), and it leads us to pursue the understanding of the profound, pervasive, and never-ending nature of the creativity process: this is the aim of the present work. In pursuing this goal, we will encounter the definition of creativity episodes and their mechanisms for extension in both time and space, the concepts of concatenation potential and evolutionary tree of creativity, to culminate in the discussion of the dynamic universal creativity process and its layers: material, biological, psycho-social, and artificial. While creativity in the strict-sense only pertains to the psycho-social layer, we will discuss the theoretical and practical reasons why it is useful to integrate also other layers in a universal wide-sense view of creativity. From a metaphysical perspective, our intention is to advance on the path traced by Alfred North Whitehead in his cosmology (1978/1929), addressing the ontological question by establishing that *creativity existed since the origin of our universe, and potentially permeates all of our universe.* We believe that the consideration of wide-sense creativity alongside with strict-sense creativity helps reducing the dramatic divarication between science and the arts, which has plagued our culture for centuries.

We start by observing the difficulty, which turns out to be an impossibility, to delimit the creative process with fixed boundaries.

17.2 Creativity Process: A Never Ending Story

Assuming a local, or microscopic, perspective, the creativity process can be shown to contain a minimum of three elements (Corazza and Agnoli 2015): (a) gathering and structuring of input elements (goal and relevant information); (b) generation of outcomes (ideation); (c) estimation and verification of the effects (assessment and implementation). Many additions and variations would be possible around this core, but this is not the point here. What matters is that it would seem possible to delimit the start and the end of the process quite precisely, both in time and in space, as well as in the involved actors. But taking on a global perspective, a macroscopic approach that considers all possible instances of creativity, it becomes apparent, perhaps surprisingly, that the creativity process cannot have a clean slate start nor a unique end, anywhere at anytime. The observation of a time-limited instance remains a very useful simplification, but it always amounts to a form of reduction. And this interconnectivity between creative instances may in fact be one of the *strongest reasons for advocating a dynamic approach in creativity studies*. Four mechanisms are identified below that lead to the extended development of the creativity process in the time and space domains.

First, and most obvious, is the case of *continued exploration*, which can be pursued in case the creative agent (or agents) is not yet satisfied by the achieved outcomes (even though outside observers would think that the results are already of great value, as was evident for example in the correspondence between Vincent Van Gogh and his brother Theo; Van Gogh 1978) or, more often, in case of creative inconclusiveness (Corazza 2016): no result of value has been obtained yet, exploration should continue, other solutions should be tried out, content improvement or better aesthetic representation would be necessary, and so on. Upon reflection, it is clear that in principle there is no intrinsic and fixed boundary to delimit the amount of resources that can be invested in continued exploration during a creative task.

Second, it is very interesting to realize that, even in the presence of significant, satisfying, and presently acclaimed creative achievements, the creativity process will still continue, in a very natural sense: in fact, the process always includes the *estimation* of the impact of its represented outcomes; but the evaluation of the originality and effectiveness of an outcome is bound to dynamically change over time and space (Corazza 2016; Glăveanu 2014), depending on what can be defined as the cultural state of those who are confronted and interact with the product itself. Given the fact that the process contains the impact over time of its products, both within and outside the domain of relevance, it follows that the creative process can go on well beyond the production of its outcomes: every creative instance has the potential to generate long waves of cultural interaction.

Third, as a consequence of cultural communication, the outcome of a creative task might become an ingredient of yet another creative activity, carried out by the same or different agent. In a metaphoric sense, creative products can be thought of as stairs in a ladder: each one is important but only as an element of the whole, without which the function and the overall purpose would be lost. And for any achievement of today, we can identify the fundamental elements introduced by previous generations that are the essential enablers for this progress. In the accumulation of culture, serial and parallel *concatenation* links can be identified between different local instances of the creativity process. These concatenations are not accidental but necessary, so much so that it is impossible to truly understand the creativity of today without considering the creativity of yesterday, and therefore of the day before, and so on indefinitely.

Fourth, and perhaps most surprising, it is important to realize that the potential for originality and effectiveness of an outcome is not limited nor restricted by the intentions or goals that characterized the process that generated the product itself. In the ensuing dynamics, *the very same product might acquire a totally new function*, clearly distinct from the original goals, and thus become a completely different creative achievement, which in some cases can even be seminal in giving life to a new branch of knowledge. This phenomenon may be identified as *exaptation*, following a terminology introduced by Gould and Vrba (1982) in evolutionary biology, to indicate those features that in the present enhance the fitness of an organism, but that were not historically selected by nature for their current role. The classic example is that of feathers, which evolved in certain variations of dinosaurs (e.g. the Archaeopteryx) for thermal regulation, and later on exapted for flight by birds (Gould and Vrba 1982). The phenomenon of exaptation has been shown to be more a norm than an exception not only in biology but also in many technological fields (Andriani and Cattani 2016; Garud et al. 2016). A paradigmatic case is given by the business evolution of Corning, which in the seventies of the twentieth century exapted the technology previously used for glass production to develop optical fibers, turning its consolidated, standard venture into a cutting-edge, high-technology firm (Cattani 2005, 2006). Exaptation points to the fact that it is effectively impossible for anyone to foresee all the possible future implications of an innovative idea. For this very reason, we introduced the term *estimation* in place of judgment or assessment of creative ideas in (Corazza 2016): estimation is an open-ended and dynamic step in the creativity process.

Table 17.1 recaps these four fundamental mechanisms identified for the dynamic extension of the development of a creativity instance.

From this discussion, agreement should follow on the fact that the dynamic process representing the creativity phenomenon from a macroscopic perspective cannot really be considered to be definitely concluded at any fixed time instant: it can certainly be locally interrupted because it was just an educational exercise or a test, or because of exhaustion of resources or motivation in the case of creative inconclusiveness, or because of reaching sufficient satisfaction in the case of a creative achievement; but the interruption is never an intrinsic property of the process. Surprisingly, this is independent from the fact that the outcomes of a creative process

Table 17.1 Mechanisms for the extended development of a creativity process instance

Mechanism for extension	Description
Continued exploration	All creativity processes involve the possibility for different outcomes, with unprestatable multiplicity and variable degrees of originality and effectiveness. Exploration of this space of possibilities can continue indefinitely, in spite of failures or successes occurred during the search.
Estimation of creative outcomes	The outcomes of a creativity process must be evaluated for their originality and effectiveness: there can be no final judgment by anyone, but only an estimation that depends on time, space and culture. Estimation extends dynamically throughout the cultural lifetime of the outcome.
Concatenation	Any outcome of a creative process has predecessors and successors, containing inherently both traces of past creative instances and the possibility to become an ingredient of a subsequent or parallel creativity instance, as part of a concatenation of creativity episodes.
Exaptation	The outcome of a creative process may subsequently acquire new functionalities and purposes, possibly completely different from those that drove the originating process.

are generated and exist (and that they are possibly exploited for their utility): the process can be carried on irrespectively. On the other hand, for the practical purposes of description, it is useful to enucleate an instance whereby an agent or agents define a goal, enact a creativity process instance, produce outcomes, and possibly enjoy a creative achievement as judged by themselves, or by fellow peers, or by experts and judges. Let's identify this instance as a *creativity episode*. In this view, when models and frameworks for the creativity process have been proposed (e.g., Corazza and Agnoli 2015; Kaufman and Baer 2004; Mumford et al. 1991; Sternberg 2006; Wallas 1926), it can be stated that they fulfilled the goal of describing with variable levels of detail the development of *a single creativity episode*, i.e. from a microscopic perspective. On the other hand, due to the fundamental dynamicity of the phenomenon, these episodes are never effectively concluded nor disjoint, as discussed above. In Fig. 17.1 a graphical representation of a creativity episode with its relevant mechanisms for dynamic extension is drawn.

The input to the creativity episode is represented in general as a concatenation to previous knowledge, excluding creation ex-nihilo. Previous knowledge is of course consolidated in culture and exchanged through social learning, but we underline here that its origin can in any case be ascribed to some past creativity episode, to which current creativity episodes are conceptually concatenated. Continued exploration forms essentially an iterative loop on the episode, which can persist irrespective of the fact that either achievement or inconclusiveness occur; bidirectional dynamic interaction with the environment (including concatenation with parallel creativity episodes) is always present to influence the development of the episode under observation; three further mechanisms are then envisaged as extensions in the time and space dimensions of a creativity episode: (a) estimation of the value and originality of the episode's outcomes, which can lead to dynamic appreciation/criticism across time and cultures; (b) concatenation of this episode into future creativity episodes (either through its outcomes, its methodologies, or simply by information exchange); (c) exaptation of the outcomes for new and unpredictable purposes, with no appreciable change to the ideas/products themselves. Clearly, as

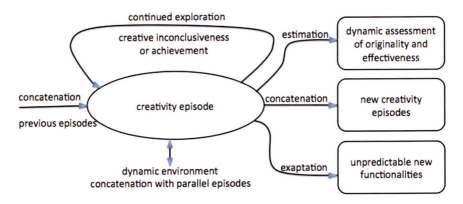

Fig. 17.1 A creativity episode and its possible extension mechanisms

it was argued that the subdivision into creativity episodes can be somewhat arbitrary, it follows that the boundary between two interconnected episodes can most often be debatable: it is in fact a matter of modelling. Perhaps, an identifiable discontinuity can be related to a change in the agents involved in the episode; but even this case can have exceptions, for example considering diverse teams collaborating on research and innovation focused on the same technology.

A crucial point should be made here: *none of the foreseen extension mechanisms should be interpreted as producing cause-effect relationships with creative achievement*. In fact, if there were a direct cause-effect relationship between a mechanism and the subsequent outcomes, the originality element of the products would irremediably be lost. Therefore, the extension mechanisms only provide a *potential* for future achievements, but no certainty. In particular, the availability of past creativity episodes provides a *concatenation potential* for further achievements, which is reminiscent of the *adjacent possible* concept by Stuart Kauffman (2016); but this concatenation potential cannot be ascribed of causing those achievements. Originality emerges out of the ingredients provided by the concatenation with extant cultural elements, but it cannot be reduced to them. If it could, the process would entail induction or deduction, but not creativity.

Let's focus now onto the main consequence of this section: accepting the proposition that the creativity process does not have an intrinsic end, irrespective of the fact that the agents involved can and do change over time and space, all creativity episodes can conceptually be concatenated and concur to form an overall process. *The creativity process appears to transcend its actors*, or in other words *all actors are contributing to one collective process*. This realization leads us to pose a number of ultimate questions: What is the nature of this unified creativity process? Can it be identified as a universal entity? Can its origin be traced? What is its role in our cosmos?

17.3 The Dynamic Universal Creativity Process

While a great number of scientific articles address the definition of a creativity episode (see for example Corazza 2016; Martin and Wilson 2017; Mayer 1999; Parkhurst 1999; Runco and Jaeger 2012; Simonton 2012; Weisberg 2015), this is likely to be the first proposal for a definition of the *dynamic universal creativity process* (DUCP), as follows:

> *The active ensemble of all creativity episodes in the course of cosmic evolution.*

Several comments are in order to justify the choice of the terms used in this attempt for a DUCP definition. First, the ensemble of all creativity episodes should be intended as a tree-shaped set that grows throughout history, containing items that are linked together either directly (through adjacent concatenation, exaptation, estimation) or indirectly (through common ancestors and remote interaction). In other words, this DUCP definition implies that even considering creativity episodes with goals and outcomes that appear to be completely unrelated, by going back in time it should always be possible to find a common ancestor. In this sense, the ensemble of all episodes can be thought of as an "*evolutionary tree of creativity.*" We will return on the ontological problem of the origin, or root, of this tree, and its cosmologic implications. But why is this ensemble "active"? Essentially, this is due to the fact that it is virtually impossible to take a permanent picture of this ensemble, in the sense that any two pictures taken at different times will always be significantly different, not only for the new additions, but also observing the past. This fundamental attribute of the evolutionary tree of creativity is due to the process dynamics, through its mechanisms of continued exploration, concatenation, estimation, and exaptation: as an example, once the outcomes of an episode are linked to a new creativity episode, the estimation of the former is also actively modified, by acquiring new values, new interpretations, and new impact. In other words, a present time creativity episode will actively lead to modifications in a past creativity episode. The same applies to parallel (contemporaneous) episodes: knowing that other agents are working creatively in a specific area actively modifies the process under consideration. This requires that inter-episode communication takes place at some stage, or that posthumous interconnection is created by those analyzing the relevant subject. The active ensemble of all creativity episodes is therefore a live tree, dynamically interconnecting past, present, as well as future elements of the universal creativity process, and producing the exponentially growing accumulation of culture.

But why is there a need in the DUCP definition to extend the tree span to the entire course of cosmic evolution, well beyond the boundaries of human and animal evolution? This is a very delicate step, which requires careful consideration. As many philosophers would argue, creativity appears to require intention, understanding, communication and judgment, and as such only a species capable of those constructs could be the agent of proper episodes of this phenomenon. For example, on this page we find the work of Berys Gaut (2010), who states (p. 1040): "Creativity is a property of agents, not of mere things or plants. […] The kinds of action that are creative are ones that exhibit at least a relevant purpose (in not being purely accidental), some degree of understanding (not using merely mechanical search procedures), a degree of judgment […] and an evaluative ability directed to the task at hand." While we agree with Gaut that this position describes creativity in a strict sense, we still want to be open to other wider sense forms, if they turn out to be useful in pragmatist terms. Possibly, the widest appreciation of the creativity phenomenon is the one proposed by Alfred North Whitehead, who in his famous work "Process and Reality" (1978/1929), delineates a cosmologic theory in which creativity is the ultimate metaphysical principle (p. 21): "Creativity is the universal of universals, characterizing ultimate matter of fact. It is the ultimate principle by which the many, which are the universe disjunctively, become the one actual occasion, which is the universe conjunctively. It lies in the nature of things that the many enter into complex unity." Clearly, in Whitehead's view there is no need for explicit intentionality, as creativity is intrinsic in nature, instantiated moment by moment and thus forming ("creating") actuality. In this wide-sense perspective, all episodes that have a potential to generate elements showing attributes of originality and effectiveness in our universe qualify as proper elements of the DUCP. By accepting this wide-sense view on creativity, the need to consider the entire evolution of our cosmos in the definition of DUCP descends directly. This entails the acceptance of a much greater variety of episodes inside the creativity realm. But before we proceed, let's ask ourselves if is this truly useful, from both theoretical and practical perspectives.

Considering first the theoretical perspective of creativity studies, the benefit in taking a wide-sense view on creativity should be searched in its resonance with existing movements towards the unification of all disciplines of knowledge. In this direction, it is possible to refer to the work of Gregg Henriques regarding the so-called Tree of Knowledge (ToK) and the theoretical unification of the field of psychology (Henriques 2003, 2011), whereby an integrated epistemological view is presented as based on four layers: matter (the domain of physical sciences), life (the domain of biology), mind (the domain of psychology), and culture (the domain of social sciences). Each layer is characterized by growing levels of complexity. Interestingly, Henriques points out that each layer is fundamentally based on the layers underneath, yet it cannot be reduced to them. For example, in moving from matter to life, Henriques notes (2003, p. 158): "Although genes are coordinated populations of molecules, individual molecules are not "small" genes. Genes are irreducible points of complexity […]." In doing so, the notion of consilience introduced by Edward O. Wilson (1998) is acknowledged but also apparently surpassed, in the sense that there seems to be no possibility to unify all knowledge under a definite number of natural laws: this is prevented by the irreducibility of disciplines from higher layers into lower layers. Another epistemologically unifying point of view is that presented by Chaisson (2009), based on the ubiquity of change and the transversal concept of energy to give rise to all forms of complexity in our universe, along a non-reversible progress of time. Let's note that in (Chaisson 2009) the "creativity" keyword is apparently missing: from a theoretical point of view, we argue that there is a necessity to open a discussion about *the role of creativity in cosmic evolution*. We start an attempt to address it here; clearly, given the ambition of such a task, it will not be possible to come to a complete framework or definite conclusions: initial considerations will have to suffice. Further, there is yet another theoretical reason behind this extension of DUCP to multiple layers of existence, brought in by taking proper account of dynamic and circular interrelationships: originality in one layer of existence can actually be the reason for creativity in another layer, which in turn might create an iterative feedback loop. For example, technological creativity of humans may affect the environment (e.g., temperature increase), which spurs biological variations (e.g., selected species hyper-flourishing through adaptation or exaptation) as well as geo-thermic and atmospheric reactions (e.g., ozone-layer depletion), which in turn require and spur more technological innovations (hopefully in more sustainable directions), as we are seeing today. Taking a macroscopic perspective, these inter-layer DUCP loops do become visible, thus allowing a holistic view on reality from the perspective of creativity studies.

On the other hand, from a practical point of view, to justify our DUCP definition we resort to pragmatism as also elected in (Corazza 2016), drawing upon the pragmatist maxim by Peirce (1992–1999, p. 132): "Consider what effects, which might conceivably have practical bearings, we conceive the object of our conception to have. Then, our conception of those effects is the whole of our conception of the object." Therefore, considering a wide-sense creativity construct that extends the DUCP reach to the entire realm of cosmic evolution (as opposed to confining it only to human and possibly animal evolution) can be usefully conceived only based on its practical bearings, i.e. its utility in terms of the development of creativity studies and in particular of the understanding of the creativity construct for the purpose of contributing to the establishment of a scientific discipline (Corazza 2017b; Corazza and Agnoli 2015). Therefore, our task should be to show that extending the consideration of creativity also to other layers of complexity, beyond those of life, mind, and culture, does provide unifying and useful perspectives that have practical bearings onto creativity studies for humans. We believe that this is indeed the case; we will provide a few examples later in this chapter, but this will also constitute a goal for future work.

The above discussion, which of course would also merit to be expanded but is deemed to be sufficient for our present purposes, contains all the essential elements of our theoretical and practical justifications to define DUCP as the active ensemble of creativity episodes in the course of cosmic evolution. In doing so, and in line with Whitehead's philosophical perspective, we can address the ontological question by establishing that *creativity existed since the origin of our universe and potentially permeates all of our universe*, in all its layers of existence.

In other words, we argue that creativity has been and is the engine for extended evolution in all layers of existence reported in Table 17.2, which are reminiscent of the ToK classification (Henriques 2003) but are actually only partially the same. In particular, both the "mind" and "culture" ToK layers are included here in the Psycho-Social layer, given the difficulty or even the impossibility of separating individual from social aspects in creativity; secondly, we introduce an additional layer of complexity due to the rise of artificial intelligence, the effect of which can be seen today but will become ever more evident in the next decades. As indicated in Table 17.2, the first two layers share the fact that the creative process occurs without apparent forms of "intelligence": agency is intrinsic in nature, following Whitehead's cosmology. On the other hand, the third layer is characterized by intelligent and purposeful forms of creativity, which is in line with the position held by Gaut, still without contradicting Whitehead. Regarding the fourth layer, the pertinent

Table 17.2 DUCP forms in the four layers of existence

Layer of existence	DUCP form	Creativity sense	Creativity form
Material layer	Material creativity process	Wide-sense	Emergent and energy-driven
Biological layer	Biological creativity process	Wide-sense	Emergent and aptive
Psycho-social layer	Psycho-social creativity process	Strict-sense	Intelligent and goal-driven
Artificial layer	Artificial creativity process	Wide-sense	Artificially intelligent

philosophical discussion is but in its infancy: can one really admit a form of creativity produced by machines?

Our next step is to consider these four layers of existence in turn, to describe the specific DUCP characteristics and extract those principles that may prove to be useful for a discipline of creativity, in pragmatist terms.

17.4 The Material Creativity Layer in the DUCP

Adding the adjective *material* to *creativity*, thus implying the generation of novelty with the exclusion of any form of life-based agency, is certainly a remarkable conceptual challenge. Our intention is to include in this domain all those phenomena taking place in the physical world that have a potential to generate originality and effectiveness, without the necessity of the action of any living form that could be ascribed the causing, estimating, or even perceiving of the corresponding outcomes. By observing our universe, at least the small portion that is available to our present-day exploration, it is immediate to realize that the vast majority of the cosmic environments are indeed purely material and inanimate. For what we know so far, life appears to be a beautiful exception reserved to the Earth. Even accepting the idea that there *must* be life somewhere else in our universe, it would be difficult to hypothesize that life is a widespread phenomenology. Therefore, the ontological issue about the *material creativity* construct can be translated into the following questions: Does creativity exist in our universe at large? Or is it a very special exception, related to special forms of life? Can the physical, material world generate original products which are also effective? Who or what can estimate this originality and effectiveness, and does this matter? The issue is first and foremost philosophical and, as we discussed above, it would see on opposite fronts thinkers such as Gaut (critical) and Whitehead (favourable). To progress in our discussion, it is important to note that of all possible entities that the human mind has been able to approach scientifically, the material world is the one that is most amenable to be described with mathematical laws, mainly pertaining to the realms of physics and chemistry. Therefore, for us to admit that creativity can exist in the material world, it must be that the laws of physics and chemistry, at least in specific conditions, allow the existence of "solutions" that are unpredictable, surprising, novel, i.e., in a word, original, but also effective, in terms of having an impact on the evolution of our cosmos. The laws of classical mechanics do not appear to have these characteristics: they are deterministic, and given that the initial conditions are known with a sufficient accuracy, the future evolution of the system under consideration can be predicted with any wanted precision. No surprises and therefore no creativity is allowed by those equations. Even the laws of statistical and quantum mechanics, although they describe phenomena which are probabilistic in nature, still produce solutions that are predictable, albeit only in a statistical sense. Very problematic appears also to be the fact that the second theorem of thermodynamics dictates that "in a closed system at equilibrium, entropy can never decrease". Given that entropy can be largely interpreted as the opposite of order, and therefore of effectiveness in a cosmologic sense, it would appear that this mathematical framework leaves no room for material creativity in our world. However, how could the universe have developed and continue to expand, starting from a big bang and henceforth giving birth to particles, galaxies, stars and planets, if creativity did not have a place in the material world? Could anyone deny surprise, beauty, and astounding complexity to the universe in which we exist? And how could the conditions to support life in general, and the human mind in particular, have been generated on Earth and not anywhere else, without a surprising process of creativity happening at the material layer? These would seem to be hardly solvable dilemmas from a scientific point of view, unless a new theoretical framework is invoked. In passing, we should note that, starting from the seventeenth century, this apparent incompatibility between the laws of classical physics and creativity contributed to divaricate a dichotomy between science and the arts, between positivism and romanticism, from which our culture has been and is still suffering dreadfully. It would be extremely important to re-integrate our culture into a unity, and this is one of the main practical reasons why it is important to accept a wide-sense view in creativity studies, along with the standard strict-sense perspective.

Luckily, in the last five decades a solution path to the above dilemmas has emerged: the thermodynamics of irreversible processes (Prigogine 1967), or the study of physical systems that are far from equilibrium, which are dissipative in nature and therefore require an exchange of energy to exist: these systems can behave in ways that have a potential to be a-priori unpredictable, original, but also effective; in our terminology, they can be creative in the wide sense. Ilya Prigogine, the Nobel prize for chemistry in 1977, played a key role in establishing this new approach to the study of the inanimate world, which contributed fundamentally to the science of complex and chaotic systems, and in particular to the phenomenon of emergence of surprising behaviour out of physical matter, leading to the end of the "certainty" provided by the previous physical-mathematical frameworks (Prigogine 1996). In what sense, then, can material originality be generated? Imagine a physical system existing in conditions of strong energy exchange with the surrounding world to keep it away from a static equilibrium, and that it is desired to predict the evolution in time of the physical behaviour of that system, given certain starting conditions. Now, Prigogine and others have proved that, under specific assumptions, even infinitely close but different starting conditions can give rise to solutions that diverge exponentially with time (Prigogine 1996). This ensuing uncertainty can also produce new forms of order that *emerge* from the system's behaviour, but that cannot be reduced to a cause-effect relation according to any physical law. When an unpredictable behaviour that demonstrates superior effectiveness in terms of order and sustainability emerges out of a physical system, we state that a *material creative achievement* has occurred. We should note the fundamental role played by *energy* in creating the potential conditions for emergence: only with a sufficient energy supply is it possible to create those far from equilibrium conditions that are conducive to material creativity. In other words, material creativity is related one-to-one with the availability and expenditure of amounts of energy which are much larger than those that would be needed to keep a system in equilibrium. And the Big Bang is our scientific explanation of the largest and seminal energy surge in the history of our universe, giving rise to all of its material richness.

Let's observe that the study of physical complex systems and the phenomenon of emergence has been taken as a useful metaphoric and explanatory framework for human creativity by a number of authors (e.g., Ambrose 2014; Gabora 2017; Loreto et al. 2016). Under this light, the construct of material creativity that is proposed here should be easily acceptable. At the same time, we underline that here we go beyond the metaphor: this may be the first instance in which material creativity and human creativity are seen as different elements of a unique, universal creativity process: the DUCP.

We close this chapter by a sort of quantification of the production of material wide-sense creativity in the course of the evolution of our cosmos. The current estimate for the extant number of galaxies could be a reasonable measure in this case: Conselice et al. (2016) calculate that there should be in the order of two trillion galaxies in our universe, each with billions of stars, each with the possibility to have planetary systems around them. This astonishing richness constitutes the first layer of DUCP production. And these systems of planets produced by material creativity open up new worlds of concatenation potential, where original outcomes might imply the opportunity to go beyond the material layer itself: this is certainly the case for our planet Earth.

17.5 The Biological Creativity Layer in the DUCP

Current estimates date the formation of the Earth at around 4.5–4.6 billion years ago (Wetherill 1990; Allegre et al. 1995). The formation of a new planet is a clear evidence for the growth of order in the universe, which we classify as an impressive material creative achievement, given its originality and time-lasting effectiveness. Clearly, conditions for life were not yet in place on Earth at the end of the accretion of its materials: our planet was still blind of any biological possibility, but it had a sort of mysterious potential for it. The insurgence of life on Earth, which from a disciplinary viewpoint could be interpreted as the emergence of biology from chemistry and physics, is the first, most surprising, extraordinary creative achievement to be accounted for in the biological layer of the DUCP. Could any other wide-sense or strict-sense creative achievement compete with the instantiation of *life* in a completely inanimate and therefore hostile environment, in terms of its beautiful originality and breathtaking effectiveness? We believe the answer is no. It is very important to underline that even though life emerged in an inanimate material world, life cannot be reduced to the material world with any form of cause-effect relationships. Biology builds on chemistry and physics, but it cannot be reduced to them (Henriques 2003). Life forms a completely distinct layer of creative activity in the DUCP, the biological creativity process driven by *aptation*, which includes both adaptation (Darwin 1859) and exaptation mechanisms (Gould and Vrba 1982). The general outcome of the biological DUCP layer can in general be identified as *biodiversity*.

There are many theories and beliefs regarding the insurgence and development of life on Earth, and this chapter is clearly not the place for a review of such an intricate, sensitive, and amply debated matter. For our purposes, it will suffice to refer to the recent work by Olivia Judson (2017) on the relationship between the various sources of available energy and the evolution of life on Earth. As a matter of fact, it appears that the history of the evolution of life and biodiversity on Earth can be partitioned into five epochs, based on the prevailing energy source utilized by living organisms. On the one hand, two of these sources were provided directly by the material layer: geochemical energy, produced by reactions of water with basalt and other rocks, and sunlight produced by our star at the center of the solar system. On the other hand, three of the sources were original and effective consequences of the biological DUCP process itself: oxygen, flesh, and fire. This is a powerful evidence for the concatenation potential between creativity episodes, both intra- and inter-layer. Let's briefly review the overall process, following Judson (2017). During energy epoch one, phylogenetic and biochemical evidence shows that the earliest organisms were chemoautotrophs exploiting geochemical energy to perform simple chemical reactions (their primitive form of "life"). These proto-organisms could survive only near geochemical sources, so that distribution of life was scattered and erratic on the Earth surface. Energy epoch two started when, around 3.7 billion years ago, an original behaviour emerged: some bacteria evolved to harness sunlight to accelerate and drive their chemical reactions. At first, these reactions were anoxygenic (did not produce oxygen), and oxygen remained at trace levels on Earth. A crucial innovation happened when one phylum, the cyanobacteria, developed oxygenic photosynthesis: in the course of about 300 million years, this would produce the Great Oxidation event, completely transforming the atmosphere of the Earth. It is important to note here that this great biological creative achievement had an impact on the material layer, transforming the physical environment and allowing completely new opportunities for concatenation potential. Oxygen was provided by the DUCP biological layer and not by the material layer, but it completely transformed the latter along with the former. We classify this phenomenon as inter-layer concatenation. Given its availability, the exploitation of oxygen as an energy source constitutes epoch three, starting around 2.4 billion years ago: the ozone layer was established, minerals were largely diversified, new areas of the Earth were colonized by those organisms that evolved to become able to exploit the concatenation potential offered by oxygen, in particular the possibility to construct original and effective molecules such as collagen. It is during this epoch that eukaryotes emerged, that would eventually produce vegetation: flora was born, and the Earth became green. One innovation by the eukaryotes is particularly of relevance: phagocytosis, or the engulfment of particles and other life forms. This led to the start of a completely new epoch, one in which energy for an organism could be derived by eating other organisms: energy epoch four, whereby flesh was an additional and phenomenal source of energy. Around 575 million years ago, animals became abundant and energy could be acquired through hunting, rapidly transforming the Earth ecosystem:

before this epoch, most of the life forms were microbial, but by eating flesh organism sizes grew rapidly and enormously, opening up the possibility for an exponential growth in biodiversity. Fire is the last innovative source of energy to be considered to conclude this overview. Throughout the solar system, only on Earth the three requirements for the existence of fire are satisfied: lightning for ignition, oxygen for combustion, and wood for fuel. The necessary concatenation of material and biological creativity episodes should be evident: without oxygen and/or without vegetation, fire would not be possible. Somewhat surprisingly, fire turned out to be a powerful promoter of biodiversity: it drove the initial growth of flowering plants, which in turn led to diversification in fauna species such as ants, bees, and mammals; fire also produced concatenations back to the material layer through the introduction of original and effective materials such as charcoal, ash, and soot. But, undoubtedly, the most crucial concatenation potential afforded by fire was the evolution of a fire creature: *Homo*. Indeed, hominids learned to control the use of fire, using it for protection, metal molding, and especially for cooking. The ability to cook changed completely the energy acquisition of hominids, because cooked food, be it meat or vegetable, is essentially pre-digested and thus delivers more energy for the same quantity. Diet diversification and thus the ability to live in many places on Earth were original and effective consequences carrying astonishing concatenation potential for hominids.

Also in the case of the biological layer of the DUCP, it would be interesting to give a quantitative measure of the overall wide-sense creative production. Perhaps, a useful number could be the total number of extant species on Earth, which is actually a subject of active debate (Caley et al. 2014). At any rate, most of the available figures circle around five million species, of which we have named about 1.5 millions (Costello et al. 2013). Indeed, the complexity produced by biodiversity goes beyond our imagination.

Finally, let's note that, similarly to the theory of complex systems, also biological evolution and biodiversity have been taken as inspiration for the modelling and explanation of the creative thinking process, starting with Campbell (1960), and later followed by Simonton (2012). This is certainly a powerful metaphor, and its use is legitimate even though subject to debate. What we must underline here is that, in the theoretical architecture of DUCP, biological evolution is not simply a useful metaphorical framework but an integral part of the wide-sense creativity process, concatenated in hardly extricable ways to the strict-sense creativity of the psycho-social layer.

17.6 The Psycho-Social Creativity Layer in the DUCP

Amongst the creative achievements of the biological layer in the DUCP, the advent of species harnessed with a brain should receive major recognition. Indeed, the overall exercise of biological evolution could be interpreted as an immense and longitudinal problem-solving exercise, aimed at expanding life, colonizing all of the

Earth, surviving as individuals, avoiding species extinction, and all of this in spite of an ever-changing physical environment, plagued by earthquakes, volcano explosions, atmospheric fluctuations, as well as glaciations. The necessary adaptations and exaptations for survival required major investments in terms of both individual sacrifices and/or time, in many cases occurring in the course of millions of years. Now, a drastic reduction in this required investment was afforded by the introduction of the immense flexibility of the brain, allowing a multitude of alternative behaviours in front of the same conditions, which can be tried and assessed even by a single individual in the course of its own lifetime. A much faster and effective modality for adaptation and exaptation. In addition, although social behaviour does not necessarily require an encephalon, it is a fact that species endowed with brains show much higher levels of mutual interrelationships and an ability to exploit these in order to improve their own sustainability. Overall, this leads to the emergence of another DUCP layer, the psycho-social layer, in which *Homo Sapiens* is without a single doubt the most prominent actor, and where individual minds collaborate for a variety of goals, increasing DUCP productivity and complexity by orders of magnitude. Given that material and biological layers are already part of the DUCP, it should be taken for granted that variable levels of potential for originality and effectiveness are a feature of all animal species (for a review, see Kaufman and Kaufman 2004); but, for the sake of brevity, we shall focus here only on hominids, and *Homo Sapiens* in particular. Given the intentionality and conscience afforded in particular by the human mind, the DUCP psycho-social layer constitutes what we consider to be the creativity process *in the strict sense*. However, when we try to identify the conditions that were conducive to the emergence of strict-sense creative behaviour in hominids, it is interesting to note that once again concatenations with significant events in the DUCP material and biological layers become evident.

The history of the human side of the DUCP psycho-social layer necessarily starts in Africa. As noted by Van Couvering et al. (2004), no other continent can rival with Africa in terms of its importance for human evolution. Briefly, around ten million years ago the displacement of the Western and Eastern African tectonic plates produced an original and effective reconfiguration of the environment: the Great Rift Valley was created, a depression of approximately 6000 km in length from North to South. The Great Rift Valley formed an obstacle to Atlantic atmospheric perturbations, so much so that the Eastern territories of the African continent became more and more arid. This produced a drastic reduction of the rainforest in vast areas, and opened up the concatenated potential for a new ecosystem: the savanna. Until then, hominids could easily live out of fruits and roots picked up in the forest. But without the forest, new sources of food were necessary. The new environment thus opened a new opportunity which was also a great challenge: how to hunt prey, without exposing oneself to excessive risk? Hominids were certainly neither the fastest nor the strongest of animals. It was in these conditions that an idea with a great potential for originality and effectiveness was generated: bipedalism. Bipedalism carried with itself numerous advantages: seeing far (particularly useful in the savanna), the possibility to wade waters, a great variety of diversified movements, and most of all the freeing of hands. On the other hand, just like any other disruptive idea, bipedalism implied also a series of negative sides: it required anatomical reorganization and with that new difficulties in giving birth, vital organs were more exposed, joints wore out more rapidly, and it was a difficult skill to learn for babies. Nonetheless, this innovation was gradually adopted to become a major biological and psycho-social creative achievement in spite of all the underlying obstacles. This was truly a crucial step forward, as underlined from a biomechanical point of view by Vaughan (2003) and from a philosophical perspective by Gallagher, considering its implications in terms of embodied cognition (Gallagher 2015, p. 99): "If humans had not attained the upright posture [...], the human brain would likely be much smaller, our sensory and motor systems would be different (more attuned to the olfactory than to vision), and none of it would function in the specific way it functions now. Indeed, we would likely have to redefine what we mean by rationality". And, we add, we would have to redefine what we mean by creativity.

A second crucial step in the development of strict-sense psycho-social creativity in humans should be underlined: neoteny, or the persistence of immature behaviour for long periods of life, up to adulthood (Bjorklund 1997). Also in this case, the are both advantages and disadvantages to take into account. On the negative side, neoteny implies much longer care periods for our babies than any other animal species, with children who are not capable of searching or hunting safely, which forced a reorganization of social roles between males and females. On the other hand, this feature brought positive sides of exceptional importance from the point of view of enhancing creativity, i.e. the potential for original and effective behaviour: long time available for playing and a strong mother-child relationship, whereby the development and refinement of language and metacognition took place, with grand implications for the future of our species.

Hominids thus became the major force inside the psycho-social layer of the DUCP: they began to shape their environment and to produce inventions, starting from stone-tools, and they affected at the same time the material and biological layers. To date, the earliest account for the inception of the stone-tool industry appears to be given by the archaeological findings in Lomekwi 3, West Turkana, Kenya (Harmand et al. 2015): they are dated at 3.3 million years ago. Building stone tools is characteristic of a psycho-social creative activity in that the potential effectiveness is projected into the future, implying the existence and use of mind. Now, 3.3 million years ago is about three million years earlier than the advent of *Homo Sapiens*, and almost one million years before *Homo Abilis*, who was also identified as one of the initiators of human creative activity (Gabora and Kaufman 2010). We want to highlight again that this finding is in line with Whitehead's hypothesis that the agent in the DUCP is the universe as a whole, so that in the psycho-social layer all hominid species can and should be accredited of creative behaviour at various degrees. However, no one could argue against the fact that DUCP productivity exploded in the hands of *Homo Sapiens*, thanks to our unprecedented ability for learning and communication, thus enhancing enormously the potential for concatenation, exploration, exaptation, and estimation. *Homo Sapiens'* cumulative culture has been shown to be growing exponentially across all times (Lehman 1947), and this exponential growth has been attributed to our creativity (Enquist et al. 2008), as noted before. Even though it is patently self-referential, we cannot avoid being astonished at the cumulative culture that *Homo Sapiens* has been able to produce in the course of its evolution.

Let's conclude this section by noting that our view of the psycho-social layer of the DUCP is in accord with the approach to economics by Koppl et al. (2015), whereby they theorize that economic dynamics are "creative", in the sense that the relevant phase space changes continually in ways that cannot be prestated. Reminiscent of biodiversity, they introduce the concept of *cambiodiversity*, or diversity in traded goods, with an estimated dimension of ten billion goods for sale in New York city in 2015. This, along the findings by Lehman (1947) on the exponential growth of cumulative culture in all disciplines across history, can be taken as forms of quantification of psycho-social productivity of the DUCP.

17.7 The Artificial Creativity Layer in the DUCP

The action of *Homo Sapiens* in the psycho-social layer of the DUCP has produced vast numbers of inventions based on scientific discoveries, opening up new professions and disciplines, among which those pertaining to information and communication technologies (ICT). Cybernetics, or the science of communication and control theory, was born in the middle of the twentieth century, when computing machines were in their pre-history, foreseeing a progression path which turned out to be very close to reality: today, modern supercomputers are reaching computational powers that are comparable to those of the biological human brain. Given the rate of increase in computational power and density, we can expect that machines might surpass the human brain in terms of raw computational power, while they already outperform us for specific tasks, such as for example arithmetic calculus or chess playing. At the same time, telecommunication infrastructures have interconnected the developed world, upon which the Internet and the World Wide Web have introduced services that have soon become pervasive and in some cases even necessary to our everyday and professional lives. Artificial intelligence has been developed to a sufficient level to enter into our everyday life, most of the times without being noticed. The Internet, with its powerful search engines, constitutes nothing less than the most powerful form of non-anthropomorphic distributed artificial intelligence, of which the majority of the world's population makes daily use. Our minds are now extended by these technologies (Menary 2010), and the job market is undergoing radical transformations (Brynjolfsson and McAfee 2014). The question for us is: should we include any of the outcomes of artificially intelligent processes as part of the DUCP? Is there a philosophical as well as practical possibility for machines to behave creatively? Since originality contains an element of authenticity, shouldn't creativity be an impossibility from the computational point of view? These are crucial questions which will require much more space than what we can dedicate here. Let's only say that the field of computational creativity is today open (see for example Colton et al. 2009, and the references therein), and that as a minimum we should consider the fact that machines can provide useful tools to enhance psycho-social creativity. Indeed, as discussed in (Corazza 2017b), we believe that the collaboration between humans and machines will be a fundamental characteristic of the future Post-Information Society.

17.8 Conclusions and Further Developments

This chapter represents but a quick initial flight over the vast territory to be covered in order to transform Whitehead's cosmological interpretation of creativity as the ultimate universal metaphysical principle into a fully-fledged theoretical framework, with practical consequences in a pragmatist sense. The first fundamental step into this process is the realization that once a dynamic definition for creativity is given in terms of potential originality and effectiveness, it becomes virtually impossible to fragment the creativity process into separate elements: creativity episodes can be carried on indefinitely, transcending their actors, and they are all interrelated. The consequence of this realization is the definition of the Dynamic Universal Creativity Process (DUCP) as the active ensemble of all creativity episodes in the course of cosmic evolution, to form an evolutionary tree of creativity. This definition allows to place into a single theoretical framework the original and effective outcomes of the material layer (mainly the domain of physics and inorganic chemistry), the biological layer (mainly the domain of biology and organic chemistry), the psycho-social layer (mainly the domain of psychology, social sciences, and economics) and the artificial layer (mainly the domain of engineering, computer science, and cybernetics). The successive layers build on, but can never be reduced to, one another, due to the intrinsic and emerging characteristics of each layer. It can be shown however that DUCP outcomes at one layer can spur iterations of innovations at other layers, with recursive mutual influences. This kind of circularity is one justification for an integrated approach to creativity: other justifications have been provided in terms of both theoretical and practical benefits. Clearly, a large amount of work will be needed to consolidate this theoretical framework and deliver practical implications, involving multiple disciplines among which psychology, philosophy, anthropology, cosmology, evolutionary biology, economics, design, engineering and cybernetics will have prominent roles.

One question which remains to be answered is the following: which implications can be derived from the adoption of the DUCP framework in terms of education, and in particular of education for creativity? Answering this fundamental question will require extensive future work, but we can start drafting preliminary answers here. Indeed, the impact appears to be far from negligible. First of all, the dynamic definition for creativity allows to take into account in a unified framework not only the desired creative achievements, but also episodes of creative inconclusiveness, which put to a test the resilience and self-efficacy of students. Therefore, the fundamental attitudes and mindsets for persistence can be recognized and developed under this dynamic perspective. Second, from an epistemological point of view, adopting DUCP implies that teachers and students should be formed and informed about a search for the possible unification of knowledge, going beyond barriers and dichotomies that are typically the result of historical disciplinary subdivisions as sorts of fenced gardens. We are specifically concerned with bridging the gap between science and technology on one side, human sciences and art on the other. Third, recognizing that creativity has a universal and metaphysical character should convince teachers and students that this is not a topic that can be excluded from any educational strategy; rather, it should find its proper collocation, one that can well exploit the material, biological, psycho-social, and artificial transversality of the DUCP, letting those willing to be involved in the DUCP become part of an endless flux of creativity episodes. Fourth, and perhaps most important, given that creativity will be essential to the survival of the human species in the post-information society, the development and measurement of skills and abilities related to creative performance, the understanding of the socio-cultural implications of creative activity, as well as the search for the overall conditions that can optimize the potential for originality and effectiveness in any circumstances should be addressed and become a positive element in the design of future education systems. We add a sense of urgency to these guidelines, given the accelerating pace of societal transformations (Corazza 2017b).

The attentive reader will have noticed that, throughout this discussion, we have avoided completely the question of whether the advancements produced by the DUCP at the various layer could or could not be supervised or guided in any teleological form. This was done on purpose to let each reader find her/his own position on this fundamental metaphysical question, which also touches upon the sphere of personal spirituality. Indeed, an intimate place which we intend to respect.

Acknowledgements The Author would like to thank Sergio Agnoli, Baptiste Barbot, Vlad Glăveanu, Roni Reiter-Palmer, and Julia Von Thienen for useful discussions.

References

Albert, R. S. (1983). Genius and eminence: The social psychology of creativity and exceptional achievement. In *International series in experimental social psychology: International series in experimental social psychology* (Vol. 5). Oxford/New York: Pergamon Press.

Alessi, G. (1992). Models of proximate and ultimate causation in psychology. *American Psychologist, 47*(11), 1359–1370.

Allegre, C. J., Manhes, G., & Göpel, C. (1995). The age of the Earth. *Geochimica et Cosmochimica Acta, 59*(8), 1445–1456.

Ambrose, D. (2014). Creative Emergence, Order, and Chaos. In D. Ambrose, B. Sriraman, & K. M. Pierce (Eds.), *A critique of creativity and complexity, Advances in creativity and giftedness* (Vol. 25). Rotterdam: Sense Publishers.

Andriani, P., & Cattani, G. (2016). Exaptation as source of creativity, innovation, and diversity: introduction to the special section. *Industrial and Corporate Change, 25*(1), 115–131.

Beer, R. D. (2000). Dynamical approaches to cognitive science. *Trends in Cognitive Sciences, 4*, 91–99.

Beghetto, R. A. (2010). Creativity in the classroom. In Kaufman & Sternberg (Eds.), *The Cambridge handbook of creativity* (pp. 447–463). New York: Cambridge University Press.

Bjorklund, D. F. (1997). The role of immaturity in human development. *Psychological Bulletin, 122*(2), 153.

Brynjolfsson, E., & McAfee, A. (2014). *The second machine age: Work, progress, and prosperity in a time of brilliant technologies.* New York: WW Norton.

Caley, M. J., Fisher, R., & Mengersen, K. (2014). Global species richness estimates have not converged. *Trends in Ecology & Evolution, 29*(4), 187–188.

Campbell, D. T. (1960). Blind variation and selective retention in creative thought as in other knowledge processes. *Psychological Review, 67,* 380–400.

Cattani, G. (2005). Preadaptation, firm heterogeneity, and technological performance: A study on the evolution of fiber optics, 1970–1995. *Organization Science, 16*(6), 563–580.

Cattani, G. (2006). Technological pre-adaptation, speciation, and emergence of new technologies: How corning invented and developed fiber optics. *Industrial and Corporate Change, 15*(2), 285–318.

Chaisson, E. J. (2009). Cosmic evolution. In S. J. Dick & M. L. Lupisella (Eds.), *Cosmos & culture: Cultural evolution in a cosmic context* (pp. 3–23). E-book: NASA SP-2009-4802.

Colton, S., de Mántaras, R. L., & Stock, O. (2009). Computational creativity: Coming of age. *AI Magazine, 30*(3), 11.

Conselice, C. J., Wilkinson, A., Duncan, K., & Mortlock, A. (2016). The evolution of galaxy number density at z < 8 and its implications. *The Astrophysical Journal, 830,* 83 (17pp).

Corazza, G. E. (2016). Potential originality and effectiveness: the dynamic definition of creativity. *Creativity Research Journal, 28*(3), 258–267.

Corazza, G. E. (2017a). Creativity and anticipation. In R. Poli (Ed.), *Handbook of anticipation. Theoretical and applied aspects of the use of future in decision making.* Basel: Springer.

Corazza, G. E. (2017b). Organic creativity for well-being in the post-information society. *Europe's Journal of Psychology, 13*(4), 599.

Corazza, G. E., & Agnoli, S. (2015). On the path towards the science of creative thinking. In G. E. Corazza & S. Agnoli (Eds.), *Multidisciplinary contributions to the science of creative thinking* (pp. 3–20). Singapore: Springer.

Corazza, G. E., Pedone, R., & Vanelli-Coralli, A. (2010). Technology as a need: Trends in the evolving information society. *Advances in Electronics and Telecommunications, 1,* 124–132.

Costello, M. J., May, R. M., & Stork, N. E. (2013). Can we name Earth's species before they go extinct? *Science, 339*(6118), 413–416.

Darwin, C. (1859). On the origin of species by means of natural selection.

Edison, T. A. (1948). *The diary and sundry observations of Thomas Alva Edison.* New York: Philosophical library.

Enquist, M., Ghirlanda, S., Jarrick, A., & Wachtmeister, C. A. (2008). Why does human culture increase exponentially? *Theoretical Population Biology, 74*(1), 46–55.

Eysenck, H. J. (1995). *Genius: The natural history of creativity* (Vol. 12). Cambridge: Cambridge University Press.

Feather, J. (2013). *The information society: A study of continuity and change.* London: Facet Publishing.

Gabora, L. (2017). Honing theory: A complex systems framework for creativity. *Nonlinear Dynamics, Psychology, and Life Sciences, 21*(1), 35–88.

Gabora, L., & Kaufman, S. B. (2010). Evolutionary approaches to creativity. *The Cambridge handbook of creativity,* 279–300.

Gallagher, S. (2015). How embodied cognition is being disembodied. *The Philosophers' Magazine, 68,* 96–102.

Galton, F. (1869). *Hereditary genius.* New York: Appleton.

Garud, R., Gehman, J., & Giuliani, A. P. (2016). Technological exaptation: A narrative approach. *Industrial and Corporate Change, 25*(1), 149–166.

Gaut, B. (2010). The philosophy of creativity. *Philosophy Compass, 5*(12), 1034–1046.

Glăveanu, V. P. (2011). Creativity as cultural participation. *Journal for the Theory of Social Behaviour, 41*(1), 48–67.
Glăveanu, V. P. (2014). The psychology of creativity: A critical reading. *Creativity. Theories – Research – Applications, 1*, 10–32.
Gould, S. J., & Vrba, E. S. (1982). Exaptation—A missing term in the science of form. *Paleobiology, 8*(1), 4–15.
Harmand, S., et al. (2015). 3.3-million-year-old stone tools from Lomekwi 3, West Turkana, Kenya. *Nature, 521*(7552), 310–315.
Henriques, G. (2003). The tree of knowledge system and the theoretical unification of psychology. *Review of General Psychology, 7*(2), 150.
Henriques, G. (2011). *A new unified theory of psychology*. New York: Springer Science & Business Media.
Judson, O. P. (2017). The energy expansions of evolution. *Nature Ecology & Evolution, 1*, 0138.
Kauffman, S. A. (2016). *Humanity in a creative universe*. New York: Oxford University Press.
Kaufman, J. C., & Baer, J. (2004). The amusement park theoretical (APT) model of creativity. *The International Journal of Creativity & Problem Solving, 14*(2), 15–25.
Kaufman, J. C., & Kaufman, A. B. (2004). Applying a creativity framework to animal cognition. *New Ideas in Psychology, 22*(2), 143–155.
Koppl, R., Kauffman, S., Felin, T., & Longo, G. (2015). Economics for a creative world. *Journal of Institutional Economics, 11*(1), 1–31.
Lehman, H. C. (1947). The exponential increase in man's cultural output. *Social Forces, 25*(3), 281–290.
Loreto, V., Servedio, V. D., Strogatz, S. H., & Tria, F. (2016). Dynamics on expanding spaces: Modeling the emergence of novelties. In *Creativity and universality in language* (pp. 59–83). Cham: Springer.
Martin, L., & Wilson, N. (2017). Defining creativity with discovery. *Creativity Research Journal, 29*(4), 417–425.
Mayer, R. E. (1999). Fifty years of creativity research. In R. J. Sternberg (Ed.), *Handbook of creativity* (pp. 449–460). Cambridge: Cambridge University Press.
Menary, R. (Ed.). (2010). *The extended mind*. Cambridge, MA: Mit Press.
Mumford, M. D., Mobley, M. I., Uhlman, C. E., Reiter-Palmon, R., & Doares, L. M. (1991). Process analytic models of creative capacities. *Creativity Research Journal, 4*, 91–122.
Parkhurst, H. B. (1999). Confusion, lack of consensus, and the definition of creativity as a construct. *Journal of Creative Behavior, 33*, 1–21.
Peirce, C. S. (1992–1999). *The Essential Peirce*. Bloomington: Indiana University Press.
Prigogine, I. (1967). *Introduction to thermodynamics of irreversible processes* (3rd ed.). New York: Interscience.
Prigogine, I. (1996). *La fin dès certitudes: temps, chaos et les lois de la nature*. Paris: Editions Odile Jacob.
Rhodes, M. (1961). An analysis of creativity. *Phi Delta Kappan, 42*, 305–310.
Rosa, H. (2003). Social acceleration: Ethical and political consequences of a desynchronized high–speed society. *Constellations, 10*(1), 3–33.
Runco, M. A., & Jaeger, G. J. (2012). The standard definition of creativity. *Creativity Research Journal, 24*, 92–96.
Simonton, D. K. (1984). *Genius, creativity, and leadership: Historiometric inquiries*. Cambridge, MA: Harvard University Press.
Simonton, D. K. (2012). Creativity, problem solving, and solution set sightedness: Radically reformulating BVSR. *The Journal of Creative Behavior, 46*(1), 48–65.
Stein, M. I. (1953). Creativity and culture. *Journal of Psychology, 36*, 311–322.
Sternberg, R. J. (2006). The nature of creativity. *Creativity Research Journal, 18*(1), 87–98.
Sternberg, R. J., & Lubart, T. I. (1991). An investment theory of creativity and its development. *Human Development, 34*(1), 1–31.

Van Couvering, J. A., Delson, E., Fleagle, J. G., Grine, F. E., & Brooks, A. S. (2004). Africa. In E. Delson, I. Tattersall, J. Van Couvering, & A. S. Brooks (Eds.), *Encyclopedia of human evolution and prehistory*. New York: Routledge.

Van Gogh, V. (1978). *Complete letters of Vincent van Gogh*. Boston: New York Graphic Society.

Vaughan, C. L. (2003). Theories of bipedal walking: An odyssey. *Journal of Biomechanics, 36*(4), 513–523.

Wallas, G. (1926). *The art of thought*. New York: Harcourt Brace.

Weisberg, R. W. (2015). On the usefulness of "Value" in the definition of creativity. *Creativity Research Journal, 27*, 111–124.

Wetherill, G. W. (1990). Formation of the Earth. *Annual Review of Earth and Planetary Sciences, 18*(1), 205–256.

Whitehead, A. N. (1978/1929). *Process and reality: An essay in cosmology*, Corrected Edition, eds. David Ray Griffin and Donald W. Sherburne. New York: Free Press.

Wilson, E. (1998). *Consilience: The unity of knowledge*. New York: Konpf.

CODA

Ronald A. Beghetto and Giovanni Emanuele Corazza

If we were to boil down the organizing assertion of this volume in one statement it would be: *Creativity is a dynamic phenomenon that cannot be adequately accounted for by fixed conceptions or one-and-done assessments.* Contributors to this volume responded to our invitation to work within this broader assertion and offer a dynamic perspective on creativity in educational settings.

Authors responded to this invitation in various ways in an effort to present how their perspective builds on and moves beyond more static representations of creativity. This resulted in a compelling set of chapters that illustrate how creative phenomena, including creative outcomes, are much more volatile and mercurial than how they have been typically represented in creativity theory, research, and practice.

What then are the implications of adopting a more dynamic perspective of creativity in education settings? Taken together, the contributors to this volume have offered a two part response to this question. The chapters found in Part 1 highlight implications for current and emergent practices; whereas the chapters comprising Part 2 focus more on theoretical conceptions and future directions.

In what follows, we briefly summarize key assertions from each of the chapters, organized along the lines of the major themes of Part 1 and 2 of this volume. These assertions are those that stand out to us as particular provocative, compelling, or important. We acknowledge that these highlights are limited to our interpretation. Other readers may interpret these implications differently. Still, we offer the following as a quick summary of what we feel are key assertions in and across the chapters of this volume.

Implications for Current and Emergent Practices

- **Use micro-longitudinal methods.** *Dynamic approaches to studying creativity are underway and researchers can draw from and build on various promising analytic and methodological options in an effort to move from more static to more dynamic, micro-longitudinal approaches to studying creative phenomena in classrooms, such as creative confidence beliefs* (Chap. 2, Beghetto and Karwowski).
- **Engage young people in participatory creative endeavours.** *Educators can engage young people in participatory creative endeavours, such as biographies of ideas, which represent a dynamic approach for understanding and experiencing the more complex, changing, and socio-cultural roles people play in the development of creative ideas, identities, and outcomes* (Chap. 3, Clapp and Hanchett Hanson).
- **Incorporate emotions into models of creative thinking.** *Emotional reactions are a main determinant of the creative process, representing the spinal cord of creative thought. Researchers can use creative thinking models, such as the DIMAI model (drive, information, movement, assessment, and implementation), to understand how emotional mechanisms control the creative thinking process* (Chap. 4, Agnoli and Corazza).
- **Develop dynamic styles of idea assessment.** *How teachers and coaches assess ideas as part of the creative process is critical. Movement from more static to dynamic styles of idea assessment are possible through training, but come with challenges (e.g., discrepant conceptions of the value of ideas between practitioners and researchers, in particular original ideas). Researchers and practitioners can benefit from understanding the benefits and challenges that inhere in adopting more dynamic assessment styles* (Chap. 5, von Thienen, Ney, and Meinel).
- **Engage in acts of exploration.** *Acts of exploration represent a promising, dynamic approach to creative schooling. Acts of exploration involve engaging in new and emerging combinations, connections, and interpretations. In this way, acts of exploration take teachers and students on a dynamic creative learning path and can be incorporated in research-education with teachers and research-action with students* (Chap. 6, Guerra and Villa).
- **Understand and develop a creative world view.** *The creative mind is a complex, dynamical system. Understanding the role and features that a creative worldview plays in creative thought and action can go a long way in cultivating creative classrooms.* (Chap. 7, Maland and Gabora)
- **Explore how to dynamically adapt existing models of creativity to understand educational practice.** *Existing models of creativity can be dynamically shaped to help inform, interpret, and understand creative educational practice in and across cultures. New applications of these models can shine the light on "hidden-c creativity", which is the dynamic potential to be found in all educational settings* (Chap. 8, Mullen).

- **Don't lose sight of content knowledge.** *Content matters when it comes to teaching about, for, and with creativity. Teachers can model the enjoyment to be found in deep subject matter knowledge, experimentation with that subject matter, encouraging students to meaningfully and critically engage with it – even in seemingly "boring" subject areas* (Chap. 9, Tanggaard)

Theoretical Implications and Future Directions

- **Much can be learned from focusing on the dynamic processes of creativity.** *Creativity involves a dynamic process, which results from an interplay of bottom-up and top-down processes. Understanding how people create requires looking beyond the product and focusing on understanding the dynamic processes involved in producing creative products* (Chap. 10, Runco).
- **Creativity can be conceptualized as a dialogic relationship.** *Creativity can be thought of as a dynamic, evolving quality of the relationships people develop with others in a shared, sociocultural environment (rather than a static object). The concept of polyphonic orchestration highlights how creativity is simultaneously an individual and social, personal and cultural, process* (Ness and Glăveanu, Chap. 11).
- **Dynamic definitions require new conceptualizations of creativity assessment.** *A dynamic definition of creativity requires new ways of conceptualizing and adapting measures of creativity to better account for more dynamic features of creative phenomena, such as inconclusiveness* (Chap. 12, Carruthers and MacLean).
- **Dynamic perspectives of creativity help us get beyond competing binaries.** *Understanding the dynamic trajectory of creativity requires moving beyond the typical binaries of choosing an interdisciplinary versus domain specific-expertise. A more dynamic concept calls for a recognition of how these two different approaches can be mutually reinforce the broader effort to understand creative phenomena* (Chap. 13, Ambrose).
- **Dynamic approaches offer new insights into internal mental processes.** *Previous work has demonstrated mixed findings with respect to relationship between internal mental process, such as mind wandering (MW), and creativity. Viewing these phenomena through a multidimensional, dynamic lens can offer researchers new ways for understanding different facets of MW (e.g., spontaneous vs. deliberate) and creative thought* (Chap. 14, Vannucci and Agnoli).
- **Adopting a dynamic conception of creativity requires developing new approaches for specifying the complex, changing, and unpredictable features of the creative process.** *Previous models of creativity which offer a sequential or step-by-step approach to understanding creative processes and outcomes fall short when viewed from a dynamic perspective. New models are needed to help conceptualize, test out, and assess the dynamics of the process in and across fields* (Chap. 15, Botella and Lubart).

- **Working through the prevalent ideologies of creativity can provide new and more dynamic ways of understanding and developing creativity in education.** *Exploring the question of how educators and researchers might become aware of and work within exisiting creative ideologies can offer new directions for promoting more participatory forms of creative work and scholarship in education* (Chap. 16, Hanchett Hanson).
- **Creative episodes can be conceptualized within a dynamic universal creative process.** *Broad, encompassing frameworks such as the Dynamic University Creativity Process (DUCP) offer new directions for conceptualizing creative phenomena in and beyond educational settings. The DUCP offers theorists, researchers, and practitioners multiple entry points (layers) for exploring and (re)conceptualizing creativity in a more dynamic, encompassing, and active ensemble of creative phenomena* (Chap. 17, Corazza).

Concluding Thoughts

When attempting to read a volume brimming with new ideas and concepts, such as this one, you may quickly feel a sense of being overwhelmed by possibilities and perspectives. We therefore hope that this coda offers you a quick refresher of key assertions in and across the chapters, which will help you reflect on and integrate some of the major themes offered herein. We also hope that it represents an invitation for you to go back and revisit the chapters in an effort to explore how your own interpretation of these ideas changes over time and in light of your engagement with these ideas in your own professional endeavours.

Indeed, in the spirit of the dynamic theme of this volume, the creative insights and interpretations you draw from engaging and revisiting the chapters of this volume likely will continue to change over time and across settings. Reading through this volume is therefore not about "finishing it," but continually engaging with, revisiting, and monitoring the changes in your own perspective on creativity in educational settings.